LEARNING ORGANIZATIONAL INNOVATION STRATEGIES

JOHN LOK

Made with ♥ on the Notion Press Platform
www.notionpress.com

Contents

Preface

Introduction

Nowadays, business society is experiencing high technology stage. Can human apply AI technology to help businessmen to reduce cost. Any businessmen must hope to learn how to reduce business cost in long time. The question is what methods can be real useful to help them to reduce long time cost aim. In nowadays business socical behavioral economic view, I shall indicate real useful business cost reducing methods in order to let businessmen can learn how to reduce their business costs in long term.

How will (AI) influence human job change?Advances in artificial intelligence (AI) technology is for the progress in critical areas, such as health, education, energy, economy inclusion, social welfare and the environment.

Thus, it brings this question: Which (AI) workers be instead of traditional human workers in these different new markets? In recent years, machines had been used to be human's tasks in the performance of certain tasks related to intelligence , such as aspects of image recognition. Experts also forecast that rapid progress in the field of specialized artificial intelligence will continue. Then, it also brings this question: Does (AI) exceed that of human performance on more and more tasks? If it is truth, will some of human jobs to be disappeared? (AI) will be instead of human some simple jobs, then unemployment rate to the low skillful and low educated workers will be increased.

Whether (AI) will be raised either production or performance or unemployment to bring human job market more advantages or more disadvantages? In my this book, I shall explain whether (AI) will bring benefits or disadvantages to change to future human job market. If one day, (AI) technology can be applied to any human job aspects. Whether human will face unemployment disadvantages or human won't face unemployment disadvantages. Whether (AI) technology will be applied to assist to future human job to raise productivities or economic growth to any societies or improve performance for any employers' benefits and workers' benefits.

How and why technology may help human to improve talent job behavior ? What methods may help human to create clever as well as creative ability? What method may improve organizational performance ? I shall indicate robot technology invention how to train human creative ability , also I shall explain whether robot tool may help human to improve economy development or help businessmen to reduce cost, I shall explain what skills may help human to raise clever, I shall explain what method may help organizations to improve performance. Readers can learn new knowledge how to improve human development.

In my this book, I shall attempt to explain how and why human may apply AI machine or other methods to help our business activities to reduce long term cost. Readers can learn fresh behavioral economic knowledge whether businessmen may choose what methods to help them to reduce business cost.

Prologue

Content of table

CHAPTER ONE

Explaining supply and demand and savng cost business relationship

The difference between past and nowadays economists their demand and supply economic theory explanation? Why cost saving and supply and demand have close relationship?

The law of supply and demand defines the relationship between the price of a given good or product and the willingness of people to either buy or sell it. Generally, as the price of a good increases, people are willing to supply more and demand less. These economists had explained economic demand and supply theory as below:

Philosopher John Locke is credited with one of the earliest written descriptions of this economic principle in his 1691 publication, Some Considerations of the Consequences of the Lowering of Interest and the Raising of the Value of Money. Locke addressed the concept of supply and demand as part of a discussion about interest rates in 17th-century England. Many merchants wanted the government to lower the cap on interest rates charged by private lenders so that people could borrow more money and thus purchase more goods. Locke argued that the free-market economy should set rates because government regulation could have unintended consequences. If the lending industry were left alone, interest rates would regulate themselves, Locke wrote: "The price of any commodity rises or falls by the proportion of the number of buyers and sellers."

Sir James Steuart's Inquiry into the Principles of Political Economy, published in 1796, was the first known printed use of the term "supply and demand." When Steuart wrote his treatise on political economy, one of his main concerns was the impact of supply and demand on laborers.

Adam Smith dealt extensively with the topic in his 1776 epic economic work, The Wealth of Nations. Often referred to as the Father of Economics, Smith explained the concept of supply and demand as an "invisible hand" that naturally guides the economy. According to Smith, the invisible hand is the automatic pricing and distribution mechanisms in the economy. Smith described a society in which bakers and butchers provide products that individuals need and want, providing a supply that meets demand and developing an economy that benefits everyone. It is important to note that Smith's ideas haven't gone without critique over the years since his ideas were first published, though. Over time, his ideas have been added to in order to represent the changing times and include concepts such as marginal utility, comparative advantage, entrepreneurship, the time-preference theory of interest, and monetary theory.

One of Marshall's most important contributions to microeconomics was his introduction of the concept of price elasticity of demand, which examines how price changes affect demand. In theory, people buy less of a particular product if the price increases, but Marshall noted that in real life, this behavior was not always true. The prices of some goods can increase without reducing demand, which means their prices are inelastic. Inelastic goods tend to include items such as medication or food that consumers deem crucial to daily life. Marshall argued that supply and demand, costs of production, and price elasticity all work together.

Nowadays economists they explain demand and supply economic theory, they have some different to past economists whose explanation as below:

How Does Supply and Demand Work? The law of supply and demand is a theory that explains the interaction between the sellers of a resource and the buyers of that resource. Generally, as price increases, people are willing to supply more and demand less and vice versa when the price falls. What does the bottom line mean. Despite the origins of the law of supply and demand beginning hundreds of years ago, it's still a topic frequently referenced and utilized today in economic theory and discussions. The theory has developed over time to accommodate recent technological and economical advancements, but the basic ideas of the theory remain largely the same.

Does demand depend on supply?

Supply and Demand Determine the Price of Goods and Quantities Produced and Consumed. Consumers may exhaust the available supply of a good by purchasing a given good or service at a high volume. This leads to an increase in demand. As demand increases, the available supply also decreases.

What does market demand depend on?

Market factors affecting demand of consumer goods. The demand for a good increases or decreases depending on several factors. This includes the product's price, perceived quality, advertising spend, consumer income, consumer confidence, and changes in taste and fashion.

Who controls the demand in supply and demand?

Supply and demand are in turn determined by technology and the conditions under which people operate. At one extreme, the market could be populated by a large number of virtually identical sellers and buyers (for example, the market for ballpoint pens).

What are the two laws of demand and supply?

The law of demand holds that the demand level for a product or a resource will decline as its price rises, and rise as the price drops. Conversely, the law of supply says higher prices boost supply of an economic good while lower ones tend to diminish it.

What factors affect demand and supply?

Price fluctuations are a strong factor affecting supply and demand. When a product gets expensive enough that the average consumer no longer feels it is worth it to buy the product, then the demand declines. This leads to cuts in production that will hopefully stabilize the product's value.

What factors affect demand and demand?

Demand may be defined as the quantity of a commodity that a consumer is able and willing to buy, at each possible price, over a given period of time. • Essential elements of demand are quantity, ability, willingness, prices, and period of time.

Which factors affect supply?

Generally, the supply of a product depends on its price and other variables such as the cost of production.

a. Price. Price can be understood as what the consumer is willing to pay to receive a good or service. ...

b. Cost of production. ...

c. Technology. ...

d. Governments' policies. ...

e. Transportation condition.

How does supply and demand work together?

It's a fundamental economic principle that when supply exceeds demand for a good or service, prices fall. When demand exceeds supply, prices tend to rise. There is an inverse relationship between the supply and prices of goods and services when demand is unchanged.

What happens to supply when demand increases?

An increase in demand, all other things unchanged, will cause the equilibrium price to rise; quantity supplied will increase. A decrease in demand will cause the equilibrium price to fall; quantity supplied will decrease.

What is the theory of demand?

Demand theory describes the way that changes in the quantity of a good or service demanded by consumers affects its price in the market, The theory states that the higher the price of a product is, all else equal, the less of it will be demanded, inferring a downward sloping demand curve.

What are the 4 basic laws of supply and demand?

1) If the supply increases and demand stays the same, the price will go down. 2) If the supply decreases and demand stays the same, the price will go up. 3) If the supply stays the same and demand increases, the price will go up. 4) If the supply stays the same and demand decreases, the price will go down.

The different types of demand are as follows:
i. Individual and Market Demand: ...
ii. Organization and Industry Demand: ...
iii. Autonomous and Derived Demand: ...
iv. Demand for Perishable and Durable Goods: ...
v. Short-term and Long-term Demand:
What creates demand for a product?
You can create demand for a unique product if you can manage to solve a persistent problem for the consumer. People are always running away from pain, and providing them with an outlet is a sure-fire way to create massive demand for your goods.
What are the 7 factors that affect supply?
The seven factors which affect the changes of supply are as follows: (i) Natural Conditions (ii) Technical Progress (iii) Change in Factor Prices (iv) Transport Improvements (v) Calamities (vi) Monopolies (vii) Fiscal Policy.
What can affect demand?
Factors Affecting Demand
Price of the Product. ...
The Consumer's Income. ...
The Price of Related Goods. ...
The Tastes and Preferences of Consumers. ...
The Consumer's Expectations. ...
The Number of Consumers in the Market.
What are the three factors affecting demand?
The demand for a product will be influenced by several factors:
Price. Usually viewed as the most important factor that affects demand. ...
Income levels. ...
Consumer tastes and preferences. ...
Competition. ...
Fashions.
What are the 4 factors of supply?
The four factors that can shift the supply curve include natural conditions, input prices, technology, and government.
What causes increase in supply?
If the cost of production is lower, the profits available at a given price will increase, and producers will produce more. With more produced at every price, the supply curve will shift to the right, meaning an increase in supply.
What causes supply changes?
A change in supply is an economic term that describes when the suppliers of a given good or service alter production or output. A change in supply can occur as a result of new technologies, such as more efficient or less expensive production processes, or a change in the number of competitors in the market.
Is supply and demand a good strategy?
When it comes to profit placement, supply and demand zones can be a great tool as well. Always place your profit target ahead of a zone so that you don't risk giving back all your profits when the open interest in that zone is filled.
How is demand created?
Demand creation is a process that fuels the revenue pipeline so the sales team can meet or exceed their quotas. In other words, it takes your big idea — the creative appeal of your brand — and turns it into sales. That sounds a lot like demand generation, which often gets confused with lead generation.
What are the two parts of demand?
Economists define demand as the quantity of a good or service that buyers are willing and able to buy at all possible prices during a certain time period. Notice that there are two components to demand: willingness to purchase and ability to pay.

Can we control demand?

If you're willing to think and act strategically, you can easily manipulate the laws of supply and demand. It should be surprising to learn, however, that by manipulating the laws of supply and demand, you can make more profit in less time and with far fewer headaches

How do you control demand?

Here are five short-term actions to improve your demand variability management plans in this time of uncertainty:

Maintain transparent, proactive relationships with your suppliers. ...

Activate alternate sources of supply. ...

Reduce lead times. ...

Update inventory policy and planning. ...

Align supply and demand management.

What are the 8 types of demand?

There are 8 states of demand: negative demand, no demand, latent demand, falling demand, irregular demand, full demand, overfull demand and unwholesome demand.

What is Demand?

Types of Determinants of Demand. Every factor has a unique impact on demand. ...

Price of the Product. ...

The Income of the Consumers. ...

Number of Buyers in the Market. ...

Consumer's Expectations. ...

Tastes and Preferences of The Consumers. ...

Complement Goods. ...

Substitute Product.

What is theory of supply?

The law of supply is a fundamental principle of economic theory which states that, keeping other factors constant, an increase in price results in an increase in quantity supplied. In other words, there is a direct relationship between price and quantity: quantities respond in the same direction as price changes.

What are the types of supply?

There are five types of supply—market supply, short-term supply, long-term supply, joint supply, and composite supply.

Which comes first supply or demand?

Demand comes first and it's followed by the corresponding supplies. Supply and demand are both very important to economic activity. Supply is the total amount of a particular good or service available at a given time to consumers at a given price. Demand is a representation of a consumer's desire to purchase goods and services; it acts as a measurement of a consumer's willingness to purchase a specific good or service at a given price. These two economic forces influence each other; they are both important for the economy because they impact the prices of consumer goods and services within an economy and the quantities produced and consumed. Supply and demand are both keys to understanding the economy because they reflect the prices and quantities of consumer goods and services within an economy.

What are the relationship between demand and supply?

According to market economy theory, the relationship between supply and demand balances out at a point in the future; this point is called the equilibrium price.

Economists and companies analyze the relationship between supply and demand when making strategic product decisions. Both economists and companies analyze the relationship between supply and demand when making strategic product decisions. The assumption behind a market economy is that supply and demand are the best determinants for an economy's growth and health.

Consumer Behavior Influences Demand

One way that companies or economists might analyze this relationship is to create graphs that chart the equilibrium price of certain goods and services in order to determine product development and their production schedule. Consumer behavior dictates which products are produced and sold because consumers create the demand that companies attempt to meet. As a result, companies may study consumer behavior in an attempt to understand the current demand and predict future demand. It is vital that companies maintain the capacity to produce enough of a good or service that they can satisfy consumer demands.

Supply and demand are two sides of the same market coin. Generally, supply is how much of something is available or will be produced at a certain price. Demand is how much of something people want to purchase or consume at a certain price. One way to develop a more precise relationship between the two is to consider how the price of something affects its supply and its demand. Generally when the price of a good goes up, so does the supply, since firms are willing to create more when they can sell at higher prices. But when the price of a good goes up consumers will, at the same time, generally demand less. It is the interaction of supply and demand that determines how much will be produced and consumed and at what price, converging to a state known as equilibrium. Hence, I believe supply and demand and manufacture cost which have close cause and effect relationship.

CHAPTER TWO

Learning invisible hand economic method

How may " inivisible hand " factor influence the smart phone manufacturer products demand number increase?
The invisible hand is for the law of supply and demand explains how the pull and push of these two factors serve to benefit sciety as a whole. In simple, every consumer choose to buy the product, he/she pursues to earn the most more interest to the manufacturer needs to produce the product as its product may be of the greatest value to let the consumer intends only his/her own gain, led by an invisible hand to promote the product to let the consumer to make satisfaction to choose to buy the product.
In behavioral economic view, the invisible hand to the product manufacturer may be " the consumer whose satisfactory feeling to use the product".So, the invisible hand meant that ir can not be touch , seen, it only brings feeling to let the consumer to feel. This feeling to the product is very mportant factor to excite the consumer to choose to buy the product, e.g. smart phone product the smart phone buyer's invisible hand factor may include: The smart phone can link to app to use internet service, download documents from smart phone , taking phonoes, watching movie, listening music, clock time etc. function, seeling different countries street locations, instead of general mobile talking function.
So, all of above factors will be future new smart phone main " invisible hand" factors to excite future smart phone buyers to make purchase decision to choose to buy the kind of smart phone among different kinds of smart phone products innovation , when they are manufactured to promote to smart phone market to sell.
So, in smart phone market supply and demand view, the smart phone manufacturer needs to innovate new smart phone products in order to let smart phone buyers fee its news phone buyers feel itsnew smart phone products have unique functions or features to excite its smart phone buyers to choose to buy its new kind of smart phone products, because smart phone buyers will be influences to make final smart phone purchase decision by invisible hand factors from smart phone different new function .
Smart phone manufacturers need to innovate many new functions o future new kinds of smart phone manufacturing in order to bring new invisible hand satisfactory feeling to let any one smart phone buyer to feel whose new smart phone can bring the most unique satisfactory feeling to let them to feel. So, smart phone 's invisible hand factor is main influential factor to bring smart phone manufacturer's new smart phone demand number will increase or decrease. If the smart phone manufacturer can often innovate its smart phone products to let smart phone buyers feel more using satisfactory feeling to its new kind of smart phone more than its other similar kinds of smart phone manufacturers. Then, the smart phone manufacturer ought raise its smart phone purchase number demand easily.
What is smart phone opportunity cost?
Hence, the concept of opportunity cost factor means smart phone manufacturers need to forgone opportunities of time cost , design new kinds of smart phone products, e.g. smart phone pictures, colour and shape , future smart phone manufacturers need to concentrate more time to research how to innovate new featurers and function to let every potential smart phone buyers to bring more functions using satisfactory feeling in order to attract they choose to buy its smart phone product.
On conclusion, opportunity cost to smart phone manufacturers may be forgone spend more time on smart phone design, colour choice, shape choice aspects. Smart phone manufacturers need to spend more time on innovate new feature and function aspects in order to satisfy future smart phone using needs in global competitive smart phone

smart.

Reference

Howlwy, M (2002). The role of consultancies in New Product Development. Journal of product & brand management, 11(7), 477-58.

Rogers,E.M. (2003) Diffusion of innovation, 5th edition, New York: Simon & Schuster.

The Times (2002) Mobile phone sales fall, The Times , 12 mar 25.

Wong, V. (2002). Antecedents of international New product pollout timeliness. Internaional marketing review, 19 (2/3), 120-32

CHAPTER THREE

Manufacturing robots reduce warehouse cost strategy

Explaining the relationship between increasing proficient workers number and avoiding excess resource waste
In organizational behavioral economic view, whether they have cause and effect relationship between employees how to use resources behaviors and organizational resource excess use within organizations ?

In organizational behavioral economic view, whether they have cause and effect relationship between employees how to use resources behaviors and organizational resource excess use within organizations. For example, if the organization has many employees number, whether the organization will use its any internal tangible and intangible resources easily per day.

For construction organization example, one construction organization must need to buy different kinds of construction materials to prepare to let workers to help it to manufacture different kinds of properties or houses (products) in order to sell to property buyers. In its every building construction site, it will need more or less workers, they are needed to use different kinds of construction materials to build housess in different construction sites. I assume that construction site (A), it has 100 construction workers number, every day, construction site (A) 100 workers need to use different kinds of construction materials to help them to build 3 building floors wall at least floor number in the construction site (A).

I assume that these 100 construction workers , they include proficient workers and not proficient workers. For proficient construction workers group, they have 50 number, and not proficient construction workers group, they also have 50 number . Hence, the proficient construction workers only need to spend 3 hours maximum and use less number of constructoin materials, then they can finish to build 3 building floors wall per day.

I also assume that all constructoin material supply number is limited. It means that due to this construction firm needs to pre-booking to purchase this kind of the best quality of constructoin material from overseas before three worths. So, it must not have enough time to pre-booking to purchase this kind of best quality of constructoin materials when they are used rapaidly within one month, due to this one month is the final finishing time to this construction firm within one month. Hence, limited construction material supply number and limited finishing time to build this new 40 floors house within this final one month .

So , not proficient construction workers number , limit number of construction material and per day 8 hours which is its limited resources in behavioral eocnomy view. Moreover, total 50 proficient and not proficient 50 construction workers (human resource employees number) will cause this constructoin firm , it will possible need to build this new 40 floors house are more than one month, if these 50 proficient construction workers , they have more than 30 at least number, they are absent to cause their overall construction workers' efficiency to be fallen down, due to the other 50 not proficient constuction numbers must need their teaching how to cooperate ad how use less materials to build this new 40 floor hourse rapidly in order to raise overall constructon team efficiency and avoid to delay more than one month time to build this 40 floors new house successfully within this final one month time.

Hence, it explains that when one organization has more employees, it does not represent that this organization must need to use more resource to achieve its any mission, such as this construction firm case, although it has 50 not proficient construction workers, they need to use more construction materials to build this new 40 floors house in this construction site (A). But, in fact, it has other 50 proficient construction workers, they know how to reduce construction materials to build every building floor wall for this new 40 floors building house. So, they can teach the not proficient building workers to know hoe to avoid to use extra excess constructon material to finish to construct every building fllor wall. SO, although, it has 50 not proficient construction workers number, but they can be taught to learn how to reduce to use these limited the best quality of construction materials to build this 40 floors new house. It implies that if the construction workers number can increase, e.g. increases more 50 not proficient construction workers, this the best quality of construction material resource number must not need to increase demand, because this construction site (A) has 50 proficient construction workers , they can teach these 50 not proficient construction workers how to avoid to use extra excess this kind of high quality construction material to build this new 40 floor house efficiently and effectively within this one month.

Hence, if this construction firm won't have more than 30 proficient workers number is absent in this final one month, it will have enough proficient construction workers to teach these 50 not proficient construction workers to know how to use this high quality of construction materials to build this 40 floors new house building in order to avoid waste or construction material need shortage challenge occurs in this final one month time.

Consequently , it ought finish to build this 40 floors new house building within this month. Hence, it explains why its this kind of high quality of construction material resource need must not increase, because if its all proficient construction workers is absent and their absent number is less than 30, then they have enough proficient construction workers number , they can teach this 50 not proficient construction workers how to avoid to use extra excess construction materials resource number in order to have enough construction material resource supply to satisfy this new 40 floors building house to finish construction within one month finishing date need.

On conclusion, in organizational behavioral economic view, it explains that resource use need must not be influenced to increase when the organization's employees number increase. It depends on whether the organization has how many talent and proficient workers number in order to assist them and teach the not proficient employees how to use resource to manufacture any kinds of products in order to avoid to spend extra excess of resource need. Hence, organizational behavioral economic view, it can explain that any organization's increase to employees number, it does not mean that its resource number is also needed to increase. Moreover, in organizational behavioral economic view, it also explains that if the organization can have many proficient workers to help it to do any complex tasks, they will help it to bring avoiding waste or excess extra resource to use advantage, because they ought know whether how they work, they can help the organization to improve performance or raise efficiency e.g. car manufacture, computer manufacture, television manufcture etc. home electronic products or car leisure products. Due to that manufacturre processes are complex, if the organization can have more proficient high skillful workers to help it to manufacture their products. They ought help it to use lesser manufacturing time and less manufacturing resource to finish any above these products to compare not proficient or low skillful manufacture workers. So, in long time, the organization must may earn economic low cost benefits from proficient worker individual high manufacturing skillful knowledge behavior or performance. So, organizational behavioral economic theory explains why even the organization plans to increase employees number, it's resources number won't be influenced to increase rapidly because when the organization's proficient high skillful workers number is more 2 times at least than not proficient low skillful workers number. They ought have enough effort to train and teach and cooperate with the not proficient low skillful manufacture workers to improve their manufacture skills in order to raise manufacturing efficiency and reduce extra excess resources waste and avoid to bring long term resource waste economic loss. So, any manufacturing organizations must need to increase proficient workers number to assist the not proficient low skillful workers to learn how to improve their skills and know how to reduce to use excess resources to keep to manufacture the highest number of products aim frequently. Consequently, the organization will bring long term low resource use manufacturing economic benefit.

How manufacturing robots help warehouse to reduce cost ?

What does AI prediction machine mean? Why AI machine can make more accurate economic prediction to compare human economists? How to apply AI machine to make more accurate economic prediciton to compare human economists? In tradition, economists can gather data to make statistics to analysis how to predict this year

or next year either economic growth or recession occurrence in possible. But, since AI machine tool, it can apply to manufacturing, service , logistic , office, hospital, shopping center etc. difference business working environment aspects, whether it can help economists to make more economic prediction in possible or economists will need AI machine to help them to make more accurate economic prediction for businessmen or societies needs. I shall attempt to give evidence to explain as
below:

Economists view our world is differently than most people. Businessmen are influenced everything by forces such as supply and demand, production and consumption, prices and costs economic concept.
However, AI machine is needed to everywhere, such as packed into your smart phones apps, warehouse logistic workers, non manual vehicles. So, AI machine may innovate our lives. Human needs AI machine to assist our tasks from complex to simple. Businessmen may bring economic time and saving long time cost benefits. Such as online shopping method, AI can help consumers find any kinds of different products prices and photos to compare in order to make reasonable purchase decision more easily from webstores channel as well as businessmen can apply ecommerce sale channel to help them to sell products to different countries in short time.

Prediction is being used for traditional tasks in business environment, such as inventional management and demand and supply forecasting. For example, because the smart phone seller predicts smart phone buyers number will reduce when he feels every family, old and young age adult who have owned at least one smart phone to every family in the country. SO, the smart phone seller ought reduce to manufacture and sell the old smart phones in order to avoid the kind of old smart phone price to reduce, due to the kind of smart phone demand purchase number will reduce,but he ouhgt to continue to innovate new kind of smart phone in order to supply new innovative smart phones products to satisfy future smart phone users needs. It is general economists judgement.Such as this smart phone case, when smart phone prediction is cheap, there has two simple economic forces drive the new opportunities, such as new kind of innovative smart phones need that predction new kind of innovative smart phones will be needed to creat in order to keep this smart phone manufacturer competitive ability in the country.

However, at low levels, a prediction machine, such as AI machine can relieve humans of predictive tasks and save on costs, when AI machine help economists or businessmen to do gather this smart phone manufacturer to manufacturing and selling this kind of smart phones data in this country consumption market every day. AI machine can gather data in short time and then it can give this kind of smart phone manufacturing and sale number data to this smart phone company every day in order to make statistic conclusion. So, AI will affect the economic of a business so dramatically, that they will no longer be used to simply enchance productivity in executing against the strategy, they will help this smart phone manufacturewr to change the strategy itself, such as whether
it ought continue to improve or innovate another kind of new smart phone design and function in order to satisfy future smart phone users needs. So, smart phones daily manufacturing and selling data is the most influential point to help this smart phone manufacturer to make decision whether it is the right time to innovate its another new kind of smart phone design and function or not in order to keep its smart phone sale competitive ability in this country.

Amazon can apply AI machine to help it reduces warehouse seeking goods time from shelves. Because Amazon has many shevles, it putted many kinds of products in shelves. Every one of worker will need long time to seek the kind of goods in order to transport to customers when they had bought the kind of goods. Amazon found this long time seeking goods problem to avoid transport time waste. It applied AI transport machine to help human worker to seek any kinds of goods from shelves. On consequently, AI transport machine help every warehouse worker to reduce at least 5 to 10 minutes to seek ths right kind of product from shelves. So, if the warehouse has 600 different kinds of products to prepare to transport to global buyers homes in the day. Every product seeking time from shelves will reduce 600 x 5 minutes or 600 x 10 minutes seeking time. So, this 600 different kinds of products will reduce 3,000 minutes or 6,000 minutes transport time to deliver to global buyers homes. So, AI machine had helped Amazon to reduce goods transport time in this day. It can help Amazon bring economic transport time shorten benefits to let global buyers can get their products within the day or tomorrow rapidly. In this case, AI machine help Amazon 's business model from shopping -then -shipping to shipping -then -shopping , AI helps Amazon to avoid buyers whose purchase goods return occurrence chance when they can be transported to their homes in short time. and accelerates the timing of investment.

Hence, it seems that AI machine may help businesses to bring these economic benefits: mahcine learning is often referred to as advances in artificial intelligence because systems prediction on this technique learn and improve over time, these systems produce significantly more accurate predictions than human economists or businessmen, traditoinal statistics methods require the articulation of hypotheses or at least of human economists analysis. In fact, AI technology is called " machine learning) for a reason. The mahines leearn form data. The prediction machine has to learn how the data is associated with actual incidences of irregular heart problem, such as Amazon transport time reducing case, when Amazon discover it will have many buyers choose either goods return decision more than non -goods return decision. AI mahcine help Amazon to seek goods from shelves to avoid goods long time seeking from human workers when AI transport delivery machine help human workers to do " goods seeking from shelves tasks working first step, then human worker only need to spend time to put the goods to lorry to transport to lorries to drive to airport in order to fly the goods to overseas customers in second time. So, AI machine may help Amazon to gather warehouse different kinds of goods shelves location data any where in order to help human workers to reduce goods seeking timr from shelves. AI mahcine may Amazon warehouse workers to avoid to spend long time to seek goods from shelves, they can concentrate on spending time to put goods on lorries.Also, AI machine help Amazon to reduce warehouse workers number or reduce salaries expenditure, when AI warehouse machine can replace human workers to do goods seeking tasks from shelves.

Ai machine help organizaitons to achieve new division of labour aim. Such as, a law firm may apply AI mahcine help human lawyers to take legal documents and predicted which

information was condfidential. This product is valuable to law firms because when they are required to disclose documents, they have to black out comnfidential information. Historically,

redaction was done by hand, with humans reading documents and blacking out confidential information. SO, AI machine help lawyers to save time and effort. Such as Amazon case, AI machine

creates new division of labor strategy in any one of Amazon warehouse. AI machine will concentrate time on doing " goods seeking tasks from shelves in first step", then human workers will concentrate on time on doing " goods are putting on lorries tasks in second step ". Traditoinal , warehouse workers need to spend time to do seek goods from shelves task and putting goods to lorries tasks both. Nowadays,warehouse AI machine only need to spend time to do seek goods from shelves task , but human workers only need to spend time to do goods are putting to lorries tasks. So, AI machine will change traditional divisoin of labor to warehouse tasks in the future. Because AI machine will help workers to reduce goods transportation time and reducing goods return chance occurrence.

CHAPTER FOUR

Technology innovation strategy

Human Behavioral network job brings social economic benefits

What does human network job mean ? Why may human network job be popular? Why human network job behavior may influence economy ?

Nowadays internet is popular to use. We can apply internet to find data , search any new things, even earn money. Why does internet

may become huma network job source. For example, e-publish may be one kind of new human network job. Any authors may apply internet

channel to help them to sell electronic or paper books from e-publisher web store. They may apply facebook, you tub etc. any online

channel to promote themselves new books to let new readers to know whether when they may buy themselves favourable new topic books to read

from electronic publisher web store.

Thus, future electronic publisher industry may help any authors to build internet network platform to help them to sell and promote

ot advertise their any one new electronic or paper book topic to let global any one reader to choose to buy their any new topic books from electronic publisher web store easily and conveniently. However, it implies that electronic network platform author may be one kind of future new human network job in our societies.

How electronic network platform author job may bring economy benefit in macro economy view? A person can have few friends, contacts and still be very influential if these few

friends and contacts are themselves highly influential, e.g. one author must not need to know any one reader in global society. When they like to choose any electronic books from electronic internet network platform. They may become the author's any one topic book buyer, when they feel the author's any one topic book is fun and attract they make decision to buth the strange author whose the topic book from electronic book publisher's platform web store conventiently in short time. Although, they are strangers, they do not know themselves , but the reader can understand what it way that made Google from writing platofrm to create new creative mind and typing network job method to replace traditional hand writing book method for global authors. It will be one kind of new human network writing job.

Hence, global any one reader can apply an innovative search engine , such as google.com to find whether whom author personal new topic books are value to read from internet.

Then, the electroniuc publisher's web store may be new book store platform sale network to help the author to sell many electronic or paper books from electronic network platform

in short time. So, internet may be future new network plaform to help global any one author to create network writing job absolutely. Furthermore, internet may be popular social media

to help any one author to build goold relationship between his/her readers. It is one kind of new network, human network job. New authors do not need to buy many paper books to prepare to put in any one book shop warehouse. Their every book can print on demand to reduce out of book stock in any one book shop. They may choose to sell either electronic books or paper books both from any one book publisher web store. So, electronic network platform may be one kind of good writing channel to help human authors to create income and it can also help authors to bring new creative mind and new topic fun content books to let readers to know and buy to read from electronic publisher network platform.

Why does human behavior may be one kind of new human network job to bring global economic advantages. ALthough, it may be free income or without inocme, but the person does the network behavior, his/her behavior may be bring advantages to influence many other people's health. For this case, when a worker in a coffee shop in an airport gets a vaccination aganinst the flu, it does not only helps him or her stay healthy, but also helps the many travellers who might otherwise have been inflected if that workers caught the flu. So, the externality , the result implies the vaccination of even a part of a community conveys benefits to the whole community. For example, governments pay special attention to the vaccinations of school children, teachers, health mothers, and the elderly, categories of people particularly susceptible not only to catching, but also to transmitting a disease.

It is not accidential that governments are heavily involved with vaccination . When there are externalities, free market, fail to persuade individual incentives with society's
their the worker's decision of whether to get a vaccine ends up attracting whether other people get sick. The workers might not fully take all these other people's potential suffering into account when making her or his vaccination decision.

As Stanford University does many suggestions, understand this and tries to help them make the right decisions and so providers free flu vaccines for its staff and students.
Small pockets of unvaccinated individuals can allow a disease to gain a spread more widely well-being. For example, parent weighing the costs and benefits of a vaccine for their child is not always thinking of the consequences of that vaccination to other people. THese are markets in which subsidizing or regulating behavior can make everyone better off. Because the reason for requiring that a child be vaccinated before enrolling in school is not just to protect that child, because each child's vaccination affects others via potential contagions.

Robots take our jobs behavioral and economy influences

Robot job behavior brings economy influences

If one day robots can replace human to do simple, even complex jobs. They will bring what influences to our global societial economy.The popular economic refrain declares that the
global middle class is dying and robots will soon take our jobs, e.g. shopping center customer service jobs, library service jobs, cinema ticket sale jobs, restaurant kitchen cooker jobs,
even, bus drivers, taxi drivers etc. public transport driving jobs, accountant, doctors etc. professional jobs. Whether it is beautiful or petty matter if our future societies have many human jobs can be replaced to do from robots. Businessman must may reduce to employ employees and reduce to pay salary or wage, when robots can be replaced to do their employees tasks. But, societies must bring unemployement rate rises , due to societies will have many people loss jobs when their employers choose to buy robots to serve their clients or do any office tasks or customer service or cleaning etc. tasks.

In micro economy view, employers may save money in long term, but in macro economy view, it will cause unemployment ratio rises , even crime rate rises when there are many people lose
jobs in societies. These models of doom, though, fail to account for the hundreds of businesses riding the waves of change in their industries when robots may be invented to replace human to do many simple , even complex tasks in our future societies.

WE may image that one small factory needs to manufacture fishes canes to sell to supermarket, the small , cheaper stuff and higher margin parts of the fishes manufacture industry. Before, this factory needs to employe many human factory workers need to help every fresh customer makeing the perfect fishing gear, designed for performance, durability, and cost in order to achieve to manufacture every fish cane in whole fished processing manufacturing stages. Every worker needs to spend about 15 to twenty minutes to finish every fish cane , till to delivery to any supermarket to sell. If this fish canes manufacturing factory can apply manufacturing robots to help them to finish

any one working tasks , every robot can only spend five minutes to finish whole fresh fish cane manufacturing process. Thus, every robot can
help this factory save 10 to 15 minutes time to finsh every fish cane manufacturing process. IN fact, time is money, because when every robot can help this factory to reduce 10 to 15 minutes time to compare human worker. Then, this factory can finish about 20 fish canes in one hour if it can use robot to help it to manufacture fish canes. Otherwise, if this factory still use human workers to help it to manufacture fish canes, then it can finsh about 3 to 4 fish canes in one hour. SO, the manufacturing efficiency ensures that robots must help this fish manufacturing factory to raise fish canes number more than human workers. So, in robotic behavioral economy view, manufacturing robots must help this fish canes manufacturing factory to raise fish canes manufacturing number and deliver increasing number to supermarkets to prepare to sell every day. Robots can help this fish canes manufacturing factory bring manufacturing time saving, rising manufacturing efficiency, improving performance and reducing wages expenditure long time advantages in micro economy view. However, manufacturing robots can also bring disadvanages to society, e.g. increasing unemployment ratio, increasing crime rate,
this factory workers will lose jobs and income, they need earn social welfare from government and increasing government finance pressure in short time, even long time in macro economic view.

Stanford University graduate program in economics, Scott lecturer explained that "in demand and supply economic theory for robots supply and demand case, robots supply number increasing may influence human workers demand number decrease. It sometimes calls " the efficient frontier".
No specific human beings were mentioned in any of economics classes. As robots supply and demand in market case, They (robots) may be purely theoretical " agents" who reached to the most reasonable sale prices in order to persuade any one businessman buyer to make manufacturing robot buying decision whether robots can help him / her to bring how much saving time , saving money, saving cost, improving performance, efficiency economic benefit before he/she plans to reduce workers number when he/she decides to apply robots to replace human workers in his/her factory or office or any service department, e.g. cinema ticket sale service, shopping center customer service, shopping center cleaning , supermarket customer service etc. service or sale tasks. When robots can replace human to do any one of these tasks in any organizations. So, robots may be human worker agents who reached to prices the way robots would react to a software
command. There was nothing that explained why some people thrived and others did n't or why truly brilliant, hardworking people could fail when much lazier folks succeeded." Having been admitted to the Stanford University graduate program in economics, Scott lecturer hoped to get his answers there.

How robots influence our future social changing? Using the right technology can be a boon to your business in this economy. For internet example, it is easier than ever to find well-matched customers all around the world, to stay in contact with them, and to more quickly design the products they want. If you focus solely on being cutting -edge, though you risk letting the technology
take over what should be very robust relationships with your customers , employees, and colleagues. IN nowaddays society, technoligical advances and cutomation, personal
relationships in business are more crucial than ever. I mean that robots can not replace human to serve clients to let them to feel more comfortable and passion more easily. For shoe shop case example, if the shoe shop apply one robot to serve its clients to replace human shoe salesperson to serve its shoe customers. Robots ensure that they can not persuade every shoe potential buyer to make shoe buying decision more easily when robots need to contact every shoe potential buyer. The reason is simple, because robots can not touch any one shoe buyer individual emotion very easier.
If the shoe buyer needs the robots to help him/her to choose any right shoe styles when he/she can not feel himself / herself can make the most right shoe style choice decision. The robots can not replace human shoe salesperson to make shoe style choice judgement more easily. They must need longer time to analyze whether which shoe style may be the most suitable to the shoe buyer. Otherwise, human shoe salesperson may attempt to make the most right shoe style choice decision to help any one shoe buyer to chooce the most right style shoe because he/she owns shoe style sale experience, shoe style knowledge, the most important reason is that they can feel every shoe customer

individual emotion to touch whether he/she will feel comfortable or happy when they attempt to help every shoe customer to seek the most right shoe style in every shoe customer whole shoe searching processing. Othwerwise, serving robots are only one machine, they can not touch or feel every shoe customer individual emotion whether he/she feel comfortable or unhappy or happy when they need to contact them in whole shoe searching processing. Hence, I believe that some tasks robots can

not repalce human staff to do very easily. Otherwise, robots may bring disadvanatges to let any one businessman to loss his/her customers, due to robots can not touch every customer

emotion to compare human staff in service tasks more easily. Robots serving customer behaviors may cause money lose and customers number lose to the shop in micro economic view.

Intellectual human economic behaviors

What does intellectual human economic behaviors mean ? I believe that when we choose or decide to do intellectual behaviors, then our societies will be influenced to bring economic growth in consequence.I shall attempt to indicate pollution case to explain how and why eithet our intellectual or foolish behaviors may bring economic growth or recession in consequence as below:

On one hand, for air pollution social case aspect example, if we only consider to buy cars to drive for working aimr or holiday leisure aim. Then, our societies air will be polluted. Our health will be influenced to bad. Our car driving behaviors may cause global environment air pollution serously. In long tiem, global air pollution will bring our bodies health to be bad. Although, ourselves car driving behaviors may bring our driving travelling leisure enjoyment and comfortable feeling in short time, also we so not need to pay public transport fare often, but we need to compensate ourselves health economic intangible loss due to air pollution , when cars number increases, dirty air will cause ouselves health to become bad.

In the result, we will need to pay more medical expenditure when we are old age, due to ourselves bodies will become bad, due to we breathe global dirty air every day, due to ourselves cars pollute air in long time, e.g. 10 to 20 years, even 30 more without limited air pollution environment. So, driving cars behavior may be one kind of human foolish behavior and our foolish behavior may bring ourselves future long time medical expenditure absolutely.

One the other hand, water pollution social aspect, if we often keep much rubblish to pollute sea, oil exploration porcessing pollute ocean , ships gas pollute ocaen, then fishes will eat polluted food and drive dirty water, due to global ocean is polluted.

In fact, because human only to conside how to buy boats to carry on leisure enjoyment activities, or catch cruises to travel on the sea. Also, oil manufacturers only consider researching anywhere to find new oil exploration places to manufacture oil product, when their oil exploration processes pollute ocarn . Consequently, global fishes drink polluted warer or eat polluted food. They will have poison. SO, human will have high chance to eat poison polluted fishes, due to fishes are poison or are polluted.

So, human is doing foolish activities, we only hope to find oil exploration places to pollute ocean or we only spend money to buy ticket to catch ships to travel anywhere in global ocean. All of these human foolish behaviors will bring pollution to global ocean. On consequently, we will need to compensate to eat polluted or dirty or poision fishes, ourselves bodies health will be bad. In long time, we need have high chance to pay medical expenditure when we are old. So, pollution case may be one good example to explain how and why human foolish behavior may influence ourselves future need to compensate serious medical loss.

All of these human foolish behavior will bring pollution to global ocean. On consequently, we will need to compensate to eat polluted or dirty or poison fished , ourselves bodies health will be bad. In long time, we will have high chance to pay medical expenditure, when we are old. So, pollution case may be one good example to explain how and why human ourselves intellectual or foolish behaviors may influence future long time economic loss or economic growth or recession in micro and micro economic view.

On another water pollution aspect hand, if we often keep rubbish to sea, oil exploration processing pollutes ocean and ships' gas pollute ocean, then fishes will eat polluted food and drink dirty water, due to fishes will eat polluted food and drink dirty sea water because the global ocean is polluted seriously.

In fact, because human only consider how to buy boats to carry on any leisure water activities, or catches cruises

to travel on the sea. Also, oil manufacturers only consider any where to find oil exploratin places to manufacture oil products from ocean, when their pol exploration processes can plooute ocean. Consequently, global fishes drink polluted water or eat direty food. They will have poison. So, human will have high chance to eat poison fishes.
Otherwise, such as pollutin case, it can infuence inflation or deflation. Consequently, the reason indicates supply and demand theory. If air pollution is serious, then we will consider health issue, global cars demand number may be influenced to reduce, when global cars number demand will reduce, global car prices and supply number will need to change to fall down in order to attract or persuade global car consumers choose to make car purchase decision.
Hence, global car manufacture number and car price will be influenced to reduce, due to global air pollution issue. Consequently, deflation will occur because when the country citizen usually does not spend much extra saving money to buy car expensive goods. Money value will be low. Otherwise, if global cair pollution is not serious, human considers to buy cars to enjoy driving leisure lives. So, global car demand is influenced to increase , also global car price will also influenced to increase.

Consequently, gobal human will choose to buy cars to drive. Due to we accept to spend extra saving to buy expensive car goods. Car sale price and supply may be influenced to rise up. Money value is influenced to reduce. Inflation may be influenced, due to global car consumers number increases, we would not have extra money to spend easily. Car expensive goods expenditure influences our spending habit to avoid to make car purchase decision more easily. So, human intellectual or foolish activities may bring inflation or deflation consequency in possible indirectly in macro economic view.

On conclusion, above pollution case explain that how and why human intellectual or foolish economic behaviors may bring inflation or deflation consequency as wll as economic growth or recession consequency as well as any goods demand and supply increasing or decreasing consequency. It implies that human behavior may have indirect relationship to influence any goods demand and supply number to either increase or decrease result as well as any goods price will be influenced to increase or decrease in micro and macro economic view.

The relationship between social change and human behavior

Why does economic changes may influence human individual behavioral change? I shall attempt to indicate shopping behavior and staying at home behavior to explain their case and effect relationsip as below:

Human behavior can be influenced by economic change or economic change can be influenced by human behavior? Why does recession may influence consumers reduce shopping desire? In social recession suitation, it is possible that many people lose jobs suddenly, due to businessmen lose many customers. They need to make decision to reduce employees number in order to continue to keep businesses. Consequently, many firms (organizations) their employees may lose jobs. When they have much time, due to lose jobs, they will feel to avoid to spend too much time and money to go to shopping often. Many losing jobs people, they will often stay at homes.

So, they will reduce time to go to shopping, then non essential products won't their preferable choice purchase products. Hence, recession will change many losing jobs people their shopping or consumption desires to avoid to buy non essential products often . Usually when economic boom, many people have jobs to do because consumers number must increase when many people have jobs to do. Then, many people can accept to spend money to buy non essential products often. Many people feel spend time to go to shopping can satisfy their purchase of any kinds of new products useful psychology or desire. So, recession is one good example to explain it can influence many people do not like often to leave homes to go to shopping easily. Many people like to stay at homes, becaue they feel worry about spending too much shopping time when they leave homes. Their staying home time is one good negative shopping behavior example. So, economic change may influence human individual behavior changes , they have direct cause and efect relationship in behavioral economic view.

May human behavior influence economic change? Is it possible that human behavior may bring the country social economic change in macro economic or micro behavioral economic view ? I shall indicate publishing industry example. Do you feel that if there are many students feel learning is very important when they read many books or many of students feel interesting to read or they have reading new books in habit, then it is possible that the country will have many students like to spend time to go to any book shops to choose the books, they feel that they can help they learn new knowledge. Then the country will increase students number, they often spend time to visit any one book shop every week. Their visiting book shops behavior which may become their habits. So, the country will increase students number, they often spend time to visit book shops. Also, it implies that visiting book shops behaviors may be their behavioral habits.

So, when the country has many students often spend time to visit book shops , their visiting book shops behaviors may help any one book shop to raise books sale chance. So, the country's student individual often visiting book shop behaviors, their habitual visiting book shops behaviors must may assist help any one book shop to increase books sale number absolutely.

Consequently, any one book shop , its books sale bumber must be influenced to increase to increase because the country will have many students like or feel need visit book shops habit in order to choose any suitable books to buy to read at home in order to raise themselves learning effort. When the country has many bok shops often have many students visit their book shops, then their books sale number may be influenced to increase. It explain why student individual visiting book shop behavior may help any one book shop sale number increases also.

How human productive behavior may influence economic development

May any country which citizen behavior assist themselves country development? It is one cause and effect economic question. I mean that if the country itself citicen can not concentrate mind or energy to choose to do one kind of industry in order to let themselves country can bring the most benefit, then whether the counry itself economy can bring the most serious economic benefit. I shall attempt to indicate these countries themselves indistry choice to explain whether these countries themselves citizen productive behavior may help themselves countries to achieve the largest economic benefits. I shall indicate as below:

New Zealand farmer individual wine productive behavior

For New Zealand country example, this country concerns itself effort is foucs on farming agricultural aspect. So, this country has many farmers concentrate on farming agricultural aspect. May New Zealanders choose to spend time to produce different kinds of wines, e.g. wine or red grape wine is for the people are eating meat, or they are eating dinner.

When these New Zealanders their behaviors choose to do farming or agriculture to grow and produce different kinds of taste of white or red grape wine drinking products job. Themselves grape agriculture behavior will influence these New Zealanders themselves, they can learn how to improve different kinds of grape wine drinking products in order to achieve every kinds of white or read grape wines taste improving aim during their white or red grape producing process.

Why can New Zealander every individual white or read grape wine producers improve their white or read grape wine taste more easily? In behavioral economic view, it can explain that why any one New Zealander white or read grape wine producer can be encouraged or excited or persuaded to concentrate nervous and energy and effort to learn how to improve their white or red grape wine products easily.

In fact, New Zealand is one agricultural food export country. It has good natural environment resource , e.g. land, seed to provide any one farmer to produce themselves any kinds of agricultrual food products, e.g. fruit, or wine food products. Because New Zealanders know themselves country has enough natural resource . So, in common, many New Zealanders choose to attempt to do farming agricultural jobs in order to export themselves any kinds of fruit or meat or wine products to overseas or sell to domestic in order to earn profit.

So, when these New Zealand farmers number has been increasing every year. This country farmers will feel themsleves competition between this New Zealand farmers themselves are serious due to they may feel New Zealanders choose to do agriculture businesses in order to export themselves different kinds of farming food to overseas or sell to local to earn profit.

Hence, when many New Zealand farmers feel that farmers number has been increasing every year. They will feel themselves competition is serious. They must need to spend much time and nervous and effort to research what method is the best how to produce the best taste of white or red grape wine products in order to let local or overseas wine buyers to choose to buy his/her producing white or read grpae products to drink.

Hence, in competition psychological view, may influence many New Zealand white or reaad wine producers had been beginning to change their learning behavior on researching what method is the best in order to produce the best quality of taste red or white wine products to sell in order to attract overseas or local white or read grape wine drinkers to choose to buy his/her wine products. Their behavior will focus on learning how to raising or improving white or read grape wine taste method more than only focus on producing a large number white or red grape wine products. They believe wine quality is more important to compare wine producing number. So, New Zealand wine producers themselves wine producers behaviors have been changing on concentrating on researching wine quality method aspect more then wine producing number aspect in behavioral economic view.

America high technological productive behavior

For America example, US is one high technological country, it owns many high technological knowledge talent inventors, e.g. computer science inventors. Hence, US must attract many diferent countries owning high technological computer inventors choose to go to US to develop their computer science profession career. Also, it seems that when many computer science inventors or professions choose to go to US to develop themselves computer science new career. In behavioral economic view, due to their leaving themselves countries choice, which may bring influence themselve country job behaviors need to be changed. They must need to adapt US new live. Because they will forgive their past computer science job. These computer science professionals need to spend time to adapt US new lives. They " past computer science job behaviors" will need to be changed to their new US any computer employer's new computer science job model.

Because their traditional computer science jobs needed to be forgot in their themselves countries. They will feel their old computer science job knowledge and behavior needed to change in order to let their US any one new of computer company employer feels satisfactory to accept their new working behavior in any one US computer organization.

So, on the other hand, many US computer company employer will feel that they must need time to accept any one new overseas computer science professions their working behaviors, their working attitude daily, because these foreign comouter science professional, their past computer working behaviors and working attitude must be different to US domestic computer science professions.

In behavioral economic view, these overseas computer science professions, their working behaviors and attitude must be needed to change in order to adapt any one US new computer company itself domestic or local computer science professional stafs themselves daily working behaviors and attitude because these overseas and local computer science professionals must need to team work together.

In behavioral economic view, it is only one way that foreign computer science professionals must need to change themselves past country traditiona daily working behaviors and attitude in order to cooperate with these US local computer science professionals in teams more easily.

Consequently, if these foreign compute science professionals can change their past working behaviors and attitude to let any one US local computer science professional feels to cooperate with them easily in short time. Then, the US computer company itself whole computer professional teams themselves efficiencies will be influenced to raised or improved by the changing past working attitude and working behaviors of these foreign computer science professionals. So, in behavioral economic view, only if US any one computer company hopes itself computer teams themselves efficiency can be raised or improved when it decides to employ foreign computer science professionals and US domestic computer science professionals. They need to work in teams together. They must need to let these foreign computer science professionals to know how to change their working behaviors and attitude to let their domestic computer science professionals feel easy to work together. Then, the US computer company itself whole team efficiency must be rasied or improved easily in short time.

- China share market investing behavior

For China share market example, economic development depends on financial market. Because if many Chinese have interest to invest to carry on shares buying and selling activities in orde to learn how to earn shares interest and share profit when the China shareholder can make decision to sell himself/herself shares in the the high price, then he/she can earn money when he/she can sell the China company's shares in the high sale share price position.

If China has many Chinese like to spend time to carry on investing shares activities. Themselves shares buying and selling behaviors will influence China has many companies can increase fund from many Chinese shareholders in order to have enough money to expand or develop themselves businesses in China in long term.

Consequently, when China can have many Chinese like to attempt to carry on buying and selling shares investing behaviors in China share market. Themselves buying and selling shares behaviors can help many Chinese companies have effort to increase enough money or capital in order to continue to do their businesses in long term absolutely. So, it explains why when many Chinese become shareholders , they can assist China will have many companies continue to develop their businesses if many Chinese like to carry on shares buying and selling investing behaviors in long time in China financial investment market nowadays in behavioral economic view.

Why has any individual country have many people invest share behavior which can influence the country's macro consumption desire?

I shall apply shares market buying and selling investment behavior to explaiin why shares investment behavior which may impact the country's overal consumption desire as below:

In behavioral economic view, I assume that when the coutry has many people have interest to attempt to carry on shares buying and selling investment behavior, then their frequent shares buying and selling behaviors which may bring negactive consumption desire or shopping desire of these shares investors their consumer behavior.

The reason is simple, when the country has many share buyers number suddenly been increasing rapidly. Consequently, these large group share investors must need to spend much time to research any kinds of company shares variations, whether when their share prices will rise up of fall down in order to achieve buying the company's shares in the lowest price and selling the company's shares in the highest price level in order to earn profit.

Basic on this reason, they must need to spend much extra time to research share prices changing behavior every day, e.g. one working person will wait to leave his/her job, after he/she can spend time to gather data to research the day's share price changing behavior after dinner. So, the working person's right time may be his/her share price market research behavior. Before he/she may spend his/her night time to go to shopping after dinner, but nowadays, he/ she will fogive to do his/her shopping behavior before dinner or after dinner at hight sometime. He/she will make decision to spend much night time to turn on computer to click on share market website to research his/her share purchase choice to investigate whether his/her share price whether it rises up or falls down at the moment in order to make his/her share buying or selling decision at ever night time.

I mean the when the country has many people are share investors, their shares investment behavioral spenging time which will influence many shops lose customers at might often because the country will have many people feel need to spend night time to turn on computer or watch television to investigate share price variation. So, the country will have many people / share investors choose to stay at home in order to carry on share price variation investigation behavior, they need to listen share market update news from radios or watch the share market update news from computer or TV at home every night. Consequenly, they must reduce times to leave themselves homes at night. So, their shopping behavior also will be reduced. Because these share investors feel need to spend time to investigate share price variation news at homes which can bring economic benefits (high opportunity benefits) when they choose to forgive to leave homes to go to shopping times (opportunity cost) every night.

On conclusion, it seems that when the country has many people are share investors, then their share price investigating behavior may bring negative shopping emotion at night. Consequently, the country's any one shop may lose many customers from this share investor consumer group in behavioral economic view. Hence, when the country's share investors number had been increasing rapidly, it will influence any shops lose many customers from this share investing customer group at night frequenly in short time, even long time in behavioral economic view, because their shopping desires or shopping emotion will be brought negative feeling when they make decisions to spend much time to listen radios or watch TV or computers share price update nes at night. Hence, share market will bring negative impact to influence consumer shopping desire or negative shopping emotion in behavioral economic view.

Can technology influence human shopping behavioral change?

Nowadays, technological development has reached mature stage, whether technological mature stage may bring positive or negative shopping emotion influence to global consumers. I shall aplly internet inventin or ecommerce shopping channel tool to explain whether internet technology can bring postive or negative influence to global consumer behavior in behavioral economic view.

Internet is a good technological tool, it brings e-commerce business chance. In fact, commonly, global has have many businessmen choose to use internet channel to carry on their products transactions between global online-buyers and their electronic websites. So, global many shoppers had begun to feel online shopping is more convenient to compare visiting shops shopping. Their shopping behaviors have been changed from internet technological tool. Global has many shoppers choose to buy any products from any overseas or local businessmen their web stores. They only need to spend time to find any businessmen their webstores to choose the most suitable products to pay visa to buy from their webstores. at homes. So, in general, global had have may shoppers had changed their shopping behaviors from visiting shops to visiting webstores at homes often.

So, it seems that internet technological tool had influenced global many shops disappear, but internet webstores will be replaced their actual shops on streets. Some of businessmen either they choose webstores to replace shops or choose websotes and shops both or still keep shops only. Hence, internet tool influences global businessmen have three kinds of products sale channels to let globa local and overseas consumers to choose how to buy their products. However, in fact, many of global shoppers, youngers and olders had begun to accept to buy any products from webstores. They feel to spend time to leave homes to visit shops , their shopping behaviors will be wasted time to not essential part to their daily lives. Hence, since internet technological invention, it had changed many consumers their traditional visiting shops shopping habit to change to buying products from webstores channel.

However, on the one hand, internet creates webstores ecommerce shopping channel to let global many consumers do not need to leave homes to go to shopping. It brings negative visiting shops shopping emotion to global general consumers nowadays. But on the other hand, it also brings positive visiting internet webstores shopping emotion to global general consumer nowadays. So, it seems that global many consumers feel that they often do not need to spend much time to go out shopping. Many global consumers feel convenient and enjoy to choose any products to buy from different internet webstores, when the online buyer chooses the most suitable product, he she only needs to pay visa card to buy the product from the online seller's webstore conveniently at home.

Hence, online shopping can bring economic benefit to online buyers, e.g. avoiding walking time or spending transport fare to visit the shop to go to shopping, shortening or reducing shopping time to do another important matter.

On conclusion, global many consumers began feel online shopping can bring more economic benefits on shortening shopping time, avoiding transport fare spending aspect. So, online shopping will be popular shopping behavior for future long time. It may encourage global many shoppers can make rapid shopping decision in short time in order to carry on any products buying transaction to global any one online shopper in short time easily in behavioral economic view. So, global many businessmen had begun to build themselves one attraction webstore in order to persuade different countries consumers to choose to click themselves webstores from internet channel to buy any kinds of products in short time easily.

So, internet technology had changed consumers traditional shopping behaviors to build positive online shopping emotion as well as raise online sellers' any products sale chance easily in behavioral economic view.

Why and how human behavior may influence the country's economic growth or recession?

When one country has many people choose to do the same matter for one period, whether their behavior may influence the country's pvera; economic growth or recession . I shall attempt to indicate cases toexplain their relationship as below:

For flowing rubblish behavioral case example, do you feel that when the country has many people often flow rubblish on the streets, instead of their flowing rubblish behavior may bring streets dirty? But, their flowing rubblish behavior may explain that this country has people may have enough money to buy food to ear, or enough cloths to wear, enough bottles of water to drink, even they may have enough money to buy new television, radio, refrigeraters , washing machines, desktops or laptops electronic home products from old to new to use in order to satisfy their living needs. So, when they flow old electronic home products, their flowing old home electronic products behaviors may seem that they have enough money to buy other new home electronic products to replace old home electronic products to use at homes.

However, it seems thaat this country ought have many people have jobs to do. So, many of them, they can easy to make purchase decison to flow any old home electronic products and buy any new home electronic products to use . Because this country has many people have jobs to do. So, they can often not use old home electonic products to become rubblishs to flow on streets after they had bought any kinds of new home electronic homes.

In fact, it also implies that this country's economy grows rapidly. So, many businesses can glow up rapdly. When they expanded their businesses, they must need to increase employees number in order to let they help themselves to raise productivity or serve their clients absolutely. So, when the country has many businesses can grow up, it seems that its economy must be better or it is improved to compare past. Due to many different kinds of home electronic products had been often bought to use by this country people in this period. So, this country's any streets can be observed that expensive electronic home products were flowed on streets anywhere. then, this country will have many electronic home products sellers can sell their home electronic products very easily. When this country has many people can find any kinds of jobs to do easily. So, due to unemploymen rate had been decreasing.

In behavioral economic view, as this many electronic home products rubblish country case, we can observe this country may have many people have jobs to do. So, consumption number has been increased long time. So, cheap food, or expensive home electronic products may be rubblish on any streets. This country's people , their flowing rubblish behaviors may be explained that many of people have enough jobs to do, so they have ability to buy any good taste food to eat or buy any kinds of expensive electronic home products to use. So, this country's economy may be improved for this long period. So, in behavioral economic view, when this country can have many electronic home products rubblishs are flowed on anywherer in streets frequently. It seems that this country will have many people have jobs to do, so it causes they often change old home electronic products or replaced them easily, when they have enough income to spend to buy any kinds of new home electronic products to use at homes easily. Moreover, their flowing old electronic home products behaviors also indicate that this country has many people their salaries may be increased in possible from their emplyers. When this country can have many different kinds of home electornic products are sold. It means that this country's electronic home products needs or demand had been increasing, due to many people have jobs to do and income increases to excite their living of needs also improve. Consequently, this country may seem have better economic improvement. We can observe from this country's electronic home products rubblish increasing income in theis period.

On conclusion, this country ought experience economic growth at this period. So, " flowing expensive electronic home rubblish increasing number " may seem that this country's economic growth is rapidly in this period, due to many people have jobs to do as well as salaries increase in this period.

Technology how impacts human behavior changing?

Technology how influences human behavior to bring changing? For example, online share purchase and sale transaction from smart phone brings share investor can do share buying or selling transation in any where and any time conveniently, non manual driving auto vehicle, bring car owner feels comfortable and spends free time to do other matter, e.g. reading, listening mucis in himself or herself car freely. electrical energy vehicle can help car owner to reduce air polluton and it can brings the drivers do not feel drive long time in any journeys in order to avoid air pollution for environmental protection responsible car drivers in our societies. Thus, they will drive long time in any journeys when they can drive electronic energy cars to replace oil energy cars.

However, online technology can also bring consumers can choose to stay at homes to buy any things from seller individual online webstore conveniently. Such as online technology can bring shoppers do not need to spend much time to visit shops to buy any things. They can choose any kinds of products from any online sellers individual online webstores conveniently at homes. Online technology excite busy consumers can make purchase decision easily as well as it can help online sellers sell any kinds of products from internet easily.

In behavioral economic view, technology can change human behavior to be improved, it can let human feels comfortable, more free time ro use, rapid making any decisions, such as apply smart phones to make share purchase or sale transaction decision, online shopping decision, even travelling any where decision in short time, when the traveller finds the most cheap hotel accommodation room price and air ticket price frm any travel agent online tourism webstore, then the potential travel customer can follow the online hotel accommodation price and air ticket price data to make decision when to buy the air ticket from the airline travel agent or make decision when to prebook which hotel accommodation room to go to the country to travel from online travel agent tourism webstores. So, technology can encourage global any country travelers to make anywhere to trvel rapidly. If the traveler can find the country's general hotel rooms and airline tickets prices had been decreasing more sightly. The traveler may make travel decision to choose the country to travel in short time, then he/she can prebook the country;s any hotel room and airline ticket to pay by visa fraom the country's any hotel and airline travel agent webstores., before one week, even one month or more easily. Hence, online technology can also encourage traveler individual frequent travel times to be increased, due to global travelers can find any hotel rooms and airline tickets prices from internet conveniently at homes. They do not need to spend time to visit any airline travel agent to enquire travel choice country's hotel rooms prices and airline ticket prices. They can compare global travel of countries choices ' all hotels rooms and airline agents air tickets prices to make prebook airline seat and hotel room decision before one week, one month even six months early.

On conclusion, online technology can encourage global travelers can make travelling any where and when traveling time desicions easily. It can excite tourism industry develops in long time. Also, such as electricity cars invention can encourage environment protection car owners do car purchase decision easily, because they can choose to drive electronic energy cars to replace oil energy cars in order to avoid air pollution occurs easily. So, electronic cars can increase electronic car purchasrs number, due to many of environmental protection attitude of car owners can choose to drive electricity cars to bring air cleans, even non -manual driving cars can encourage lazy driving and free time driving car owners to choose to buy non-manual (artificial intelligent) cars to drive , because they can spend much free time to read, listen music or do any matters in themselves cars, they do not need to drive cars, robotic (AI) auto driving machine is such one non-manual driver to help them to drive themselves cars confidently. So, non-manual driving cars can attract lazy and enjoying free time driving car owners to choose to buy to replace traditional manual cars to drive easily. Moreover, online share transaction can help any share investors to make share buying and selling decision in short time easily. When they can apply smart phones technological tool to carry on share buying and selling activities easily. They can observe any share rising or falling price suitation from smart phones in any where any any time easily. So, smart phone technology can help global any shareholders to make share purchase and sale transaction easily. So, technology can encourage human makes decision in short time rapidly.

How and why employees behaviors may influence economy development?

In behavioral economy view,I believe the country's any organizational employees behavior may bring indirect relationship to influence the country's long term economic development. I shall indicate past manufacture industry social development period to explain their relationship. For many countries' past business activities had belonged to manufacturing industry, such as US, UK past before 1980 year, it focused on steel manufacturing and steel manufacturing related machine products. So, US, Uk developed countries manufacturing industries may be past main country's economic income sources. I assume US , UK past had one million number different kinds of industries. They ought had about seven houndred thousand number organizational businesses were belonged to manufactured industry. They may include:

Steel manufacturing and steel related machine manufacturing, e.g. vehicle manufacturing, home appliances, e.g. washing machine, television, radio, refrigerate cooler, heater, air condition etc. different kinds of different kinds of steel -related manufacturing machine, they were manufactured from US, UK steel machine manufacturers. So, US, Uk the other three hundred thousand number industry may be general service industry, e.g. hotel service, restaurent, cinema, public transport service, tourism lesiure , wine bar, supermarket etc. different kinds of non-manufacturing industries business organizations were operated in UK, US past before 1980 year.

So, in UK, US developed countries industry development history, they ought have high percentage of businesses belonged to steel related manufacturing machine and steel products. Also, in the past before 1980 year, US, Uk business employers , they employed many workers are manufacturing workers. They needed to spend long time to work in factories. They were skillful workers, and they are trained to manufacturing cars, washing machine, television, heater, etc. even steel itself different kinds of steel related products to prepare to deliver to their shops to sell to US, Uk local or overseas clients.

So, I believe that past UK, US ought employ many employees, they belonged to skillful manufacturing workers, manufacture increasing steel machine or steel related machine number of products rapidly daily. So, if UK, US had had many of these manufacturing factories owned high skillful workers, then their manufacturing steel-related machine or steel both kinds of products number must be influenced to raise rapidly. Consequently, their steel machine manufacturing products would been exported to overseas or would been sold to local both markets , they may be influenced to raise sale number. They (these manufacturing workers) needed to be trained to know how to manufactur these different kinds of machine products in the efficient teams and they ought to be trained to raise their efficiencies in order to shorten time to manufacturing many kinds of steel related manufacturing machine or steel itself products rapidly. So , if their efficiencies and manufacturing performance was improved, these US, UK any one manufacturing worker and their teams ought achieve raising productivities significantly.

Hence, when past UK, US manufacturing industry development period, if these two countries‘ any manufacturing factories could have many manufacturing workers could be trained to be skillful and proficient manufacturing workers. Then, in past every day to these factories workers, they ought help their steel or steel related manufacturing employers to raise any kinds of machine or steel products number in every team. So, when past in the manufacturing industry development, US, UK could have many factories' manufacturing workers themselves steel or steel related machine products manufacturing skill could be trained to to improve to any kinds of these machine or steel manufacuring products quality as well as their products number could be influenced to raise by themselves skillful improvement significantly every day.

Then, what would be influenced to occur to past UK, US manufacturing industry period? In behavioral economic view, when these two manufacturing industry developed countries, such as UK, US , if they had many factories workers can be trained to improve their skill in order to achieve any kinds of steel or steel-related machine products quality could be improved as well as products manufacturing number could be also increased absolutely.

In consequence, past UK and US both countries ought increase themselves any kinds of steel and steel related machine products number to be supplied to themselves local shops to let local clients to choose any one kind of machine manufacturing products to buy easily as well as they could also export to supply overseas any countries to buy their different kinds of steel or steel related machine products to let overseas steel or steel related manufacturing machine product buyers, they can have many of these different kinds of these steel or steel-related different kinds of manufacturing machine from UK and UK these both countries easily to compare other countries.

On conclusion, I believe that past US, and UK macro manufacturing industry income GDP would increase significantly. So, they would have good economic growth performance because when many of these manufacturing workers themselves manufacturing effort could be improved. So, it explained when employees manufacturing abilities can influence economic growth indirectly.

Robots invention whether they can help organizations to raise efficiencies or inefficiencies?

In behavioral economic view, in any organizations, when the organization hopes its worker teams can raise efficiencies , the organization may choose to increase more workers number and/or it can provide training to improve these workets themselves skills in order to raise their efficiencies. For one warehouse example, when the warehouse increases many goods , they are needed to delivered these goods from the shelves to the delivering destination locations. If this warehouse supervisors feel these workers themselves goods delivery speeds are slow, which is possible due to this warehouse's workers number is not enough. So, this warehouse supervisor ought increase workers number in order to increase their goods delivery speed in order to deliver goods from the shelves to every indicated goods delivery destination in order to let any one lorry driver can transport the right kinds of goods and ensure the accurate goods number to transport to any one client home rapidly.

However, if this warehouse supervisor planed to buy several warehouse goods delivery robots to assist these warehouse workers to find the right kinds of goods from shelves and then deliver to the right destination location in the warehouse. So, these warehouse orkers can concentrate on counting the accurate goods number and ensuring the right kinds of goods in order to prepare to let lorry drivers to transport these goods to these goods of buyers themselvers homes rapidly. Consequently, in the first step, robots can concentrate on finding th right goods from shelves and delivers them to the right goods transportation of location destination. Then, in the second step, these warehouse workers can concentrate on counting the accurate goods number and ensuring the right kinds of goods in order to prepare to put them to the lorry. Consequently, when warehouse robots and warehouse workers can cooperate to work together, the most important, robots, can deal on finding the right kinds of goods and deal on delivering the accurate number of goods of job duty as well as these warehouse workers can only concentrte on counting the right kinds of goods number in order to avoid it has none any mistake of wrong kinds of goods and inaccurate goods of delivery number to be transported to the lorry and to deliver to any one buyer's home.

So, it seems that warehouse robots ought help any one warehouse worker to raise himself efficiency and avoid goods delivery of mistake occurrence easily as well as their help to warehouse workers that can let any one goods buyer feels their goods can be delivered to their homes rapidly. Moreover, warehouse robots can also help these warehouse workers to raise efficiencies because warehouse robots can help them to shorten goods delivery time between any one shelf and any one goods delivery destination of location in the warehuse because robots may help them to find the right kinds of goods from the right shelf in the short time. So, any one worker does not need to spend long time to seek anywhere is the right shelf location for the kind of goods when the kind of goods are needed to deliver to the buyer's home from lorry. Warehouse robots can help them to do this aspect of " finding the goods from the right shelf in short time job duty". So, any one warehouse worker only needed tospend less time to do the counting of any right kind of goods number and ensuring the right kind of goods job duty. Consequently, this warehouse 's any one worker, his any one kind of goods delivery time may be reduced, because robots' assistance and they may have more confidence to avoid mistake to deliver the wrong number of goods and/or the wrong kind of goods to any one goods buyer's home.

On conclusion, it seems that warehouse robots ought may help any one warehouse worker to raise efficiency for any one team in the warehouse as well as the warehouse any one supervisor does not need to spend much time to observe any one worker individual performance for " goods delivery job duty aspect" because their goods delivery job duty that had been replaced to do by these several warehouse robots. Robots can achieve the more accurate of right kinds of goods and the right number of goods delviery job performance to compare any one of human warehouse worker themselves right kinds of goods of delivery and right number of goods of delivery job performance. So, when robots can participate to cooperate with this warehouse's any one worker to do their goods of delivery job duty in this warehouse every day. Then, robots can raies any one of supervisor individual confidence in order to let they do not need to spend time to observe any one of worker individual whose goods of delivery job performane. They can concentrate on supervising any one worker whose goods transport to lorry in the final step in order to avoid to deliver wrong goods number and / or wrong kind of goods to any one goods buyer's home every day. Consequently, this warehouse's overall teams of their delviery of goods performance many be improved by robotss' participatin to goods of delivery task as well as this warehouse's oveall teams themselves efficiencies may be influenced to raise by robots' goods of delivery task participation.

Why social behavior may influence organizational strategy needs to be changed ?

Why any organizations need to know whether nowadays social behaivor how has been changing in order to implement the kind of the most right strategy to achieve the profit aim pursue in possible. I shall indicate nowadays ecommerce or online, customer shopping behavior to explain above question concerns they ought have close relationship between social behavior and organizational strategic choice or organizational behavioral changing need.

On nowadays ecommerce business, or online shopping model, this kind of shopping model in global many young and old age consumers like to apply internet tool to choose any country sellers website stores in order to stay at home to buy any kinds of products from themselves webstores in global societies.

In fact, online shopping model had been popular for long time above to twenty years. Most of global sellers will make decision to design themselves webstores in order to attract global many online buyers to choose to buy their products from themselves webstores. So, it seems that social consumers purchase behaviors had been changed to online shopping from internet invention.

Hence, social consumers purchase behavioral changes may influence any organizations' strategies need to be changed from visiting shops purchase strategy model to online purchase strategy model, if the seller still concentrate on concentrate on considerate how to design itelf , but neglects to considerate how to design itself webstore, e.g. how to design attract product photos to put on itself webstore, how to arrange sale price information location to be putted on webstore and visa card payment location on itself webstore in order to let any one online buyer can feel very easier to buy itself any kinds of products from itself webstore. Then, its potential online buyers will be influenced to increase number when they can find this online seller itself any kinds of products photes and every kinds of product sale price information and visa card payment channel locations easily from itself webstore.

So, it implies that nowadays any one seller ought need to design one webstore to let any one online overseas and domestic consumers can have chance to click itself webstore to choose any one kind of product to buy conveniently when he/she does not hope to leave him/her home to go to shop, because nowadays social shopping behaviors had been influenced to change when internet invention, them it gives another online purchase method to replace visiting shops purchase method to global any one buyer in nowadays societies.

So, if nowadays any one seller still concentrate on how to design itself shop display in order to put any kinds of product on shelf in order to let any one visiting shop customer to find the kind of product to buy, but it neglects to change to choose to pursue another new technological shopping method, such as webstore purchase method in order to implement effective strategy to design the most right webstore as well as in order to attract global overseas and local consumers to find itself webstore easily from website and find its any one kind of product phots and sale price and visa card payment button in order to choose to buy itself any kinds of products in the short time. Consequently I believe that the seller will lose many customers from overseas and local when its other same or similar product sellers choose to design themselves webstores in order to let global any one product buyer can buy themselves any one kind of product when they can pay visa card to buy their products from them webstores conveniently when they stay at home habitly. Then, the seller will lose many global potential customers in long time.

On conclusion, in behavioral economic view, any consumer behavioral social changing, which will influence any in order to avoid customers number loses significantly . In future time, organizations need to make rapid decision in order to implement the most reasonable and the most useful strategy in order to avoid global potential customers number reduces or lose them in long time. So, social behavioral changing environment ought influence any global organizations need to decide how to change themselves strategies in order to avoid customers loses significantly in future time.

How and why human behavior may influence economic growth or recession?

May ourselves daily behaviors influence our global societial continue economic growth or recession? Do they have cause and effect close relationship between human behaviors and global economic growth or recession? I shall apply behavioral economic theory to analyze and explain whether ourselves daily behaviors and our global societial economic growth or recession which have close cause and effect relationship as below:

Every country itself economic development must depend on any business activities, otherwise, any kinds of business activities must need ourselves business activities or behaviors in order to achieve any business activities as well as achieve the country's overall economic development in macro view.

However, any country's overall business activites or behaviors which must depend on any kinds of individual businessmen, themselves employees daily working behavior or activity or performance in order to help them to attract or increase many clients number to acieve " earning profit" aim. So, it seems that any individual business, itself overall every department individual working behavior is one main factor to influence the company's overall business performance.

For agricultural fruit and meat food farming industry example, such as New Zealand is a farming main target industry country. It had had many New Zealanders were daily themselves own farming businesses for many years. Their farming businesses include growing fruit, sheep, cow, pig pork, meat etc. food sale business. If the New Zealand farmer owned a large size farming land, then he will choose either growing fruit or feeding sheeps, pigs, cows to be meat to to transport to New Zealand supermarkets to help them to sell to their farmers meet to New Zealanders in order to earn profit. Thus, if the New Zealand farmer owned large size of farming lands, then he needs to employ many farming employees (farming workers) to help him to carry on farming business daily tasks, e.g. picking up friuts, feeding pigs, cows, sheeps to eat food daily. These daily farming jobs are very important to influence this New Zealand farmer's meats or fruits sale number whether they can be easy or diffcult to sell in New Zealand supermarkets , if these farming workers can own encough farming knowledge or skill to know how to pick up fruits method and make judgement to know whether it is right time to pick up the kind of fruits from the trees , as well as know how feed this pigs, sheeps, cows to eat food in order to let they are better health. Consequently, their farming behaviors which can let these animals can provide the best taste and enough meat from these animals to let New Zealander to buy to eat from New Zealand any one supermarket. Even these New Zealand farming workers can know whether the kinds of fruits, e.g. oranges, apples, gapes etc. fruits whether they ought be picked up from the trees at the right time. Consequently, they can make judgement to decide to pick up any kinds of the best taste fruits to let any one New Zealander to buy to eat from any one supermarket in New Zealand. Otherwise, if they do not make judegement to know whether the kind of fruit ought not be picked up because they still need longer time to continue grow up to increase fruit size and better taste from the trees in order to let any one fruit buyer can feel better taste when they eat this kind of fruit later. If they can buy this kind of fruit to eat later, then this New Zealand farmer's his fruit buyers can buy the best taste of this kind of fruit to eat from an yone supermarket in New Zealand. Consequently, many New Zealand supermarkets will choose to buy any kinds of fruits from this farmer fruit supplier when they feel this farmer's fruits can provide more better taste fruits to compare other farmers' fruits.

Thus, due to New Zealand is one farming main income source country. It's any kinds of fruits and meats need to be export to overseas to sell , instead of local sale. It's GDP percent is very high to whole country 's overall income source. So, any one New Zealand farmer individual and any one farming worker individual working behavior will influence its economy whether it is influenced to grow or recession possible. Moreover, it also seems that farming workers' farming knowledge and skill will influence themselves farming daily activities to achieve the aim of the number of increase or decrease to any kinds of fruits whether they are better taste or the number of increase of decrease to any kinds of meats whether they are better taste to supply to any one New Zealand fruit or meat buyers to eat from any one New Zealand supermarket. So, it implies that any one New Zealand farming worker individual farming behavior may influence any kinds of fruits or any kinds of meat taste because they are transported to any one supermarket to sell in New Zealand.

Consequently, if New Zealans had many farmers can teach god farming knowledge and skill to let their any one farming workers know how to decide judgement to decide when it is right time to pick up any kinds of fruits from trees , or how to grow them on soil in order to let they can grow rapidly. Then, many different kinds of fruits can be provided to let any one New Zealanders can eat the best taste of fruits when their fruits are supplied to any one New Zealand supermarkets. Even, if they knew how to feed foods to pigs, cows, sheeps to eat daily. Then they can be more health and they can provide the best taste of meats to let any one New Zealanders can buy their meats from any one New Zealand supermarkets. Moreover, their fruits and meats can be transported to overseas to let any one country fruits or meats buyers can choose any kinds of New Zealand meats and fruits to buy to eat from themselves countries supermarkets. Then, many overseas fruit and meat buyers will perfer to choose New Zealand any kinds of fruits or meats to buy to compare other countries fruits or meats to buy when they go to any one local supermarkets. On conclusion, it seems that New Zealand farming workers themselves farming behavior may influence their farming employers any kinds of fruits or meats sale number and income because their farming task behaviors must influence whether their fruits or meats taste are the better taste or worse taste to compare their other local farmers (the farmer competitors) whose fruits or meats taste. If tthe farmer's any one farming worker can be trained to learn how to know to feed animals skill and when is the most right time to pick up any kinds of fruits from trees or how to grow them on the soil methods. Due to these farming worker individual farming behavior may influence his different finds of fruits and meats sale number to be increase or decrease, so these any one New Zealand farmer must need to depend on any one farming worker whose farming working methods, if their farming working behaviors can be the best to influence any kinds of fruits to grow rapid or any kinds of pigs, cows, sheeps animals grow up rapidly , then their sale number may be increase significantly and their taste can be improved to let any New Zealand or overseas meat or fruit buyer to buy to eat to feel from any one New Zealand or overseas supermarkets, then New Zealand's agriculture industry must be influenced to increase. In the world, any one fruit or meat buyer must choose to buy New Zealand's fruit and meat to eat in prefer to compare other countries' fruits and meats. So, New Zealand's GDP may be influenced to raise from any one New Zealand farming worker individual farming working behaviors.

Reasons why human behavior may influence economic recession or growth?

Can ourselves daily behaviors or activies influence ourselves countries' economic growth or recession? I shall attempt to explain the reasons why they have direct or indirect relationship between human behavior and economy growth or recession as below:

I shall indicate environment pollution case to attempt to explain above question. Our societies had been experiencing servious environment pollution challenge. However, environment pollution , such as air pollution is caused by air planes and vehicles emission by air planes and vehicles emission as well as water pollution is caused by plastic rubblish, or dirty water or oil or gas chemical material, these both kinds of pollution ought may bring economic recession and this both kinds of pollution are caused by human ourselves daily foolish activities.

I believe human behavior and economy and pollution which have cause and effect relationship. I shall analyze this environment pollution case to explain why they have case and effect relationship between human foolish behavior and environment pollution and economic recession as below:

When global societies had many people like to buy cars to drive to bring emission to fresh air on the roads as well as many manufacturing factories will bring emission to pollute fresh air in their manufacturing processes. Factories and cars will bring air pollution , due to factories need to pollute fresh air in order to manufacture many products and car owners need to drive their cars to go to offices or leisure places. Their cars will also bring emisson to pollute fresh air. On consequence, car owners themselves frequent driving behaviors and factory workers themselves frequent manufacturing behaviors may bring environment pollution. Technology or human behavior whether may influence economic growth or recession. Moreover, air planes also brings emission to pollute air when they are flying in sky. Also, when ships bring oil pollution or sea plastic rubblishs bring pollution to global oceans.

In fact, manufactuers and cars owners, such as factories workers manufacturing behaviours ans car owners driving behaviors and pilots driving air planes flying behaviors and ships transport behaviors, which may cause plastic rubblish, oil or gas emission to sky or sea or on the road to cause ocean and air pollution is serious. However, human ourselves need to buy cars to drive to satisfy ourselves driving leisure or enjoyment, travelers need to catch air planes to travel to enjoy leisure needs, factories workers need help factories to manufacture many products to sell to customers to satisfy their using needs. oil exploration needs to find lands to explore new oil lands.

All of these business and leisure activites may bring serious air and water pollution. However, due to serious air and water pollution will bring earth warming challenge , such as some countries temperature will be influences to rise up to 40 degree or higher br earth warming. However, earth warming is caused by air and ocean pollution. Pollution must be caused by human ourselves, driving cars leisure and factories manufacturing business activities. Hence, if human decided to continue to do these foolish behaviors, we only pursue to manufacture different kinds of industrial products or drive cars to enjoy leisure aims, but we also neglect ourselves behaviors may bring environment pollution. Then, earth warming or earth temperature will be influenced to rise up absolutely in long term. Moreover, if our future earth will be influenced to bring serious high temperature effect by human ourselves these foolish behaviors.

On consequencey, warth warming will bring serious economic losses in possible because when ourselves earth temperature had been influenced to rise up to 40 degree or high. Ourselves health will be caused poor, due to we will feel difficult breath, we must need often tried and hard to work, due to our nervous and health will be influenced to poor by pollution and earth warming effect. Also, we need to pay more money to see doctors when we had long life. Then, our societies will lose may strong labors to help manufacturers to work, e.g. factories will reduce workers number to help manufacturers to produce more different kinds of products, due to workers health is general poor. Due to lacking enough workers to manufacture products, our societies will begin to reduce enough supply number of products to sell to global consumers to satisfy their use needs.

On conclusion, in behaviroal economic view, our societies will lose many labors due to their bodies are not health by air and water pollution. Global economic and business activities will be influenced to worse by global workers reducing number reason. So, economic recession will begin to occur in possible when pollution reaches the serious level.

How employee behavior influences organizational development?

Can any organizational department employee individual behavior may help the organization to bring long term development? When one employee individual behavior, manager won't feel whose task behavior may help organizational development, but when the department has many teams cooperate to work together , all of these team employees whose task behaviors may help their organization to bring long term development.

I shall explain how any why when the organization has many departments, as well as when every team memmber individual behavior may help whole organization to bring long term development in possible as below:

Every organization must need efficient department to cooperate to work together. They may include human resource, finance, logistic, facility management, sales, marketing , operateional , warehouse , factory manufacture , research and development, purchase, customer service etc. different kinds of departments to cooperate to work together. So, any one employee individual behavior, include manager, leader, supervisor, worker, salesperson, manufacture worker, adminisration staff, factory or logistic worker etc. themselves task behavior whether his/her performance is worse or better , whose task behavior ought bring long term good or bad influence to cause the organization's whose efficiency, or performance , whether it can be influenced to improve significantly. For car factory manufacture workers department example, it exmploys 100 car manufacturing workers. They need to manufacture at least 50 cars in order to bring enough car manufacture number to supply to global car buyers to choose to buy (satisfaction to car buyers their driving leisure activity needs). However, if this car manufacture firm employs many low skilful car manufacture workers, their inefficient car skill may bring cars manufacture number reduces, they can not achieve to reach the at least 50 cars manufacture number, if these 100 car manufacture workers. They have half number of workers, they only manufacture 30 to 40 cars number at least daily. So, it seems that this car manufacture firm will have half car manufacture workers bring the low cars manufacture number to compare the another half cars manufacture workers, when this proficient car manufacture workers may manufacture at least 60 or more cars manufacture number daily. So, it explains that this inefficient car manufacture workers will not help this car manufacture company to manufacture enough cars number in order to supply to global car market to sell to satisfy global car buyers needs, when car buyers demand number is more thn car manufacture supply number in supply and demand view. Hence, in long term, if this car manufacture company can not employ new proficient car manufacture workers to replace those inefficient or low skillful car workers. Consequently, its car manufacture number must be influenced to reduce and it can not satisfy global car buyers driving leisure needs.

However, if this car manufacture firm also has shop to sell itself any kinds of cars, instead of manufacturing cars product. So, it needs have both main departments to help it to earn profit. The first step, it needs have proficient car manufacture workers to help it to manufacture at least 50 cars from every car worker in order to have enough cars number to be provided to global car sellers to help it to sell to global car customers. Second step, if it decided to attempt to sell itself cars. Then, it needs to set up car shops in global to different countries in order to let global car buyers may visit its global any one car shop to enquire any one car etc. salesperson about any car quality, speed, gas useful, price, safety, etc. information questions and they can attempt to sit in any one car to feel whether which car can let them to feel more comfortable to make final car purchase decision in any one shop. So, if this car company can provide good sale speaking skillful training to any one car salesperson to let his/her to know whether how to explain every kind of car function and feature, manufacture method etc. questions, then I believe that they can influence any one car buyer to makecar purchase choice decision more easily. So, it this car manufacturer hopes it may attempt to earn profit from different countries car sellers and car buyers both. It ought also provide training course to all general car salespeople to be proficient owning sale speaking skillful professional skill in order to prepare having more confidence to persuade any one car customer to make car purchase choice from any one car salesperson more easily to compare global other car sellers.

Hence, if this car manufacturer could build both car manufacturing team and car sale team more proficient. However, if this car manufacturer hopes to develop itself car manufacture busness to expend to car sale business both in success. It must need to spend long term to provide training courses to general car manufacture workers and general car salespeople both to be proficient car skillful manufacture workers and proficient car skillful salespeople in order to help they can manufacture enough car numbers and help they can persuade may car customers can make car purchase decision in short time when they visit its any one car shop.

However, this car manufacture company explains why every car manufacture worker whose manufacturing behavior and every car salesperson sale persuading speaking ability may help this car manufacture company to expand from its car manufacture market to car sale market development in sussess in possible. So, this car manufacture firm must need these two kinds of essential human resource elements in order to achieve its cars sale number and cars manufacture number increasing aim. They may include proficient car manufacture workers and proficient car salespeople both human resource elements. These both human resource daily task behavior may influence its long term task efficient performance in order to expand itself car sale business in success from itself car manufacture business easily. If it hopes to expand its car manufacture business to car sale business in success. It must need to provide training to these two departments general staffs to be proficient staffs in order to supply enough cars number to its global car shops to let global car buyers can choose its any kinds of cars to buy in any time.

Morevoer, if this car manufacture company can have good skillful of car research and development department , it aims to research and innovate any new technological cars invention in order to improve its any traditional old kinds of cars to be innovative new kinds of cars from every year. Consequently, its any new innovative cars ought attract global any one car buyer to make car purchase choice final decision more easily, because its any kinds of manufacturng cars can be innovated rapidly to compare its any one car manufacturing competitors, when its nay kinds of cars can be shorten time to innovate within three months, but its any one car manufacturing competitors need to spend more than three months, even one year to innovate themselves traditional old cars products in long term.

Hence, its car staffs research and development department staffs must need own good car product design ability, proficient car engineering knowledge , even car invention knowledge in order to innovate its any one kind of car product in short time and introduce to let its global car proficient car buyers feel surprise to its any one kind of innovative car products to compare its any one car manufacturer.Hence, these four departments: car manufacture, car sale and car research and development anr car training departments must need concentrate resource to provide enough training to any one staffs in order to achieve the best performance.

On conclusion, all these departments staffs their performance can influence car manufacture aim to chance to car manufacture and sale aim more significantly. it explains why some main department staffs whole behaviors may influence any organizational performance significantly.

Artificial intelligent Human clever and art creating ability methods

How robots create human clever and art creating ability? Nowadays robots invention may help businesses to reduce employees number, improve performance, raise productivities, reduce cost in service industry,manufacturing industry, office , warehouse, restaurant, hotel , factory, cinema etc. different kinds of business environments, even public transport tools. However, instead of robots may bring these above advantages to any kinds of business working and service environments, whether robots may also help human to create clever and image creating ability. I shall attempt to answer this question:

On the one hand, I believe that past technology ,e.g. machine , it should not have ability to help human to create clever and image creative ability,but nowadays, robots invention that I believe it had had enough ability to help future human to raise more clever and more creating image or painting picture, art design etr. image ability, after robots had been experienced above more than ten years improvement stage from early research stage to invention stage, till to nowadays improvement stage, e.g. non-manual driving auto vehicels, even future non-manual driving skill may be improved to apply to public transport tools, e.g. trams, trains,buses, airplanes, ships etc. public transport tools, when non-manual driving skills can be improved to own the most safe driving skillful ability to compare human driving skills.

On another hand, when robots could be invented to be applied to medical or hospital surgery aspect, e.g. roboting surgerys may help surgery doctors to do complex surgery in surgery rooms, or serving patients tasks in any hospital working environments. They can help nurses and doctors to spend more time to do more important tasks urgently, so medical or surgery serving robots may help nurses and surgery doctors to reduce task load pressure and create clever or improve their surgery skills to when they can cooperate to work in hospitals.

On the other hand, robots can be invented to help any public transport drivers to avoid more traffic accidents occurrence on any countries roads. So, it seems that non-manual driving public transport tools invention may also help human drivers to improve driving skills in possible, when they can learn how to avoid sudden traffic accidents occurrence in any countries roads in any time. so, any kindsof public transport tool drivers ought learn how to avoid traffic accidents skills from future non-manual driving robots invention. Instead of non-manual driving robots and hospital patients medical care or surgery service robots may help public transport tools drivers and hospital nurses and doctors to concentrate on spending time to treat any more important and urgent matters every days. Even, future restaurants may let cooking restaurants may let cooking robots to help human cookers to cook more different kinds of good taste food, to human cookers may learn cooking robots cooking skills in order to improve themselves traditional cooking skills often, in order to compare their cooking skills between human cookers and cooking robots.

On conclusion, it seems that cooking robots ought help human cookers to create any kinds of new cooking skills. Moremove, futuer robot cookers ought be future human cookers their cooking coaches. These robot cookers will help human cookers to create clever cooking skills in possible. Also, future non-manual driving robots ought help human drivers to create new driving skills in order to improve their driving skills to reduce sudden traffic accidents occurrence easily on any countries roads in any time, future hospital surgery or patient care service robots may help surgeons or nurses to do any surgerys in surgery rooms or looking care patients in hospitals. So, when robot surgeons help human surgeons to do complex surgerys in surgerical rooms, human surgeons can learn how to do more complex surgerical tasks for every surgeons when human surgeons can observate every surgerical robots how to do surgeons together. Hence, it seems that robot surgeons also may create future human surgeons themselves innovate surgerical skills from traditional surgerical skills improvement. So, future artificial intelligent technology ought help any kinds of human occupations to create clever, even improvement themselves traditional skills to new innovative skills absolutely.

Why does technology raise online products sale demand and reduces shops products sale demand?

Nowadays robot technology is popular to be applied to different aspects of our daily lives. They may include: non-manual driving vehicles, smart phones, space rockets, kitchen cookers, shopping centres service, cinema ticket sale, etc. different kinds of businesses demand. However, instead of internet invention may influence global communication, media channel is changed to computer internet, media channel is changed to computer internet, media communication from traditional newspaper, letter, TV, radio etc. communication channel. So, any internet users may click to yahoo.com news website to read global news from computer yahoo.com website easily.

In fact, internet technology is also used from businesses. They attempt to set up themselves web stores to sell their products from themselves webstores. So, any one product buyers may buy any kinds of products from any one webstores when they stay at homes. It is very convenient and common to future any one webstore shoppers. It brings this question: Can webstores help online product purchases needs raise and influence shop product purchases need reduce?

In demand and supply view, when one product price raises, its sale demand ought reduce, unless, it can attract to influence customers need consideration or its supply number decreases. But, when one product is increasing sale price to seel from the seller's webstore, whether its sale number will be influenced to reduce. Also, when the kind of product is selling and its sale price is raised, whether it can still keep demand number increase as well as whether it can influence its similar kinds of competitor their products sale demand number to reduce from shop sale channel.

In demand and supply view, when one product price raises, its sale demand ought reduce, unless, it can attract to influence customers need consideration or its supply number decreases. But when one product is increasing sale price to sell from the seller's webstore, whether its sale number will be influenced to reduce. Also, when the kind of product is selling and its sale price is raised, whether it can still keep demand number increases as well as whether it

can influence its similar kinds of competitors their products sale demand number to reduce from shop sale channel.
I suppose that webstore sale may influence shop sale demand number decreases, because when internet is popular to use, when one country's buyer wants to buy one kind of product, but he/she can not find the kind of product can be bought from himself/herself home country. If he/she can findthe kind of product to buy from any one of overseas webstore from internet channel at home in any time. Then, he/she will be influenced to make purchase decision from the seller's websote immediately. So, it implies that when on consumer plans to buy one kind of product, he / she will attempt to find the kind of product from any one seller's webstore in preferat home, if he/she spend long time to find the kind of product from many of webstores, but he /she still does not find the kind of product from many of webstores, then he/she will choose to visit any one shop to attempt to buy the kind of product.Hence, online shopping purchase channel will be prefer choice to compare visiting shopd purchase channel in nowadays society.
So, it explains that why the kind of product online sale number may influence the kind of similar product visiting shop sale number either increases or decreases. It means that the kind of product visiting shops sale number may still increases , if the kind of similar products supply number is not enough , they are difficult to let any one online buyer to find to buy from any one webstore. Otherwise, if the kind of similar products sale supply number is enough to let any one online buyer to find from many webstores. Then, they can influence the similar kinds of shop products purchase demand to reduce and their shops purchase demand will be also influenced to reduce from webstores purchase channel.
On conclusion, it explains that the kind of shop products demand number ought be influenced to increase or decrease, when the similar kind of products can be bought easily from many webstores from internet (e-commerce) shopping channel. Internet (online) technology may help the seller to raise the kind of product competitive ability on purchase demand aspect, when there are not many other sellers can provide webstores to sell the similar kind of products and they only concentrate on selling the kind of similar products from shops to let any one online buyer to frind from may webstores. Then, they can influence the similar kinds of shop products purchase demand to reduce and their shops purchase demand will be also influenced to reduce from webstores purchase channel. Hence, webstore and shop both purchase channel explains that the similar kinds of shop products demand number will be influenced to increase or decrease , when the kinds of product can be bought easily from many webstores from internet shopping channel. Internet technology may help the seller to raise the kind of product competitive abilty to raise purchase demand when there are not many other sellers can provide webstores to sell the kind of similar products and they only concentrate on selling the kind of similar products from shops.

Does car technological development helps economic development?
Our societies had been developing too many years. In our past technological aspect, machine invention had began till to computer invention till to internet invention. It seems that our technological development stage may reach mature stage. Why do I feel our technological development had reached mature stage. I shall apply demand and supply economic theory to explain this question as below:
I shall indicate car development industry to explain whether when car development stage can reach mature stage, it may help global economic growth. In our car technological development stage, it is from gas energy car invention till to nowadays battery energy car invention till to even future non-manual driving car invention. Do you feel that when human (car buyers) felt environmental protecion need to avoid air pollution. So, battery energy cars demand number may increase , it will influence gas energy cars demand number reduces. Even, if future non0manula driving cars invention succeed, lazy driving car buyers will choose to buy non-manual driving (robot driving cars) in preference. So, it is possible that , it will influence future gas energy cars demand number reduces much. I mean that when car buyers can choose many different kinds of non-manual driving cars and battery energy cars to buy. Then, gas energy cars demand number must be influenced to reduce very much as well as gas energy cars supply number will be influenced to reduce to avoid sale prices reduce.
Hence, it explains why future car technological development will reach mature stage when both kinds of non-manual driving cars and battery energy cars are invented to the mature stage. When these two kinds of cars invention can satisfy future global car buyers driving needs. Then, car maufacturers won't need to spend too much time to continue

to attempt to invent any new kinds of cars in order to excite future car buyers' purchase decision. So, I believe that car technological development will reach mature stage within five years, if non-manual driving cars and battery energy cars are invented in success and they can be popular to accept to drive to global car buyers.

On conclusion, when car technological development reaches matural stage, it will help future economy continue grows because when car manufacturers had invented many new kinds of non-manual driving cars and new kinds of non-manual driving cars and new battery energy car sale market. Then, they will encourage or attract global many car buyers choose to buy these both kinds of cars products in preference to compare to traditional gas energy car products. So, they will influence many traditional gas- energy car buyers forgive to drive gas energy cars to avoid non pollution and lazy driving behavioral feeling. So, gas energy car reselling number will increase between gas energy car drivers and past non-owning any car buyers. Also, non-manual driving cars and battery energy car supplying number will be influenced to increase when battery energy car buyers and non-manual driving car buyers driving needs increase.

Consequently, these factors will influence global gas energy cars, non-manual driving cars and battery energy cars their cars purchase and sale transactions increase in future global car market. So, I believe that global car technological development could reach matural stage, then it will infuence global car buyers number increases as well as this car technological mature development stage may also bring global rapid economic growth future non-manual driving car buyers and battery energy car buyers both number increases.

CHAPTER FIVE

Reengineering Management Science Method

What does reengineering management science mean? It is one kind of process reengineering is about innovating and changing , innovating the way work is done and changing the way people work together to get the task done. In fact, any organizations plan to survive, improvement is not an option. Hence, dramatic improvement is essential. However, I shall suggest " reengineering management skill" to help any organizations to achieve effective improvement, or raising efficiency or performance. But, process reengineering is difficult. To achieve effective reengineering managment skill, it must need time, creativity, even if the organization doe snot achieve effective reengineering management skill, if it ususally achieves more than 50% or more. Consequently, it can be achieved to effective reengineering managment skill absolutely. I shall explain whether how organization ought implement reengineering managment skill in order to achieve effective more than 50% level objective as below:

I assume that you are one organization CEO, a vice president,a trainer , a manager or a supervisor. You may attempt to implement process reengineering in action in order to design changes. However, each phase builds on the vision and research of the previous phase. If you desire dramatic improvement in one or more processes within your organization. You need to learn how to succeed plan for, design and implement a reengineered process. However, effective process reengineering may be your organization's chance to break ahead in an increasingly competitive business environment.

What is process reengineering ? It can be defined as the fundamental rethinking and redesigning of existing process tasks and operating structure to achieve dramatic improvement in process performance. What is the different between continuous process improvement and process reengineering. Although process reengineering needs to be spent cost and too time consuming. But, it can assist any organizations to lead to changing organizational structure lead to changing organizational structure and redesigning jobs to be better or to be improved.

Process reengineering is periodic and focuses on the achievement of dramatic improvement, redesigning how a process operates without being constrained by how things were previously long done. It aims to assist the traditional organization to add up to significant improvements, focuses on outcome and multiple gains. With process reengineering, process changes often go hand in hand with changes in job design, managment systems, training and retraining, organizational structure and information technology, e.g. improving frontline employees subprocess that is part of a higher-level process, with process reengineering, information systems technology often helps to improve in cycle-time reduction , informtation access, and avoiding paper waste for administration task.

Reengineering management skill may include these several aspects: Marketplace changes, e.g. your products or services is rapid changes, making incremental improvement, to existing processes, new product/service development, geographic spread, if the process is typically " housed" within one or more physical locations (e.g. work groups / departments etc.) , multiple locations, particularly crossing countries and critical data exhange, customers / suppliers involvement (hand-on customer and supplier is desired with key customer and supplier of the process being reengineering, cost and staffing allocation is when to limited financial resources and periodic , part time involvement, part time reengineering efforts have commonly resulted in limited resources, increased frustration on the part of team members and missed expectations on the part of senior management for disadvantages, level of urgency is relatively low on the quality improvement.

Reengineering is more appropriate if an existing process is failing or when the suitation is drastic and significant improvement must be achieved in a relatively short period of time. Core elements of process reengineering may include: Purchases new hardware and software, redesigns jobs and train representatives when the way customer service representatives need often to handle customer complaints. For example, reengineering aims to help the representatives to attract a greater number of customers to become repeat customers and to raise the turnover of customer service to climb up within six months.

In general, the three phases for reenginerring management strategy include: Phase one: plan , determine " new process requirements, seek opportunities, analysis as is capability, envision desired state, indentify process performance gaps ; Phase two: Design, map the ideal process, complete preliminary work, set new goals and establish measures, create a new process flow chart. It aims to redefine process support requirements, develop change management plan. Final phase: Implement on the " trial run" basis, standardize the reengineered process, evaluate process performance on an ongoing basis.

How to select a process reengineering team? Should an interim team looks at the need for reengineering first? Should the team manage the process reengineering effort from beginning to end? Should team members be assigned to the team for the entire duration or just need? Should team members be selected for first-hand knowledge of the process being reengineering, authority level or for other reasons?

Determining new process requirements involves researching what your customers want and what the marketplace offers and determining what operating requirements you need set for the new process to meer demands.

In the reginnering process, cost of labor is essential. The end result is that profitability decreases, because they had to hire additional help to spead up the time. Now if the goal was time, reduction because customers demanded it and profitability was not a factor, then the effort could be considered successful.

Consequently, when you feel that your organization needs to be implement any kinds of new reengineering management strategy , you must need to consider these issues, such as are there any parts of the process than can be eliminated ? Can technology help, what tools or equipment can improves the process? How will they improve it? Is new computer hardware or software necessary for your reengineering effort, will you need to provide training for any new equipment or to use already existing equipment? Where the delays in your current processes are, steps are designed in the correct order? Where you are getting the least account of return?

Organizational change and development reengineering strategy case

Giornl coffee company is a small collection of individuals with many ideas and a pressing need for financial capital. The founding partner, provided expertise in unscale speciality coffees and European style coffee bars and coffee houses. It hopes to raise capital. it decided to do little advertiseing, relying instead of seattle's established coffee culture to provide initial interest among potential customers. It also needs to handle the increasing customer traffic challenge. It decided to hire additional people and planned for expansion. Everyone did every thing. One staff needs to make sandwich meat at his desk in the business office, when another waited on customers, cleaned tables, and obtaned additional financial capital. Everyone worked long hours, but motivation was high. Owners , managers and baristas who made and served the various coffee drinks were in the venture together and were inspired by the possibility of fundamentally elevating the coffee experience in Seattle and beyond. It is one good reengineering strategy to change this coffee shop employee attitude to be positive emotion in order to satisfy coffee customer service and coffee taste provision need.

New technology reengineering strategy case

Polaroid corporation has become a classic case, showing the outcome of being too slow to change. It introduced instant photography to the market and at time was among the top 50 corporation in U.S. However, in 2001, it declared bankruptcy. Polaroid's problem was its failure to adapt in a timely way to technological change. It lost its market because it was too slow in recognizating the importance of digital imaging technology and then too slow in changing after competitors developed digital cameras.

The development of a new technology created the need for the change. Although the top managers are responsible for instituting such changes, managers and accociates lower in the organization must help because of their knowledge of the environment (markets, customers, competitors, technology, government regulations). All managers should actvely scan the environment for changes and help to identify external opportunities and threats. Unfortunately, managers did bot perceive the threat to their existing business quickly enough to transform the firm. After learning of the need for a change. These managers began the difficult process of designing and implementing a new approach, but they were able to do so in time to avoid failure. Competitors developed and introduced new cameras using digital technology before Polaroid could do and it lose a substantial share of its market. So this camera manufacturing firm can not achieve reengineering strategy before competition market increases. So it became loss.

In general, this camera firm encountered ought feel these pressures for its organizational reengineering change. They may include: aspiration performance discrepances, technology advances, introduction of removal of government regulations, changes in societal values, shifting political dynamics, changes in demogrpahics, growing international interdependence, life cycle forces. All of these factors may influences it can not achieve reengineering change strategy easily.

Life cycle forces

When any organizations feel need reengineering change. Organizations tend to encounter predictable life-cycle forces as they grow. Not every organization experiences the same forces in the same way as others, but most organizations face similar pressures. Although several models of the organizational life cycle have been proposed, an integrative model best highlights the key pressures that organizations experience. The model had four stages. Entrepreneurial , collectively , formalization and control, and elaboration.

In the entreprensurial stage, founders and perhaps a fre initial managers and associates develop ideas for products and services, acquire capital and take actions to enter a niche in the marketplace. This is an exciting time, but after the market is entered and success is achieved, growth requires founders to add managers and associates. Processes must be introduced for selecting , training and corrdinating these individuals.

In the collectivity stage, founders, managers and associates continue to emphasize product or service development and fund raising. Individuals in the young firm tend to feel like a family as they pursue the vision that attracted them to the firm. Individuals often work long hours for relatively low pay. As the firm continues to grow, formal process mus tbe incorporated to resolve or prevent coordination and control problems.

In the formalization and control stage, staffs are guided by formal processes and rules, a strict division of labour, and a stable organizational structure. And they emphasize efficiency more than innovation. Functional disciplines , such as accounting and operation managemenr are elevated in status. As the firm contiues to grow, more rules and procedures are often added, along with a greater number of management levels.

Finally, in the elaboration stage, managers and associates experience a more balances, mature organization. formal rules and processes exist empowered lower level managers and associate. Efficiency concerns with concerns for innovation and renewal. (reenginering changing strategy) is needed.

Why does reenginering strategy need to plan change?

How does an organization respond to pressure for change? On possibility is planned change, which involves deliberate efforts to move an organization or a subunit from its current state to a new state. Planned change may be evoluation, or can be more revolutionary, involving major changes in a shorter period of time. To effectively move the organization from one state to another. Those managing the change must consider a number of issues in three distinct parts of the change process.

Process of planned change is typically thought of as a three phase process that moves an organization from an undersirable stte through a difficult transition period to a desireable new state. Although, researchers tend to agree on the nature of these three phases, different names for the phases have been used by different people. However, the process of planned change may include these three stages:

Unfreezing stage: provide rational for change, create minor level of anxiety about not changing, create sense of psychological safety , concerning change.

Moving stage: provide information that supports proposed changes, bring about actual shifts in behavior.

Refreezing stage: implement new evaluation systems, create levels of anxiety about not changing, implement new hiring and promotion systems.

However, style of change may include: urgency level, if the change is urgent, a participatory approach should not be used, as it tends to be time consuming. Degree of support, if the idea of changing is supported by a wide variety of people, a particpatory approach is less necesary as well as referent and expert power of change leaders, when change leaders are admired and are known to be knowledgeable about pertinent issues, a participatory approach is less necessary. So, reeengineer strategy must need to consider change style in order to achieve the right time change.

CHAPTER SIX

How technology improves consumer behavior

Can technology influence human shopping behavioral change?
Nowadays, technological development has reached mature stage, whether technological mature stage may bring positive or negative shopping emotion influence to global consumers. I shall aplly internet inventin or ecommerce shopping channel tool to explain whether internet technology can bring postive or negative influence to global consumer behavior in behavioral economic view.
Internet is a good technological tool, it brings e-commerce business chance. In fact, commonly, global has have many businessmen choose to use internet channel to carry on their products transactions between global online-buyers and their electronic websites. So, global many shoppers had begun to feel online shopping is more convenient to compare visiting shops shopping. Their shopping behaviors have been changed from internet technological tool. Global has many shoppers choose to buy any products from any overseas or local businessmen their web stores. They only need to spend time to find any businessmen their webstores to choose the most suitable products to pay visa to buy from their webstores. at homes. So, in general, global had have may shoppers had changed their shopping behaviors from visiting shops to visiting webstores at homes often.
So, it seems that internet technological tool had influenced global many shops disappear, but internet webstores will be replaced their actual shops on streets. Some of businessmen either they choose webstores to replace shops or choose websotes and shops both or still keep shops only. Hence, internet tool influences global businessmen have three kinds of products sale channels to let globa local and overseas consumers to choose how to buy their products. However, in fact, many of global shoppers, youngers and olders had begun to accept to buy any products from webstores. They feel to spend time to leave homes to visit shops , their shopping behaviors will be wasted time to not essential part to their daily lives. Hence, since internet technological invention, it had changed many consumers their traditional visiting shops shopping habit to change to buying products from webstores channel.
However, on the one hand, internet creates webstores ecommerce shopping channel to let global many consumers do not need to leave homes to go to shopping. It brings negative visiting shops shopping emotion to global general consumers nowadays. But on the other hand, it also brings positive visiting internet webstores shopping emotion to global general consumer nowadays. So, it seems that global many consumers feel that they often do not need to spend much time to go out shopping. Many global consumers feel convenient and enjoy to choose any products to buy from different internet webstores, when the online buyer chooses the most suitable product, he she only needs to pay visa card to buy the product from the online seller's webstore conveniently at home.
Hence, online shopping can bring economic benefit to online buyers, e.g. avoiding walking time or spending transport fare to visit the shop to go to shopping, shortening or reducing shopping time to do another important matter.
On conclusion, global many consumers began feel online shopping can bring more economic benefits on shortening shopping time, avoiding transport fare spending aspect. So, online shopping will be popular shopping behavior for future long time. It may encourage global many shoppers can make rapid shopping decision in short time in order to carry on any products buying transaction to global any one online shopper in short time easily in behavioral economic view. So, global many businessmen had begun to build themselves one attraction webstore in order to

persuade different countries consumers to choose to click themselves webstores from internet channel to buy any kinds of products in short time easily.
So, internet technology had changed consumers traditional shopping behaviors to build positive online shopping emotion as well as raise online sellers' any products sale chance easily in behavioral economic view.

Why and how human behavior may influence the country's economic growth or recession?
When one country has many people choose to do the same matter for one period, whether their behavior may influence the country's pvera; economic growth or recession . I shall attempt to indicate cases toexplain their relationship as below:
For flowing rubblish behavioral case example, do you feel that when the country has many people often flow rubblish on the streets, instead of their flowing rubblish behavior may bring streets dirty? But, their flowing rubblish behavior may explain that this country has people may have enough money to buy food to ear, or enough cloths to wear, enough bottles of water to drink, even they may have enough money to buy new television, radio, refrigeraters , washing machines, desktops or laptops electronic home products from old to new to use in order to satisfy their living needs. So, when they flow old electronic home products, their flowing old home electronic products behaviors may seem that they have enough money to buy other new home electronic products to replace old home electronic products to use at homes.
However, it seems thaat this country ought have many people have jobs to do. So, many of them, they can easy to make purchase decison to flow any old home electronic products and buy any new home electronic products to use . Because this country has many people have jobs to do. So, they can often not use old home electonic products to become rubblishs to flow on streets after they had bought any kinds of new home electronic homes.
In fact, it also implies that this country's economy grows rapidly. So, many businesses can glow up rapdly. When they expanded their businesses, they must need to increase employees number in order to let they help themselves to raise productivity or serve their clients absolutely. So, when the country has many businesses can grow up, it seems that its economy must be better or it is improved to compare past. Due to many different kinds of home electronic products had been often bought to use by this country people in this period. So, this country's any streets can be observed that expensive electronic home products were flowed on streets anywhere. then, this country will have many electronic home products sellers can sell their home electronic products very easily. When this country has many people can find any kinds of jobs to do easily. So, due to unemploymen rate had been decreasing.
In behavioral economic view, as this many electronic home products rubblish country case, we can observe this country may have many people have jobs to do. So, consumption number has been increased long time. So, cheap food, or expensive home electronic products may be rubblish on any streets. This country's people , their flowing rubblish behaviors may be explained that many of people have enough jobs to do, so they have ability to buy any good taste food to eat or buy any kinds of expensive electronic home products to use. So, this country's economy may be improved for this long period. So, in behavioral economic view, when this country can have many electronic home products rubblishs are flowed on anywherer in streets frequently. It seems that this country will have many people have jobs to do, so it causes they often change old home electronic products or replaced them easily, when they have enough income to spend to buy any kinds of new home electronic products to use at homes easily. Moreover, their flowing old electronic home products behaviors also indicate that this country has many people their salaries may be increased in possible from their emplyers. When this country can have many different kinds of home electornic products are sold. It means that this country's electronic home products needs or demand had been increasing, due to many people have jobs to do and income increases to excite their living of needs also improve. Consequently, this country may seem have better economic improvement. We can observe from this country's electronic home products rubblish increasing income in theis period.
On conclusion, this country ought experience economic growth at this period. So, " flowing expensive electronic home rubblish increasing number " may seem that this country's economic growth is rapidly in this period, due to many people have jobs to do as well as salaries increase in this period.

Technology how impacts human behavior changing?

Technology how influences human behavior to bring changing? For example, online share purchase and sale transaction from smart phone brings share investor can do share buying or selling transation in any where and any time conveniently, non manual driving auto vehicle, bring car owner feels comfortable and spends free time to do other matter, e.g. reading, listening mucis in himself or herself car freely. electrical energy vehicle can help car owner to reduce air polluton and it can brings the drivers do not feel drive long time in any journeys in order to avoid air pollution for environmental protection responsible car drivers in our societies. Thus, they will drive long time in any journeys when they can drive electronic energy cars to replace oil energy cars.

However, online technology can also bring consumers can choose to stay at homes to buy any things from seller individual online webstore conveniently. Such as online technology can bring shoppers do not need to spend much time to visit shops to buy any things. They can choose any kinds of products from any online sellers individual online webstores conveniently at homes. Online technology excite busy consumers can make purchase decision easily as well as it can help online sellers sell any kinds of products from internet easily.

In behavioral economic view, technology can change human behavior to be improved, it can let human feels comfortable, more free time ro use, rapid making any decisions, such as apply smart phones to make share purchase or sale transaction decision, online shopping decision, even travelling any where decision in short time, when the traveller finds the most cheap hotel accommodation room price and air ticket price frm any travel agent online tourism webstore, then the potential travel customer can follow the online hotel accommodation price and air ticket price data to make decision when to buy the air ticket from the airline travel agent or make decision when to prebook which hotel accommodation room to go to the country to travel from online travel agent tourism webstores. So, technology can encourage global any country travelers to make anywhere to trvel rapidly. If the traveler can find the country's general hotel rooms and airline tickets prices had been decreasing more sightly. The traveler may make travel decision to choose the country to travel in short time, then he/she can prebook the country;s any hotel room and airline ticket to pay by visa fraom the country's any hotel and airline travel agent webstores., before one week, even one month or more easily. Hence, online technology can also encourage traveler individual frequent travel times to be increased, due to global travelers can find any hotel rooms and airline tickets prices from internet conveniently at homes. They do not need to spend time to visit any airline travel agent to enquire travel choice country's hotel rooms prices and airline ticket prices. They can compare global travel of countries choices ' all hotels rooms and airline agents air tickets prices to make prebook airline seat and hotel room decision before one week, one month even six months early.

On conclusion, online technology can encourage global travelers can make travelling any where and when traveling time desicions easily. It can excite tourism industry develops in long time. Also, such as electricity cars invention can encourage environment protection car owners do car purchase decision easily, because they can choose to drive electronic energy cars to replace oil energy cars in order to avoid air pollution occurs easily. So, electronic cars can increase electronic car purchasrs number, due to many of environmental protection attitude of car owners can choose to drive electricity cars to bring air cleans, even non -manual driving cars can encourage lazy driving and free time driving car owners to choose to buy non-manual (artificial intelligent) cars to drive , because they can spend much free time to read, listen music or do any matters in themselves cars, they do not need to drive cars, robotic (AI) auto driving machine is such one non-manual driver to help them to drive themselves cars confidently. So, non-manual driving cars can attract lazy and enjoying free time driving car owners to choose to buy to replace traditional manual cars to drive easily. Moreover, online share transaction can help any share investors to make share buying and selling decision in short time easily. When they can apply smart phones technological tool to carry on share buying and selling activities easily. They can observe any share rising or falling price suitation from smart phones in any where any any time easily. So, smart phone technology can help global any shareholders to make share purchase and sale transaction easily. So, technology can encourage human makes decision in short time rapidly.

How and why employees behaviors may influence economy development?

In behavioral economy view,I believe the country's any organizational employees behavior may bring indirect relationship to influence the country's long term economic development. I shall indicate past manufacture industry social development period to explain their relationship. For many countries' past business activities had belonged to manufacturing industry, such as US, UK past before 1980 year, it focused on steel manufacturing and steel manufacturing related machine products. So, US, Uk developed countries manufacturing industries may be past main country's economic income sources. I assume US , UK past had one million number different kinds of industries. They ought had about seven houndred thousand number organizational businesses were belonged to manufactured industry. They may include:

Steel manufacturing and steel related machine manufacturing, e.g. vehicle manufacturing, home appliances, e.g. washing machine, television, radio, refrigerate cooler, heater, air condition etc. different kinds of different kinds of steel -related manufacturing machine, they were manufactured from US, UK steel machine manufacturers. So, US, Uk the other three hundred thousand number industry may be general service industry, e.g. hotel service, restaurent, cinema, public transport service, tourism lesiure , wine bar, supermarket etc. different kinds of non-manufacturing industries business organizations were operated in UK, US past before 1980 year.

So, in UK, US developed countries industry development history, they ought have high percentage of businesses belonged to steel related manufacturing machine and steel products. Also, in the past before 1980 year, US, Uk business employers , they employed many workers are manufacturing workers. They needed to spend long time to work in factories. They were skillful workers, and they are trained to manufacturing cars, washing machine, television, heater, etc. even steel itself different kinds of steel related products to prepare to deliver to their shops to sell to US, Uk local or overseas clients.

So, I believe that past UK, US ought employ many employees, they belonged to skillful manufacturing workers, manufacture increasing steel machine or steel related machine number of products rapidly daily. So, if UK, US had had many of these manufacturing factories owned high skillful workers, then their manufacturing steel-related machine or steel both kinds of products number must be influenced to raise rapidly. Consequently, their steel machine manufacturing products would been exported to overseas or would been sold to local both markets , they may be influenced to raise sale number. They (these manufacturing workers) needed to be trained to know how to manufactur these different kinds of machine products in the efficient teams and they ought to be trained to raise their efficiencies in order to shorten time to manufacturing many kinds of steel related manufacturing machine or steel itself products rapidly. So , if their efficiencies and manufacturing performance was improved, these US, UK any one manufacturing worker and their teams ought achieve raising productivities significantly.

Hence, when past UK, US manufacturing industry development period, if these two countries' any manufacturing factories could have many manufacturing workers could be trained to be skillful and proficient manufacturing workers. Then, in past every day to these factories workers, they ought help their steel or steel related manufacturing employers to raise any kinds of machine or steel products number in every team. So, when past in the manufacturing industry development, US, UK could have many factories' manufacturing workers themselves steel or steel related machine products manufacturing skill could be trained to to improve to any kinds of these machine or steel manufacuring products quality as well as their products number could be influenced to raise by themselves skillful improvement significantly every day.

Then, what would be influenced to occur to past UK, US manufacturing industry period? In behavioral economic view, when these two manufacturing industry developed countries, such as UK, US , if they had many factories workers can be trained to improve their skill in order to achieve any kinds of steel or steel-related machine products quality could be improved as well as products manufacturing number could be also increased absolutely.

In consequence, past UK and US both countries ought increase themselves any kinds of steel and steel related machine products number to be supplied to themselves local shops to let local clients to choose any one kind of machine manufacturing products to buy easily as well as they could also export to supply overseas any countries to buy their different kinds of steel or steel related machine products to let overseas steel or steel related manufacturing machine product buyers, they can have many of these different kinds of these steel or steel-related different kinds of manufacturing machine from UK and UK these both countries easily to compare other countries.

On conclusion, I believe that past US, and UK macro manufacturing industry income GDP would increase significantly. So, they would have good economic growth performance because when many of these manufacturing workers themselves manufacturing effort could be improved. So, it explained when employees manufacturing abilities can influence economic growth indirectly.

Robots invention whether they can help organizations to raise efficiencies or inefficiencies?

In behavioral economic view, in any organizations, when the organization hopes its worker teams can raise efficiencies , the organization may choose to increase more workers number and/or it can provide training to improve these workets themselves skills in order to raise their efficiencies. For one warehouse example, when the warehouse increases many goods , they are needed to delivered these goods from the shelves to the delivering destination locations. If this warehouse supervisors feel these workers themselves goods delivery speeds are slow, which is possible due to this warehouse's workers number is not enough. So, this warehouse supervisor ought increase workers number in order to increase their goods delivery speed in order to deliver goods from the shelves to every indicated goods delivery destination in order to let any one lorry driver can transport the right kinds of goods and ensure the accurate goods number to transport to any one client home rapidly.

However, if this warehouse supervisor planed to buy several warehouse goods delivery robots to assist these warehouse workers to find the right kinds of goods from shelves and then deliver to the right destination location in the warehouse. So, these warehouse orkers can concentrate on counting the accurate goods number and ensuring the right kinds of goods in order to prepare to let lorry drivers to transport these goods to these goods of buyers themselvers homes rapidly. Consequently, in the first step, robots can concentrate on finding th right goods from shelves and delivers them to the right goods transportation of location destination. Then, in the second step, these warehouse workers can concentrate on counting the accurate goods number and ensuring the right kinds of goods in order to prepare to put them to the lorry. Consequently, when warehouse robots and warehouse workers can cooperate to work together, the most important, robots, can deal on finding the right kinds of goods and deal on delivering the accurate number of goods of job duty as well as these warehouse workers can only concentrte on counting the right kinds of goods number in order to avoid it has none any mistake of wrong kinds of goods and inaccurate goods of delivery number to be transported to the lorry and to deliver to any one buyer's home.

So, it seems that warehouse robots ought help any one warehouse worker to raise himself efficiency and avoid goods delivery of mistake occurrence easily as well as their help to warehouse workers that can let any one goods buyer feels their goods can be delivered to their homes rapidly. Moreover, warehouse robots can also help these warehouse workers to raise efficiencies because warehouse robots can help them to shorten goods delivery time between any one shelf and any one goods delivery destination of location in the warehuse because robots may help them to find the right kinds of goods from the right shelf in the short time. So, any one worker does not need to spend long time to seek anywhere is the right shelf location for the kind of goods when the kind of goods are needed to deliver to the buyer's home from lorry. Warehouse robots can help them to do this aspect of " finding the goods from the right shelf in short time job duty". So, any one warehouse worker only needed tospend less time to do the counting of any right kind of goods number and ensuring the right kind of goods job duty. Consequently, this warehouse 's any one worker, his any one kind of goods delivery time may be reduced, because robots' assistance and they may have more confidence to avoid mistake to deliver the wrong number of goods and/or the wrong kind of goods to any one goods buyer's home.

On conclusion, it seems that warehouse robots ought may help any one warehouse worker to raise efficiency for any one team in the warehouse as well as the warehouse any one supervisor does not need to spend much time to observe any one worker individual performance for " goods delivery job duty aspect" because their goods delivery job duty that had been replaced to do by these several warehouse robots. Robots can achieve the more accurate of right kinds of goods and the right number of goods delviery job performance to compare any one of human warehouse worker themselves right kinds of goods of delivery and right number of goods of delivery job performance. So, when robots can participate to cooperate with this warehouse's any one worker to do their goods of delivery job duty in this warehouse every day. Then, robots can raies any one of supervisor individual confidence in order to let they do not need to spend time to observe any one of worker individual whose goods of delivery job performane. They can concentrate on supervising any one worker whose goods transport to lorry in the final step in order to avoid to deliver wrong goods number and / or wrong kind of goods to any one goods buyer's home every day. Consequently, this warehouse's overall teams of their delviery of goods performance many be improved by robotss' participatin to goods of delivery task as well as this warehouse's oveall teams themselves efficiencies may be influenced to raise by robots' goods of delivery task participation.

Why social behavior may influence organizational strategy needs to be changed ?
Why any organizations need to know whether nowadays social behaivor how has been changing in order to implement the kind of the most right strategy to achieve the profit aim pursue in possible. I shall indicate nowadays ecommerce or online, customer shopping behavior to explain above question concerns they ought have close relationship between social behavior and organizational strategic choice or organizational behavioral changing need.

On nowadays ecommerce business, or online shopping model, this kind of shopping model in global many young and old age consumers like to apply internet tool to choose any country sellers website stores in order to stay at home to buy any kinds of products from themselves webstores in global societies.
In fact, online shopping model had been popular for long time above to twenty years. Most of global sellers will make decision to design themselves webstores in order to attract global many online buyers to choose to buy their products from themselves webstores. So, it seems that social consumers purchase behaviors had been changed to online shopping from internet invention.
Hence, social consumers purchase behavioral changes may influence any organizations' strategies need to be changed from visiting shops purchase strategy model to online purchase strategy model, if the seller still concentrate on concentrate on considerate how to design itelf , but neglects to considerate how to design itself webstore, e.g. how to design attract product photos to put on itself webstore, how to arrange sale price information location to be putted on webstore and visa card payment location on itself webstore in order to let any one online buyer can feel very easier to buy itself any kinds of products from itself webstore. Then, its potential online buyers will be influenced to increase number when they can find this online seller itself any kinds of products photes and every kinds of product sale price information and visa card payment channel locations easily from itself webstore.
So, it implies that nowadays any one seller ought need to design one webstore to let any one online overseas and domestic consumers can have chance to click itself webstore to choose any one kind of product to buy conveniently when he/she does not hope to leave him/her home to go to shop, because nowadays social shopping behaviors had been influenced to change when internet invention, them it gives another online purchase method to replace visiting shops purchase method to global any one buyer in nowadays societies.
So, if nowadays any one seller still concentrate on how to design itself shop display in order to put any kinds of product on shelf in order to let any one visiting shop customer to find the kind of product to buy, but it neglects to change to choose to pursue another new technological shopping method, such as webstore purchase method in order to implement effective strategy to design the most right webstore as well as in order to attract global overseas and local consumers to find itself webstore easily from website and find its any one kind of product phots and sale price and visa card payment button in order to choose to buy itself any kinds of products in the short time. Consequently I believe that the seller will lose many customers from overseas and local when its other same or similar product sellers choose to design themselves webstores in order to let global any one product buyer can buy themselves any one kind of product when they can pay visa card to buy their products from them webstores conveniently when they stay at home habitly. Then, the seller will lose many global potential customers in long time.
On conclusion, in behavioral economic view, any consumer behavioral social changing, which will influence any in order to avoid customers number loses significantly . In future time, organizations need to make rapid decision in order to implement the most reasonable and the most useful strategy in order to avoid global potential customers number reduces or lose them in long time. So, social behavioral changing environment ought influence any global organizations need to decide how to change themselves strategies in order to avoid customers loses significantly in future time.

How and why human behavior may influence economic growth or recession?

May ourselves daily behaviors influence our global societial continue economic growth or recession? Do they have cause and effect close relationship between human behaviors and global economic growth or recession? I shall apply behavioral economic theory to analyze and explain whether ourselves daily behaviors and our global societial economic growth or recession which have close cause and effect relationship as below:

Every country itself economic development must depend on any business activities, otherwise, any kinds of business activities must need ourselves business activities or behaviors in order to achieve any business activities as well as achieve the country's overall economic development in macro view.

However, any country's overall business activites or behaviors which must depend on any kinds of individual businessmen, themselves employees daily working behavior or activity or performance in order to help them to attract or increase many clients number to acieve " earning profit" aim. So, it seems that any individual business, itself overall every department individual working behavior is one main factor to influence the company's overall business performance.

For agricultural fruit and meat food farming industry example, such as New Zealand is a farming main target industry country. It had had many New Zealanders were daily themselves own farming businesses for many years. Their farming businesses include growing fruit, sheep, cow, pig pork, meat etc. food sale business. If the New Zealand farmer owned a large size farming land, then he will choose either growing fruit or feeding sheeps, pigs, cows to be meat to to transport to New Zealand supermarkets to help them to sell to their farmers meet to New Zealanders in order to earn profit. Thus, if the New Zealand farmer owned large size of farming lands, then he needs to employ many farming employees (farming workers) to help him to carry on farming business daily tasks, e.g. picking up friuts, feeding pigs, cows, sheeps to eat food daily. These daily farming jobs are very important to influence this New Zealand farmer's meats or fruits sale number whether they can be easy or diffcult to sell in New Zealand supermarkets , if these farming workers can own encough farming knowledge or skill to know how to pick up fruits method and make judgement to know whether it is right time to pick up the kind of fruits from the trees , as well as know how feed this pigs, sheeps, cows to eat food in order to let they are better health. Consequently, their farming behaviors which can let these animals can provide the best taste and enough meat from these animals to let New Zealander to buy to eat from New Zealand any one supermarket. Even these New Zealand farming workers can know whether the kinds of fruits, e.g. oranges, apples, gapes etc. fruits whether they ought be picked up from the trees at the right time. Consequently, they can make judgement to decide to pick up any kinds of the best taste fruits to let any one New Zealander to buy to eat from any one supermarket in New Zealand. Otherwise, if they do not make judegement to know whether the kind of fruit ought not be picked up because they still need longer time to continue grow up to increase fruit size and better taste from the trees in order to let any one fruit buyer can feel better taste when they eat this kind of fruit later. If they can buy this kind of fruit to eat later, then this New Zealand farmer's his fruit buyers can buy the best taste of this kind of fruit to eat from an yone supermarket in New Zealand. Consequently, many New Zealand supermarkets will choose to buy any kinds of fruits from this farmer fruit supplier when they feel this farmer's fruits can provide more better taste fruits to compare other farmers' fruits.

Thus, due to New Zealand is one farming main income source country. It's any kinds of fruits and meats need to be export to overseas to sell , instead of local sale. It's GDP percent is very high to whole country 's overall income source. So, any one New Zealand farmer individual and any one farming worker individual working behavior will influence its economy whether it is influenced to grow or recession possible. Moreover, it also seems that farming workers' farming knowledge and skill will influence themselves farming daily activities to achieve the aim of the number of increase or decrease to any kinds of fruits whether they are better taste or the number of increase of decrease to any kinds of meats whether they are better taste to supply to any one New Zealand fruit or meat buyers to eat from any one New Zealand supermarket. So, it implies that any one New Zealand farming worker individual farming behavior may influence any kinds of fruits or any kinds of meat taste because they are transported to any one supermarket to sell in New Zealand.

Consequently, if New Zealans had many farmers can teach god farming knowledge and skill to let their any one farming workers know how to decide judgement to decide when it is right time to pick up any kinds of fruits from trees , or how to grow them on soil in order to let they can grow rapidly. Then, many different kinds of fruits can be provided to let any one New Zealanders can eat the best taste of fruits when their fruits are supplied to any one New Zealand supermarkets. Even, if they knew how to feed foods to pigs, cows, sheeps to eat daily. Then they can be more health and they can provide the best taste of meats to let any one New Zealanders can buy their meats from any one New Zealand supermarkets. Moreover, their fruits and meats can be transported to overseas to let any one country fruits or meats buyers can choose any kinds of New Zealand meats and fruits to buy to eat from themselves countries supermarkets. Then, many overseas fruit and meat buyers will perfer to choose New Zealand any kinds of fruits or meats to buy to compare other countries fruits or meats to buy when they go to any one local supermarkets. On conclusion, it seems that New Zealand farming workers themselves farming behavior may influence their farming employers any kinds of fruits or meats sale number and income because their farming task behaviors must influence whether their fruits or meats taste are the better taste or worse taste to compare their other local farmers (the farmer competitors) whose fruits or meats taste. If tthe farmer's any one farming worker can be trained to learn how to know to feed animals skill and when is the most right time to pick up any kinds of fruits from trees or how to grow them on the soil methods. Due to these farming worker individual farming behavior may influence his different finds of fruits and meats sale number to be increase or decrease, so these any one New Zealand farmer must need to depend on any one farming worker whose farming working methods, if their farming working behaviors can be the best to influence any kinds of fruits to grow rapid or any kinds of pigs, cows, sheeps animals grow up rapidly , then their sale number may be increase significantly and their taste can be improved to let any New Zealand or overseas meat or fruit buyer to buy to eat to feel from any one New Zealand or overseas supermarkets, then New Zealand's agriculture industry must be influenced to increase. In the world, any one fruit or meat buyer must choose to buy New Zealand's fruit and meat to eat in prefer to compare other countries' fruits and meats. So, New Zealand's GDP may be influenced to raise from any one New Zealand farming worker individual farming working behaviors. It seems that New Zealand farmer fruit and meat sale number is depended on their eatting consumers demand more than their meat and fruit supply because if these NZ farmers can apply high technology method to grow good taste fruit or feed good taste meat to let global eatting customers to feel, their demand will increase, then NZ farmers will need to increase good taste fruit and good taste meat supply number to satisfy global meat and fruit eatting customer taste need.

CHAPTER SEVEN

How facility management helps organizations to save cost

How green building helps organizations to reduce resource waste
green building avoids resource waste
The relationship between organization resource and earth resource in behavioral economic view, global organizations use any kinds of resource, such as office, warehouse facility building resource to build any new offices, warehouses, supermarkets, shopping centers, car parks, whether they can bring global building resources reducing number to satisfy human houses living needs, if one day building resources are facing any kinds building material is reducing number, but global applying steel, wood, brick etc. different kinds of building material number increases, when global population number is still increasingm any high houses' building materials need increase, even low wood houses' wood natural resource needs increase in order to let many people can live in the expensive wood houses. SO, it brings this question: Would wood, natural resource, steel, brick resource have shortage supply challenge, due to office, warehouse, shopping center,manufacturer, ther fixed assets number building need increases, but the same time, global houses need number also increases, when polulation increases? Can businessmen their fixed assets : offices , warehouse, shopping centers, factories, supermarkets, etc. building need bring negative impact to influence future human living house resource nu mber decreases?
I assume that global businessmen their offices, warehouses, shopping centers, hospitals, private school education organizations, supermarkets etc. business organizations their buildings number is sudden increasing high, due to many organizations can earn more profit to expand their businesses. So, they will need to spend much woods, steels, bricks etc. different kinds nature resources to build any high , height offices buildings in different countries. So, wood, steel brick etc. different kinds of offices building material need must also sudden be influenced to sudden increase by global business organizations increasing number. When global businesses organizations number increases, it will cause global high height offices number increases, because every business organizations must need to rent any building office to operate their businesses. If global has many new businesses are continue growing, they will influence offices building need in possibe, even for food business , e.g. supermarke, restaurant building material need will also increase, if the reestaurant can earn more profit, then it will need to expand itself restaurant vacancy floor to let many food customers do not need to spend long queue time to wait table in order to avoid to loss these food customers, even it will buy any shopping center location to build one or more than one restaurant to satisfy food customers need . So building material needs to the new restaurant design, it may decide to decorate all restaurant location, to feel food customers to feel more comfortable when they are sitting in its restaurant.SO, when the restaurant changes its inside design , it needs to find designers to buy any new building materials to design its restaurant to be new one in order to attract food customer choice.
I assume that global many old restaurants need to recorate their inside, or many global restaurants number increases, then any restaurants material natural resource need number may also be influenced to increase. Then, our earth building material resource for restaurants need will influence general office buildings material resource, shopping center building material resource decreases to supply. When, global many restaurants are needed to build, more building material resource is needed to be used build new restaurants or is needed to decorate to change old

restaurants design . So, our earth will have much building material resources to be used to build new restaurants or they are be used to decorate the old restaurants design in order to change new restaurants design function. So, our earth building material natural resources for new or old restuarants , which must increase, when global has many restaurants need any kinds of building materials to be used to help them to build new or old restaurants. Then, they must influence natural resources of building material supply number to be reduced to satisfy any office building matierals user need, even any house building material user need, if global offices and houses number sudden increase. Consequently, due to global building material natural resource can not be produced rapidly in order to satisfy any office building, shopping center, house, supermarket etc. different kinds business organizations or private houses needs. Then, the natural resource of building resources shortage, it may influence any kinds of building material production price increases. It may influence global business organizations need to pay high price to rent office or build office, or build supermarket, or build shopping center, even any private houses prices increase, when global building material natural resource has no enough number to be supplied to satisfy builders‘ need in order to help any office, supermarket, shopping center, supermarket warehouse etc. business organization users to build their properties to operate their businesses. SO, these businessmen must need to spend much money for building expenditure, when they begin to do their businesses. Even, public or private house buyers also need to pay more expenditure to buy houses to live , when any kinds of building material price increases.

So, it explains why global business organizations number increases may influence global public or private houses prices increase, when our earth has no enough natural resource to be building matieral supplied to satisfy global construction properties development need. Finally, when global construction properties developers feel our earth building material natural resource encounters supply shortage challengem due to they need to pay higher price to buy any kinds of building material to help any business organizations to build their offices, restaurants, supermarkets, shopping centers, wareshouses etc. different fixed assets buildings or they need to ehlp any public or private houses buyers to build their houses. Consequently, any one businessmen or house livers must need to pay high price to buy any houses or offices , restaurants, hospitals etc. different buildings either to live or to use for business operations. Hence, it seems that they have chose resource supply surplus or shortage relationship between business organizations and private house buyers.

ON conclusion, I recommend that any business office buildings ought choose green buildings orrice, their advantages may include to avoid nature resource waste, improved indoor environment, quality of life , saving water, reduce , reuse, enhanced health, eco-friendly for life, reducing operational cost and maintenance , energy -efficient, non-renewable, vs renesable resource, keep it clean, protecting our ecosystem . Hence, green buildings can not only reduce or eliminate negative impacts on the environment, by using less water, energy, or natural resources.

Moreover, green buildings, or substainable design, is the practice of increasing the efficiency with wich buildings and their sites use energy , water and materials, and reducing impaction human health and the environments for lifecycle of a building. So, on environmental benefits of grren building aspect, it can enhance and protect bio-diversity and ecosystems , imprive air and water quality, reducing waste streams, conserve and restore natural resources, on economic benefits of green building aspect, it can reduce operating costs, improve occupant productiviity, enhance asset value and profits optimize life-cycle economic performance, on social bebefits of green building aspct, it can enhance occupant health and comfort, improve indoor air quality, minimize strain on local utility infrastracture, improve overall qualty of life.

Consequently, if any organizations can apply green building concept to design and build their offices, waterhouses, restaurants, shopping centers etc. different kinds of business green buildings, even ourselves houses design is chosen by green building concept. On behavioral economic view, green building concept is the best moethod to help us to reduce natural resource waste nowadays. Then, I beleive that our earth nature resources won't be easte easily.

facility management helps organizations to avoid resource waste

Can facility management helps organizations to avoid resource waste? How waste management helps in productivity improvement? Waste management is more long term, which involves investment in new technology processes, product and training that can improve production efficiency and reduce waste in using least amount og materials to make and package the products can reduce the materials ,cost and waste.

Why the facility management of waste dosposal is important? When waste is disposed of or recycled in a safe, ethical and responsible manner, it helps reduce the negative impacts of the environment, ensuring that waste management procedures are carried our with regularly helps ensure the fewer waste materials go to the general waste system. som if any organizations can implement the most efficient facility management system, then it can help the organization's internal any building material to keep long ife time. When the organization can have the best building facility materials , it doed not need to spend much money to carry on repairment. Then, building resource cost must not often changed new, it's fised repairment or building material purchase expenditure must reduce as well as the organization's building materials do not waste easily.

Why does facility management help organization to reduce waste cost? This is because of a company can manage its waste properly, reduction in waste can help the company to reduce its cost. Waste minization is a set of processes and practices intended to help managers to see waste minimisation as a primary focus for most waste management strategies. It can reduce waste and usually much improves resources optimisation. Why is facility management software important for productivity? Can efficient facility management bring efficient resource management for organizations?

For organization, building efficiency is absolutely critical for reducing overhead and contributes directly to corporate green initiatives. Building efficiency also improves the operations of the business as whole, and it ensures that employees are able to work productivity in a comfortable environment. Beside having the potential to directly improve productivity, facility management can influence other of employees' lives that contribute to the overall output of an organization. FM can improve social interaction among colleges as well as enabling them to work in an effective, focuses and motivated manner. So, FM has close relationship to let organizations can use resources efficiently, even avoiding wastes resources ad reduces long term cost. Organizing maintanance, repairs and security of the building and premises. This protects employees and FM in organizations may include: claening offices, handware inspection and maintenance, environment health and safety, space management, efficient transportation space parking resource arrangement, operational efficient resources implemenation . So, facility management and efficient resource has relationship of a multiple disciplines to ensure functinality , comfort, safety and efficiency of the build environment by people, place, process and technology resource management.

Today, many organizaions recognize the importance of FM to efficiently manage its properties . Their data to increase productivity by FM, are heating and coolong tasks carried out efficiently? To meet organizations every day needs, some organizations require spaces , such as meeting rooms, or huddle spaces. Hence, facilities management and corporate real estate provisions are becoming increasing need, on efficient resource management business, goals in the most , effective, efficient are quitable way aspect, FM can optimize and implement solutions which fit the organization's trategic . FM aims to help offices, and building resources facilities empower orgsanizations to function at their most efficient and effective level to use their resources.

From manufacturing platns to healthcare facility boosting efficiency is a goals logistics resource management is important to have proper organizatin policies in plan throughtout every facility. For example, high performance building, are characterized by their efficient use of resources and their ability to enhance the safety, health and productivity. So FM can help organizations to achieve to se resources in high performance effectiveness.

FM can also help organizations to save time. Any organizations must have offices to let employees can work together. If the organization lasks efficient and enough space to let many employees to feel comfortable to work together all working days. Their performance will be caused worse. So, efficient facility management to office rooms spaces, it can let employees to work in the most efficient manner.

Organization facility managment (FM) strategy aims to keep the best facility equipment repair improvement to let any organizational equipment can be used in long time. Hence, FM aims to help organizations to avoid to spend much expenditure on long time repair. When any organizational equipment can be improved to achieve good quality. Instead of improvement equipment quality aspect, can improvement facility equipment bring good customer emotion? How FM may help entertainment theme parks to save long time cost?

In entertainment theme park organizations, they must need to have different kinds of leisure playing machine facilities to supply to visitors to choose to play. So, facility management (FM) must need to imrpove any one entertainment theme parkj machine facility quality, it aims to avoid accidents occur , due to any leisure machine facilities are old or damage when they are used to operate in daily long opening time. Hence, FM must be needed to improve any entertainment theme parks' different kinds of leisure playing machine equipment frequently. If any one theme park leisure machine facility has poor FM in order to improve its machine quality. Consequently, this kind of leisure theme park leisure playing mahcine may be sudden to bring accidents occur, when any one visitor chooses this one of leisure playing machine facility to play. It may cause the player to hurt, even die in possible. Hence, FM to any entertainment theme park playing machine equipment , it may be one major facility repair management srtategy to any entertainment theme parks leisure playing machine facilities, because any one leisure playing machine facilities may bring any one visiot body hurt when the playing machine is old. Instead of FM can bring safety and playinf machine facilities quality improvement benefits to any one entertainment theme park leisure playing machine, whether FM to entertainment theme parks can bring psotive playing of leisure emotion to any one theme park visitor. I shall attempt to discuss as below:

Firstly, we need to know that any kinds of entertainment theme parks why they need to implement FM strategy. Why FM can bring advantages to any kinds of entertainment theme parks. In fact, the benefits of facility management to entertainment theme parks, it enables a more cost-effective working process within any kinds of the theme park any leisure playing machine facilities, such as theme park leisure playing sevice business. It improves the efficiency and it can help the theme park to manage health and safety requirements in accordance with industry regulations. It increases lifespan of a theme park any kinds of leisure playing machines, they are the theme park fixed assets, such as theme park's any kinds of leisure playing machine facilities. New theme parks and attractions can also improve the image of a destination increase tourism and hence economic benefits for the local community , and provide education and entertainment opportunities to the public.

Hence, it is common sense, if the theme park can have good FM to improve its any leisure playing facilities in order to avoid any accident occurrence , when any one visitor chooses to play its any one lesiure machine. Then, it can bring positive safe emotion feeling to satisfy any one visitor whose individual playing safe need to any kinds of playing leisure machines. I believe that its visitors number will not decrease, even increases significantly forever. Hence , the major roles of a theme park facility manager, is that to ensure the upkeep and manintenance of its any one entertainment playing machines, e.g. rolling rides, water rides etc. So, that they meet both safety and health standards to let any one visitors to feel safe to play.

In fact, the scope of facilities management covers two main areas: space and infrastructure , such as planning, design and workplace, construction, occupancy , maintenance and furniture as well as people and organization (such as catering, cleaning and HR, hospitality, accounting and marketing efficient operation in office) both aspects. Hence, these are 6 main facilities to ensure one available for any familiry theme plars. For leisure theme park case, rides and attractions are needed for all ages of any one theme park visitors. This is perhaps the most imprtant, as different parks will have different target audiences, e.g. refreshments, shops, toilets, and parking , access facilities and any one kind of leisure playing machines, such as rolling rides, water rides etc.

Hence, a theme park is a type of amusement park that bases its choice of which kinds of leisure playing facility structures and attractions around a central theme often featureing multiple areas with different themes. Unlike temporary and mobile fun fairs and carnivals, amusement parks are stationary and built for long lasting operation. Hence, every theme park must need have a photogenic, iconic landmark that draws people into the park, beautiful landscaping , enough available attraction capacity to keep peak waits for non-new attractions under 90 minutes, all of these are other faciliities. They must also need to manage to keep more attraction to theme park any one visitor to feel enjoyable and comfortable to play any one theme park leisure playing machines.

What advantages to the theme park implements FM strategy? For Ocean Park example, it aims to let visitors feel themed ocean animal recreational and educational and leisure park experience. So, it must need to upgrade to improve its any facilities to avoid long time repaire spending expenditure. FM project may include: modifying sections of ocean park road, which is a local distributor, around the existing bus terminus , drain works, tunneling and geotechnical works, bulk excavation and slope works, site clearance, modification to bus terminus, taxi stands as well as utilities works including power supply distribution, electrical substations, freshwater and saltwater reservoirs, water supply distribution, gas supply distribution, telecommunications networks, landscope irrigation network to the ocean park any one ocean fish reservoirs, primary life support system works for animal keeping, area development works include elevated walkways, external lighting, external escalators, bridges, parkwide systems works include: signage, background, music system, toilet facilities, guard sheds, first and facilities, communication systems , CCTV systems and waste facilities, landscape or theming works, themed concern pavements, hardscape soft landscaping, water and rockwork features, visual intrusion screens, area props and artwork etc. works for the attractions venues include: animal exhibits, marine animal, terrestrial animal, aviaries , bind exhibits, individual life support systems for animal , exhibits and non- animal related attractions, e.g. shipwreck play area, bamboo maze etc. installation of rides interactive rides , transportation rides etc. , works for venues include : event halls, outdoor live show area, cinema band stands, work for the merchandise / retail facilities include souvonir stores, novelty stores, games ascade, photo shops etc. in the ocean park.

Moreover, any ocean park also have works for the food and baverage facilities include: restaurants, ballery, food casrts as well as back of house facilities include: ocean park offices, break areas, warehouses , centralized facilities, operational facilities etc. , even the ocean park inside hotel development facilities. All of these may bring positive or negative leisure activities impacts to influence any one of this ocean park visitor individual emotion significantly, if he /she feel comfortable and enjoyable , when they enter this ocean park. This ocean park whole natural environment may influence they like to stay long time in this ocean park. So, when they can stay long time in this ocean park, they may spend money to live hotels, spend money to play any leisure machines and spend time to go to shopping, or buying tickets to see any movies in this ocean park. All of this ocean park natural environment facilities and leisure playing machines improvement may influence any one visitor individual emotion either negative or positive feeling. On conclusion, any theme parks must need to implement FM strategy to improve their theme parks inside natural environment and leisure playing machines quality and hotel living facilities and theme park external transport tool stations facilities, e.g. taxi, bus , railway station distance to convenience any one visitor can catch any one kind of public transport tool to arrive this theme park in short time easily. Also, any theme parks need to impove environment facilities in order to let any one visitor feels comfortable and enhoyable feeling when they choose this theme park to play. Consequently, the theme park's visitors number may be influenced to increase by their positive playing emotion feeling.

Organization facility managment (FM) strategy aims to keep the best facility equipment repair improvement to let any organizational equipment can be used in long time. Hence, FM aims to help organizations to avoid to spend much expenditure on long time repair. When any organizational equipment can be improved to achieve good quality. Instead of improvement equipment quality aspect, can improvement facility equipment bring good customer emotion? How FM may help entertainment theme parks to save long time cost?

In entertainment theme park organizations, they must need to have different kinds of leisure playing machine facilities to supply to visitors to choose to play. So, facility management (FM) must need to imrpove any one entertainment theme parkj machine facility quality, it aims to avoid accidents occur , due to any leisure machine facilities are old or damage when they are used to operate in daily long opening time. Hence, FM must be needed to improve any entertainment theme parks' different kinds of leisure playing machine equipment frequently. If any one theme park leisure machine facility has poor FM in order to improve its machine quality. Consequently, this kind of leisure theme park leisure playing mahcine may be sudden to bring accidents occur, when any one visitor chooses this one of leisure playing machine facility to play. It may cause the player to hurt, even die in possible. Hence, FM to any entertainment theme park playing machine equipment , it may be one major facility repair management srtategy to any entertainment theme parks leisure playing machine facilities, because any one leisure playing machine facilities may bring any one visiot body hurt when the playing machine is old. Instead of FM can bring safety and playinf machine facilities quality improvement benefits to any one entertainment theme park leisure playing machine, whether FM to entertainment theme parks can bring psotive playing of leisure emotion to any one theme park visitor. I shall attempt to discuss as below:

Firstly, we need to know that any kinds of entertainment theme parks why they need to implement FM strategy. Why FM can bring advantages to any kinds of entertainment theme parks. In fact, the benefits of facility management to entertainment theme parks, it enables a more cost-effective working process within any kinds of the theme park any leisure playing machine facilities, such as theme park leisure playing sevice business. It improves the efficiency and it can help the theme park to manage health and safety requirements in accordance with industry regulations. It increases lifespan of a theme park any kinds of leisure playing machines, they are the theme park fixed assets, such as theme park's any kinds of leisure playing machine facilities. New theme parks and attractions can also improve the image of a destination increase tourism and hence economic benefits for the local community , and provide education and entertainment opportunities to the public.

Hence, it is common sense, if the theme park can have good FM to improve its any leisure playing facilities in order to avoid any accident occurrence , when any one visitor chooses to play its any one lesiure machine. Then, it can bring positive safe emotion feeling to satisfy any one visitor whose individual playing safe need to any kinds of playing leisure machines. I believe that its visitors number will not decrease, even increases significantly forever. Hence , the major roles of a theme park facility manager, is that to ensure the upkeep and manintenance of its any one entertainment playing machines, e.g. rolling rides, water rides etc. So, that they meet both safety and health standards to let any one visitors to feel safe to play.

In fact, the scope of facilities management covers two main areas: space and infrastructure , such as planning, design and workplace, construction, occupancy , maintenance and furniture as well as people and organization (such as catering, cleaning and HR, hospitality, accounting and marketing efficient operation in office) both aspects. Hence, these are 6 main facilities to ensure one available for any familiry theme plars. For leisure theme park case, rides and attractions are needed for all ages of any one theme park visitors. This is perhaps the most imprtant, as different parks will have different target audiences, e.g. refreshments, shops, toilets, and parking , access facilities and any one kind of leisure playing machines, such as rolling rides, water rides etc.

Hence, a theme park is a type of amusement park that bases its choice of which kinds of leisure playing facility structures and attractions around a central theme often featureing multiple areas with different themes. Unlike temporary and mobile fun fairs and carnivals, amusement parks are stationary and built for long lasting operation. Hence, every theme park must need have a photogenic, iconic landmark that draws people into the park, beautiful landscaping , enough available attraction capacity to keep peak waits for non-new attractions under 90 minutes, all of these are other faciliities. They must also need to manage to keep more attraction to theme park any one visitor to feel enjoyable and comfortable to play any one theme park leisure playing machines.

What advantages to the theme park implements FM strategy? For Ocean Park example, it aims to let visitors feel themed ocean animal recreational and educational and leisure park experience. So, it must need to upgrade to improve its any facilities to avoid long time repaire spending expenditure. FM project may include: modifying sections of ocean park road, which is a local distributor, around the existing bus terminus , drain works, tunneling and geotechnical works, bulk excavation and slope works, site clearance, modification to bus terminus, taxi stands as well as utilities works including power supply distribution, electrical substations, freshwater and saltwater reservoirs, water supply distribution, gas supply distribution, telecommunications networks, landscope irrigation network to the ocean park any one ocean fish reservoirs, primary life support system works for animal keeping, area development works include elevated walkways, external lighting, external escalators, bridges, parkwide systems works include: signage, background, music system, toilet facilities, guard sheds, first and facilities, communication systems , CCTV systems and waste facilities, landscape or theming works, themed concern pavements, hardscape soft landscaping, water and rockwork features, visual intrusion screens, area props and artwork etc. works for the attractions venues include: animal exhibits, marine animal, terrestrial animal, aviaries , bind exhibits, individual life support systems for animal , exhibits and non- animal related attractions, e.g. shipwreck play area, bamboo maze etc. installation of rides interactive rides , transportation rides etc. , works for venues include : event halls, outdoor live show area, cinema band stands, work for the merchandise / retail facilities include souvonir stores, novelty stores, games ascade, photo shops etc. in the ocean park.

Moreover, any ocean park also have works for the food and baverage facilities include: restaurants, ballery, food casrts as well as back of house facilities include: ocean park offices, break areas, warehouses , centralized facilities, operational facilities etc. , even the ocean park inside hotel development facilities. All of these may bring positive or negative leisure activities impacts to influence any one of this ocean park visitor individual emotion significantly, if he /she feel comfortable and enjoyable , when they enter this ocean park. This ocean park whole natural environment may influence they like to stay long time in this ocean park. So, when they can stay long time in this ocean park, they may spend money to live hotels, spend money to play any leisure machines and spend time to go to shopping, or buying tickets to see any movies in this ocean park. All of this ocean park natural environment facilities and leisure playing machines improvement may influence any one visitor individual emotion either negative or positive feeling. On conclusion, any theme parks must need to implement FM strategy to improve their theme parks inside natural environment and leisure playing machines quality and hotel living facilities and theme park external transport tool stations facilities, e.g. taxi, bus , railway station distance to convenience any one visitor can catch any one kind of public transport tool to arrive this theme park in short time easily. Also, any theme parks need to impove environment facilities in order to let any one visitor feels comfortable and enhoyable feeling when they choose this theme park to play. Consequently, the theme park's visitors number may be influenced to increase by their positive playing emotion feeling.

Organization facility managment (FM) strategy aims to keep the best facility equipment repair improvement to let any organizational equipment can be used in long time. Hence, FM aims to help organizations to avoid to spend much expenditure on long time repair. When any organizational equipment can be improved to achieve good quality. Instead of improvement equipment quality aspect, can improvement facility equipment bring good customer emotion? How FM may help entertainment theme parks to save long time cost?

In entertainment theme park organizations, they must need to have different kinds of leisure playing machine facilities to supply to visitors to choose to play. So, facility management (FM) must need to imrpove any one entertainment theme parkj machine facility quality, it aims to avoid accidents occur , due to any leisure machine facilities are old or damage when they are used to operate in daily long opening time. Hence, FM must be needed to improve any entertainment theme parks‘ different kinds of leisure playing machine equipment frequently. If any one theme park leisure machine facility has poor FM in order to improve its machine quality. Consequently, this kind of leisure theme park leisure playing mahcine may be sudden to bring accidents occur, when any one visitor chooses this one of leisure playing machine facility to play. It may cause the player to hurt, even die in possible. Hence, FM to any entertainment theme park playing machine equipment , it may be one major facility repair management srtategy to any entertainment theme parks leisure playing machine facilities, because any one leisure playing machine facilities may bring any one visiot body hurt when the playing machine is old. Instead of FM can bring safety and playinf machine facilities quality improvement benefits to any one entertainment theme park leisure playing machine, whether FM to entertainment theme parks can bring psotive playing of leisure emotion to any one theme park visitor. I shall attempt to discuss as below:

Firstly, we need to know that any kinds of entertainment theme parks why they need to implement FM strategy. Why FM can bring advantages to any kinds of entertainment theme parks. In fact, the benefits of facility management to entertainment theme parks, it enables a more cost-effective working process within any kinds of the theme park any leisure playing machine facilities, such as theme park leisure playing sevice business. It improves the efficiency and it can help the theme park to manage health and safety requirements in accordance with industry regulations. It increases lifespan of a theme park any kinds of leisure playing machines, they are the theme park fixed assets, such as theme park's any kinds of leisure playing machine facilities. New theme parks and attractions can also improve the image of a destination increase tourism and hence economic benefits for the local community , and provide education and entertainment opportunities to the public.

Hence, it is common sense, if the theme park can have good FM to improve its any leisure playing facilities in order to avoid any accident occurrence , when any one visitor chooses to play its any one lesiure machine. Then, it can bring positive safe emotion feeling to satisfy any one visitor whose individual playing safe need to any kinds of playing leisure machines. I believe that its visitors number will not decrease, even increases significantly forever. Hence , the major roles of a theme park facility manager, is that to ensure the upkeep and manintenance of its any one entertainment playing machines, e.g. rolling rides, water rides etc. So, that they meet both safety and health standards to let any one visitors to feel safe to play.

In fact, the scope of facilities management covers two main areas: space and infrastructure , such as planning, design and workplace, construction, occupancy , maintenance and furniture as well as people and organization (such as catering, cleaning and HR, hospitality, accounting and marketing efficient operation in office) both aspects. Hence, these are 6 main facilities to ensure one available for any familiry theme plars. For leisure theme park case, rides and attractions are needed for all ages of any one theme park visitors. This is perhaps the most imprtant, as different parks will have different target audiences, e.g. refreshments, shops, toilets, and parking , access facilities and any one kind of leisure playing machines, such as rolling rides, water rides etc.

Hence, a theme park is a type of amusement park that bases its choice of which kinds of leisure playing facility structures and attractions around a central theme often featureing multiple areas with different themes. Unlike temporary and mobile fun fairs and carnivals, amusement parks are stationary and built for long lasting operation. Hence, every theme park must need have a photogenic, iconic landmark that draws people into the park, beautiful landscaping , enough available attraction capacity to keep peak waits for non-new attractions under 90 minutes, all of these are other faciliities. They must also need to manage to keep more attraction to theme park any one visitor to feel enjoyable and comfortable to play any one theme park leisure playing machines.

What advantages to the theme park implements FM strategy? For Ocean Park example, it aims to let visitors feel themed ocean animal recreational and educational and leisure park experience. So, it must need to upgrade to improve its any facilities to avoid long time repaire spending expenditure. FM project may include: modifying sections of ocean park road, which is a local distributor, around the existing bus terminus , drain works, tunneling and geotechnical works, bulk excavation and slope works, site clearance, modification to bus terminus, taxi stands as well as utilities works including power supply distribution, electrical substations, freshwater and saltwater reservoirs, water supply distribution, gas supply distribution, telecommunications networks, landscope irrigation network to the ocean park any one ocean fish reservoirs, primary life support system works for animal keeping, area development works include elevated walkways, external lighting, external escalators, bridges, parkwide systems works include: signage, background, music system, toilet facilities, guard sheds, first and facilities, communication systems , CCTV systems and waste facilities, landscape or theming works, themed concern pavements, hardscape soft landscaping, water and rockwork features, visual intrusion screens, area props and artwork etc. works for the attractions venues include: animal exhibits, marine animal, terrestrial animal, aviaries , bind exhibits, individual life support systems for animal , exhibits and non- animal related attractions, e.g. shipwreck play area, bamboo maze etc. installation of rides interactive rides , transportation rides etc. , works for venues include : event halls, outdoor live show area, cinema band stands, work for the merchandise / retail facilities include souvonir stores, novelty stores, games ascade, photo shops etc. in the ocean park.

Moreover, any ocean park also have works for the food and baverage facilities include: restaurants, ballery, food casrts as well as back of house facilities include: ocean park offices, break areas, warehouses , centralized facilities, operational facilities etc. , even the ocean park inside hotel development facilities. All of these may bring positive or negative leisure activities impacts to influence any one of this ocean park visitor individual emotion significantly, if he /she feel comfortable and enjoyable , when they enter this ocean park. This ocean park whole natural environment may influence they like to stay long time in this ocean park. So, when they can stay long time in this ocean park, they may spend money to live hotels, spend money to play any leisure machines and spend time to go to shopping, or buying tickets to see any movies in this ocean park. All of this ocean park natural environment facilities and leisure playing machines improvement may influence any one visitor individual emotion either negative or positive feeling.

On conclusion, any theme parks must need to implement FM strategy to improve their theme parks inside natural environment and leisure playing machines quality and hotel living facilities and theme park external transport tool stations facilities, e.g. taxi, bus , railway station distance to convenience any one visitor can catch any one kind of public transport tool to arrive this theme park in short time easily. Also, any theme parks need to impove environment facilities in order to let any one visitor feels comfortable and enhoyable feeling when they choose this theme park to play. Consequently, the theme park's visitors number may be influenced to increase by their positive playing emotion feeling.

Organization facility managment (FM) strategy aims to keep the best facility equipment repair improvement to let any organizational equipment can be used in long time. Hence, FM aims to help organizations to avoid to spend much expenditure on long time repair. When any organizational equipment can be improved to achieve good quality. Instead of improvement equipment quality aspect, can improvement facility equipment bring good customer emotion? How FM may help entertainment theme parks to save long time cost?

In entertainment theme park organizations, they must need to have different kinds of leisure playing machine facilities to supply to visitors to choose to play. So, facility management (FM) must need to imrpove any one entertainment theme parkj machine facility quality, it aims to avoid accidents occur , due to any leisure machine facilities are old or damage when they are used to operate in daily long opening time. Hence, FM must be needed to improve any entertainment theme parks' different kinds of leisure playing machine equipment frequently. If any one theme park leisure machine facility has poor FM in order to improve its machine quality. Consequently, this kind of leisure theme park leisure playing mahcine may be sudden to bring accidents occur, when any one visitor chooses this one of leisure playing machine facility to play. It may cause the player to hurt, even die in possible. Hence, FM to any entertainment theme park playing machine equipment , it may be one major facility repair management srtategy to any entertainment theme parks leisure playing machine facilities, because any one leisure playing machine facilities may bring any one visiot body hurt when the playing machine is old. Instead of FM can bring safety and playinf machine facilities quality improvement benefits to any one entertainment theme park leisure playing machine, whether FM to entertainment theme parks can bring psotive playing of leisure emotion to any one theme park visitor. I shall attempt to discuss as below:

Firstly, we need to know that any kinds of entertainment theme parks why they need to implement FM strategy. Why FM can bring advantages to any kinds of entertainment theme parks. In fact, the benefits of facility management to entertainment theme parks, it enables a more cost-effective working process within any kinds of the theme park any leisure playing machine facilities, such as theme park leisure playing sevice business. It improves the efficiency and it can help the theme park to manage health and safety requirements in accordance with industry regulations. It increases lifespan of a theme park any kinds of leisure playing machines, they are the theme park fixed assets, such as theme park's any kinds of leisure playing machine facilities. New theme parks and attractions can also improve the image of a destination increase tourism and hence economic benefits for the local community , and provide education and entertainment opportunities to the public.

Hence, it is common sense, if the theme park can have good FM to improve its any leisure playing facilities in order to avoid any accident occurrence , when any one visitor chooses to play its any one lesiure machine. Then, it can bring positive safe emotion feeling to satisfy any one visitor whose individual playing safe need to any kinds of playing leisure machines. I believe that its visitors number will not decrease, even increases significantly forever. Hence , the major roles of a theme park facility manager, is that to ensure the upkeep and manintenance of its any one entertainment playing machines, e.g. rolling rides, water rides etc. So, that they meet both safety and health standards to let any one visitors to feel safe to play.

In fact, the scope of facilities management covers two main areas: space and infrastructure , such as planning, design and workplace, construction, occupancy , maintenance and furniture as well as people and organization (such as catering, cleaning and HR, hospitality, accounting and marketing efficient operation in office) both aspects. Hence, these are 6 main facilities to ensure one available for any familiry theme plars. For leisure theme park case, rides and attractions are needed for all ages of any one theme park visitors. This is perhaps the most imprtant, as different parks will have different target audiences, e.g. refreshments, shops, toilets, and parking , access facilities and any one kind of leisure playing machines, such as rolling rides, water rides etc.

Hence, a theme park is a type of amusement park that bases its choice of which kinds of leisure playing facility structures and attractions around a central theme often featureing multiple areas with different themes. Unlike

temporary and mobile fun fairs and carnivals, amusement parks are stationary and built for long lasting operation. Hence, every theme park must need have a photogenic, iconic landmark that draws people into the park, beautiful landscaping , enough available attraction capacity to keep peak waits for non-new attractions under 90 minutes, all of these are other faciliities. They must also need to manage to keep more attraction to theme park any one visitor to feel enjoyable and comfortable to play any one theme park leisure playing machines.
What advantages to the theme park implements FM strategy? For Ocean Park example, it aims to let visitors feel themed ocean animal recreational and educational and leisure park experience. So, it must need to upgrade to improve its any facilities to avoid long time repaire spending expenditure. FM project may include: modifying sections of ocean park road, which is a local distributor, around the existing bus terminus , drain works, tunneling and geotechnical works, bulk excavation and slope works, site clearance, modification to bus terminus, taxi stands as well as utilities works including power supply distribution, electrical substations, freshwater and saltwater reservoirs, water supply distribution, gas supply distribution, telecommunications networks, landscope irrigation network to the ocean park any one ocean fish reservoirs, primary life support system works for animal keeping, area development works include elevated walkways, external lighting, external escalators, bridges, parkwide systems works include: signage, background, music system, toilet facilities, guard sheds, first and facilities, communication systems , CCTV systems and waste facilities, landscape or theming works, themed concern pavements, hardscape soft landscaping, water and rockwork features, visual intrusion screens, area props and artwork etc. works for the attractions venues include: animal exhibits, marine animal, terrestrial animal, aviaries , bind exhibits, individual life support systems for animal , exhibits and non- animal related attractions, e.g. shipwreck play area, bamboo maze etc. installation of rides interactive rides , transportation rides etc. , works for venues include : event halls, outdoor live show area, cinema band stands, work for the merchandise / retail facilities include souvonir stores, novelty stores, games ascade, photo shops etc. in the ocean park.
Moreover, any ocean park also have works for the food and baverage facilities include: restaurants, ballery, food casrts as well as back of house facilities include: ocean park offices, break areas, warehouses , centralized facilities, operational facilities etc. , even the ocean park inside hotel development facilities. All of these may bring positive or negative leisure activities impacts to influence any one of this ocean park visitor individual emotion significantly, if he /she feel comfortable and enjoyable , when they enter this ocean park. This ocean park whole natural environment may influence they like to stay long time in this ocean park. So, when they can stay long time in this ocean park, they may spend money to live hotels, spend money to play any leisure machines and spend time to go to shopping, or buying tickets to see any movies in this ocean park. All of this ocean park natural environment facilities and leisure playing machines improvement may influence any one visitor individual emotion either negative or positive feeling.
On conclusion, any theme parks must need to implement FM strategy to improve their theme parks inside natural environment and leisure playing machines quality and hotel living facilities and theme park external transport tool stations facilities, e.g. taxi, bus , railway station distance to convenience any one visitor can catch any one kind of public transport tool to arrive this theme park in short time easily. Also, any theme parks need to impove environment facilities in order to let any one visitor feels comfortable and enhoyable feeling when they choose this theme park to play. Consequently, the theme park's visitors number may be influenced to increase by their positive playing emotion feeling.

Organization facility managment (FM) strategy aims to keep the best facility equipment repair improvement to let any organizational equipment can be used in long time. Hence, FM aims to help organizations to avoid to spend much expenditure on long time repair. When any organizational equipment can be improved to achieve good quality. Instead of improvement equipment quality aspect, can improvement facility equipment bring good customer emotion? How FM may help entertainment theme parks to save long time cost?

In entertainment theme park organizations, they must need to have different kinds of leisure playing machine facilities to supply to visitors to choose to play. So, facility management (FM) must need to imrpove any one entertainment theme parkj machine facility quality, it aims to avoid accidents occur , due to any leisure machine facilities are old or damage when they are used to operate in daily long opening time. Hence, FM must be needed to improve any entertainment theme parks' different kinds of leisure playing machine equipment frequently. If any one theme park leisure machine facility has poor FM in order to improve its machine quality. Consequently, this kind of leisure theme park leisure playing mahcine may be sudden to bring accidents occur, when any one visitor chooses this one of leisure playing machine facility to play. It may cause the player to hurt, even die in possible. Hence, FM to any entertainment theme park playing machine equipment , it may be one major facility repair management srtategy to any entertainment theme parks leisure playing machine facilities, because any one leisure playing machine facilities may bring any one visiot body hurt when the playing machine is old. Instead of FM can bring safety and playinf machine facilities quality improvement benefits to any one entertainment theme park leisure playing machine, whether FM to entertainment theme parks can bring psotive playing of leisure emotion to any one theme park visitor. I shall attempt to discuss as below:

Firstly, we need to know that any kinds of entertainment theme parks why they need to implement FM strategy. Why FM can bring advantages to any kinds of entertainment theme parks. In fact, the benefits of facility management to entertainment theme parks, it enables a more cost-effective working process within any kinds of the theme park any leisure playing machine facilities, such as theme park leisure playing sevice business. It improves the efficiency and it can help the theme park to manage health and safety requirements in accordance with industry regulations. It increases lifespan of a theme park any kinds of leisure playing machines, they are the theme park fixed assets, such as theme park's any kinds of leisure playing machine facilities. New theme parks and attractions can also improve the image of a destination increase tourism and hence economic benefits for the local community , and provide education and entertainment opportunities to the public.

Hence, it is common sense, if the theme park can have good FM to improve its any leisure playing facilities in order to avoid any accident occurrence , when any one visitor chooses to play its any one lesiure machine. Then, it can bring positive safe emotion feeling to satisfy any one visitor whose individual playing safe need to any kinds of playing leisure machines. I believe that its visitors number will not decrease, even increases significantly forever. Hence , the major roles of a theme park facility manager, is that to ensure the upkeep and manintenance of its any one entertainment playing machines, e.g. rolling rides, water rides etc. So, that they meet both safety and health standards to let any one visitors to feel safe to play.

In fact, the scope of facilities management covers two main areas: space and infrastructure , such as planning, design and workplace, construction, occupancy , maintenance and furniture as well as people and organization (such as catering, cleaning and HR, hospitality, accounting and marketing efficient operation in office) both aspects. Hence, these are 6 main facilities to ensure one available for any familiry theme plars. For leisure theme park case, rides and attractions are needed for all ages of any one theme park visitors. This is perhaps the most imprtant, as different parks will have different target audiences, e.g. refreshments, shops, toilets, and parking , access facilities and any one kind of leisure playing machines, such as rolling rides, water rides etc.

Hence, a theme park is a type of amusement park that bases its choice of which kinds of leisure playing facility structures and attractions around a central theme often featureing multiple areas with different themes. Unlike temporary and mobile fun fairs and carnivals, amusement parks are stationary and built for long lasting operation. Hence, every theme park must need have a photogenic, iconic landmark that draws people into the park, beautiful landscaping , enough available attraction capacity to keep peak waits for non-new attractions under 90 minutes, all of these are other faciliities. They must also need to manage to keep more attraction to theme park any one visitor to feel enjoyable and comfortable to play any one theme park leisure playing machines.

What advantages to the theme park implements FM strategy? For Ocean Park example, it aims to let visitors feel themed ocean animal recreational and educational and leisure park experience. So, it must need to upgrade to improve its any facilities to avoid long time repaire spending expenditure. FM project may include: modifying sections of ocean park road, which is a local distributor, around the existing bus terminus , drain works, tunneling and geotechnical works, bulk excavation and slope works, site clearance, modification to bus terminus, taxi stands as well as utilities works including power supply distribution, electrical substations, freshwater and saltwater reservoirs, water supply distribution, gas supply distribution, telecommunications networks, landscope irrigation network to the ocean park any one ocean fish reservoirs, primary life support system works for animal keeping, area development works include elevated walkways, external lighting, external escalators, bridges, parkwide systems works include: signage, background, music system, toilet facilities, guard sheds, first and facilities, communication systems , CCTV systems and waste facilities, landscape or theming works, themed concern pavements, hardscape soft landscaping, water and rockwork features, visual intrusion screens, area props and artwork etc. works for the attractions venues include: animal exhibits, marine animal, terrestrial animal, aviaries , bind exhibits, individual life support systems for animal , exhibits and non- animal related attractions, e.g. shipwreck play area, bamboo maze etc. installation of rides interactive rides , transportation rides etc. , works for venues include : event halls, outdoor live show area, cinema band stands, work for the merchandise / retail facilities include souvonir stores, novelty stores, games ascade, photo shops etc. in the ocean park.

Moreover, any ocean park also have works for the food and baverage facilities include: restaurants, ballery, food casrts as well as back of house facilities include: ocean park offices, break areas, warehouses , centralized facilities, operational facilities etc. , even the ocean park inside hotel development facilities. All of these may bring positive or negative leisure activities impacts to influence any one of this ocean park visitor individual emotion significantly, if he /she feel comfortable and enjoyable , when they enter this ocean park. This ocean park whole natural environment may influence they like to stay long time in this ocean park. So, when they can stay long time in this ocean park, they may spend money to live hotels, spend money to play any leisure machines and spend time to go to shopping, or buying tickets to see any movies in this ocean park. All of this ocean park natural environment facilities and leisure playing machines improvement may influence any one visitor individual emotion either negative or positive feeling. On conclusion, any theme parks must need to implement FM strategy to improve their theme parks inside natural environment and leisure playing machines quality and hotel living facilities and theme park external transport tool stations facilities, e.g. taxi, bus , railway station distance to convenience any one visitor can catch any one kind of public transport tool to arrive this theme park in short time easily. Also, any theme parks need to impove environment facilities in order to let any one visitor feels comfortable and enhoyable feeling when they choose this theme park to play. Consequently, the theme park's visitors number may be influenced to increase by their positive playing emotion feeling.

Organization facility managment (FM) strategy aims to keep the best facility equipment repair improvement to let any organizational equipment can be used in long time. Hence, FM aims to help organizations to avoid to spend much expenditure on long time repair. When any organizational equipment can be improved to achieve good quality. Instead of improvement equipment quality aspect, can improvement facility equipment bring good customer emotion? How FM may help entertainment theme parks to save long time cost?

In entertainment theme park organizations, they must need to have different kinds of leisure playing machine facilities to supply to visitors to choose to play. So, facility management (FM) must need to imrpove any one entertainment theme parkj machine facility quality, it aims to avoid accidents occur , due to any leisure machine facilities are old or damage when they are used to operate in daily long opening time. Hence, FM must be needed to improve any entertainment theme parks' different kinds of leisure playing machine equipment frequently. If any one theme park leisure machine facility has poor FM in order to improve its machine quality. Consequently, this kind of leisure theme park leisure playing mahcine may be sudden to bring accidents occur, when any one visitor chooses this one of leisure playing machine facility to play. It may cause the player to hurt, even die in possible. Hence, FM to any entertainment theme park playing machine equipment , it may be one major facility repair management srtategy to any entertainment theme parks leisure playing machine facilities, because any one leisure playing machine facilities may bring any one visiot body hurt when the playing machine is old. Instead of FM can bring safety and playinf machine facilities quality improvement benefits to any one entertainment theme park leisure playing machine, whether FM to entertainment theme parks can bring psotive playing of leisure emotion to any one theme park visitor. I shall attempt to discuss as below:

Firstly, we need to know that any kinds of entertainment theme parks why they need to implement FM strategy. Why FM can bring advantages to any kinds of entertainment theme parks. In fact, the benefits of facility management to entertainment theme parks, it enables a more cost-effective working process within any kinds of the theme park any leisure playing machine facilities, such as theme park leisure playing sevice business. It improves the efficiency and it can help the theme park to manage health and safety requirements in accordance with industry regulations. It increases lifespan of a theme park any kinds of leisure playing machines, they are the theme park fixed assets, such as theme park's any kinds of leisure playing machine facilities. New theme parks and attractions can also improve the image of a destination increase tourism and hence economic benefits for the local community , and provide education and entertainment opportunities to the public.

Hence, it is common sense, if the theme park can have good FM to improve its any leisure playing facilities in order to avoid any accident occurrence , when any one visitor chooses to play its any one lesiure machine. Then, it can bring positive safe emotion feeling to satisfy any one visitor whose individual playing safe need to any kinds of playing leisure machines. I believe that its visitors number will not decrease, even increases significantly forever. Hence , the major roles of a theme park facility manager, is that to ensure the upkeep and manintenance of its any one entertainment playing machines, e.g. rolling rides, water rides etc. So, that they meet both safety and health standards to let any one visitors to feel safe to play.

In fact, the scope of facilities management covers two main areas: space and infrastructure , such as planning, design and workplace, construction, occupancy , maintenance and furniture as well as people and organization (such as catering, cleaning and HR, hospitality, accounting and marketing efficient operation in office) both aspects. Hence, these are 6 main facilities to ensure one available for any familiry theme plars. For leisure theme park case, rides and attractions are needed for all ages of any one theme park visitors. This is perhaps the most imprtant, as different parks will have different target audiences, e.g. refreshments, shops, toilets, and parking , access facilities and any one kind of leisure playing machines, such as rolling rides, water rides etc.

Hence, a theme park is a type of amusement park that bases its choice of which kinds of leisure playing facility structures and attractions around a central theme often featureing multiple areas with different themes. Unlike temporary and mobile fun fairs and carnivals, amusement parks are stationary and built for long lasting operation. Hence, every theme park must need have a photogenic, iconic landmark that draws people into the park, beautiful landscaping , enough available attraction capacity to keep peak waits for non-new attractions under 90 minutes, all of these are other faciliities. They must also need to manage to keep more attraction to theme park any one visitor to feel enjoyable and comfortable to play any one theme park leisure playing machines.

What advantages to the theme park implements FM strategy? For Ocean Park example, it aims to let visitors feel themed ocean animal recreational and educational and leisure park experience. So, it must need to upgrade to improve its any facilities to avoid long time repaire spending expenditure. FM project may include: modifying sections of ocean park road, which is a local distributor, around the existing bus terminus , drain works, tunneling and geotechnical works, bulk excavation and slope works, site clearance, modification to bus terminus, taxi stands as well as utilities works including power supply distribution, electrical substations, freshwater and saltwater reservoirs, water supply distribution, gas supply distribution, telecommunications networks, landscope irrigation network to the ocean park any one ocean fish reservoirs, primary life support system works for animal keeping, area development works include elevated walkways, external lighting, external escalators, bridges, parkwide systems works include: signage, background, music system, toilet facilities, guard sheds, first and facilities, communication systems , CCTV systems and waste facilities, landscape or theming works, themed concern pavements, hardscape soft landscaping, water and rockwork features, visual intrusion screens, area props and artwork etc. works for the attractions venues include: animal exhibits, marine animal, terrestrial animal, aviaries , bind exhibits, individual life support systems for animal , exhibits and non- animal related attractions, e.g. shipwreck play area, bamboo maze etc. installation of rides interactive rides , transportation rides etc. , works for venues include : event halls, outdoor live show area, cinema band stands, work for the merchandise / retail facilities include souvonir stores, novelty stores, games ascade, photo shops etc. in the ocean park.

Moreover, any ocean park also have works for the food and baverage facilities include: restaurants, ballery, food casrts as well as back of house facilities include: ocean park offices, break areas, warehouses , centralized facilities, operational facilities etc. , even the ocean park inside hotel development facilities. All of these may bring positive or negative leisure activities impacts to influence any one of this ocean park visitor individual emotion significantly, if he /she feel comfortable and enjoyable , when they enter this ocean park. This ocean park whole natural environment may influence they like to stay long time in this ocean park. So, when they can stay long time in this ocean park, they may spend money to live hotels, spend money to play any leisure machines and spend time to go to shopping, or buying tickets to see any movies in this ocean park. All of this ocean park natural environment facilities and leisure playing machines improvement may influence any one visitor individual emotion either negative or positive feeling. On conclusion, any theme parks must need to implement FM strategy to improve their theme parks inside natural environment and leisure playing machines quality and hotel living facilities and theme park external transport tool stations facilities, e.g. taxi, bus , railway station distance to convenience any one visitor can catch any one kind of public transport tool to arrive this theme park in short time easily. Also, any theme parks need to impove environment facilities in order to let any one visitor feels comfortable and enhoyable feeling when they choose this theme park to play. Consequently, the theme park's visitors number may be influenced to increase by their positive playing emotion feeling.

Organization facility managment (FM) strategy aims to keep the best facility equipment repair improvement to let any organizational equipment can be used in long time. Hence, FM aims to help organizations to avoid to spend much expenditure on long time repair. When any organizational equipment can be improved to achieve good quality. Instead of improvement equipment quality aspect, can improvement facility equipment bring good customer emotion? How FM may help entertainment theme parks to save long time cost?

In entertainment theme park organizations, they must need to have different kinds of leisure playing machine facilities to supply to visitors to choose to play. So, facility management (FM) must need to imrpove any one entertainment theme parkj machine facility quality, it aims to avoid accidents occur , due to any leisure machine facilities are old or damage when they are used to operate in daily long opening time. Hence, FM must be needed to improve any entertainment theme parks‘ different kinds of leisure playing machine equipment frequently. If any one theme park leisure machine facility has poor FM in order to improve its machine quality. Consequently, this kind of leisure theme park leisure playing mahcine may be sudden to bring accidents occur, when any one visitor chooses this one of leisure playing machine facility to play. It may cause the player to hurt, even die in possible. Hence, FM to any entertainment theme park playing machine equipment , it may be one major facility repair management srtategy to any entertainment theme parks leisure playing machine facilities, because any one leisure playing machine facilities may bring any one visiot body hurt when the playing machine is old. Instead of FM can bring safety and playinf machine facilities quality improvement benefits to any one entertainment theme park leisure playing machine, whether FM to entertainment theme parks can bring psotive playing of leisure emotion to any one theme park visitor. I shall attempt to discuss as below:

Firstly, we need to know that any kinds of entertainment theme parks why they need to implement FM strategy. Why FM can bring advantages to any kinds of entertainment theme parks. In fact, the benefits of facility management to entertainment theme parks, it enables a more cost-effective working process within any kinds of the theme park any leisure playing machine facilities, such as theme park leisure playing sevice business. It improves the efficiency and it can help the theme park to manage health and safety requirements in accordance with industry regulations. It increases lifespan of a theme park any kinds of leisure playing machines, they are the theme park fixed assets, such as theme park's any kinds of leisure playing machine facilities. New theme parks and attractions can also improve the image of a destination increase tourism and hence economic benefits for the local community , and provide education and entertainment opportunities to the public.

Hence, it is common sense, if the theme park can have good FM to improve its any leisure playing facilities in order to avoid any accident occurrence , when any one visitor chooses to play its any one lesiure machine. Then, it can bring positive safe emotion feeling to satisfy any one visitor whose individual playing safe need to any kinds of playing leisure machines. I believe that its visitors number will not decrease, even increases significantly forever. Hence , the major roles of a theme park facility manager, is that to ensure the upkeep and manintenance of its any one entertainment playing machines, e.g. rolling rides, water rides etc. So, that they meet both safety and health standards to let any one visitors to feel safe to play.

In fact, the scope of facilities management covers two main areas: space and infrastructure , such as planning, design and workplace, construction, occupancy , maintenance and furniture as well as people and organization (such as catering, cleaning and HR, hospitality, accounting and marketing efficient operation in office) both aspects. Hence, these are 6 main facilities to ensure one available for any familiry theme plars. For leisure theme park case, rides and attractions are needed for all ages of any one theme park visitors. This is perhaps the most imprtant, as different parks will have different target audiences, e.g. refreshments, shops, toilets, and parking , access facilities and any one kind of leisure playing machines, such as rolling rides, water rides etc.

Hence, a theme park is a type of amusement park that bases its choice of which kinds of leisure playing facility structures and attractions around a central theme often featureing multiple areas with different themes. Unlike temporary and mobile fun fairs and carnivals, amusement parks are stationary and built for long lasting operation. Hence, every theme park must need have a photogenic, iconic landmark that draws people into the park, beautiful landscaping , enough available attraction capacity to keep peak waits for non-new attractions under 90 minutes, all of these are other faciliities. They must also need to manage to keep more attraction to theme park any one visitor to feel enjoyable and comfortable to play any one theme park leisure playing machines.

What advantages to the theme park implements FM strategy? For Ocean Park example, it aims to let visitors feel themed ocean animal recreational and educational and leisure park experience. So, it must need to upgrade to improve its any facilities to avoid long time repaire spending expenditure. FM project may include: modifying sections of ocean park road, which is a local distributor, around the existing bus terminus , drain works, tunneling and geotechnical works, bulk excavation and slope works, site clearance, modification to bus terminus, taxi stands as well as utilities works including power supply distribution, electrical substations, freshwater and saltwater reservoirs, water supply distribution, gas supply distribution, telecommunications networks, landscope irrigation network to the ocean park any one ocean fish reservoirs, primary life support system works for animal keeping, area development works include elevated walkways, external lighting, external escalators, bridges, parkwide systems works include: signage, background, music system, toilet facilities, guard sheds, first and facilities, communication systems , CCTV systems and waste facilities, landscape or theming works, themed concern pavements, hardscape soft landscaping, water and rockwork features, visual intrusion screens, area props and artwork etc. works for the attractions venues include: animal exhibits, marine animal, terrestrial animal, aviaries , bind exhibits, individual life support systems for animal , exhibits and non- animal related attractions, e.g. shipwreck play area, bamboo maze etc. installation of rides interactive rides , transportation rides etc. , works for venues include : event halls, outdoor live show area, cinema band stands, work for the merchandise / retail facilities include souvonir stores, novelty stores, games ascade, photo shops etc. in the ocean park.

Moreover, any ocean park also have works for the food and baverage facilities include: restaurants, ballery, food casrts as well as back of house facilities include: ocean park offices, break areas, warehouses , centralized facilities, operational facilities etc. , even the ocean park inside hotel development facilities. All of these may bring positive or negative leisure activities impacts to influence any one of this ocean park visitor individual emotion significantly, if he /she feel comfortable and enjoyable , when they enter this ocean park. This ocean park whole natural environment may influence they like to stay long time in this ocean park. So, when they can stay long time in this ocean park, they may spend money to live hotels, spend money to play any leisure machines and spend time to go to shopping, or buying tickets to see any movies in this ocean park. All of this ocean park natural environment facilities and leisure playing machines improvement may influence any one visitor individual emotion either negative or positive feeling.

On conclusion, any theme parks must need to implement FM strategy to improve their theme parks inside natural environment and leisure playing machines quality and hotel living facilities and theme park external transport tool stations facilities, e.g. taxi, bus , railway station distance to convenience any one visitor can catch any one kind of public transport tool to arrive this theme park in short time easily. Also, any theme parks need to impove environment facilities in order to let any one visitor feels comfortable and enhoyable feeling when they choose this theme park to play. Consequently, the theme park's visitors number may be influenced to increase by their positive playing emotion feeling.

Organization facility managment (FM) strategy aims to keep the best facility equipment repair improvement to let any organizational equipment can be used in long time. Hence, FM aims to help organizations to avoid to spend much expenditure on long time repair. When any organizational equipment can be improved to achieve good quality. Instead of improvement equipment quality aspect, can improvement facility equipment bring good customer emotion? How FM may help entertainment theme parks to save long time cost?

In entertainment theme park organizations, they must need to have different kinds of leisure playing machine facilities to supply to visitors to choose to play. So, facility management (FM) must need to imrpove any one entertainment theme parkj machine facility quality, it aims to avoid accidents occur , due to any leisure machine facilities are old or damage when they are used to operate in daily long opening time. Hence, FM must be needed to improve any entertainment theme parks' different kinds of leisure playing machine equipment frequently. If any one theme park leisure machine facility has poor FM in order to improve its machine quality. Consequently, this kind of leisure theme park leisure playing mahcine may be sudden to bring accidents occur, when any one visitor chooses this one of leisure playing machine facility to play. It may cause the player to hurt, even die in possible. Hence, FM to any entertainment theme park playing machine equipment , it may be one major facility repair management srtategy to any entertainment theme parks leisure playing machine facilities, because any one leisure playing machine facilities may bring any one visiot body hurt when the playing machine is old. Instead of FM can bring safety and playinf machine facilities quality improvement benefits to any one entertainment theme park leisure playing machine, whether FM to entertainment theme parks can bring psotive playing of leisure emotion to any one theme park visitor. I shall attempt to discuss as below:

Firstly, we need to know that any kinds of entertainment theme parks why they need to implement FM strategy. Why FM can bring advantages to any kinds of entertainment theme parks. In fact, the benefits of facility management to entertainment theme parks, it enables a more cost-effective working process within any kinds of the theme park any leisure playing machine facilities, such as theme park leisure playing sevice business. It improves the efficiency and it can help the theme park to manage health and safety requirements in accordance with industry regulations. It increases lifespan of a theme park any kinds of leisure playing machines, they are the theme park fixed assets, such as theme park's any kinds of leisure playing machine facilities. New theme parks and attractions can also improve the image of a destination increase tourism and hence economic benefits for the local community , and provide education and entertainment opportunities to the public.

Hence, it is common sense, if the theme park can have good FM to improve its any leisure playing facilities in order to avoid any accident occurrence , when any one visitor chooses to play its any one lesiure machine. Then, it can bring positive safe emotion feeling to satisfy any one visitor whose individual playing safe need to any kinds of playing leisure machines. I believe that its visitors number will not decrease, even increases significantly forever. Hence , the major roles of a theme park facility manager, is that to ensure the upkeep and manintenance of its any one entertainment playing machines, e.g. rolling rides, water rides etc. So, that they meet both safety and health standards to let any one visitors to feel safe to play.

In fact, the scope of facilities management covers two main areas: space and infrastructure , such as planning, design and workplace, construction, occupancy , maintenance and furniture as well as people and organization (such as catering, cleaning and HR, hospitality, accounting and marketing efficient operation in office) both aspects. Hence, these are 6 main facilities to ensure one available for any familiry theme plars. For leisure theme park case, rides and attractions are needed for all ages of any one theme park visitors. This is perhaps the most imprtant, as different parks will have different target audiences, e.g. refreshments, shops, toilets, and parking , access facilities and any one kind of leisure playing machines, such as rolling rides, water rides etc.

Hence, a theme park is a type of amusement park that bases its choice of which kinds of leisure playing facility structures and attractions around a central theme often featureing multiple areas with different themes. Unlike temporary and mobile fun fairs and carnivals, amusement parks are stationary and built for long lasting operation. Hence, every theme park must need have a photogenic, iconic landmark that draws people into the park, beautiful landscaping , enough available attraction capacity to keep peak waits for non-new attractions under 90 minutes, all of these are other faciliities. They must also need to manage to keep more attraction to theme park any one visitor to feel enjoyable and comfortable to play any one theme park leisure playing machines.

What advantages to the theme park implements FM strategy? For Ocean Park example, it aims to let visitors feel themed ocean animal recreational and educational and leisure park experience. So, it must need to upgrade to improve its any facilities to avoid long time repaire spending expenditure. FM project may include: modifying sections of ocean park road, which is a local distributor, around the existing bus terminus , drain works, tunneling and geotechnical works, bulk excavation and slope works, site clearance, modification to bus terminus, taxi stands as well as utilities works including power supply distribution, electrical substations, freshwater and saltwater reservoirs, water supply distribution, gas supply distribution, telecommunications networks, landscope irrigation network to the ocean park any one ocean fish reservoirs, primary life support system works for animal keeping, area development works include elevated walkways, external lighting, external escalators, bridges, parkwide systems works include: signage, background, music system, toilet facilities, guard sheds, first and facilities, communication systems , CCTV systems and waste facilities, landscape or theming works, themed concern pavements, hardscape soft landscaping, water and rockwork features, visual intrusion screens, area props and artwork etc. works for the attractions venues include: animal exhibits, marine animal, terrestrial animal, aviaries , bind exhibits, individual life support systems for animal , exhibits and non- animal related attractions, e.g. shipwreck play area, bamboo maze etc. installation of rides interactive rides , transportation rides etc. , works for venues include : event halls, outdoor live show area, cinema band stands, work for the merchandise / retail facilities include souvonir stores, novelty stores, games ascade, photo shops etc. in the ocean park.

Moreover, any ocean park also have works for the food and baverage facilities include: restaurants, ballery, food casrts as well as back of house facilities include: ocean park offices, break areas, warehouses , centralized facilities, operational facilities etc. , even the ocean park inside hotel development facilities. All of these may bring positive or negative leisure activities impacts to influence any one of this ocean park visitor individual emotion significantly, if he /she feel comfortable and enjoyable , when they enter this ocean park. This ocean park whole natural environment may influence they like to stay long time in this ocean park. So, when they can stay long time in this ocean park, they may spend money to live hotels, spend money to play any leisure machines and spend time to go to shopping, or buying tickets to see any movies in this ocean park. All of this ocean park natural environment facilities and leisure playing machines improvement may influence any one visitor individual emotion either negative or positive feeling.

On conclusion, any theme parks must need to implement FM strategy to improve their theme parks inside natural environment and leisure playing machines quality and hotel living facilities and theme park external transport tool stations facilities, e.g. taxi, bus , railway station distance to convenience any one visitor can catch any one kind of public transport tool to arrive this theme park in short time easily. Also, any theme parks need to impove environment facilities in order to let any one visitor feels comfortable and enhoyable feeling when they choose this theme park to play. Consequently, the theme park's visitors number may be influenced to increase by their positive playing emotion feeling.

Organization facility managment (FM) strategy aims to keep the best facility equipment repair improvement to let any organizational equipment can be used in long time. Hence, FM aims to help organizations to avoid to spend much expenditure on long time repair. When any organizational equipment can be improved to achieve good quality. Instead of improvement equipment quality aspect, can improvement facility equipment bring good customer emotion? How FM may help entertainment theme parks to save long time cost?

In entertainment theme park organizations, they must need to have different kinds of leisure playing machine facilities to supply to visitors to choose to play. So, facility management (FM) must need to imrpove any one entertainment theme parkj machine facility quality, it aims to avoid accidents occur , due to any leisure machine facilities are old or damage when they are used to operate in daily long opening time. Hence, FM must be needed to improve any entertainment theme parks' different kinds of leisure playing machine equipment frequently. If any one theme park leisure machine facility has poor FM in order to improve its machine quality. Consequently, this kind of leisure theme park leisure playing mahcine may be sudden to bring accidents occur, when any one visitor chooses this one of leisure playing machine facility to play. It may cause the player to hurt, even die in possible. Hence, FM to any entertainment theme park playing machine equipment , it may be one major facility repair management srtategy to any entertainment theme parks leisure playing machine facilities, because any one leisure playing machine facilities may bring any one visiot body hurt when the playing machine is old. Instead of FM can bring safety and playinf machine facilities quality improvement benefits to any one entertainment theme park leisure playing machine, whether FM to entertainment theme parks can bring psotive playing of leisure emotion to any one theme park visitor. I shall attempt to discuss as below:

Firstly, we need to know that any kinds of entertainment theme parks why they need to implement FM strategy. Why FM can bring advantages to any kinds of entertainment theme parks. In fact, the benefits of facility management to entertainment theme parks, it enables a more cost-effective working process within any kinds of the theme park any leisure playing machine facilities, such as theme park leisure playing sevice business. It improves the efficiency and it can help the theme park to manage health and safety requirements in accordance with industry regulations. It increases lifespan of a theme park any kinds of leisure playing machines, they are the theme park fixed assets, such as theme park's any kinds of leisure playing machine facilities. New theme parks and attractions can also improve the image of a destination increase tourism and hence economic benefits for the local community , and provide education and entertainment opportunities to the public.

Hence, it is common sense, if the theme park can have good FM to improve its any leisure playing facilities in order to avoid any accident occurrence , when any one visitor chooses to play its any one lesiure machine. Then, it can bring positive safe emotion feeling to satisfy any one visitor whose individual playing safe need to any kinds of playing leisure machines. I believe that its visitors number will not decrease, even increases significantly forever. Hence , the major roles of a theme park facility manager, is that to ensure the upkeep and manintenance of its any one entertainment playing machines, e.g. rolling rides, water rides etc. So, that they meet both safety and health standards to let any one visitors to feel safe to play.

In fact, the scope of facilities management covers two main areas: space and infrastructure , such as planning, design and workplace, construction, occupancy , maintenance and furniture as well as people and organization (such as catering, cleaning and HR, hospitality, accounting and marketing efficient operation in office) both aspects. Hence, these are 6 main facilities to ensure one available for any familiry theme plars. For leisure theme park case, rides and attractions are needed for all ages of any one theme park visitors. This is perhaps the most imprtant, as different parks will have different target audiences, e.g. refreshments, shops, toilets, and parking , access facilities and any one kind of leisure playing machines, such as rolling rides, water rides etc.

Hence, a theme park is a type of amusement park that bases its choice of which kinds of leisure playing facility structures and attractions around a central theme often featureing multiple areas with different themes. Unlike temporary and mobile fun fairs and carnivals, amusement parks are stationary and built for long lasting operation. Hence, every theme park must need have a photogenic, iconic landmark that draws people into the park, beautiful landscaping , enough available attraction capacity to keep peak waits for non-new attractions under 90 minutes, all of these are other faciliities. They must also need to manage to keep more attraction to theme park any one visitor to feel enjoyable and comfortable to play any one theme park leisure playing machines.

What advantages to the theme park implements FM strategy? For Ocean Park example, it aims to let visitors feel themed ocean animal recreational and educational and leisure park experience. So, it must need to upgrade to improve its any facilities to avoid long time repaire spending expenditure. FM project may include: modifying sections of ocean park road, which is a local distributor, around the existing bus terminus , drain works, tunneling and geotechnical works, bulk excavation and slope works, site clearance, modification to bus terminus, taxi stands as well as utilities works including power supply distribution, electrical substations, freshwater and saltwater reservoirs, water supply distribution, gas supply distribution, telecommunications networks, landscope irrigation network to the ocean park any one ocean fish reservoirs, primary life support system works for animal keeping, area development works include elevated walkways, external lighting, external escalators, bridges, parkwide systems works include: signage, background, music system, toilet facilities, guard sheds, first and facilities, communication systems , CCTV systems and waste facilities, landscape or theming works, themed concern pavements, hardscape soft landscaping, water and rockwork features, visual intrusion screens, area props and artwork etc. works for the attractions venues include: animal exhibits, marine animal, terrestrial animal, aviaries , bind exhibits, individual life support systems for animal , exhibits and non- animal related attractions, e.g. shipwreck play area, bamboo maze etc. installation of rides interactive rides , transportation rides etc. , works for venues include : event halls, outdoor live show area, cinema band stands, work for the merchandise / retail facilities include souvonir stores, novelty stores, games ascade, photo shops etc. in the ocean park.

Moreover, any ocean park also have works for the food and baverage facilities include: restaurants, ballery, food casrts as well as back of house facilities include: ocean park offices, break areas, warehouses , centralized facilities, operational facilities etc. , even the ocean park inside hotel development facilities. All of these may bring positive or negative leisure activities impacts to influence any one of this ocean park visitor individual emotion significantly, if he /she feel comfortable and enjoyable , when they enter this ocean park. This ocean park whole natural environment may influence they like to stay long time in this ocean park. So, when they can stay long time in this ocean park, they may spend money to live hotels, spend money to play any leisure machines and spend time to go to shopping, or buying tickets to see any movies in this ocean park. All of this ocean park natural environment facilities and leisure playing machines improvement may influence any one visitor individual emotion either negative or positive feeling. On conclusion, any theme parks must need to implement FM strategy to improve their theme parks inside natural environment and leisure playing machines quality and hotel living facilities and theme park external transport tool stations facilities, e.g. taxi, bus , railway station distance to convenience any one visitor can catch any one kind of public transport tool to arrive this theme park in short time easily. Also, any theme parks need to impove environment facilities in order to let any one visitor feels comfortable and enhoyable feeling when they choose this theme park to play. Consequently, the theme park's visitors number may be influenced to increase by their positive playing emotion feeling.

Organization facility managment (FM) strategy aims to keep the best facility equipment repair improvement to let any organizational equipment can be used in long time. Hence, FM aims to help organizations to avoid to spend much expenditure on long time repair. When any organizational equipment can be improved to achieve good quality. Instead of improvement equipment quality aspect, can improvement facility equipment bring good customer emotion? How FM may help entertainment theme parks to save long time cost?

In entertainment theme park organizations, they must need to have different kinds of leisure playing machine facilities to supply to visitors to choose to play. So, facility management (FM) must need to imrpove any one entertainment theme parkj machine facility quality, it aims to avoid accidents occur , due to any leisure machine facilities are old or damage when they are used to operate in daily long opening time. Hence, FM must be needed to improve any entertainment theme parks' different kinds of leisure playing machine equipment frequently. If any one theme park leisure machine facility has poor FM in order to improve its machine quality. Consequently, this kind of leisure theme park leisure playing mahcine may be sudden to bring accidents occur, when any one visitor chooses this one of leisure playing machine facility to play. It may cause the player to hurt, even die in possible. Hence, FM to any entertainment theme park playing machine equipment , it may be one major facility repair management srtategy to any entertainment theme parks leisure playing machine facilities, because any one leisure playing machine facilities may bring any one visiot body hurt when the playing machine is old. Instead of FM can bring safety and playinf machine facilities quality improvement benefits to any one entertainment theme park leisure playing machine, whether FM to entertainment theme parks can bring psotive playing of leisure emotion to any one theme park visitor. I shall attempt to discuss as below:

Firstly, we need to know that any kinds of entertainment theme parks why they need to implement FM strategy. Why FM can bring advantages to any kinds of entertainment theme parks. In fact, the benefits of facility management to entertainment theme parks, it enables a more cost-effective working process within any kinds of the theme park any leisure playing machine facilities, such as theme park leisure playing sevice business. It improves the efficiency and it can help the theme park to manage health and safety requirements in accordance with industry regulations. It increases lifespan of a theme park any kinds of leisure playing machines, they are the theme park fixed assets, such as theme park's any kinds of leisure playing machine facilities. New theme parks and attractions can also improve the image of a destination increase tourism and hence economic benefits for the local community , and provide education and entertainment opportunities to the public.

Hence, it is common sense, if the theme park can have good FM to improve its any leisure playing facilities in order to avoid any accident occurrence , when any one visitor chooses to play its any one lesiure machine. Then, it can bring positive safe emotion feeling to satisfy any one visitor whose individual playing safe need to any kinds of playing leisure machines. I believe that its visitors number will not decrease, even increases significantly forever. Hence , the major roles of a theme park facility manager, is that to ensure the upkeep and manintenance of its any one entertainment playing machines, e.g. rolling rides, water rides etc. So, that they meet both safety and health standards to let any one visitors to feel safe to play.

In fact, the scope of facilities management covers two main areas: space and infrastructure , such as planning, design and workplace, construction, occupancy , maintenance and furniture as well as people and organization (such as catering, cleaning and HR, hospitality, accounting and marketing efficient operation in office) both aspects. Hence, these are 6 main facilities to ensure one available for any familiry theme plars. For leisure theme park case, rides and attractions are needed for all ages of any one theme park visitors. This is perhaps the most imprtant, as different parks will have different target audiences, e.g. refreshments, shops, toilets, and parking , access facilities and any one kind of leisure playing machines, such as rolling rides, water rides etc.

Hence, a theme park is a type of amusement park that bases its choice of which kinds of leisure playing facility structures and attractions around a central theme often featureing multiple areas with different themes. Unlike temporary and mobile fun fairs and carnivals, amusement parks are stationary and built for long lasting operation. Hence, every theme park must need have a photogenic, iconic landmark that draws people into the park, beautiful landscaping , enough available attraction capacity to keep peak waits for non-new attractions under 90 minutes, all of these are other faciliities. They must also need to manage to keep more attraction to theme park any one visitor to feel enjoyable and comfortable to play any one theme park leisure playing machines.

What advantages to the theme park implements FM strategy? For Ocean Park example, it aims to let visitors feel themed ocean animal recreational and educational and leisure park experience. So, it must need to upgrade to improve its any facilities to avoid long time repaire spending expenditure. FM project may include: modifying sections of ocean park road, which is a local distributor, around the existing bus terminus , drain works, tunneling and geotechnical works, bulk excavation and slope works, site clearance, modification to bus terminus, taxi stands as well as utilities works including power supply distribution, electrical substations, freshwater and saltwater reservoirs, water supply distribution, gas supply distribution, telecommunications networks, landscope irrigation network to the ocean park any one ocean fish reservoirs, primary life support system works for animal keeping, area development works include elevated walkways, external lighting, external escalators, bridges, parkwide systems works include: signage, background, music system, toilet facilities, guard sheds, first and facilities, communication systems , CCTV systems and waste facilities, landscape or theming works, themed concern pavements, hardscape soft landscaping, water and rockwork features, visual intrusion screens, area props and artwork etc. works for the attractions venues include: animal exhibits, marine animal, terrestrial animal, aviaries , bind exhibits, individual life support systems for animal , exhibits and non- animal related attractions, e.g. shipwreck play area, bamboo maze etc. installation of rides interactive rides , transportation rides etc. , works for venues include : event halls, outdoor live show area, cinema band stands, work for the merchandise / retail facilities include souvonir stores, novelty stores, games ascade, photo shops etc. in the ocean park.

Moreover, any ocean park also have works for the food and baverage facilities include: restaurants, ballery, food casrts as well as back of house facilities include: ocean park offices, break areas, warehouses , centralized facilities, operational facilities etc. , even the ocean park inside hotel development facilities. All of these may bring positive or negative leisure activities impacts to influence any one of this ocean park visitor individual emotion significantly, if he /she feel comfortable and enjoyable , when they enter this ocean park. This ocean park whole natural environment may influence they like to stay long time in this ocean park. So, when they can stay long time in this ocean park, they may spend money to live hotels, spend money to play any leisure machines and spend time to go to shopping, or buying tickets to see any movies in this ocean park. All of this ocean park natural environment facilities and leisure playing machines improvement may influence any one visitor individual emotion either negative or positive feeling. On conclusion, any theme parks must need to implement FM strategy to improve their theme parks inside natural environment and leisure playing machines quality and hotel living facilities and theme park external transport tool stations facilities, e.g. taxi, bus , railway station distance to convenience any one visitor can catch any one kind of public transport tool to arrive this theme park in short time easily. Also, any theme parks need to impove environment facilities in order to let any one visitor feels comfortable and enhoyable feeling when they choose this theme park to play. Consequently, the theme park's visitors number may be influenced to increase by their positive playing emotion feeling.

Organization facility managment (FM) strategy aims to keep the best facility equipment repair improvement to let any organizational equipment can be used in long time. Hence, FM aims to help organizations to avoid to spend much expenditure on long time repair. When any organizational equipment can be improved to achieve good quality. Instead of improvement equipment quality aspect, can improvement facility equipment bring good customer emotion? How FM may help entertainment theme parks to save long time cost?

In entertainment theme park organizations, they must need to have different kinds of leisure playing machine facilities to supply to visitors to choose to play. So, facility management (FM) must need to imrpove any one entertainment theme parkj machine facility quality, it aims to avoid accidents occur , due to any leisure machine facilities are old or damage when they are used to operate in daily long opening time. Hence, FM must be needed to improve any entertainment theme parks' different kinds of leisure playing machine equipment frequently. If any one theme park leisure machine facility has poor FM in order to improve its machine quality. Consequently, this kind of leisure theme park leisure playing mahcine may be sudden to bring accidents occur, when any one visitor chooses this one of leisure playing machine facility to play. It may cause the player to hurt, even die in possible. Hence, FM to any entertainment theme park playing machine equipment , it may be one major facility repair management srtategy to any entertainment theme parks leisure playing machine facilities, because any one leisure playing machine facilities may bring any one visiot body hurt when the playing machine is old. Instead of FM can bring safety and playinf machine facilities quality improvement benefits to any one entertainment theme park leisure playing machine, whether FM to entertainment theme parks can bring psotive playing of leisure emotion to any one theme park visitor. I shall attempt to discuss as below:

Firstly, we need to know that any kinds of entertainment theme parks why they need to implement FM strategy. Why FM can bring advantages to any kinds of entertainment theme parks. In fact, the benefits of facility management to entertainment theme parks, it enables a more cost-effective working process within any kinds of the theme park any leisure playing machine facilities, such as theme park leisure playing sevice business. It improves the efficiency and it can help the theme park to manage health and safety requirements in accordance with industry regulations. It increases lifespan of a theme park any kinds of leisure playing machines, they are the theme park fixed assets, such as theme park's any kinds of leisure playing machine facilities. New theme parks and attractions can also improve the image of a destination increase tourism and hence economic benefits for the local community , and provide education and entertainment opportunities to the public.

Hence, it is common sense, if the theme park can have good FM to improve its any leisure playing facilities in order to avoid any accident occurrence , when any one visitor chooses to play its any one lesiure machine. Then, it can bring positive safe emotion feeling to satisfy any one visitor whose individual playing safe need to any kinds of playing leisure machines. I believe that its visitors number will not decrease, even increases significantly forever. Hence , the major roles of a theme park facility manager, is that to ensure the upkeep and manintenance of its any one entertainment playing machines, e.g. rolling rides, water rides etc. So, that they meet both safety and health standards to let any one visitors to feel safe to play.

In fact, the scope of facilities management covers two main areas: space and infrastructure , such as planning, design and workplace, construction, occupancy , maintenance and furniture as well as people and organization (such as catering, cleaning and HR, hospitality, accounting and marketing efficient operation in office) both aspects. Hence, these are 6 main facilities to ensure one available for any familiry theme plars. For leisure theme park case, rides and attractions are needed for all ages of any one theme park visitors. This is perhaps the most imprtant, as different parks will have different target audiences, e.g. refreshments, shops, toilets, and parking , access facilities and any one kind of leisure playing machines, such as rolling rides, water rides etc.

Hence, a theme park is a type of amusement park that bases its choice of which kinds of leisure playing facility structures and attractions around a central theme often featureing multiple areas with different themes. Unlike temporary and mobile fun fairs and carnivals, amusement parks are stationary and built for long lasting operation. Hence, every theme park must need have a photogenic, iconic landmark that draws people into the park, beautiful landscaping , enough available attraction capacity to keep peak waits for non-new attractions under 90 minutes, all of these are other faciliities. They must also need to manage to keep more attraction to theme park any one visitor to feel enjoyable and comfortable to play any one theme park leisure playing machines.

What advantages to the theme park implements FM strategy? For Ocean Park example, it aims to let visitors feel themed ocean animal recreational and educational and leisure park experience. So, it must need to upgrade to improve its any facilities to avoid long time repaire spending expenditure. FM project may include: modifying sections of ocean park road, which is a local distributor, around the existing bus terminus , drain works, tunneling and geotechnical works, bulk excavation and slope works, site clearance, modification to bus terminus, taxi stands as well as utilities works including power supply distribution, electrical substations, freshwater and saltwater reservoirs, water supply distribution, gas supply distribution, telecommunications networks, landscope irrigation network to the ocean park any one ocean fish reservoirs, primary life support system works for animal keeping, area development works include elevated walkways, external lighting, external escalators, bridges, parkwide systems works include: signage, background, music system, toilet facilities, guard sheds, first and facilities, communication systems , CCTV systems and waste facilities, landscape or theming works, themed concern pavements, hardscape soft landscaping, water and rockwork features, visual intrusion screens, area props and artwork etc. works for the attractions venues include: animal exhibits, marine animal, terrestrial animal, aviaries , bind exhibits, individual life support systems for animal , exhibits and non- animal related attractions, e.g. shipwreck play area, bamboo maze etc. installation of rides interactive rides , transportation rides etc. , works for venues include : event halls, outdoor live show area, cinema band stands, work for the merchandise / retail facilities include souvonir stores, novelty stores, games ascade, photo shops etc. in the ocean park.

Moreover, any ocean park also have works for the food and baverage facilities include: restaurants, ballery, food casrts as well as back of house facilities include: ocean park offices, break areas, warehouses , centralized facilities, operational facilities etc. , even the ocean park inside hotel development facilities. All of these may bring positive or negative leisure activities impacts to influence any one of this ocean park visitor individual emotion significantly, if he /she feel comfortable and enjoyable , when they enter this ocean park. This ocean park whole natural environment may influence they like to stay long time in this ocean park. So, when they can stay long time in this ocean park, they may spend money to live hotels, spend money to play any leisure machines and spend time to go to shopping, or buying tickets to see any movies in this ocean park. All of this ocean park natural environment facilities and leisure playing machines improvement may influence any one visitor individual emotion either negative or positive feeling.

On conclusion, any theme parks must need to implement FM strategy to improve their theme parks inside natural environment and leisure playing machines quality and hotel living facilities and theme park external transport tool stations facilities, e.g. taxi, bus , railway station distance to convenience any one visitor can catch any one kind of public transport tool to arrive this theme park in short time easily. Also, any theme parks need to impove environment facilities in order to let any one visitor feels comfortable and enhoyable feeling when they choose this theme park to play. Consequently, the theme park's visitors number may be influenced to increase by their positive playing emotion feeling.

Organization facility managment (FM) strategy aims to keep the best facility equipment repair improvement to let any organizational equipment can be used in long time. Hence, FM aims to help organizations to avoid to spend much expenditure on long time repair. When any organizational equipment can be improved to achieve good quality. Instead of improvement equipment quality aspect, can improvement facility equipment bring good customer emotion? How FM may help entertainment theme parks to save long time cost?

In entertainment theme park organizations, they must need to have different kinds of leisure playing machine facilities to supply to visitors to choose to play. So, facility management (FM) must need to imrpove any one entertainment theme parkj machine facility quality, it aims to avoid accidents occur , due to any leisure machine facilities are old or damage when they are used to operate in daily long opening time. Hence, FM must be needed to improve any entertainment theme parks' different kinds of leisure playing machine equipment frequently. If any one theme park leisure machine facility has poor FM in order to improve its machine quality. Consequently, this kind of leisure theme park leisure playing mahcine may be sudden to bring accidents occur, when any one visitor chooses this one of leisure playing machine facility to play. It may cause the player to hurt, even die in possible. Hence, FM to any entertainment theme park playing machine equipment , it may be one major facility repair management srtategy to any entertainment theme parks leisure playing machine facilities, because any one leisure playing machine facilities may bring any one visiot body hurt when the playing machine is old. Instead of FM can bring safety and playinf machine facilities quality improvement benefits to any one entertainment theme park leisure playing machine, whether FM to entertainment theme parks can bring psotive playing of leisure emotion to any one theme park visitor. I shall attempt to discuss as below:

Firstly, we need to know that any kinds of entertainment theme parks why they need to implement FM strategy. Why FM can bring advantages to any kinds of entertainment theme parks. In fact, the benefits of facility management to entertainment theme parks, it enables a more cost-effective working process within any kinds of the theme park any leisure playing machine facilities, such as theme park leisure playing sevice business. It improves the efficiency and it can help the theme park to manage health and safety requirements in accordance with industry regulations. It increases lifespan of a theme park any kinds of leisure playing machines, they are the theme park fixed assets, such as theme park's any kinds of leisure playing machine facilities. New theme parks and attractions can also improve the image of a destination increase tourism and hence economic benefits for the local community , and provide education and entertainment opportunities to the public.

Hence, it is common sense, if the theme park can have good FM to improve its any leisure playing facilities in order to avoid any accident occurrence , when any one visitor chooses to play its any one lesiure machine. Then, it can bring positive safe emotion feeling to satisfy any one visitor whose individual playing safe need to any kinds of playing leisure machines. I believe that its visitors number will not decrease, even increases significantly forever. Hence , the major roles of a theme park facility manager, is that to ensure the upkeep and manintenance of its any one entertainment playing machines, e.g. rolling rides, water rides etc. So, that they meet both safety and health standards to let any one visitors to feel safe to play.

In fact, the scope of facilities management covers two main areas: space and infrastructure , such as planning, design and workplace, construction, occupancy , maintenance and furniture as well as people and organization (such as catering, cleaning and HR, hospitality, accounting and marketing efficient operation in office) both aspects. Hence, these are 6 main facilities to ensure one available for any familiry theme plars. For leisure theme park case, rides and attractions are needed for all ages of any one theme park visitors. This is perhaps the most imprtant, as different parks will have different target audiences, e.g. refreshments, shops, toilets, and parking , access facilities and any one kind of leisure playing machines, such as rolling rides, water rides etc.

Hence, a theme park is a type of amusement park that bases its choice of which kinds of leisure playing facility structures and attractions around a central theme often featureing multiple areas with different themes. Unlike temporary and mobile fun fairs and carnivals, amusement parks are stationary and built for long lasting operation. Hence, every theme park must need have a photogenic, iconic landmark that draws people into the park, beautiful landscaping , enough available attraction capacity to keep peak waits for non-new attractions under 90 minutes, all of these are other faciliities. They must also need to manage to keep more attraction to theme park any one visitor to feel enjoyable and comfortable to play any one theme park leisure playing machines.

What advantages to the theme park implements FM strategy? For Ocean Park example, it aims to let visitors feel themed ocean animal recreational and educational and leisure park experience. So, it must need to upgrade to improve its any facilities to avoid long time repaire spending expenditure. FM project may include: modifying sections of ocean park road, which is a local distributor, around the existing bus terminus , drain works, tunneling and geotechnical works, bulk excavation and slope works, site clearance, modification to bus terminus, taxi stands as well as utilities works including power supply distribution, electrical substations, freshwater and saltwater reservoirs, water supply distribution, gas supply distribution, telecommunications networks, landscope irrigation network to the ocean park any one ocean fish reservoirs, primary life support system works for animal keeping, area development works include elevated walkways, external lighting, external escalators, bridges, parkwide systems works include: signage, background, music system, toilet facilities, guard sheds, first and facilities, communication systems , CCTV systems and waste facilities, landscape or theming works, themed concern pavements, hardscape soft landscaping, water and rockwork features, visual intrusion screens, area props and artwork etc. works for the attractions venues include: animal exhibits, marine animal, terrestrial animal, aviaries , bind exhibits, individual life support systems for animal , exhibits and non- animal related attractions, e.g. shipwreck play area, bamboo maze etc. installation of rides interactive rides , transportation rides etc. , works for venues include : event halls, outdoor live show area, cinema band stands, work for the merchandise / retail facilities include souvonir stores, novelty stores, games ascade, photo shops etc. in the ocean park.

Moreover, any ocean park also have works for the food and baverage facilities include: restaurants, ballery, food casrts as well as back of house facilities include: ocean park offices, break areas, warehouses , centralized facilities, operational facilities etc. , even the ocean park inside hotel development facilities. All of these may bring positive or negative leisure activities impacts to influence any one of this ocean park visitor individual emotion significantly, if he /she feel comfortable and enjoyable , when they enter this ocean park. This ocean park whole natural environment may influence they like to stay long time in this ocean park. So, when they can stay long time in this ocean park, they may spend money to live hotels, spend money to play any leisure machines and spend time to go to shopping, or buying tickets to see any movies in this ocean park. All of this ocean park natural environment facilities and leisure playing machines improvement may influence any one visitor individual emotion either negative or positive feeling. On conclusion, any theme parks must need to implement FM strategy to improve their theme parks inside natural environment and leisure playing machines quality and hotel living facilities and theme park external transport tool stations facilities, e.g. taxi, bus , railway station distance to convenience any one visitor can catch any one kind of public transport tool to arrive this theme park in short time easily. Also, any theme parks need to impove environment facilities in order to let any one visitor feels comfortable and enhoyable feeling when they choose this theme park to play. Consequently, the theme park's visitors number may be influenced to increase by their positive playing emotion feeling.

Organization facility managment (FM) strategy aims to keep the best facility equipment repair improvement to let any organizational equipment can be used in long time. Hence, FM aims to help organizations to avoid to spend much expenditure on long time repair. When any organizational equipment can be improved to achieve good quality. Instead of improvement equipment quality aspect, can improvement facility equipment bring good customer emotion? How FM may help entertainment theme parks to save long time cost?

In entertainment theme park organizations, they must need to have different kinds of leisure playing machine facilities to supply to visitors to choose to play. So, facility management (FM) must need to imrpove any one entertainment theme parkj machine facility quality, it aims to avoid accidents occur , due to any leisure machine facilities are old or damage when they are used to operate in daily long opening time. Hence, FM must be needed to improve any entertainment theme parks' different kinds of leisure playing machine equipment frequently. If any one theme park leisure machine facility has poor FM in order to improve its machine quality. Consequently, this kind of leisure theme park leisure playing mahcine may be sudden to bring accidents occur, when any one visitor chooses this one of leisure playing machine facility to play. It may cause the player to hurt, even die in possible. Hence, FM to any entertainment theme park playing machine equipment , it may be one major facility repair management srtategy to any entertainment theme parks leisure playing machine facilities, because any one leisure playing machine facilities may bring any one visiot body hurt when the playing machine is old. Instead of FM can bring safety and playinf machine facilities quality improvement benefits to any one entertainment theme park leisure playing machine, whether FM to entertainment theme parks can bring psotive playing of leisure emotion to any one theme park visitor. I shall attempt to discuss as below:

Firstly, we need to know that any kinds of entertainment theme parks why they need to implement FM strategy. Why FM can bring advantages to any kinds of entertainment theme parks. In fact, the benefits of facility management to entertainment theme parks, it enables a more cost-effective working process within any kinds of the theme park any leisure playing machine facilities, such as theme park leisure playing sevice business. It improves the efficiency and it can help the theme park to manage health and safety requirements in accordance with industry regulations. It increases lifespan of a theme park any kinds of leisure playing machines, they are the theme park fixed assets, such as theme park's any kinds of leisure playing machine facilities. New theme parks and attractions can also improve the image of a destination increase tourism and hence economic benefits for the local community , and provide education and entertainment opportunities to the public.

Hence, it is common sense, if the theme park can have good FM to improve its any leisure playing facilities in order to avoid any accident occurrence , when any one visitor chooses to play its any one lesiure machine. Then, it can bring positive safe emotion feeling to satisfy any one visitor whose individual playing safe need to any kinds of playing leisure machines. I believe that its visitors number will not decrease, even increases significantly forever. Hence , the major roles of a theme park facility manager, is that to ensure the upkeep and manintenance of its any one entertainment playing machines, e.g. rolling rides, water rides etc. So, that they meet both safety and health standards to let any one visitors to feel safe to play.

In fact, the scope of facilities management covers two main areas: space and infrastructure , such as planning, design and workplace, construction, occupancy , maintenance and furniture as well as people and organization (such as catering, cleaning and HR, hospitality, accounting and marketing efficient operation in office) both aspects. Hence, these are 6 main facilities to ensure one available for any familiry theme plars. For leisure theme park case, rides and attractions are needed for all ages of any one theme park visitors. This is perhaps the most imprtant, as different parks will have different target audiences, e.g. refreshments, shops, toilets, and parking , access facilities and any one kind of leisure playing machines, such as rolling rides, water rides etc.

Hence, a theme park is a type of amusement park that bases its choice of which kinds of leisure playing facility structures and attractions around a central theme often featureing multiple areas with different themes. Unlike temporary and mobile fun fairs and carnivals, amusement parks are stationary and built for long lasting operation. Hence, every theme park must need have a photogenic, iconic landmark that draws people into the park, beautiful landscaping , enough available attraction capacity to keep peak waits for non-new attractions under 90 minutes, all of these are other faciliities. They must also need to manage to keep more attraction to theme park any one visitor to feel enjoyable and comfortable to play any one theme park leisure playing machines.

What advantages to the theme park implements FM strategy? For Ocean Park example, it aims to let visitors feel themed ocean animal recreational and educational and leisure park experience. So, it must need to upgrade to improve its any facilities to avoid long time repaire spending expenditure. FM project may include: modifying sections of ocean park road, which is a local distributor, around the existing bus terminus , drain works, tunneling and geotechnical works, bulk excavation and slope works, site clearance, modification to bus terminus, taxi stands as well as utilities works including power supply distribution, electrical substations, freshwater and saltwater reservoirs, water supply distribution, gas supply distribution, telecommunications networks, landscope irrigation network to the ocean park any one ocean fish reservoirs, primary life support system works for animal keeping, area development works include elevated walkways, external lighting, external escalators, bridges, parkwide systems works include: signage, background, music system, toilet facilities, guard sheds, first and facilities, communication systems , CCTV systems and waste facilities, landscape or theming works, themed concern pavements, hardscape soft landscaping, water and rockwork features, visual intrusion screens, area props and artwork etc. works for the attractions venues include: animal exhibits, marine animal, terrestrial animal, aviaries , bind exhibits, individual life support systems for animal , exhibits and non- animal related attractions, e.g. shipwreck play area, bamboo maze etc. installation of rides interactive rides , transportation rides etc. , works for venues include : event halls, outdoor live show area, cinema band stands, work for the merchandise / retail facilities include souvonir stores, novelty stores, games ascade, photo shops etc. in the ocean park.

Moreover, any ocean park also have works for the food and baverage facilities include: restaurants, ballery, food casrts as well as back of house facilities include: ocean park offices, break areas, warehouses , centralized facilities, operational facilities etc. , even the ocean park inside hotel development facilities. All of these may bring positive or negative leisure activities impacts to influence any one of this ocean park visitor individual emotion significantly, if he /she feel comfortable and enjoyable , when they enter this ocean park. This ocean park whole natural environment may influence they like to stay long time in this ocean park. So, when they can stay long time in this ocean park, they may spend money to live hotels, spend money to play any leisure machines and spend time to go to shopping, or buying tickets to see any movies in this ocean park. All of this ocean park natural environment facilities and leisure playing machines improvement may influence any one visitor individual emotion either negative or positive feeling.

On conclusion, any theme parks must need to implement FM strategy to improve their theme parks inside natural environment and leisure playing machines quality and hotel living facilities and theme park external transport tool stations facilities, e.g. taxi, bus , railway station distance to convenience any one visitor can catch any one kind of public transport tool to arrive this theme park in short time easily. Also, any theme parks need to impove environment facilities in order to let any one visitor feels comfortable and enhoyable feeling when they choose this theme park to play. Consequently, the theme park's visitors number may be influenced to increase by their positive playing emotion feeling.

Organization facility managment (FM) strategy aims to keep the best facility equipment repair improvement to let any organizational equipment can be used in long time. Hence, FM aims to help organizations to avoid to spend much expenditure on long time repair. When any organizational equipment can be improved to achieve good quality. Instead of improvement equipment quality aspect, can improvement facility equipment bring good customer emotion? How FM may help entertainment theme parks to save long time cost?

In entertainment theme park organizations, they must need to have different kinds of leisure playing machine facilities to supply to visitors to choose to play. So, facility management (FM) must need to imrpove any one entertainment theme parkj machine facility quality, it aims to avoid accidents occur , due to any leisure machine facilities are old or damage when they are used to operate in daily long opening time. Hence, FM must be needed to improve any entertainment theme parks' different kinds of leisure playing machine equipment frequently. If any one theme park leisure machine facility has poor FM in order to improve its machine quality. Consequently, this kind of leisure theme park leisure playing mahcine may be sudden to bring accidents occur, when any one visitor chooses this one of leisure playing machine facility to play. It may cause the player to hurt, even die in possible. Hence, FM to any entertainment theme park playing machine equipment , it may be one major facility repair management srtategy to any entertainment theme parks leisure playing machine facilities, because any one leisure playing machine facilities may bring any one visiot body hurt when the playing machine is old. Instead of FM can bring safety and playinf machine facilities quality improvement benefits to any one entertainment theme park leisure playing machine, whether FM to entertainment theme parks can bring psotive playing of leisure emotion to any one theme park visitor. I shall attempt to discuss as below:

Firstly, we need to know that any kinds of entertainment theme parks why they need to implement FM strategy. Why FM can bring advantages to any kinds of entertainment theme parks. In fact, the benefits of facility management to entertainment theme parks, it enables a more cost-effective working process within any kinds of the theme park any leisure playing machine facilities, such as theme park leisure playing sevice business. It improves the efficiency and it can help the theme park to manage health and safety requirements in accordance with industry regulations. It increases lifespan of a theme park any kinds of leisure playing machines, they are the theme park fixed assets, such as theme park's any kinds of leisure playing machine facilities. New theme parks and attractions can also improve the image of a destination increase tourism and hence economic benefits for the local community , and provide education and entertainment opportunities to the public.

Hence, it is common sense, if the theme park can have good FM to improve its any leisure playing facilities in order to avoid any accident occurrence , when any one visitor chooses to play its any one lesiure machine. Then, it can bring positive safe emotion feeling to satisfy any one visitor whose individual playing safe need to any kinds of playing leisure machines. I believe that its visitors number will not decrease, even increases significantly forever. Hence , the major roles of a theme park facility manager, is that to ensure the upkeep and manintenance of its any one entertainment playing machines, e.g. rolling rides, water rides etc. So, that they meet both safety and health standards to let any one visitors to feel safe to play.

In fact, the scope of facilities management covers two main areas: space and infrastructure , such as planning, design and workplace, construction, occupancy , maintenance and furniture as well as people and organization (such as catering, cleaning and HR, hospitality, accounting and marketing efficient operation in office) both aspects. Hence, these are 6 main facilities to ensure one available for any familiry theme plars. For leisure theme park case, rides and attractions are needed for all ages of any one theme park visitors. This is perhaps the most imprtant, as different parks will have different target audiences, e.g. refreshments, shops, toilets, and parking , access facilities and any one kind of leisure playing machines, such as rolling rides, water rides etc.

Hence, a theme park is a type of amusement park that bases its choice of which kinds of leisure playing facility structures and attractions around a central theme often featureing multiple areas with different themes. Unlike temporary and mobile fun fairs and carnivals, amusement parks are stationary and built for long lasting operation. Hence, every theme park must need have a photogenic, iconic landmark that draws people into the park, beautiful landscaping , enough available attraction capacity to keep peak waits for non-new attractions under 90 minutes, all of these are other faciliities. They must also need to manage to keep more attraction to theme park any one visitor to feel enjoyable and comfortable to play any one theme park leisure playing machines.

What advantages to the theme park implements FM strategy? For Ocean Park example, it aims to let visitors feel themed ocean animal recreational and educational and leisure park experience. So, it must need to upgrade to improve its any facilities to avoid long time repaire spending expenditure. FM project may include: modifying sections of ocean park road, which is a local distributor, around the existing bus terminus , drain works, tunneling and geotechnical works, bulk excavation and slope works, site clearance, modification to bus terminus, taxi stands as well as utilities works including power supply distribution, electrical substations, freshwater and saltwater reservoirs, water supply distribution, gas supply distribution, telecommunications networks, landscope irrigation network to the ocean park any one ocean fish reservoirs, primary life support system works for animal keeping, area development works include elevated walkways, external lighting, external escalators, bridges, parkwide systems works include: signage, background, music system, toilet facilities, guard sheds, first and facilities, communication systems , CCTV systems and waste facilities, landscape or theming works, themed concern pavements, hardscape soft landscaping, water and rockwork features, visual intrusion screens, area props and artwork etc. works for the attractions venues include: animal exhibits, marine animal, terrestrial animal, aviaries , bind exhibits, individual life support systems for animal , exhibits and non- animal related attractions, e.g. shipwreck play area, bamboo maze etc. installation of rides interactive rides , transportation rides etc. , works for venues include : event halls, outdoor live show area, cinema band stands, work for the merchandise / retail facilities include souvonir stores, novelty stores, games ascade, photo shops etc. in the ocean park.

Moreover, any ocean park also have works for the food and baverage facilities include: restaurants, ballery, food casrts as well as back of house facilities include: ocean park offices, break areas, warehouses , centralized facilities, operational facilities etc. , even the ocean park inside hotel development facilities. All of these may bring positive or negative leisure activities impacts to influence any one of this ocean park visitor individual emotion significantly, if he /she feel comfortable and enjoyable , when they enter this ocean park. This ocean park whole natural environment may influence they like to stay long time in this ocean park. So, when they can stay long time in this ocean park, they may spend money to live hotels, spend money to play any leisure machines and spend time to go to shopping, or buying tickets to see any movies in this ocean park. All of this ocean park natural environment facilities and leisure playing machines improvement may influence any one visitor individual emotion either negative or positive feeling.

On conclusion, any theme parks must need to implement FM strategy to improve their theme parks inside natural environment and leisure playing machines quality and hotel living facilities and theme park external transport tool stations facilities, e.g. taxi, bus , railway station distance to convenience any one visitor can catch any one kind of public transport tool to arrive this theme park in short time easily. Also, any theme parks need to impove environment facilities in order to let any one visitor feels comfortable and enhoyable feeling when they choose this theme park to play. Consequently, the theme park's visitors number may be influenced to increase by their positive playing emotion feeling.

Organization facility managment (FM) strategy aims to keep the best facility equipment repair improvement to let any organizational equipment can be used in long time. Hence, FM aims to help organizations to avoid to spend much expenditure on long time repair. When any organizational equipment can be improved to achieve good quality. Instead of improvement equipment quality aspect, can improvement facility equipment bring good customer emotion? How FM may help entertainment theme parks to save long time cost?

In entertainment theme park organizations, they must need to have different kinds of leisure playing machine facilities to supply to visitors to choose to play. So, facility management (FM) must need to imrpove any one entertainment theme parkj machine facility quality, it aims to avoid accidents occur , due to any leisure machine facilities are old or damage when they are used to operate in daily long opening time. Hence, FM must be needed to improve any entertainment theme parks' different kinds of leisure playing machine equipment frequently. If any one theme park leisure machine facility has poor FM in order to improve its machine quality. Consequently, this kind of leisure theme park leisure playing mahcine may be sudden to bring accidents occur, when any one visitor chooses this one of leisure playing machine facility to play. It may cause the player to hurt, even die in possible. Hence, FM to any entertainment theme park playing machine equipment , it may be one major facility repair management srtategy to any entertainment theme parks leisure playing machine facilities, because any one leisure playing machine facilities may bring any one visiot body hurt when the playing machine is old. Instead of FM can bring safety and playinf machine facilities quality improvement benefits to any one entertainment theme park leisure playing machine, whether FM to entertainment theme parks can bring psotive playing of leisure emotion to any one theme park visitor. I shall attempt to discuss as below:

Firstly, we need to know that any kinds of entertainment theme parks why they need to implement FM strategy. Why FM can bring advantages to any kinds of entertainment theme parks. In fact, the benefits of facility management to entertainment theme parks, it enables a more cost-effective working process within any kinds of the theme park any leisure playing machine facilities, such as theme park leisure playing sevice business. It improves the efficiency and it can help the theme park to manage health and safety requirements in accordance with industry regulations. It increases lifespan of a theme park any kinds of leisure playing machines, they are the theme park fixed assets, such as theme park's any kinds of leisure playing machine facilities. New theme parks and attractions can also improve the image of a destination increase tourism and hence economic benefits for the local community , and provide education and entertainment opportunities to the public.

Hence, it is common sense, if the theme park can have good FM to improve its any leisure playing facilities in order to avoid any accident occurrence , when any one visitor chooses to play its any one lesiure machine. Then, it can bring positive safe emotion feeling to satisfy any one visitor whose individual playing safe need to any kinds of playing leisure machines. I believe that its visitors number will not decrease, even increases significantly forever. Hence , the major roles of a theme park facility manager, is that to ensure the upkeep and manintenance of its any one entertainment playing machines, e.g. rolling rides, water rides etc. So, that they meet both safety and health standards to let any one visitors to feel safe to play.

In fact, the scope of facilities management covers two main areas: space and infrastructure , such as planning, design and workplace, construction, occupancy , maintenance and furniture as well as people and organization (such as catering, cleaning and HR, hospitality, accounting and marketing efficient operation in office) both aspects. Hence, these are 6 main facilities to ensure one available for any familiry theme plars. For leisure theme park case, rides and attractions are needed for all ages of any one theme park visitors. This is perhaps the most imprtant, as different parks will have different target audiences, e.g. refreshments, shops, toilets, and parking , access facilities and any one kind of leisure playing machines, such as rolling rides, water rides etc.

Hence, a theme park is a type of amusement park that bases its choice of which kinds of leisure playing facility structures and attractions around a central theme often featureing multiple areas with different themes. Unlike temporary and mobile fun fairs and carnivals, amusement parks are stationary and built for long lasting operation. Hence, every theme park must need have a photogenic, iconic landmark that draws people into the park, beautiful landscaping , enough available attraction capacity to keep peak waits for non-new attractions under 90 minutes, all of these are other faciliities. They must also need to manage to keep more attraction to theme park any one visitor to feel enjoyable and comfortable to play any one theme park leisure playing machines.
What advantages to the theme park implements FM strategy? For Ocean Park example, it aims to let visitors feel themed ocean animal recreational and educational and leisure park experience. So, it must need to upgrade to improve its any facilities to avoid long time repaire spending expenditure. FM project may include: modifying sections of ocean park road, which is a local distributor, around the existing bus terminus , drain works, tunneling and geotechnical works, bulk excavation and slope works, site clearance, modification to bus terminus, taxi stands as well as utilities works including power supply distribution, electrical substations, freshwater and saltwater reservoirs, water supply distribution, gas supply distribution, telecommunications networks, landscope irrigation network to the ocean park any one ocean fish reservoirs, primary life support system works for animal keeping, area development works include elevated walkways, external lighting, external escalators, bridges, parkwide systems works include: signage, background, music system, toilet facilities, guard sheds, first and facilities, communication systems , CCTV systems and waste facilities, landscape or theming works, themed concern pavements, hardscape soft landscaping, water and rockwork features, visual intrusion screens, area props and artwork etc. works for the attractions venues include: animal exhibits, marine animal, terrestrial animal, aviaries , bind exhibits, individual life support systems for animal , exhibits and non- animal related attractions, e.g. shipwreck play area, bamboo maze etc. installation of rides interactive rides , transportation rides etc. , works for venues include : event halls, outdoor live show area, cinema band stands, work for the merchandise / retail facilities include souvonir stores, novelty stores, games ascade, photo shops etc. in the ocean park.
Moreover, any ocean park also have works for the food and baverage facilities include: restaurants, ballery, food casrts as well as back of house facilities include: ocean park offices, break areas, warehouses , centralized facilities, operational facilities etc. , even the ocean park inside hotel development facilities. All of these may bring positive or negative leisure activities impacts to influence any one of this ocean park visitor individual emotion significantly, if he /she feel comfortable and enjoyable , when they enter this ocean park. This ocean park whole natural environment may influence they like to stay long time in this ocean park. So, when they can stay long time in this ocean park, they may spend money to live hotels, spend money to play any leisure machines and spend time to go to shopping, or buying tickets to see any movies in this ocean park. All of this ocean park natural environment facilities and leisure playing machines improvement may influence any one visitor individual emotion either negative or positive feeling.
On conclusion, any theme parks must need to implement FM strategy to improve their theme parks inside natural environment and leisure playing machines quality and hotel living facilities and theme park external transport tool stations facilities, e.g. taxi, bus , railway station distance to convenience any one visitor can catch any one kind of public transport tool to arrive this theme park in short time easily. Also, any theme parks need to impove environment facilities in order to let any one visitor feels comfortable and enhoyable feeling when they choose this theme park to play. Consequently, the theme park's visitors number may be influenced to increase by their positive playing emotion feeling.

Organization facility managment (FM) strategy aims to keep the best facility equipment repair improvement to let any organizational equipment can be used in long time. Hence, FM aims to help organizations to avoid to spend much expenditure on long time repair. When any organizational equipment can be improved to achieve good quality. Instead of improvement equipment quality aspect, can improvement facility equipment bring good customer emotion? How FM may help entertainment theme parks to save long time cost?

In entertainment theme park organizations, they must need to have different kinds of leisure playing machine facilities to supply to visitors to choose to play. So, facility management (FM) must need to imrpove any one entertainment theme parkj machine facility quality, it aims to avoid accidents occur , due to any leisure machine facilities are old or damage when they are used to operate in daily long opening time. Hence, FM must be needed to improve any entertainment theme parks' different kinds of leisure playing machine equipment frequently. If any one theme park leisure machine facility has poor FM in order to improve its machine quality. Consequently, this kind of leisure theme park leisure playing mahcine may be sudden to bring accidents occur, when any one visitor chooses this one of leisure playing machine facility to play. It may cause the player to hurt, even die in possible. Hence, FM to any entertainment theme park playing machine equipment , it may be one major facility repair management srtategy to any entertainment theme parks leisure playing machine facilities, because any one leisure playing machine facilities may bring any one visiot body hurt when the playing machine is old. Instead of FM can bring safety and playinf machine facilities quality improvement benefits to any one entertainment theme park leisure playing machine, whether FM to entertainment theme parks can bring psotive playing of leisure emotion to any one theme park visitor. I shall attempt to discuss as below:

Firstly, we need to know that any kinds of entertainment theme parks why they need to implement FM strategy. Why FM can bring advantages to any kinds of entertainment theme parks. In fact, the benefits of facility management to entertainment theme parks, it enables a more cost-effective working process within any kinds of the theme park any leisure playing machine facilities, such as theme park leisure playing sevice business. It improves the efficiency and it can help the theme park to manage health and safety requirements in accordance with industry regulations. It increases lifespan of a theme park any kinds of leisure playing machines, they are the theme park fixed assets, such as theme park's any kinds of leisure playing machine facilities. New theme parks and attractions can also improve the image of a destination increase tourism and hence economic benefits for the local community , and provide education and entertainment opportunities to the public.

Hence, it is common sense, if the theme park can have good FM to improve its any leisure playing facilities in order to avoid any accident occurrence , when any one visitor chooses to play its any one lesiure machine. Then, it can bring positive safe emotion feeling to satisfy any one visitor whose individual playing safe need to any kinds of playing leisure machines. I believe that its visitors number will not decrease, even increases significantly forever. Hence , the major roles of a theme park facility manager, is that to ensure the upkeep and manintenance of its any one entertainment playing machines, e.g. rolling rides, water rides etc. So, that they meet both safety and health standards to let any one visitors to feel safe to play.

In fact, the scope of facilities management covers two main areas: space and infrastructure , such as planning, design and workplace, construction, occupancy , maintenance and furniture as well as people and organization (such as catering, cleaning and HR, hospitality, accounting and marketing efficient operation in office) both aspects. Hence, these are 6 main facilities to ensure one available for any familiry theme plars. For leisure theme park case, rides and attractions are needed for all ages of any one theme park visitors. This is perhaps the most imprtant, as different parks will have different target audiences, e.g. refreshments, shops, toilets, and parking , access facilities and any one kind of leisure playing machines, such as rolling rides, water rides etc.

Hence, a theme park is a type of amusement park that bases its choice of which kinds of leisure playing facility structures and attractions around a central theme often featureing multiple areas with different themes. Unlike temporary and mobile fun fairs and carnivals, amusement parks are stationary and built for long lasting operation. Hence, every theme park must need have a photogenic, iconic landmark that draws people into the park, beautiful landscaping , enough available attraction capacity to keep peak waits for non-new attractions under 90 minutes, all of these are other faciliities. They must also need to manage to keep more attraction to theme park any one visitor to feel enjoyable and comfortable to play any one theme park leisure playing machines.

What advantages to the theme park implements FM strategy? For Ocean Park example, it aims to let visitors feel themed ocean animal recreational and educational and leisure park experience. So, it must need to upgrade to improve its any facilities to avoid long time repaire spending expenditure. FM project may include: modifying sections of ocean park road, which is a local distributor, around the existing bus terminus , drain works, tunneling and geotechnical works, bulk excavation and slope works, site clearance, modification to bus terminus, taxi stands as well as utilities works including power supply distribution, electrical substations, freshwater and saltwater reservoirs, water supply distribution, gas supply distribution, telecommunications networks, landscope irrigation network to the ocean park any one ocean fish reservoirs, primary life support system works for animal keeping, area development works include elevated walkways, external lighting, external escalators, bridges, parkwide systems works include: signage, background, music system, toilet facilities, guard sheds, first and facilities, communication systems , CCTV systems and waste facilities, landscape or theming works, themed concern pavements, hardscape soft landscaping, water and rockwork features, visual intrusion screens, area props and artwork etc. works for the attractions venues include: animal exhibits, marine animal, terrestrial animal, aviaries , bind exhibits, individual life support systems for animal , exhibits and non- animal related attractions, e.g. shipwreck play area, bamboo maze etc. installation of rides interactive rides , transportation rides etc. , works for venues include : event halls, outdoor live show area, cinema band stands, work for the merchandise / retail facilities include souvonir stores, novelty stores, games ascade, photo shops etc. in the ocean park.

Moreover, any ocean park also have works for the food and baverage facilities include: restaurants, ballery, food casrts as well as back of house facilities include: ocean park offices, break areas, warehouses , centralized facilities, operational facilities etc. , even the ocean park inside hotel development facilities. All of these may bring positive or negative leisure activities impacts to influence any one of this ocean park visitor individual emotion significantly, if he /she feel comfortable and enjoyable , when they enter this ocean park. This ocean park whole natural environment may influence they like to stay long time in this ocean park. So, when they can stay long time in this ocean park, they may spend money to live hotels, spend money to play any leisure machines and spend time to go to shopping, or buying tickets to see any movies in this ocean park. All of this ocean park natural environment facilities and leisure playing machines improvement may influence any one visitor individual emotion either negative or positive feeling. On conclusion, any theme parks must need to implement FM strategy to improve their theme parks inside natural environment and leisure playing machines quality and hotel living facilities and theme park external transport tool stations facilities, e.g. taxi, bus , railway station distance to convenience any one visitor can catch any one kind of public transport tool to arrive this theme park in short time easily. Also, any theme parks need to impove environment facilities in order to let any one visitor feels comfortable and enhoyable feeling when they choose this theme park to play. Consequently, the theme park's visitors number may be influenced to increase by their positive playing emotion feeling.

Organization facility managment (FM) strategy aims to keep the best facility equipment repair improvement to let any organizational equipment can be used in long time. Hence, FM aims to help organizations to avoid to spend much expenditure on long time repair. When any organizational equipment can be improved to achieve good quality. Instead of improvement equipment quality aspect, can improvement facility equipment bring good customer emotion? How FM may help entertainment theme parks to save long time cost?

In entertainment theme park organizations, they must need to have different kinds of leisure playing machine facilities to supply to visitors to choose to play. So, facility management (FM) must need to imrpove any one entertainment theme parkj machine facility quality, it aims to avoid accidents occur , due to any leisure machine facilities are old or damage when they are used to operate in daily long opening time. Hence, FM must be needed to improve any entertainment theme parks‘ different kinds of leisure playing machine equipment frequently. If any one theme park leisure machine facility has poor FM in order to improve its machine quality. Consequently, this kind of leisure theme park leisure playing mahcine may be sudden to bring accidents occur, when any one visitor chooses this one of leisure playing machine facility to play. It may cause the player to hurt, even die in possible. Hence, FM to any entertainment theme park playing machine equipment , it may be one major facility repair management srtategy to any entertainment theme parks leisure playing machine facilities, because any one leisure playing machine facilities may bring any one visiot body hurt when the playing machine is old. Instead of FM can bring safety and playinf machine facilities quality improvement benefits to any one entertainment theme park leisure playing machine, whether FM to entertainment theme parks can bring psotive playing of leisure emotion to any one theme park visitor. I shall attempt to discuss as below:

Firstly, we need to know that any kinds of entertainment theme parks why they need to implement FM strategy. Why

FM can bring advantages to any kinds of entertainment theme parks. In fact, the benefits of facility management to entertainment theme parks, it enables a more cost-effective working process within any kinds of the theme park any leisure playing machine facilities, such as theme park leisure playing sevice business. It improves the efficiency and it can help the theme park to manage health and safety requirements in accordance with industry regulations. It increases lifespan of a theme park any kinds of leisure playing machines, they are the theme park fixed assets, such as theme park's any kinds of leisure playing machine facilities. New theme parks and attractions can also improve the image of a destination increase tourism and hence economic benefits for the local community , and provide education and entertainment opportunities to the public.

Hence, it is common sense, if the theme park can have good FM to improve its any leisure playing facilities in order to avoid any accident occurrence , when any one visitor chooses to play its any one lesiure machine. Then, it can bring positive safe emotion feeling to satisfy any one visitor whose individual playing safe need to any kinds of playing leisure machines. I believe that its visitors number will not decrease, even increases significantly forever. Hence , the major roles of a theme park facility manager, is that to ensure the upkeep and manintenance of its any one entertainment playing machines, e.g. rolling rides, water rides etc. So, that they meet both safety and health standards to let any one visitors to feel safe to play.

In fact, the scope of facilities management covers two main areas: space and infrastructure , such as planning, design and workplace, construction, occupancy , maintenance and furniture as well as people and organization (such as catering, cleaning and HR, hospitality, accounting and marketing efficient operation in office) both aspects. Hence, these are 6 main facilities to ensure one available for any familiry theme plars. For leisure theme park case, rides and attractions are needed for all ages of any one theme park visitors. This is perhaps the most imprtant, as different parks will have different target audiences, e.g. refreshments, shops, toilets, and parking , access facilities and any one kind of leisure playing machines, such as rolling rides, water rides etc.

Hence, a theme park is a type of amusement park that bases its choice of which kinds of leisure playing facility structures and attractions around a central theme often featureing multiple areas with different themes. Unlike temporary and mobile fun fairs and carnivals, amusement parks are stationary and built for long lasting operation. Hence, every theme park must need have a photogenic, iconic landmark that draws people into the park, beautiful landscaping , enough available attraction capacity to keep peak waits for non-new attractions under 90 minutes, all of these are other faciliities. They must also need to manage to keep more attraction to theme park any one visitor to feel enjoyable and comfortable to play any one theme park leisure playing machines.

What advantages to the theme park implements FM strategy? For Ocean Park example, it aims to let visitors feel themed ocean animal recreational and educational and leisure park experience. So, it must need to upgrade to improve its any facilities to avoid long time repaire spending expenditure. FM project may include: modifying sections of ocean park road, which is a local distributor, around the existing bus terminus , drain works, tunneling and geotechnical works, bulk excavation and slope works, site clearance, modification to bus terminus, taxi stands as well as utilities works including power supply distribution, electrical substations, freshwater and saltwater reservoirs, water supply distribution, gas supply distribution, telecommunications networks, landscope irrigation network to the ocean park any one ocean fish reservoirs, primary life support system works for animal keeping, area development works include elevated walkways, external lighting, external escalators, bridges, parkwide systems works include: signage, background, music system, toilet facilities, guard sheds, first and facilities, communication systems , CCTV systems and waste facilities, landscape or theming works, themed concern pavements, hardscape soft landscaping, water and rockwork features, visual intrusion screens, area props and artwork etc. works for the attractions venues include: animal exhibits, marine animal, terrestrial animal, aviaries , bind exhibits, individual life support systems for animal , exhibits and non- animal related attractions, e.g. shipwreck play area, bamboo maze etc. installation of rides interactive rides , transportation rides etc. , works for venues include : event halls, outdoor live show area, cinema band stands, work for the merchandise / retail facilities include souvonir stores, novelty stores, games ascade, photo shops etc. in the ocean park.

Moreover, any ocean park also have works for the food and baverage facilities include: restaurants, ballery, food casrts as well as back of house facilities include: ocean park offices, break areas, warehouses , centralized facilities, operational facilities etc. , even the ocean park inside hotel development facilities. All of these may bring positive or negative leisure activities impacts to influence any one of this ocean park visitor individual emotion significantly, if he /she feel comfortable and enjoyable , when they enter this ocean park. This ocean park whole natural environment may influence they like to stay long time in this ocean park. So, when they can stay long time in this ocean park, they may spend money to live hotels, spend money to play any leisure machines and spend time to go to shopping, or buying tickets to see any movies in this ocean park. All of this ocean park natural environment facilities and leisure playing machines improvement may influence any one visitor individual emotion either negative or positive feeling. On conclusion, any theme parks must need to implement FM strategy to improve their theme parks inside natural environment and leisure playing machines quality and hotel living facilities and theme park external transport tool stations facilities, e.g. taxi, bus , railway station distance to convenience any one visitor can catch any one kind of public transport tool to arrive this theme park in short time easily. Also, any theme parks need to impove environment facilities in order to let any one visitor feels comfortable and enhoyable feeling when they choose this theme park to play. Consequently, the theme park's visitors number may be influenced to increase by their positive playing emotion feeling.

Organization facility managment (FM) strategy aims to keep the best facility equipment repair improvement to let any organizational equipment can be used in long time. Hence, FM aims to help organizations to avoid to spend much expenditure on long time repair. When any organizational equipment can be improved to achieve good quality. Instead of improvement equipment quality aspect, can improvement facility equipment bring good customer emotion? How FM may help entertainment theme parks to save long time cost?

In entertainment theme park organizations, they must need to have different kinds of leisure playing machine facilities to supply to visitors to choose to play. So, facility management (FM) must need to imrpove any one entertainment theme parkj machine facility quality, it aims to avoid accidents occur , due to any leisure machine facilities are old or damage when they are used to operate in daily long opening time. Hence, FM must be needed to improve any entertainment theme parks' different kinds of leisure playing machine equipment frequently. If any one theme park leisure machine facility has poor FM in order to improve its machine quality. Consequently, this kind of leisure theme park leisure playing mahcine may be sudden to bring accidents occur, when any one visitor chooses this one of leisure playing machine facility to play. It may cause the player to hurt, even die in possible. Hence, FM to any entertainment theme park playing machine equipment , it may be one major facility repair management srtategy to any entertainment theme parks leisure playing machine facilities, because any one leisure playing machine facilities may bring any one visiot body hurt when the playing machine is old. Instead of FM can bring safety and playinf machine facilities quality improvement benefits to any one entertainment theme park leisure playing machine, whether FM to entertainment theme parks can bring psotive playing of leisure emotion to any one theme park visitor. I shall attempt to discuss as below:

Firstly, we need to know that any kinds of entertainment theme parks why they need to implement FM strategy. Why FM can bring advantages to any kinds of entertainment theme parks. In fact, the benefits of facility management to entertainment theme parks, it enables a more cost-effective working process within any kinds of the theme park any leisure playing machine facilities, such as theme park leisure playing sevice business. It improves the efficiency and it can help the theme park to manage health and safety requirements in accordance with industry regulations. It increases lifespan of a theme park any kinds of leisure playing machines, they are the theme park fixed assets, such as theme park's any kinds of leisure playing machine facilities. New theme parks and attractions can also improve the image of a destination increase tourism and hence economic benefits for the local community , and provide education and entertainment opportunities to the public.

Hence, it is common sense, if the theme park can have good FM to improve its any leisure playing facilities in order to avoid any accident occurrence , when any one visitor chooses to play its any one lesiure machine. Then, it can bring positive safe emotion feeling to satisfy any one visitor whose individual playing safe need to any kinds of playing leisure machines. I believe that its visitors number will not decrease, even increases significantly forever. Hence , the major roles of a theme park facility manager, is that to ensure the upkeep and manintenance of its any one entertainment playing machines, e.g. rolling rides, water rides etc. So, that they meet both safety and health standards to let any one visitors to feel safe to play.

In fact, the scope of facilities management covers two main areas: space and infrastructure , such as planning, design and workplace, construction, occupancy , maintenance and furniture as well as people and organization (such as catering, cleaning and HR, hospitality, accounting and marketing efficient operation in office) both aspects. Hence, these are 6 main facilities to ensure one available for any familiry theme plars. For leisure theme park case, rides and attractions are needed for all ages of any one theme park visitors. This is perhaps the most imprtant, as different parks will have different target audiences, e.g. refreshments, shops, toilets, and parking , access facilities and any one kind of leisure playing machines, such as rolling rides, water rides etc.

Hence, a theme park is a type of amusement park that bases its choice of which kinds of leisure playing facility structures and attractions around a central theme often featureing multiple areas with different themes. Unlike temporary and mobile fun fairs and carnivals, amusement parks are stationary and built for long lasting operation. Hence, every theme park must need have a photogenic, iconic landmark that draws people into the park, beautiful landscaping , enough available attraction capacity to keep peak waits for non-new attractions under 90 minutes, all of these are other faciliities. They must also need to manage to keep more attraction to theme park any one visitor to feel enjoyable and comfortable to play any one theme park leisure playing machines.

What advantages to the theme park implements FM strategy? For Ocean Park example, it aims to let visitors feel themed ocean animal recreational and educational and leisure park experience. So, it must need to upgrade to improve its any facilities to avoid long time repaire spending expenditure. FM project may include: modifying sections of ocean park road, which is a local distributor, around the existing bus terminus , drain works, tunneling and geotechnical works, bulk excavation and slope works, site clearance, modification to bus terminus, taxi stands as well as utilities works including power supply distribution, electrical substations, freshwater and saltwater reservoirs, water supply distribution, gas supply distribution, telecommunications networks, landscope irrigation network to the ocean park any one ocean fish reservoirs, primary life support system works for animal keeping, area development works include elevated walkways, external lighting, external escalators, bridges, parkwide systems works include: signage, background, music system, toilet facilities, guard sheds, first and facilities, communication systems , CCTV systems and waste facilities, landscape or theming works, themed concern pavements, hardscape soft landscaping, water and rockwork features, visual intrusion screens, area props and artwork etc. works for the attractions venues include: animal exhibits, marine animal, terrestrial animal, aviaries , bind exhibits, individual life support systems for animal , exhibits and non- animal related attractions, e.g. shipwreck play area, bamboo maze etc. installation of rides interactive rides , transportation rides etc. , works for venues include : event halls, outdoor live show area, cinema band stands, work for the merchandise / retail facilities include souvonir stores, novelty stores, games ascade, photo shops etc. in the ocean park.

Moreover, any ocean park also have works for the food and baverage facilities include: restaurants, ballery, food casrts as well as back of house facilities include: ocean park offices, break areas, warehouses , centralized facilities, operational facilities etc. , even the ocean park inside hotel development facilities. All of these may bring positive or negative leisure activities impacts to influence any one of this ocean park visitor individual emotion significantly, if he /she feel comfortable and enjoyable , when they enter this ocean park. This ocean park whole natural environment may influence they like to stay long time in this ocean park. So, when they can stay long time in this ocean park, they may spend money to live hotels, spend money to play any leisure machines and spend time to go to shopping, or buying tickets to see any movies in this ocean park. All of this ocean park natural environment facilities and leisure playing machines improvement may influence any one visitor individual emotion either negative or positive feeling.

On conclusion, any theme parks must need to implement FM strategy to improve their theme parks inside natural environment and leisure playing machines quality and hotel living facilities and theme park external transport tool stations facilities, e.g. taxi, bus , railway station distance to convenience any one visitor can catch any one kind of public transport tool to arrive this theme park in short time easily. Also, any theme parks need to impove environment facilities in order to let any one visitor feels comfortable and enhoyable feeling when they choose this theme park to play. Consequently, the theme park's visitors number may be influenced to increase by their positive playing emotion feeling.

Organization facility managment (FM) strategy aims to keep the best facility equipment repair improvement to let any organizational equipment can be used in long time. Hence, FM aims to help organizations to avoid to spend much expenditure on long time repair. When any organizational equipment can be improved to achieve good quality. Instead of improvement equipment quality aspect, can improvement facility equipment bring good customer emotion? How FM may help entertainment theme parks to save long time cost?

In entertainment theme park organizations, they must need to have different kinds of leisure playing machine facilities to supply to visitors to choose to play. So, facility management (FM) must need to imrpove any one entertainment theme parkj machine facility quality, it aims to avoid accidents occur , due to any leisure machine facilities are old or damage when they are used to operate in daily long opening time. Hence, FM must be needed to improve any entertainment theme parks' different kinds of leisure playing machine equipment frequently. If any one theme park leisure machine facility has poor FM in order to improve its machine quality. Consequently, this kind of leisure theme park leisure playing mahcine may be sudden to bring accidents occur, when any one visitor chooses this one of leisure playing machine facility to play. It may cause the player to hurt, even die in possible. Hence, FM to any entertainment theme park playing machine equipment , it may be one major facility repair management srtategy to any entertainment theme parks leisure playing machine facilities, because any one leisure playing machine facilities may bring any one visiot body hurt when the playing machine is old. Instead of FM can bring safety and playinf machine facilities quality improvement benefits to any one entertainment theme park leisure playing machine, whether FM to entertainment theme parks can bring psotive playing of leisure emotion to any one theme park visitor. I shall attempt to discuss as below:

Firstly, we need to know that any kinds of entertainment theme parks why they need to implement FM strategy. Why FM can bring advantages to any kinds of entertainment theme parks. In fact, the benefits of facility management to entertainment theme parks, it enables a more cost-effective working process within any kinds of the theme park any leisure playing machine facilities, such as theme park leisure playing sevice business. It improves the efficiency and it can help the theme park to manage health and safety requirements in accordance with industry regulations. It increases lifespan of a theme park any kinds of leisure playing machines, they are the theme park fixed assets, such as theme park's any kinds of leisure playing machine facilities. New theme parks and attractions can also improve the image of a destination increase tourism and hence economic benefits for the local community , and provide education and entertainment opportunities to the public.

Hence, it is common sense, if the theme park can have good FM to improve its any leisure playing facilities in order to avoid any accident occurrence , when any one visitor chooses to play its any one lesiure machine. Then, it can bring positive safe emotion feeling to satisfy any one visitor whose individual playing safe need to any kinds of playing leisure machines. I believe that its visitors number will not decrease, even increases significantly forever. Hence , the major roles of a theme park facility manager, is that to ensure the upkeep and manintenance of its any one entertainment playing machines, e.g. rolling rides, water rides etc. So, that they meet both safety and health standards to let any one visitors to feel safe to play.

In fact, the scope of facilities management covers two main areas: space and infrastructure , such as planning, design and workplace, construction, occupancy , maintenance and furniture as well as people and organization (such as catering, cleaning and HR, hospitality, accounting and marketing efficient operation in office) both aspects. Hence, these are 6 main facilities to ensure one available for any familiry theme plars. For leisure theme park case, rides and attractions are needed for all ages of any one theme park visitors. This is perhaps the most imprtant, as different parks will have different target audiences, e.g. refreshments, shops, toilets, and parking , access facilities and any one kind of leisure playing machines, such as rolling rides, water rides etc.

Hence, a theme park is a type of amusement park that bases its choice of which kinds of leisure playing facility structures and attractions around a central theme often featureing multiple areas with different themes. Unlike temporary and mobile fun fairs and carnivals, amusement parks are stationary and built for long lasting operation. Hence, every theme park must need have a photogenic, iconic landmark that draws people into the park, beautiful landscaping , enough available attraction capacity to keep peak waits for non-new attractions under 90 minutes, all of these are other faciliities. They must also need to manage to keep more attraction to theme park any one visitor to feel enjoyable and comfortable to play any one theme park leisure playing machines.

What advantages to the theme park implements FM strategy? For Ocean Park example, it aims to let visitors feel themed ocean animal recreational and educational and leisure park experience. So, it must need to upgrade to improve its any facilities to avoid long time repaire spending expenditure. FM project may include: modifying sections of ocean park road, which is a local distributor, around the existing bus terminus , drain works, tunneling and geotechnical works, bulk excavation and slope works, site clearance, modification to bus terminus, taxi stands as well as utilities works including power supply distribution, electrical substations, freshwater and saltwater reservoirs, water supply distribution, gas supply distribution, telecommunications networks, landscope irrigation network to the ocean park any one ocean fish reservoirs, primary life support system works for animal keeping, area development works include elevated walkways, external lighting, external escalators, bridges, parkwide systems works include: signage, background, music system, toilet facilities, guard sheds, first and facilities, communication systems , CCTV systems and waste facilities, landscape or theming works, themed concern pavements, hardscape soft landscaping, water and rockwork features, visual intrusion screens, area props and artwork etc. works for the attractions venues include: animal exhibits, marine animal, terrestrial animal, aviaries , bind exhibits, individual life support systems for animal , exhibits and non- animal related attractions, e.g. shipwreck play area, bamboo maze etc. installation of rides interactive rides , transportation rides etc. , works for venues include : event halls, outdoor live show area, cinema band stands, work for the merchandise / retail facilities include souvonir stores, novelty stores, games ascade, photo shops etc. in the ocean park.

Moreover, any ocean park also have works for the food and baverage facilities include: restaurants, ballery, food casrts as well as back of house facilities include: ocean park offices, break areas, warehouses , centralized facilities, operational facilities etc. , even the ocean park inside hotel development facilities. All of these may bring positive or negative leisure activities impacts to influence any one of this ocean park visitor individual emotion significantly, if he /she feel comfortable and enjoyable , when they enter this ocean park. This ocean park whole natural environment may influence they like to stay long time in this ocean park. So, when they can stay long time in this ocean park, they may spend money to live hotels, spend money to play any leisure machines and spend time to go to shopping, or buying tickets to see any movies in this ocean park. All of this ocean park natural environment facilities and leisure playing machines improvement may influence any one visitor individual emotion either negative or positive feeling. On conclusion, any theme parks must need to implement FM strategy to improve their theme parks inside natural environment and leisure playing machines quality and hotel living facilities and theme park external transport tool stations facilities, e.g. taxi, bus , railway station distance to convenience any one visitor can catch any one kind of public transport tool to arrive this theme park in short time easily. Also, any theme parks need to impove environment facilities in order to let any one visitor feels comfortable and enhoyable feeling when they choose this theme park to play. Consequently, the theme park's visitors number may be influenced to increase by their positive playing emotion feeling.

Organization facility managment (FM) strategy aims to keep the best facility equipment repair improvement to let any organizational equipment can be used in long time. Hence, FM aims to help organizations to avoid to spend much expenditure on long time repair. When any organizational equipment can be improved to achieve good quality. Instead of improvement equipment quality aspect, can improvement facility equipment bring good customer emotion? How FM may help entertainment theme parks to save long time cost?

In entertainment theme park organizations, they must need to have different kinds of leisure playing machine facilities to supply to visitors to choose to play. So, facility management (FM) must need to imrpove any one entertainment theme parkj machine facility quality, it aims to avoid accidents occur , due to any leisure machine facilities are old or damage when they are used to operate in daily long opening time. Hence, FM must be needed to improve any entertainment theme parks' different kinds of leisure playing machine equipment frequently. If any one theme park leisure machine facility has poor FM in order to improve its machine quality. Consequently, this kind of leisure theme park leisure playing mahcine may be sudden to bring accidents occur, when any one visitor chooses this one of leisure playing machine facility to play. It may cause the player to hurt, even die in possible. Hence, FM to any entertainment theme park playing machine equipment , it may be one major facility repair management srtategy to any entertainment theme parks leisure playing machine facilities, because any one leisure playing machine facilities may bring any one visiot body hurt when the playing machine is old. Instead of FM can bring safety and playinf machine facilities quality improvement benefits to any one entertainment theme park leisure playing machine, whether FM to entertainment theme parks can bring psotive playing of leisure emotion to any one theme park visitor. I shall attempt to discuss as below:

Firstly, we need to know that any kinds of entertainment theme parks why they need to implement FM strategy. Why FM can bring advantages to any kinds of entertainment theme parks. In fact, the benefits of facility management to entertainment theme parks, it enables a more cost-effective working process within any kinds of the theme park any leisure playing machine facilities, such as theme park leisure playing sevice business. It improves the efficiency and it can help the theme park to manage health and safety requirements in accordance with industry regulations. It increases lifespan of a theme park any kinds of leisure playing machines, they are the theme park fixed assets, such as theme park's any kinds of leisure playing machine facilities. New theme parks and attractions can also improve the image of a destination increase tourism and hence economic benefits for the local community , and provide education and entertainment opportunities to the public.

Hence, it is common sense, if the theme park can have good FM to improve its any leisure playing facilities in order to avoid any accident occurrence , when any one visitor chooses to play its any one lesiure machine. Then, it can bring positive safe emotion feeling to satisfy any one visitor whose individual playing safe need to any kinds of playing leisure machines. I believe that its visitors number will not decrease, even increases significantly forever. Hence , the major roles of a theme park facility manager, is that to ensure the upkeep and manintenance of its any one entertainment playing machines, e.g. rolling rides, water rides etc. So, that they meet both safety and health standards to let any one visitors to feel safe to play.

In fact, the scope of facilities management covers two main areas: space and infrastructure , such as planning, design and workplace, construction, occupancy , maintenance and furniture as well as people and organization (such as catering, cleaning and HR, hospitality, accounting and marketing efficient operation in office) both aspects. Hence, these are 6 main facilities to ensure one available for any familiry theme plars. For leisure theme park case, rides and attractions are needed for all ages of any one theme park visitors. This is perhaps the most imprtant, as different parks will have different target audiences, e.g. refreshments, shops, toilets, and parking , access facilities and any one kind of leisure playing machines, such as rolling rides, water rides etc.

Hence, a theme park is a type of amusement park that bases its choice of which kinds of leisure playing facility structures and attractions around a central theme often featureing multiple areas with different themes. Unlike temporary and mobile fun fairs and carnivals, amusement parks are stationary and built for long lasting operation. Hence, every theme park must need have a photogenic, iconic landmark that draws people into the park, beautiful landscaping , enough available attraction capacity to keep peak waits for non-new attractions under 90 minutes, all of these are other faciliities. They must also need to manage to keep more attraction to theme park any one visitor to feel enjoyable and comfortable to play any one theme park leisure playing machines.

What advantages to the theme park implements FM strategy? For Ocean Park example, it aims to let visitors feel themed ocean animal recreational and educational and leisure park experience. So, it must need to upgrade to improve its any facilities to avoid long time repaire spending expenditure. FM project may include: modifying sections of ocean park road, which is a local distributor, around the existing bus terminus , drain works, tunneling and geotechnical works, bulk excavation and slope works, site clearance, modification to bus terminus, taxi stands as well as utilities works including power supply distribution, electrical substations, freshwater and saltwater reservoirs, water supply distribution, gas supply distribution, telecommunications networks, landscope irrigation network to the ocean park any one ocean fish reservoirs, primary life support system works for animal keeping, area development works include elevated walkways, external lighting, external escalators, bridges, parkwide systems works include: signage, background, music system, toilet facilities, guard sheds, first and facilities, communication systems , CCTV systems and waste facilities, landscape or theming works, themed concern pavements, hardscape soft landscaping, water and rockwork features, visual intrusion screens, area props and artwork etc. works for the attractions venues include: animal exhibits, marine animal, terrestrial animal, aviaries , bind exhibits, individual life support systems for animal , exhibits and non- animal related attractions, e.g. shipwreck play area, bamboo maze etc. installation of rides interactive rides , transportation rides etc. , works for venues include : event halls, outdoor live show area, cinema band stands, work for the merchandise / retail facilities include souvonir stores, novelty stores, games ascade, photo shops etc. in the ocean park.

Moreover, any ocean park also have works for the food and baverage facilities include: restaurants, ballery, food casrts as well as back of house facilities include: ocean park offices, break areas, warehouses , centralized facilities, operational facilities etc. , even the ocean park inside hotel development facilities. All of these may bring positive or negative leisure activities impacts to influence any one of this ocean park visitor individual emotion significantly, if he /she feel comfortable and enjoyable , when they enter this ocean park. This ocean park whole natural environment may influence they like to stay long time in this ocean park. So, when they can stay long time in this ocean park, they may spend money to live hotels, spend money to play any leisure machines and spend time to go to shopping, or buying tickets to see any movies in this ocean park. All of this ocean park natural environment facilities and leisure playing machines improvement may influence any one visitor individual emotion either negative or positive feeling. On conclusion, any theme parks must need to implement FM strategy to improve their theme parks inside natural environment and leisure playing machines quality and hotel living facilities and theme park external transport tool stations facilities, e.g. taxi, bus , railway station distance to convenience any one visitor can catch any one kind of public transport tool to arrive this theme park in short time easily. Also, any theme parks need to impove environment facilities in order to let any one visitor feels comfortable and enhoyable feeling when they choose this theme park to play. Consequently, the theme park's visitors number may be influenced to increase by their positive playing emotion feeling.

Organization facility managment (FM) strategy aims to keep the best facility equipment repair improvement to let any organizational equipment can be used in long time. Hence, FM aims to help organizations to avoid to spend much expenditure on long time repair. When any organizational equipment can be improved to achieve good quality. Instead of improvement equipment quality aspect, can improvement facility equipment bring good customer emotion? How FM may help entertainment theme parks to save long time cost?

In entertainment theme park organizations, they must need to have different kinds of leisure playing machine facilities to supply to visitors to choose to play. So, facility management (FM) must need to imrpove any one entertainment theme parkj machine facility quality, it aims to avoid accidents occur , due to any leisure machine facilities are old or damage when they are used to operate in daily long opening time. Hence, FM must be needed to improve any entertainment theme parks' different kinds of leisure playing machine equipment frequently. If any one theme park leisure machine facility has poor FM in order to improve its machine quality. Consequently, this kind of leisure theme park leisure playing mahcine may be sudden to bring accidents occur, when any one visitor chooses this one of leisure playing machine facility to play. It may cause the player to hurt, even die in possible. Hence, FM to any entertainment theme park playing machine equipment , it may be one major facility repair management srtategy to any entertainment theme parks leisure playing machine facilities, because any one leisure playing machine facilities may bring any one visiot body hurt when the playing machine is old. Instead of FM can bring safety and playinf machine facilities quality improvement benefits to any one entertainment theme park leisure playing machine, whether FM to entertainment theme parks can bring psotive playing of leisure emotion to any one theme park visitor. I shall attempt to discuss as below:

Firstly, we need to know that any kinds of entertainment theme parks why they need to implement FM strategy. Why FM can bring advantages to any kinds of entertainment theme parks. In fact, the benefits of facility management to entertainment theme parks, it enables a more cost-effective working process within any kinds of the theme park any leisure playing machine facilities, such as theme park leisure playing sevice business. It improves the efficiency and it can help the theme park to manage health and safety requirements in accordance with industry regulations. It increases lifespan of a theme park any kinds of leisure playing machines, they are the theme park fixed assets, such as theme park's any kinds of leisure playing machine facilities. New theme parks and attractions can also improve the image of a destination increase tourism and hence economic benefits for the local community , and provide education and entertainment opportunities to the public.

Hence, it is common sense, if the theme park can have good FM to improve its any leisure playing facilities in order to avoid any accident occurrence , when any one visitor chooses to play its any one lesiure machine. Then, it can bring positive safe emotion feeling to satisfy any one visitor whose individual playing safe need to any kinds of playing leisure machines. I believe that its visitors number will not decrease, even increases significantly forever. Hence , the major roles of a theme park facility manager, is that to ensure the upkeep and manintenance of its any one entertainment playing machines, e.g. rolling rides, water rides etc. So, that they meet both safety and health standards to let any one visitors to feel safe to play.

In fact, the scope of facilities management covers two main areas: space and infrastructure , such as planning, design and workplace, construction, occupancy , maintenance and furniture as well as people and organization (such as catering, cleaning and HR, hospitality, accounting and marketing efficient operation in office) both aspects. Hence, these are 6 main facilities to ensure one available for any familiry theme plars. For leisure theme park case, rides and attractions are needed for all ages of any one theme park visitors. This is perhaps the most imprtant, as different parks will have different target audiences, e.g. refreshments, shops, toilets, and parking , access facilities and any one kind of leisure playing machines, such as rolling rides, water rides etc.

Hence, a theme park is a type of amusement park that bases its choice of which kinds of leisure playing facility structures and attractions around a central theme often featureing multiple areas with different themes. Unlike temporary and mobile fun fairs and carnivals, amusement parks are stationary and built for long lasting operation. Hence, every theme park must need have a photogenic, iconic landmark that draws people into the park, beautiful landscaping , enough available attraction capacity to keep peak waits for non-new attractions under 90 minutes, all of these are other faciliities. They must also need to manage to keep more attraction to theme park any one visitor to feel enjoyable and comfortable to play any one theme park leisure playing machines.

What advantages to the theme park implements FM strategy? For Ocean Park example, it aims to let visitors feel themed ocean animal recreational and educational and leisure park experience. So, it must need to upgrade to improve its any facilities to avoid long time repaire spending expenditure. FM project may include: modifying sections of ocean park road, which is a local distributor, around the existing bus terminus , drain works, tunneling and geotechnical works, bulk excavation and slope works, site clearance, modification to bus terminus, taxi stands as well as utilities works including power supply distribution, electrical substations, freshwater and saltwater reservoirs, water supply distribution, gas supply distribution, telecommunications networks, landscope irrigation network to the ocean park any one ocean fish reservoirs, primary life support system works for animal keeping, area development works include elevated walkways, external lighting, external escalators, bridges, parkwide systems works include: signage, background, music system, toilet facilities, guard sheds, first and facilities, communication systems , CCTV systems and waste facilities, landscape or theming works, themed concern pavements, hardscape soft landscaping, water and rockwork features, visual intrusion screens, area props and artwork etc. works for the attractions venues include: animal exhibits, marine animal, terrestrial animal, aviaries , bind exhibits, individual life support systems for animal , exhibits and non- animal related attractions, e.g. shipwreck play area, bamboo maze etc. installation of rides interactive rides , transportation rides etc. , works for venues include : event halls, outdoor live show area, cinema band stands, work for the merchandise / retail facilities include souvonir stores, novelty stores, games ascade, photo shops etc. in the ocean park.

Moreover, any ocean park also have works for the food and baverage facilities include: restaurants, ballery, food casrts as well as back of house facilities include: ocean park offices, break areas, warehouses , centralized facilities, operational facilities etc. , even the ocean park inside hotel development facilities. All of these may bring positive or negative leisure activities impacts to influence any one of this ocean park visitor individual emotion significantly, if he /she feel comfortable and enjoyable , when they enter this ocean park. This ocean park whole natural environment may influence they like to stay long time in this ocean park. So, when they can stay long time in this ocean park, they may spend money to live hotels, spend money to play any leisure machines and spend time to go to shopping, or buying tickets to see any movies in this ocean park. All of this ocean park natural environment facilities and leisure playing machines improvement may influence any one visitor individual emotion either negative or positive feeling. On conclusion, any theme parks must need to implement FM strategy to improve their theme parks inside natural environment and leisure playing machines quality and hotel living facilities and theme park external transport tool stations facilities, e.g. taxi, bus , railway station distance to convenience any one visitor can catch any one kind of public transport tool to arrive this theme park in short time easily. Also, any theme parks need to impove environment facilities in order to let any one visitor feels comfortable and enhoyable feeling when they choose this theme park to play. Consequently, the theme park's visitors number may be influenced to increase by their positive playing emotion feeling.

Organization facility managment (FM) strategy aims to keep the best facility equipment repair improvement to let any organizational equipment can be used in long time. Hence, FM aims to help organizations to avoid to spend much expenditure on long time repair. When any organizational equipment can be improved to achieve good quality. Instead of improvement equipment quality aspect, can improvement facility equipment bring good customer emotion? How FM may help entertainment theme parks to save long time cost?

In entertainment theme park organizations, they must need to have different kinds of leisure playing machine facilities to supply to visitors to choose to play. So, facility management (FM) must need to imrpove any one entertainment theme parkj machine facility quality, it aims to avoid accidents occur , due to any leisure machine facilities are old or damage when they are used to operate in daily long opening time. Hence, FM must be needed to improve any entertainment theme parks' different kinds of leisure playing machine equipment frequently. If any one theme park leisure machine facility has poor FM in order to improve its machine quality. Consequently, this kind of leisure theme park leisure playing mahcine may be sudden to bring accidents occur, when any one visitor chooses this one of leisure playing machine facility to play. It may cause the player to hurt, even die in possible. Hence, FM to any entertainment theme park playing machine equipment , it may be one major facility repair management srtategy to any entertainment theme parks leisure playing machine facilities, because any one leisure playing machine facilities may bring any one visiot body hurt when the playing machine is old. Instead of FM can bring safety and playinf machine facilities quality improvement benefits to any one entertainment theme park leisure playing machine, whether FM to entertainment theme parks can bring psotive playing of leisure emotion to any one theme park visitor. I shall attempt to discuss as below:

Firstly, we need to know that any kinds of entertainment theme parks why they need to implement FM strategy. Why FM can bring advantages to any kinds of entertainment theme parks. In fact, the benefits of facility management to entertainment theme parks, it enables a more cost-effective working process within any kinds of the theme park any leisure playing machine facilities, such as theme park leisure playing sevice business. It improves the efficiency and it can help the theme park to manage health and safety requirements in accordance with industry regulations. It increases lifespan of a theme park any kinds of leisure playing machines, they are the theme park fixed assets, such as theme park's any kinds of leisure playing machine facilities. New theme parks and attractions can also improve the image of a destination increase tourism and hence economic benefits for the local community , and provide education and entertainment opportunities to the public.

Hence, it is common sense, if the theme park can have good FM to improve its any leisure playing facilities in order to avoid any accident occurrence , when any one visitor chooses to play its any one lesiure machine. Then, it can bring positive safe emotion feeling to satisfy any one visitor whose individual playing safe need to any kinds of playing leisure machines. I believe that its visitors number will not decrease, even increases significantly forever. Hence , the major roles of a theme park facility manager, is that to ensure the upkeep and manintenance of its any one entertainment playing machines, e.g. rolling rides, water rides etc. So, that they meet both safety and health standards to let any one visitors to feel safe to play.

In fact, the scope of facilities management covers two main areas: space and infrastructure , such as planning, design and workplace, construction, occupancy , maintenance and furniture as well as people and organization (such as catering, cleaning and HR, hospitality, accounting and marketing efficient operation in office) both aspects. Hence, these are 6 main facilities to ensure one available for any familiry theme plars. For leisure theme park case, rides and attractions are needed for all ages of any one theme park visitors. This is perhaps the most imprtant, as different parks will have different target audiences, e.g. refreshments, shops, toilets, and parking , access facilities and any one kind of leisure playing machines, such as rolling rides, water rides etc.

Hence, a theme park is a type of amusement park that bases its choice of which kinds of leisure playing facility structures and attractions around a central theme often featureing multiple areas with different themes. Unlike temporary and mobile fun fairs and carnivals, amusement parks are stationary and built for long lasting operation. Hence, every theme park must need have a photogenic, iconic landmark that draws people into the park, beautiful landscaping , enough available attraction capacity to keep peak waits for non-new attractions under 90 minutes, all of these are other faciliities. They must also need to manage to keep more attraction to theme park any one visitor to feel enjoyable and comfortable to play any one theme park leisure playing machines.

What advantages to the theme park implements FM strategy? For Ocean Park example, it aims to let visitors feel themed ocean animal recreational and educational and leisure park experience. So, it must need to upgrade to improve its any facilities to avoid long time repaire spending expenditure. FM project may include: modifying sections of ocean park road, which is a local distributor, around the existing bus terminus , drain works, tunneling and geotechnical works, bulk excavation and slope works, site clearance, modification to bus terminus, taxi stands as well as utilities works including power supply distribution, electrical substations, freshwater and saltwater reservoirs, water supply distribution, gas supply distribution, telecommunications networks, landscope irrigation network to the ocean park any one ocean fish reservoirs, primary life support system works for animal keeping, area development works include elevated walkways, external lighting, external escalators, bridges, parkwide systems works include: signage, background, music system, toilet facilities, guard sheds, first and facilities, communication systems , CCTV systems and waste facilities, landscape or theming works, themed concern pavements, hardscape soft landscaping, water and rockwork features, visual intrusion screens, area props and artwork etc. works for the attractions venues include: animal exhibits, marine animal, terrestrial animal, aviaries , bind exhibits, individual life support systems for animal , exhibits and non- animal related attractions, e.g. shipwreck play area, bamboo maze etc. installation of rides interactive rides , transportation rides etc. , works for venues include : event halls, outdoor live show area, cinema band stands, work for the merchandise / retail facilities include souvonir stores, novelty stores, games ascade, photo shops etc. in the ocean park.

Moreover, any ocean park also have works for the food and baverage facilities include: restaurants, ballery, food casrts as well as back of house facilities include: ocean park offices, break areas, warehouses , centralized facilities, operational facilities etc. , even the ocean park inside hotel development facilities. All of these may bring positive or negative leisure activities impacts to influence any one of this ocean park visitor individual emotion significantly, if he /she feel comfortable and enjoyable , when they enter this ocean park. This ocean park whole natural environment may influence they like to stay long time in this ocean park. So, when they can stay long time in this ocean park, they may spend money to live hotels, spend money to play any leisure machines and spend time to go to shopping, or buying tickets to see any movies in this ocean park. All of this ocean park natural environment facilities and leisure playing machines improvement may influence any one visitor individual emotion either negative or positive feeling.

On conclusion, any theme parks must need to implement FM strategy to improve their theme parks inside natural environment and leisure playing machines quality and hotel living facilities and theme park external transport tool stations facilities, e.g. taxi, bus , railway station distance to convenience any one visitor can catch any one kind of public transport tool to arrive this theme park in short time easily. Also, any theme parks need to impove environment facilities in order to let any one visitor feels comfortable and enhoyable feeling when they choose this theme park to play. Consequently, the theme park's visitors number may be influenced to increase by their positive playing emotion feeling.

Organization facility managment (FM) strategy aims to keep the best facility equipment repair improvement to let any organizational equipment can be used in long time. Hence, FM aims to help organizations to avoid to spend much expenditure on long time repair. When any organizational equipment can be improved to achieve good quality. Instead of improvement equipment quality aspect, can improvement facility equipment bring good customer emotion? How FM may help entertainment theme parks to save long time cost?

In entertainment theme park organizations, they must need to have different kinds of leisure playing machine facilities to supply to visitors to choose to play. So, facility management (FM) must need to imrpove any one entertainment theme parkj machine facility quality, it aims to avoid accidents occur , due to any leisure machine facilities are old or damage when they are used to operate in daily long opening time. Hence, FM must be needed to improve any entertainment theme parks' different kinds of leisure playing machine equipment frequently. If any one theme park leisure machine facility has poor FM in order to improve its machine quality. Consequently, this kind of leisure theme park leisure playing mahcine may be sudden to bring accidents occur, when any one visitor chooses this one of leisure playing machine facility to play. It may cause the player to hurt, even die in possible. Hence, FM to any entertainment theme park playing machine equipment , it may be one major facility repair management srtategy to any entertainment theme parks leisure playing machine facilities, because any one leisure playing machine facilities may bring any one visiot body hurt when the playing machine is old. Instead of FM can bring safety and playinf machine facilities quality improvement benefits to any one entertainment theme park leisure playing machine, whether FM to entertainment theme parks can bring psotive playing of leisure emotion to any one theme park visitor. I shall attempt to discuss as below:

Firstly, we need to know that any kinds of entertainment theme parks why they need to implement FM strategy. Why FM can bring advantages to any kinds of entertainment theme parks. In fact, the benefits of facility management to entertainment theme parks, it enables a more cost-effective working process within any kinds of the theme park any leisure playing machine facilities, such as theme park leisure playing sevice business. It improves the efficiency and it can help the theme park to manage health and safety requirements in accordance with industry regulations. It increases lifespan of a theme park any kinds of leisure playing machines, they are the theme park fixed assets, such as theme park's any kinds of leisure playing machine facilities. New theme parks and attractions can also improve the image of a destination increase tourism and hence economic benefits for the local community , and provide education and entertainment opportunities to the public.

Hence, it is common sense, if the theme park can have good FM to improve its any leisure playing facilities in order to avoid any accident occurrence , when any one visitor chooses to play its any one lesiure machine. Then, it can bring positive safe emotion feeling to satisfy any one visitor whose individual playing safe need to any kinds of playing leisure machines. I believe that its visitors number will not decrease, even increases significantly forever. Hence , the major roles of a theme park facility manager, is that to ensure the upkeep and manintenance of its any one entertainment playing machines, e.g. rolling rides, water rides etc. So, that they meet both safety and health standards to let any one visitors to feel safe to play.

In fact, the scope of facilities management covers two main areas: space and infrastructure , such as planning, design and workplace, construction, occupancy , maintenance and furniture as well as people and organization (such as catering, cleaning and HR, hospitality, accounting and marketing efficient operation in office) both aspects. Hence, these are 6 main facilities to ensure one available for any familiry theme plars. For leisure theme park case, rides and attractions are needed for all ages of any one theme park visitors. This is perhaps the most imprtant, as different parks will have different target audiences, e.g. refreshments, shops, toilets, and parking , access facilities and any one kind of leisure playing machines, such as rolling rides, water rides etc.

Hence, a theme park is a type of amusement park that bases its choice of which kinds of leisure playing facility structures and attractions around a central theme often featureing multiple areas with different themes. Unlike temporary and mobile fun fairs and carnivals, amusement parks are stationary and built for long lasting operation. Hence, every theme park must need have a photogenic, iconic landmark that draws people into the park, beautiful landscaping , enough available attraction capacity to keep peak waits for non-new attractions under 90 minutes, all of these are other faciliities. They must also need to manage to keep more attraction to theme park any one visitor to feel enjoyable and comfortable to play any one theme park leisure playing machines.

What advantages to the theme park implements FM strategy? For Ocean Park example, it aims to let visitors feel themed ocean animal recreational and educational and leisure park experience. So, it must need to upgrade to improve its any facilities to avoid long time repaire spending expenditure. FM project may include: modifying sections of ocean park road, which is a local distributor, around the existing bus terminus , drain works, tunneling and geotechnical works, bulk excavation and slope works, site clearance, modification to bus terminus, taxi stands as well as utilities works including power supply distribution, electrical substations, freshwater and saltwater reservoirs, water supply distribution, gas supply distribution, telecommunications networks, landscope irrigation network to the ocean park any one ocean fish reservoirs, primary life support system works for animal keeping, area development works include elevated walkways, external lighting, external escalators, bridges, parkwide systems works include: signage, background, music system, toilet facilities, guard sheds, first and facilities, communication systems , CCTV systems and waste facilities, landscape or theming works, themed concern pavements, hardscape soft landscaping, water and rockwork features, visual intrusion screens, area props and artwork etc. works for the attractions venues include: animal exhibits, marine animal, terrestrial animal, aviaries , bind exhibits, individual life support systems for animal , exhibits and non- animal related attractions, e.g. shipwreck play area, bamboo maze etc. installation of rides interactive rides , transportation rides etc. , works for venues include : event halls, outdoor live show area, cinema band stands, work for the merchandise / retail facilities include souvonir stores, novelty stores, games ascade, photo shops etc. in the ocean park.

Moreover, any ocean park also have works for the food and baverage facilities include: restaurants, ballery, food casrts as well as back of house facilities include: ocean park offices, break areas, warehouses , centralized facilities, operational facilities etc. , even the ocean park inside hotel development facilities. All of these may bring positive or negative leisure activities impacts to influence any one of this ocean park visitor individual emotion significantly, if he /she feel comfortable and enjoyable , when they enter this ocean park. This ocean park whole natural environment may influence they like to stay long time in this ocean park. So, when they can stay long time in this ocean park, they may spend money to live hotels, spend money to play any leisure machines and spend time to go to shopping, or buying tickets to see any movies in this ocean park. All of this ocean park natural environment facilities and leisure playing machines improvement may influence any one visitor individual emotion either negative or positive feeling. On conclusion, any theme parks must need to implement FM strategy to improve their theme parks inside natural environment and leisure playing machines quality and hotel living facilities and theme park external transport tool stations facilities, e.g. taxi, bus , railway station distance to convenience any one visitor can catch any one kind of public transport tool to arrive this theme park in short time easily. Also, any theme parks need to impove environment facilities in order to let any one visitor feels comfortable and enhoyable feeling when they choose this theme park to play. Consequently, the theme park's visitors number may be influenced to increase by their positive playing emotion feeling.

Organization facility managment (FM) strategy aims to keep the best facility equipment repair improvement to let any organizational equipment can be used in long time. Hence, FM aims to help organizations to avoid to spend much expenditure on long time repair. When any organizational equipment can be improved to achieve good quality. Instead of improvement equipment quality aspect, can improvement facility equipment bring good customer emotion? How FM may help entertainment theme parks to save long time cost?

In entertainment theme park organizations, they must need to have different kinds of leisure playing machine facilities to supply to visitors to choose to play. So, facility management (FM) must need to imrpove any one entertainment theme parkj machine facility quality, it aims to avoid accidents occur , due to any leisure machine facilities are old or damage when they are used to operate in daily long opening time. Hence, FM must be needed to improve any entertainment theme parks' different kinds of leisure playing machine equipment frequently. If any one theme park leisure machine facility has poor FM in order to improve its machine quality. Consequently, this kind of leisure theme park leisure playing mahcine may be sudden to bring accidents occur, when any one visitor chooses this one of leisure playing machine facility to play. It may cause the player to hurt, even die in possible. Hence, FM to any entertainment theme park playing machine equipment , it may be one major facility repair management srtategy to any entertainment theme parks leisure playing machine facilities, because any one leisure playing machine facilities may bring any one visiot body hurt when the playing machine is old. Instead of FM can bring safety and playinf machine facilities quality improvement benefits to any one entertainment theme park leisure playing machine, whether FM to entertainment theme parks can bring psotive playing of leisure emotion to any one theme park visitor. I shall attempt to discuss as below:

Firstly, we need to know that any kinds of entertainment theme parks why they need to implement FM strategy. Why FM can bring advantages to any kinds of entertainment theme parks. In fact, the benefits of facility management to entertainment theme parks, it enables a more cost-effective working process within any kinds of the theme park any leisure playing machine facilities, such as theme park leisure playing sevice business. It improves the efficiency and it can help the theme park to manage health and safety requirements in accordance with industry regulations. It increases lifespan of a theme park any kinds of leisure playing machines, they are the theme park fixed assets, such as theme park's any kinds of leisure playing machine facilities. New theme parks and attractions can also improve the image of a destination increase tourism and hence economic benefits for the local community , and provide education and entertainment opportunities to the public.

Hence, it is common sense, if the theme park can have good FM to improve its any leisure playing facilities in order to avoid any accident occurrence , when any one visitor chooses to play its any one lesiure machine. Then, it can bring positive safe emotion feeling to satisfy any one visitor whose individual playing safe need to any kinds of playing leisure machines. I believe that its visitors number will not decrease, even increases significantly forever. Hence , the major roles of a theme park facility manager, is that to ensure the upkeep and manintenance of its any one entertainment playing machines, e.g. rolling rides, water rides etc. So, that they meet both safety and health standards to let any one visitors to feel safe to play.

In fact, the scope of facilities management covers two main areas: space and infrastructure , such as planning, design and workplace, construction, occupancy , maintenance and furniture as well as people and organization (such as catering, cleaning and HR, hospitality, accounting and marketing efficient operation in office) both aspects. Hence, these are 6 main facilities to ensure one available for any familiry theme plars. For leisure theme park case, rides and attractions are needed for all ages of any one theme park visitors. This is perhaps the most imprtant, as different parks will have different target audiences, e.g. refreshments, shops, toilets, and parking , access facilities and any one kind of leisure playing machines, such as rolling rides, water rides etc.

Hence, a theme park is a type of amusement park that bases its choice of which kinds of leisure playing facility structures and attractions around a central theme often featureing multiple areas with different themes. Unlike temporary and mobile fun fairs and carnivals, amusement parks are stationary and built for long lasting operation. Hence, every theme park must need have a photogenic, iconic landmark that draws people into the park, beautiful landscaping , enough available attraction capacity to keep peak waits for non-new attractions under 90 minutes, all of these are other faciliities. They must also need to manage to keep more attraction to theme park any one visitor to feel enjoyable and comfortable to play any one theme park leisure playing machines.

What advantages to the theme park implements FM strategy? For Ocean Park example, it aims to let visitors feel themed ocean animal recreational and educational and leisure park experience. So, it must need to upgrade to improve its any facilities to avoid long time repaire spending expenditure. FM project may include: modifying sections of ocean park road, which is a local distributor, around the existing bus terminus , drain works, tunneling and geotechnical works, bulk excavation and slope works, site clearance, modification to bus terminus, taxi stands as well as utilities works including power supply distribution, electrical substations, freshwater and saltwater reservoirs, water supply distribution, gas supply distribution, telecommunications networks, landscope irrigation network to the ocean park any one ocean fish reservoirs, primary life support system works for animal keeping, area development works include elevated walkways, external lighting, external escalators, bridges, parkwide systems works include: signage, background, music system, toilet facilities, guard sheds, first and facilities, communication systems , CCTV systems and waste facilities, landscape or theming works, themed concern pavements, hardscape soft landscaping, water and rockwork features, visual intrusion screens, area props and artwork etc. works for the attractions venues include: animal exhibits, marine animal, terrestrial animal, aviaries , bind exhibits, individual life support systems for animal , exhibits and non- animal related attractions, e.g. shipwreck play area, bamboo maze etc. installation of rides interactive rides , transportation rides etc. , works for venues include : event halls, outdoor live show area, cinema band stands, work for the merchandise / retail facilities include souvonir stores, novelty stores, games ascade, photo shops etc. in the ocean park.

Moreover, any ocean park also have works for the food and baverage facilities include: restaurants, ballery, food casrts as well as back of house facilities include: ocean park offices, break areas, warehouses , centralized facilities, operational facilities etc. , even the ocean park inside hotel development facilities. All of these may bring positive or negative leisure activities impacts to influence any one of this ocean park visitor individual emotion significantly, if he /she feel comfortable and enjoyable , when they enter this ocean park. This ocean park whole natural environment may influence they like to stay long time in this ocean park. So, when they can stay long time in this ocean park, they may spend money to live hotels, spend money to play any leisure machines and spend time to go to shopping, or buying tickets to see any movies in this ocean park. All of this ocean park natural environment facilities and leisure playing machines improvement may influence any one visitor individual emotion either negative or positive feeling. On conclusion, any theme parks must need to implement FM strategy to improve their theme parks inside natural environment and leisure playing machines quality and hotel living facilities and theme park external transport tool stations facilities, e.g. taxi, bus , railway station distance to convenience any one visitor can catch any one kind of public transport tool to arrive this theme park in short time easily. Also, any theme parks need to impove environment facilities in order to let any one visitor feels comfortable and enhoyable feeling when they choose this theme park to play. Consequently, the theme park's visitors number may be influenced to increase by their positive playing emotion feeling.

Organization facility managment (FM) strategy aims to keep the best facility equipment repair improvement to let any organizational equipment can be used in long time. Hence, FM aims to help organizations to avoid to spend much expenditure on long time repair. When any organizational equipment can be improved to achieve good quality. Instead of improvement equipment quality aspect, can improvement facility equipment bring good customer emotion? How FM may help entertainment theme parks to save long time cost?

In entertainment theme park organizations, they must need to have different kinds of leisure playing machine facilities to supply to visitors to choose to play. So, facility management (FM) must need to imrpove any one entertainment theme parkj machine facility quality, it aims to avoid accidents occur , due to any leisure machine facilities are old or damage when they are used to operate in daily long opening time. Hence, FM must be needed to improve any entertainment theme parks' different kinds of leisure playing machine equipment frequently. If any one theme park leisure machine facility has poor FM in order to improve its machine quality. Consequently, this kind of leisure theme park leisure playing mahcine may be sudden to bring accidents occur, when any one visitor chooses this one of leisure playing machine facility to play. It may cause the player to hurt, even die in possible. Hence, FM to any entertainment theme park playing machine equipment , it may be one major facility repair management srtategy to any entertainment theme parks leisure playing machine facilities, because any one leisure playing machine facilities may bring any one visiot body hurt when the playing machine is old. Instead of FM can bring safety and playinf machine facilities quality improvement benefits to any one entertainment theme park leisure playing machine, whether FM to entertainment theme parks can bring psotive playing of leisure emotion to any one theme park visitor. I shall attempt to discuss as below:

Firstly, we need to know that any kinds of entertainment theme parks why they need to implement FM strategy. Why FM can bring advantages to any kinds of entertainment theme parks. In fact, the benefits of facility management to entertainment theme parks, it enables a more cost-effective working process within any kinds of the theme park any leisure playing machine facilities, such as theme park leisure playing sevice business. It improves the efficiency and it can help the theme park to manage health and safety requirements in accordance with industry regulations. It increases lifespan of a theme park any kinds of leisure playing machines, they are the theme park fixed assets, such as theme park's any kinds of leisure playing machine facilities. New theme parks and attractions can also improve the image of a destination increase tourism and hence economic benefits for the local community , and provide education and entertainment opportunities to the public.

Hence, it is common sense, if the theme park can have good FM to improve its any leisure playing facilities in order to avoid any accident occurrence , when any one visitor chooses to play its any one lesiure machine. Then, it can bring positive safe emotion feeling to satisfy any one visitor whose individual playing safe need to any kinds of playing leisure machines. I believe that its visitors number will not decrease, even increases significantly forever. Hence , the major roles of a theme park facility manager, is that to ensure the upkeep and manintenance of its any one entertainment playing machines, e.g. rolling rides, water rides etc. So, that they meet both safety and health standards to let any one visitors to feel safe to play.

In fact, the scope of facilities management covers two main areas: space and infrastructure , such as planning, design and workplace, construction, occupancy , maintenance and furniture as well as people and organization (such as catering, cleaning and HR, hospitality, accounting and marketing efficient operation in office) both aspects. Hence, these are 6 main facilities to ensure one available for any familiry theme plars. For leisure theme park case, rides and attractions are needed for all ages of any one theme park visitors. This is perhaps the most imprtant, as different parks will have different target audiences, e.g. refreshments, shops, toilets, and parking , access facilities and any one kind of leisure playing machines, such as rolling rides, water rides etc.

Hence, a theme park is a type of amusement park that bases its choice of which kinds of leisure playing facility structures and attractions around a central theme often featureing multiple areas with different themes. Unlike temporary and mobile fun fairs and carnivals, amusement parks are stationary and built for long lasting operation. Hence, every theme park must need have a photogenic, iconic landmark that draws people into the park, beautiful landscaping , enough available attraction capacity to keep peak waits for non-new attractions under 90 minutes, all of these are other faciliities. They must also need to manage to keep more attraction to theme park any one visitor to feel enjoyable and comfortable to play any one theme park leisure playing machines.

What advantages to the theme park implements FM strategy? For Ocean Park example, it aims to let visitors feel themed ocean animal recreational and educational and leisure park experience. So, it must need to upgrade to improve its any facilities to avoid long time repaire spending expenditure. FM project may include: modifying sections of ocean park road, which is a local distributor, around the existing bus terminus , drain works, tunneling and geotechnical works, bulk excavation and slope works, site clearance, modification to bus terminus, taxi stands as well as utilities works including power supply distribution, electrical substations, freshwater and saltwater reservoirs, water supply distribution, gas supply distribution, telecommunications networks, landscope irrigation network to the ocean park any one ocean fish reservoirs, primary life support system works for animal keeping, area development works include elevated walkways, external lighting, external escalators, bridges, parkwide systems works include: signage, background, music system, toilet facilities, guard sheds, first and facilities, communication systems , CCTV systems and waste facilities, landscape or theming works, themed concern pavements, hardscape soft landscaping, water and rockwork features, visual intrusion screens, area props and artwork etc. works for the attractions venues include: animal exhibits, marine animal, terrestrial animal, aviaries , bind exhibits, individual life support systems for animal , exhibits and non- animal related attractions, e.g. shipwreck play area, bamboo maze etc. installation of rides interactive rides , transportation rides etc. , works for venues include : event halls, outdoor live show area, cinema band stands, work for the merchandise / retail facilities include souvonir stores, novelty stores, games ascade, photo shops etc. in the ocean park.

Moreover, any ocean park also have works for the food and baverage facilities include: restaurants, ballery, food casrts as well as back of house facilities include: ocean park offices, break areas, warehouses , centralized facilities, operational facilities etc. , even the ocean park inside hotel development facilities. All of these may bring positive or negative leisure activities impacts to influence any one of this ocean park visitor individual emotion significantly, if he /she feel comfortable and enjoyable , when they enter this ocean park. This ocean park whole natural environment may influence they like to stay long time in this ocean park. So, when they can stay long time in this ocean park, they may spend money to live hotels, spend money to play any leisure machines and spend time to go to shopping, or buying tickets to see any movies in this ocean park. All of this ocean park natural environment facilities and leisure playing machines improvement may influence any one visitor individual emotion either negative or positive feeling.

On conclusion, any theme parks must need to implement FM strategy to improve their theme parks inside natural environment and leisure playing machines quality and hotel living facilities and theme park external transport tool stations facilities, e.g. taxi, bus , railway station distance to convenience any one visitor can catch any one kind of public transport tool to arrive this theme park in short time easily. Also, any theme parks need to impove environment facilities in order to let any one visitor feels comfortable and enhoyable feeling when they choose this theme park to play. Consequently, the theme park's visitors number may be influenced to increase by their positive playing emotion feeling.

Organization facility managment (FM) strategy aims to keep the best facility equipment repair improvement to let any organizational equipment can be used in long time. Hence, FM aims to help organizations to avoid to spend much expenditure on long time repair. When any organizational equipment can be improved to achieve good quality. Instead of improvement equipment quality aspect, can improvement facility equipment bring good customer emotion? How FM may help entertainment theme parks to save long time cost?

In entertainment theme park organizations, they must need to have different kinds of leisure playing machine facilities to supply to visitors to choose to play. So, facility management (FM) must need to imrpove any one entertainment theme parkj machine facility quality, it aims to avoid accidents occur , due to any leisure machine facilities are old or damage when they are used to operate in daily long opening time. Hence, FM must be needed to improve any entertainment theme parks' different kinds of leisure playing machine equipment frequently. If any one theme park leisure machine facility has poor FM in order to improve its machine quality. Consequently, this kind of leisure theme park leisure playing mahcine may be sudden to bring accidents occur, when any one visitor chooses this one of leisure playing machine facility to play. It may cause the player to hurt, even die in possible. Hence, FM to any entertainment theme park playing machine equipment , it may be one major facility repair management srtategy to any entertainment theme parks leisure playing machine facilities, because any one leisure playing machine facilities may bring any one visiot body hurt when the playing machine is old. Instead of FM can bring safety and playinf machine facilities quality improvement benefits to any one entertainment theme park leisure playing machine, whether FM to entertainment theme parks can bring psotive playing of leisure emotion to any one theme park visitor. I shall attempt to discuss as below:

Firstly, we need to know that any kinds of entertainment theme parks why they need to implement FM strategy. Why FM can bring advantages to any kinds of entertainment theme parks. In fact, the benefits of facility management to entertainment theme parks, it enables a more cost-effective working process within any kinds of the theme park any leisure playing machine facilities, such as theme park leisure playing sevice business. It improves the efficiency and it can help the theme park to manage health and safety requirements in accordance with industry regulations. It increases lifespan of a theme park any kinds of leisure playing machines, they are the theme park fixed assets, such as theme park's any kinds of leisure playing machine facilities. New theme parks and attractions can also improve the image of a destination increase tourism and hence economic benefits for the local community , and provide education and entertainment opportunities to the public.

Hence, it is common sense, if the theme park can have good FM to improve its any leisure playing facilities in order to avoid any accident occurrence , when any one visitor chooses to play its any one lesiure machine. Then, it can bring positive safe emotion feeling to satisfy any one visitor whose individual playing safe need to any kinds of playing leisure machines. I believe that its visitors number will not decrease, even increases significantly forever. Hence , the major roles of a theme park facility manager, is that to ensure the upkeep and manintenance of its any one entertainment playing machines, e.g. rolling rides, water rides etc. So, that they meet both safety and health standards to let any one visitors to feel safe to play.

In fact, the scope of facilities management covers two main areas: space and infrastructure , such as planning, design and workplace, construction, occupancy , maintenance and furniture as well as people and organization (such as catering, cleaning and HR, hospitality, accounting and marketing efficient operation in office) both aspects. Hence, these are 6 main facilities to ensure one available for any familiry theme plars. For leisure theme park case, rides and attractions are needed for all ages of any one theme park visitors. This is perhaps the most imprtant, as different parks will have different target audiences, e.g. refreshments, shops, toilets, and parking , access facilities and any one kind of leisure playing machines, such as rolling rides, water rides etc.

Hence, a theme park is a type of amusement park that bases its choice of which kinds of leisure playing facility structures and attractions around a central theme often featureing multiple areas with different themes. Unlike temporary and mobile fun fairs and carnivals, amusement parks are stationary and built for long lasting operation. Hence, every theme park must need have a photogenic, iconic landmark that draws people into the park, beautiful landscaping , enough available attraction capacity to keep peak waits for non-new attractions under 90 minutes, all of these are other faciliities. They must also need to manage to keep more attraction to theme park any one visitor to feel enjoyable and comfortable to play any one theme park leisure playing machines.

What advantages to the theme park implements FM strategy? For Ocean Park example, it aims to let visitors feel themed ocean animal recreational and educational and leisure park experience. So, it must need to upgrade to improve its any facilities to avoid long time repaire spending expenditure. FM project may include: modifying sections of ocean park road, which is a local distributor, around the existing bus terminus , drain works, tunneling and geotechnical works, bulk excavation and slope works, site clearance, modification to bus terminus, taxi stands as well as utilities works including power supply distribution, electrical substations, freshwater and saltwater reservoirs, water supply distribution, gas supply distribution, telecommunications networks, landscope irrigation network to the ocean park any one ocean fish reservoirs, primary life support system works for animal keeping, area development works include elevated walkways, external lighting, external escalators, bridges, parkwide systems works include: signage, background, music system, toilet facilities, guard sheds, first and facilities, communication systems , CCTV systems and waste facilities, landscape or theming works, themed concern pavements, hardscape soft landscaping, water and rockwork features, visual intrusion screens, area props and artwork etc. works for the attractions venues include: animal exhibits, marine animal, terrestrial animal, aviaries , bind exhibits, individual life support systems for animal , exhibits and non- animal related attractions, e.g. shipwreck play area, bamboo maze etc. installation of rides interactive rides , transportation rides etc. , works for venues include : event halls, outdoor live show area, cinema band stands, work for the merchandise / retail facilities include souvonir stores, novelty stores, games ascade, photo shops etc. in the ocean park.

Moreover, any ocean park also have works for the food and baverage facilities include: restaurants, ballery, food casrts as well as back of house facilities include: ocean park offices, break areas, warehouses , centralized facilities, operational facilities etc. , even the ocean park inside hotel development facilities. All of these may bring positive or negative leisure activities impacts to influence any one of this ocean park visitor individual emotion significantly, if he /she feel comfortable and enjoyable , when they enter this ocean park. This ocean park whole natural environment may influence they like to stay long time in this ocean park. So, when they can stay long time in this ocean park, they may spend money to live hotels, spend money to play any leisure machines and spend time to go to shopping, or buying tickets to see any movies in this ocean park. All of this ocean park natural environment facilities and leisure playing machines improvement may influence any one visitor individual emotion either negative or positive feeling.

On conclusion, any theme parks must need to implement FM strategy to improve their theme parks inside natural environment and leisure playing machines quality and hotel living facilities and theme park external transport tool stations facilities, e.g. taxi, bus , railway station distance to convenience any one visitor can catch any one kind of public transport tool to arrive this theme park in short time easily. Also, any theme parks need to impove environment facilities in order to let any one visitor feels comfortable and enhoyable feeling when they choose this theme park to play. Consequently, the theme park's visitors number may be influenced to increase by their positive playing emotion feeling.

Organization facility managment (FM) strategy aims to keep the best facility equipment repair improvement to let any organizational equipment can be used in long time. Hence, FM aims to help organizations to avoid to spend much expenditure on long time repair. When any organizational equipment can be improved to achieve good quality. Instead of improvement equipment quality aspect, can improvement facility equipment bring good customer emotion? How FM may help entertainment theme parks to save long time cost?

In entertainment theme park organizations, they must need to have different kinds of leisure playing machine facilities to supply to visitors to choose to play. So, facility management (FM) must need to imrpove any one entertainment theme parkj machine facility quality, it aims to avoid accidents occur , due to any leisure machine facilities are old or damage when they are used to operate in daily long opening time. Hence, FM must be needed to improve any entertainment theme parks' different kinds of leisure playing machine equipment frequently. If any one theme park leisure machine facility has poor FM in order to improve its machine quality. Consequently, this kind of leisure theme park leisure playing mahcine may be sudden to bring accidents occur, when any one visitor chooses this one of leisure playing machine facility to play. It may cause the player to hurt, even die in possible. Hence, FM to any entertainment theme park playing machine equipment , it may be one major facility repair management srtategy to any entertainment theme parks leisure playing machine facilities, because any one leisure playing machine facilities may bring any one visiot body hurt when the playing machine is old. Instead of FM can bring safety and playinf machine facilities quality improvement benefits to any one entertainment theme park leisure playing machine, whether FM to entertainment theme parks can bring psotive playing of leisure emotion to any one theme park visitor. I shall attempt to discuss as below:

Firstly, we need to know that any kinds of entertainment theme parks why they need to implement FM strategy. Why FM can bring advantages to any kinds of entertainment theme parks. In fact, the benefits of facility management to entertainment theme parks, it enables a more cost-effective working process within any kinds of the theme park any leisure playing machine facilities, such as theme park leisure playing sevice business. It improves the efficiency and it can help the theme park to manage health and safety requirements in accordance with industry regulations. It increases lifespan of a theme park any kinds of leisure playing machines, they are the theme park fixed assets, such as theme park's any kinds of leisure playing machine facilities. New theme parks and attractions can also improve the image of a destination increase tourism and hence economic benefits for the local community , and provide education and entertainment opportunities to the public.

Hence, it is common sense, if the theme park can have good FM to improve its any leisure playing facilities in order to avoid any accident occurrence , when any one visitor chooses to play its any one lesiure machine. Then, it can bring positive safe emotion feeling to satisfy any one visitor whose individual playing safe need to any kinds of playing leisure machines. I believe that its visitors number will not decrease, even increases significantly forever. Hence , the major roles of a theme park facility manager, is that to ensure the upkeep and manintenance of its any one entertainment playing machines, e.g. rolling rides, water rides etc. So, that they meet both safety and health standards to let any one visitors to feel safe to play.

In fact, the scope of facilities management covers two main areas: space and infrastructure , such as planning, design and workplace, construction, occupancy , maintenance and furniture as well as people and organization (such as catering, cleaning and HR, hospitality, accounting and marketing efficient operation in office) both aspects. Hence, these are 6 main facilities to ensure one available for any familiry theme plars. For leisure theme park case, rides and attractions are needed for all ages of any one theme park visitors. This is perhaps the most imprtant, as different parks will have different target audiences, e.g. refreshments, shops, toilets, and parking , access facilities and any one kind of leisure playing machines, such as rolling rides, water rides etc.

Hence, a theme park is a type of amusement park that bases its choice of which kinds of leisure playing facility structures and attractions around a central theme often featureing multiple areas with different themes. Unlike temporary and mobile fun fairs and carnivals, amusement parks are stationary and built for long lasting operation. Hence, every theme park must need have a photogenic, iconic landmark that draws people into the park, beautiful landscaping , enough available attraction capacity to keep peak waits for non-new attractions under 90 minutes, all of these are other faciliities. They must also need to manage to keep more attraction to theme park any one visitor to feel enjoyable and comfortable to play any one theme park leisure playing machines.

What advantages to the theme park implements FM strategy? For Ocean Park example, it aims to let visitors feel themed ocean animal recreational and educational and leisure park experience. So, it must need to upgrade to improve its any facilities to avoid long time repaire spending expenditure. FM project may include: modifying sections of ocean park road, which is a local distributor, around the existing bus terminus , drain works, tunneling and geotechnical works, bulk excavation and slope works, site clearance, modification to bus terminus, taxi stands as well as utilities works including power supply distribution, electrical substations, freshwater and saltwater reservoirs, water supply distribution, gas supply distribution, telecommunications networks, landscope irrigation network to the ocean park any one ocean fish reservoirs, primary life support system works for animal keeping, area development works include elevated walkways, external lighting, external escalators, bridges, parkwide systems works include: signage, background, music system, toilet facilities, guard sheds, first and facilities, communication systems , CCTV systems and waste facilities, landscape or theming works, themed concern pavements, hardscape soft landscaping, water and rockwork features, visual intrusion screens, area props and artwork etc. works for the attractions venues include: animal exhibits, marine animal, terrestrial animal, aviaries , bind exhibits, individual life support systems for animal , exhibits and non- animal related attractions, e.g. shipwreck play area, bamboo maze etc. installation of rides interactive rides , transportation rides etc. , works for venues include : event halls, outdoor live show area, cinema band stands, work for the merchandise / retail facilities include souvonir stores, novelty stores, games ascade, photo shops etc. in the ocean park.

Moreover, any ocean park also have works for the food and baverage facilities include: restaurants, ballery, food casrts as well as back of house facilities include: ocean park offices, break areas, warehouses , centralized facilities, operational facilities etc. , even the ocean park inside hotel development facilities. All of these may bring positive or negative leisure activities impacts to influence any one of this ocean park visitor individual emotion significantly, if he /she feel comfortable and enjoyable , when they enter this ocean park. This ocean park whole natural environment may influence they like to stay long time in this ocean park. So, when they can stay long time in this ocean park, they may spend money to live hotels, spend money to play any leisure machines and spend time to go to shopping, or buying tickets to see any movies in this ocean park. All of this ocean park natural environment facilities and leisure playing machines improvement may influence any one visitor individual emotion either negative or positive feeling. On conclusion, any theme parks must need to implement FM strategy to improve their theme parks inside natural environment and leisure playing machines quality and hotel living facilities and theme park external transport tool stations facilities, e.g. taxi, bus , railway station distance to convenience any one visitor can catch any one kind of public transport tool to arrive this theme park in short time easily. Also, any theme parks need to impove environment facilities in order to let any one visitor feels comfortable and enhoyable feeling when they choose this theme park to play. Consequently, the theme park's visitors number may be influenced to increase by their positive playing emotion feeling.

Organization facility managment (FM) strategy aims to keep the best facility equipment repair improvement to let any organizational equipment can be used in long time. Hence, FM aims to help organizations to avoid to spend much expenditure on long time repair. When any organizational equipment can be improved to achieve good quality. Instead of improvement equipment quality aspect, can improvement facility equipment bring good customer emotion? How FM may help entertainment theme parks to save long time cost?

In entertainment theme park organizations, they must need to have different kinds of leisure playing machine facilities to supply to visitors to choose to play. So, facility management (FM) must need to imrpove any one entertainment theme parkj machine facility quality, it aims to avoid accidents occur , due to any leisure machine facilities are old or damage when they are used to operate in daily long opening time. Hence, FM must be needed to improve any entertainment theme parks' different kinds of leisure playing machine equipment frequently. If any one theme park leisure machine facility has poor FM in order to improve its machine quality. Consequently, this kind of leisure theme park leisure playing mahcine may be sudden to bring accidents occur, when any one visitor chooses this one of leisure playing machine facility to play. It may cause the player to hurt, even die in possible. Hence, FM to any entertainment theme park playing machine equipment , it may be one major facility repair management srtategy to any entertainment theme parks leisure playing machine facilities, because any one leisure playing machine facilities may bring any one visiot body hurt when the playing machine is old. Instead of FM can bring safety and playinf machine facilities quality improvement benefits to any one entertainment theme park leisure playing machine, whether FM to entertainment theme parks can bring psotive playing of leisure emotion to any one theme park visitor. I shall attempt to discuss as below:

Firstly, we need to know that any kinds of entertainment theme parks why they need to implement FM strategy. Why FM can bring advantages to any kinds of entertainment theme parks. In fact, the benefits of facility management to entertainment theme parks, it enables a more cost-effective working process within any kinds of the theme park any leisure playing machine facilities, such as theme park leisure playing sevice business. It improves the efficiency and it can help the theme park to manage health and safety requirements in accordance with industry regulations. It increases lifespan of a theme park any kinds of leisure playing machines, they are the theme park fixed assets, such as theme park's any kinds of leisure playing machine facilities. New theme parks and attractions can also improve the image of a destination increase tourism and hence economic benefits for the local community , and provide education and entertainment opportunities to the public.

Hence, it is common sense, if the theme park can have good FM to improve its any leisure playing facilities in order to avoid any accident occurrence , when any one visitor chooses to play its any one lesiure machine. Then, it can bring positive safe emotion feeling to satisfy any one visitor whose individual playing safe need to any kinds of playing leisure machines. I believe that its visitors number will not decrease, even increases significantly forever. Hence , the major roles of a theme park facility manager, is that to ensure the upkeep and manintenance of its any one entertainment playing machines, e.g. rolling rides, water rides etc. So, that they meet both safety and health standards to let any one visitors to feel safe to play.

In fact, the scope of facilities management covers two main areas: space and infrastructure , such as planning, design and workplace, construction, occupancy , maintenance and furniture as well as people and organization (such as catering, cleaning and HR, hospitality, accounting and marketing efficient operation in office) both aspects. Hence, these are 6 main facilities to ensure one available for any familiry theme plars. For leisure theme park case, rides and attractions are needed for all ages of any one theme park visitors. This is perhaps the most imprtant, as different parks will have different target audiences, e.g. refreshments, shops, toilets, and parking , access facilities and any one kind of leisure playing machines, such as rolling rides, water rides etc.

Hence, a theme park is a type of amusement park that bases its choice of which kinds of leisure playing facility structures and attractions around a central theme often featureing multiple areas with different themes. Unlike temporary and mobile fun fairs and carnivals, amusement parks are stationary and built for long lasting operation. Hence, every theme park must need have a photogenic, iconic landmark that draws people into the park, beautiful landscaping , enough available attraction capacity to keep peak waits for non-new attractions under 90 minutes, all of these are other faciliities. They must also need to manage to keep more attraction to theme park any one visitor to feel enjoyable and comfortable to play any one theme park leisure playing machines.

What advantages to the theme park implements FM strategy? For Ocean Park example, it aims to let visitors feel themed ocean animal recreational and educational and leisure park experience. So, it must need to upgrade to improve its any facilities to avoid long time repaire spending expenditure. FM project may include: modifying sections of ocean park road, which is a local distributor, around the existing bus terminus , drain works, tunneling and geotechnical works, bulk excavation and slope works, site clearance, modification to bus terminus, taxi stands as well as utilities works including power supply distribution, electrical substations, freshwater and saltwater reservoirs, water supply distribution, gas supply distribution, telecommunications networks, landscope irrigation network to the ocean park any one ocean fish reservoirs, primary life support system works for animal keeping, area development works include elevated walkways, external lighting, external escalators, bridges, parkwide systems works include: signage, background, music system, toilet facilities, guard sheds, first and facilities, communication systems , CCTV systems and waste facilities, landscape or theming works, themed concern pavements, hardscape soft landscaping, water and rockwork features, visual intrusion screens, area props and artwork etc. works for the attractions venues include: animal exhibits, marine animal, terrestrial animal, aviaries , bind exhibits, individual life support systems for animal , exhibits and non- animal related attractions, e.g. shipwreck play area, bamboo maze etc. installation of rides interactive rides , transportation rides etc. , works for venues include : event halls, outdoor live show area, cinema band stands, work for the merchandise / retail facilities include souvonir stores, novelty stores, games ascade, photo shops etc. in the ocean park.

Moreover, any ocean park also have works for the food and baverage facilities include: restaurants, ballery, food casrts as well as back of house facilities include: ocean park offices, break areas, warehouses , centralized facilities, operational facilities etc. , even the ocean park inside hotel development facilities. All of these may bring positive or negative leisure activities impacts to influence any one of this ocean park visitor individual emotion significantly, if he /she feel comfortable and enjoyable , when they enter this ocean park. This ocean park whole natural environment may influence they like to stay long time in this ocean park. So, when they can stay long time in this ocean park, they may spend money to live hotels, spend money to play any leisure machines and spend time to go to shopping, or buying tickets to see any movies in this ocean park. All of this ocean park natural environment facilities and leisure playing machines improvement may influence any one visitor individual emotion either negative or positive feeling. On conclusion, any theme parks must need to implement FM strategy to improve their theme parks inside natural environment and leisure playing machines quality and hotel living facilities and theme park external transport tool stations facilities, e.g. taxi, bus , railway station distance to convenience any one visitor can catch any one kind of public transport tool to arrive this theme park in short time easily. Also, any theme parks need to impove environment facilities in order to let any one visitor feels comfortable and enhoyable feeling when they choose this theme park to play. Consequently, the theme park's visitors number may be influenced to increase by their positive playing emotion feeling.

Organization facility managment (FM) strategy aims to keep the best facility equipment repair improvement to let any organizational equipment can be used in long time. Hence, FM aims to help organizations to avoid to spend much expenditure on long time repair. When any organizational equipment can be improved to achieve good quality. Instead of improvement equipment quality aspect, can improvement facility equipment bring good customer emotion? How FM may help entertainment theme parks to save long time cost?

In entertainment theme park organizations, they must need to have different kinds of leisure playing machine facilities to supply to visitors to choose to play. So, facility management (FM) must need to imrpove any one entertainment theme parkj machine facility quality, it aims to avoid accidents occur , due to any leisure machine facilities are old or damage when they are used to operate in daily long opening time. Hence, FM must be needed to improve any entertainment theme parks' different kinds of leisure playing machine equipment frequently. If any one theme park leisure machine facility has poor FM in order to improve its machine quality. Consequently, this kind of leisure theme park leisure playing mahcine may be sudden to bring accidents occur, when any one visitor chooses this one of leisure playing machine facility to play. It may cause the player to hurt, even die in possible. Hence, FM to any entertainment theme park playing machine equipment , it may be one major facility repair management srtategy to any entertainment theme parks leisure playing machine facilities, because any one leisure playing machine facilities may bring any one visiot body hurt when the playing machine is old. Instead of FM can bring safety and playinf machine facilities quality improvement benefits to any one entertainment theme park leisure playing machine, whether FM to entertainment theme parks can bring psotive playing of leisure emotion to any one theme park visitor. I shall attempt to discuss as below:

Firstly, we need to know that any kinds of entertainment theme parks why they need to implement FM strategy. Why FM can bring advantages to any kinds of entertainment theme parks. In fact, the benefits of facility management to entertainment theme parks, it enables a more cost-effective working process within any kinds of the theme park any leisure playing machine facilities, such as theme park leisure playing sevice business. It improves the efficiency and it can help the theme park to manage health and safety requirements in accordance with industry regulations. It increases lifespan of a theme park any kinds of leisure playing machines, they are the theme park fixed assets, such as theme park's any kinds of leisure playing machine facilities. New theme parks and attractions can also improve the image of a destination increase tourism and hence economic benefits for the local community , and provide education and entertainment opportunities to the public.

Hence, it is common sense, if the theme park can have good FM to improve its any leisure playing facilities in order to avoid any accident occurrence , when any one visitor chooses to play its any one lesiure machine. Then, it can bring positive safe emotion feeling to satisfy any one visitor whose individual playing safe need to any kinds of playing leisure machines. I believe that its visitors number will not decrease, even increases significantly forever. Hence , the major roles of a theme park facility manager, is that to ensure the upkeep and manintenance of its any one entertainment playing machines, e.g. rolling rides, water rides etc. So, that they meet both safety and health standards to let any one visitors to feel safe to play.

In fact, the scope of facilities management covers two main areas: space and infrastructure , such as planning, design and workplace, construction, occupancy , maintenance and furniture as well as people and organization (such as catering, cleaning and HR, hospitality, accounting and marketing efficient operation in office) both aspects. Hence, these are 6 main facilities to ensure one available for any familiry theme plars. For leisure theme park case, rides and attractions are needed for all ages of any one theme park visitors. This is perhaps the most imprtant, as different parks will have different target audiences, e.g. refreshments, shops, toilets, and parking , access facilities and any one kind of leisure playing machines, such as rolling rides, water rides etc.

Hence, a theme park is a type of amusement park that bases its choice of which kinds of leisure playing facility structures and attractions around a central theme often featureing multiple areas with different themes. Unlike temporary and mobile fun fairs and carnivals, amusement parks are stationary and built for long lasting operation. Hence, every theme park must need have a photogenic, iconic landmark that draws people into the park, beautiful landscaping , enough available attraction capacity to keep peak waits for non-new attractions under 90 minutes, all of these are other faciliities. They must also need to manage to keep more attraction to theme park any one visitor to feel enjoyable and comfortable to play any one theme park leisure playing machines.

What advantages to the theme park implements FM strategy? For Ocean Park example, it aims to let visitors feel themed ocean animal recreational and educational and leisure park experience. So, it must need to upgrade to improve its any facilities to avoid long time repaire spending expenditure. FM project may include: modifying sections of ocean park road, which is a local distributor, around the existing bus terminus , drain works, tunneling and geotechnical works, bulk excavation and slope works, site clearance, modification to bus terminus, taxi stands as well as utilities works including power supply distribution, electrical substations, freshwater and saltwater reservoirs, water supply distribution, gas supply distribution, telecommunications networks, landscope irrigation network to the ocean park any one ocean fish reservoirs, primary life support system works for animal keeping, area development works include elevated walkways, external lighting, external escalators, bridges, parkwide systems works include: signage, background, music system, toilet facilities, guard sheds, first and facilities, communication systems , CCTV systems and waste facilities, landscape or theming works, themed concern pavements, hardscape soft landscaping, water and rockwork features, visual intrusion screens, area props and artwork etc. works for the attractions venues include: animal exhibits, marine animal, terrestrial animal, aviaries , bind exhibits, individual life support systems for animal , exhibits and non- animal related attractions, e.g. shipwreck play area, bamboo maze etc. installation of rides interactive rides , transportation rides etc. , works for venues include : event halls, outdoor live show area, cinema band stands, work for the merchandise / retail facilities include souvonir stores, novelty stores, games ascade, photo shops etc. in the ocean park.

Moreover, any ocean park also have works for the food and baverage facilities include: restaurants, ballery, food casrts as well as back of house facilities include: ocean park offices, break areas, warehouses , centralized facilities, operational facilities etc. , even the ocean park inside hotel development facilities. All of these may bring positive or negative leisure activities impacts to influence any one of this ocean park visitor individual emotion significantly, if he /she feel comfortable and enjoyable , when they enter this ocean park. This ocean park whole natural environment may influence they like to stay long time in this ocean park. So, when they can stay long time in this ocean park, they may spend money to live hotels, spend money to play any leisure machines and spend time to go to shopping, or buying tickets to see any movies in this ocean park. All of this ocean park natural environment facilities and leisure playing machines improvement may influence any one visitor individual emotion either negative or positive feeling.

On conclusion, any theme parks must need to implement FM strategy to improve their theme parks inside natural environment and leisure playing machines quality and hotel living facilities and theme park external transport tool stations facilities, e.g. taxi, bus , railway station distance to convenience any one visitor can catch any one kind of public transport tool to arrive this theme park in short time easily. Also, any theme parks need to impove environment facilities in order to let any one visitor feels comfortable and enhoyable feeling when they choose this theme park to play. Consequently, the theme park's visitors number may be influenced to increase by their positive playing emotion feeling.

Organization facility managment (FM) strategy aims to keep the best facility equipment repair improvement to let any organizational equipment can be used in long time. Hence, FM aims to help organizations to avoid to spend much expenditure on long time repair. When any organizational equipment can be improved to achieve good quality. Instead of improvement equipment quality aspect, can improvement facility equipment bring good customer emotion? How FM may help entertainment theme parks to save long time cost?

In entertainment theme park organizations, they must need to have different kinds of leisure playing machine facilities to supply to visitors to choose to play. So, facility management (FM) must need to imrpove any one entertainment theme parkj machine facility quality, it aims to avoid accidents occur , due to any leisure machine facilities are old or damage when they are used to operate in daily long opening time. Hence, FM must be needed to improve any entertainment theme parks' different kinds of leisure playing machine equipment frequently. If any one theme park leisure machine facility has poor FM in order to improve its machine quality. Consequently, this kind of leisure theme park leisure playing mahcine may be sudden to bring accidents occur, when any one visitor chooses this one of leisure playing machine facility to play. It may cause the player to hurt, even die in possible. Hence, FM to any entertainment theme park playing machine equipment , it may be one major facility repair management srtategy to any entertainment theme parks leisure playing machine facilities, because any one leisure playing machine facilities may bring any one visiot body hurt when the playing machine is old. Instead of FM can bring safety and playinf machine facilities quality improvement benefits to any one entertainment theme park leisure playing machine, whether FM to entertainment theme parks can bring psotive playing of leisure emotion to any one theme park visitor. I shall attempt to discuss as below:

Firstly, we need to know that any kinds of entertainment theme parks why they need to implement FM strategy. Why FM can bring advantages to any kinds of entertainment theme parks. In fact, the benefits of facility management to entertainment theme parks, it enables a more cost-effective working process within any kinds of the theme park any leisure playing machine facilities, such as theme park leisure playing sevice business. It improves the efficiency and it can help the theme park to manage health and safety requirements in accordance with industry regulations. It increases lifespan of a theme park any kinds of leisure playing machines, they are the theme park fixed assets, such as theme park's any kinds of leisure playing machine facilities. New theme parks and attractions can also improve the image of a destination increase tourism and hence economic benefits for the local community , and provide education and entertainment opportunities to the public.

Hence, it is common sense, if the theme park can have good FM to improve its any leisure playing facilities in order to avoid any accident occurrence , when any one visitor chooses to play its any one lesiure machine. Then, it can bring positive safe emotion feeling to satisfy any one visitor whose individual playing safe need to any kinds of playing leisure machines. I believe that its visitors number will not decrease, even increases significantly forever. Hence , the major roles of a theme park facility manager, is that to ensure the upkeep and manintenance of its any one entertainment playing machines, e.g. rolling rides, water rides etc. So, that they meet both safety and health standards to let any one visitors to feel safe to play.

In fact, the scope of facilities management covers two main areas: space and infrastructure , such as planning, design and workplace, construction, occupancy , maintenance and furniture as well as people and organization (such as catering, cleaning and HR, hospitality, accounting and marketing efficient operation in office) both aspects. Hence, these are 6 main facilities to ensure one available for any familiry theme plars. For leisure theme park case, rides and attractions are needed for all ages of any one theme park visitors. This is perhaps the most imprtant, as different parks will have different target audiences, e.g. refreshments, shops, toilets, and parking , access facilities and any one kind of leisure playing machines, such as rolling rides, water rides etc.

Hence, a theme park is a type of amusement park that bases its choice of which kinds of leisure playing facility structures and attractions around a central theme often featureing multiple areas with different themes. Unlike temporary and mobile fun fairs and carnivals, amusement parks are stationary and built for long lasting operation. Hence, every theme park must need have a photogenic, iconic landmark that draws people into the park, beautiful landscaping , enough available attraction capacity to keep peak waits for non-new attractions under 90 minutes, all of these are other faciliities. They must also need to manage to keep more attraction to theme park any one visitor to feel enjoyable and comfortable to play any one theme park leisure playing machines.

What advantages to the theme park implements FM strategy? For Ocean Park example, it aims to let visitors feel themed ocean animal recreational and educational and leisure park experience. So, it must need to upgrade to improve its any facilities to avoid long time repaire spending expenditure. FM project may include: modifying sections of ocean park road, which is a local distributor, around the existing bus terminus , drain works, tunneling and geotechnical works, bulk excavation and slope works, site clearance, modification to bus terminus, taxi stands as well as utilities works including power supply distribution, electrical substations, freshwater and saltwater reservoirs, water supply distribution, gas supply distribution, telecommunications networks, landscope irrigation network to the ocean park any one ocean fish reservoirs, primary life support system works for animal keeping, area development works include elevated walkways, external lighting, external escalators, bridges, parkwide systems works include: signage, background, music system, toilet facilities, guard sheds, first and facilities, communication systems , CCTV systems and waste facilities, landscape or theming works, themed concern pavements, hardscape soft landscaping, water and rockwork features, visual intrusion screens, area props and artwork etc. works for the attractions venues include: animal exhibits, marine animal, terrestrial animal, aviaries , bind exhibits, individual life support systems for animal , exhibits and non- animal related attractions, e.g. shipwreck play area, bamboo maze etc. installation of rides interactive rides , transportation rides etc. , works for venues include : event halls, outdoor live show area, cinema band stands, work for the merchandise / retail facilities include souvonir stores, novelty stores, games ascade, photo shops etc. in the ocean park.

Moreover, any ocean park also have works for the food and baverage facilities include: restaurants, ballery, food casrts as well as back of house facilities include: ocean park offices, break areas, warehouses , centralized facilities, operational facilities etc. , even the ocean park inside hotel development facilities. All of these may bring positive or negative leisure activities impacts to influence any one of this ocean park visitor individual emotion significantly, if he /she feel comfortable and enjoyable , when they enter this ocean park. This ocean park whole natural environment may influence they like to stay long time in this ocean park. So, when they can stay long time in this ocean park, they may spend money to live hotels, spend money to play any leisure machines and spend time to go to shopping, or buying tickets to see any movies in this ocean park. All of this ocean park natural environment facilities and leisure playing machines improvement may influence any one visitor individual emotion either negative or positive feeling.

On conclusion, any theme parks must need to implement FM strategy to improve their theme parks inside natural environment and leisure playing machines quality and hotel living facilities and theme park external transport tool stations facilities, e.g. taxi, bus , railway station distance to convenience any one visitor can catch any one kind of public transport tool to arrive this theme park in short time easily. Also, any theme parks need to impove environment facilities in order to let any one visitor feels comfortable and enhoyable feeling when they choose this theme park to play. Consequently, the theme park's visitors number may be influenced to increase by their positive playing emotion feeling.

Organization facility managment (FM) strategy aims to keep the best facility equipment repair improvement to let any organizational equipment can be used in long time. Hence, FM aims to help organizations to avoid to spend much expenditure on long time repair. When any organizational equipment can be improved to achieve good quality. Instead of improvement equipment quality aspect, can improvement facility equipment bring good customer emotion? How FM may help entertainment theme parks to save long time cost?

Amusement , entertainment theme parks aim to provide good playing different kinds of lesiure facilities, and ocean fish performance shows to attract visitors to buy tickets to play lesiure activities when they are staying in the entertainment theme park. I assume that any entertainment theme park must need large lands resources to build the different kinds of entertainment machines facilities to let visitors to choose to play, as well as ocean parks can provide whales animals and human ocean peformance shows to let visitors to see their attraction whales animals performances.

So, enough land supply , it can let the theme park to build different kinds of entertainment machine facilities and ocen park to let many visitors have enough space to stay or walk in the entertainment theme park any time. Even, some theme park builds some hotels to let visitors to live several days, when they can not spend whole day to play all entertainment machine facilities. So, land resources must need , if the theme park needs to increase more different kinds of leisure mahcine facilities, it ought need to expand more leisure machine facilities and let visitors can increase number. So, they won't feel noise and crowd feeling. Because noise and crowd environment may influence some visitors feel discomfortable to enjoy to stay long time in the theme park. Then, it may bring negative lesiure emotion to these visitors.

So, any entertainment theme parks whether their land supply is enough to let it to build more different kinds of entertainment machine facilities and let many visitors can feel the entertainment theme park environment is quiest and not crowd environment factor may influence any visitors' staying time and enjoyment feeling to the theme park, instead of whether its leisure facility activities are attraction. Hence, one attraction land supply to build different kinds of entertainment machine facilities and cean parks and hotels to let visitors can enjoy quiet and not crowd comfortable feeling when they are staying to play any these entertainment facilities inthe theme park.

Entertainment machine facilities will be theme park playing resources, they may include: flat rides, rotter coasters, railways, water rides, dark rides, ferries wheels, transport rides. All of these entertainment facilities their leisure attraction , they may influence lesiure consumer individual enjoyment feeling whether is more or less. So, a theme park is s place with attractions made up of rides, such is roller coasters and water rides. They ususally contain a selection of different types of rides, along with shops, restaurants, and other entertainment outlets.

Theme park cann be enjoyed by adules, teenagers and children. So, a successful theme park must can bring memorable attractions that people want to ride to see over and over again. Great attractions are inclusive and are not overly restrictive. They should have great stroy telling elements and put visitors into unique situations.

Future trends in the theme park industry, they ought concentrate all resources on these aspects: Changes in business models, e.g. it does not consider only entertainment facilities, it ought consider park comfortable environment feeling, e.g. more free, flower, animals, performance, natural environment, more dynamic pricing, changes in interactions between empllyees and guests.So, HRM front line service employee performance will influence whether visitors can feel friendly service feeling (home family feeling), more touchless technology and arificicial intelligence, robots technological resource will be one kind excited entertainment machine facilities to every visitor, they like to play robotic entertainment machines, fresh entertainment enjoyment feeling, more augumented and virtual reality in quest experience, changes in the food experience. So, restaurant food supply resource may bring good taste to excite visitors relas feeling when they feel hungry and they need to find restaurants to eat good taste food.

So, theme park entertainment family resource expenditure must be the highest, e.g. small waterparks can assist less than one million to build, but parks of this size are considered move as water playgrounds. Generally, waterparks , cost between $10 million and $40 million to build, indoor theme parks require on average $10 million to $30 million to build. So, the main resource element is the different kinds of entertainment facilities. Any kind of model of theme park needs to make decision whether which kind of enetertainment facility will be their theme park garden, e.g. water playground or indoor theme park, or natural environment forest enjoyment feeling, ocean park seeing whale performance show etc. theme park kinds. Because capital is limited. So, themem park designer needs to consider whether what kind of theme park feature is the most suitable to build in the land in order to avoid waste building land and not suitable entertainment facilities building material resources, when they can not attract many visitors to buy tickets to enter visit the theme park. For an amusement park example, it is a park that features various attractions, such as rides as well as other events for entertainmetn purposes. A theme park is a type of amusement park that bses its structures and attractions around a central theme, often featuring multiple areas with different themes. The others for amusement park may include: Theme park, carnival, funfair, pleasure ground, safari park, water park.

So, what kind features of theme park construction choice, it may influence future what lesiure needs for the visitors. Theme park investors need to gather fata to make market decision to choose to build what kinds of theme park in

order to build what kinds of theme park in orde to attract the kind of leisure choice visitors.
for disney theme park exmample, it avoids birds play the sound in distress. It will there for keep birds away from visitors and allow for guests to eat in peace without being bothered by hungry birds. So, it increases resources for birds only. So, birds can have more gardens to let them to fly. They wont fly away the gardens in Desney. So, any gueses do not feel worry about the sound of birds in distress. Also, any theme parks need to invest resources on safety aspect when any one guest plays any kinds of entertainment facilities, e.g. the safest roller coaster is Blackpool, theme park. It can attract many guests to play its entertainment facilities. This theme park locates near to US one beach. Because , it did not cause any one guest dies before, when they go to US this beach, they will like to pay ticket to play rides entertainment facilities. Because it often spends expenditure on rides repairment aspect, so, it can bring the safest feeling to let any one beach guest feels leisure ride playing need when they visits to this US beach to feel swimming need. They also feel playing rides entertainment needs both. Hence, any kinds of theme park investors need to consider how to allocate limited resources to the different element aspect in order to safety, entertainment facilities attraction , reasonable price, enjoyment animals performance shows, restaurents good food taste providing hotel comfortable living feeling aims to all themem park guests.

In entertainment theme park organizations, they must need to have different kinds of leisure playing machine facilities to supply to visitors to choose to play. So, facility management (FM) must need to imrpove any one entertainment theme parkj machine facility quality, it aims to avoid accidents occur , due to any leisure machine facilities are old or damage when they are used to operate in daily long opening time. Hence, FM must be needed to improve any entertainment theme parks' different kinds of leisure playing machine equipment frequently. If any one theme park leisure machine facility has poor FM in order to improve its machine quality. Consequently, this kind of leisure theme park leisure playing mahcine may be sudden to bring accidents occur, when any one visitor chooses this one of leisure playing machine facility to play. It may cause the player to hurt, even die in possible. Hence, FM to any entertainment theme park playing machine equipment , it may be one major facility repair management srtategy to any entertainment theme parks leisure playing machine facilities, because any one leisure playing machine facilities may bring any one visiot body hurt when the playing machine is old. Instead of FM can bring safety and playinf machine facilities quality improvement benefits to any one entertainment theme park leisure playing machine, whether FM to entertainment theme parks can bring psotive playing of leisure emotion to any one theme park visitor. I shall attempt to discuss as below:
Firstly, we need to know that any kinds of entertainment theme parks why they need to implement FM strategy. Why FM can bring advantages to any kinds of entertainment theme parks. In fact, the benefits of facility management to entertainment theme parks, it enables a more cost-effective working process within any kinds of the theme park any leisure playing machine facilities, such as theme park leisure playing sevice business. It improves the efficiency and it can help the theme park to manage health and safety requirements in accordance with industry regulations. It increases lifespan of a theme park any kinds of leisure playing machines, they are the theme park fixed assets, such as theme park's any kinds of leisure playing machine facilities. New theme parks and attractions can also improve the image of a destination increase tourism and hence economic benefits for the local community , and provide education and entertainment opportunities to the public.
Hence, it is common sense, if the theme park can have good FM to improve its any leisure playing facilities in order to avoid any accident occurrence , when any one visitor chooses to play its any one lesiure machine. Then, it can bring positive safe emotion feeling to satisfy any one visitor whose individual playing safe need to any kinds of playing leisure machines. I believe that its visitors number will not decrease, even increases significantly forever. Hence , the major roles of a theme park facility manager, is that to ensure the upkeep and manintenance of its any one entertainment playing machines, e.g. rolling rides, water rides etc. So, that they meet both safety and health standards to let any one visitors to feel safe to play.
In fact, the scope of facilities management covers two main areas: space and infrastructure , such as planning, design and workplace, construction, occupancy , maintenance and furniture as well as people and organization (such as catering, cleaning and HR, hospitality, accounting and marketing efficient operation in office) both aspects. Hence, these are 6 main facilities to ensure one available for any familiry theme plars. For leisure theme park case, rides

and attractions are needed for all ages of any one theme park visitors. This is perhaps the most imprtant, as different parks will have different target audiences, e.g. refreshments, shops, toilets, and parking , access facilities and any one kind of leisure playing machines, such as rolling rides, water rides etc.

Hence, a theme park is a type of amusement park that bases its choice of which kinds of leisure playing facility structures and attractions around a central theme often featureing multiple areas with different themes. Unlike temporary and mobile fun fairs and carnivals, amusement parks are stationary and built for long lasting operation. Hence, every theme park must need have a photogenic, iconic landmark that draws people into the park, beautiful landscaping , enough available attraction capacity to keep peak waits for non-new attractions under 90 minutes, all of these are other faciliities. They must also need to manage to keep more attraction to theme park any one visitor to feel enjoyable and comfortable to play any one theme park leisure playing machines.

What advantages to the theme park implements FM strategy? For Ocean Park example, it aims to let visitors feel themed ocean animal recreational and educational and leisure park experience. So, it must need to upgrade to improve its any facilities to avoid long time repaire spending expenditure. FM project may include: modifying sections of ocean park road, which is a local distributor, around the existing bus terminus , drain works, tunneling and geotechnical works, bulk excavation and slope works, site clearance, modification to bus terminus, taxi stands as well as utilities works including power supply distribution, electrical substations, freshwater and saltwater reservoirs, water supply distribution, gas supply distribution, telecommunications networks, landscope irrigation network to the ocean park any one ocean fish reservoirs, primary life support system works for animal keeping, area development works include elevated walkways, external lighting, external escalators, bridges, parkwide systems works include: signage, background, music system, toilet facilities, guard sheds, first and facilities, communication systems , CCTV systems and waste facilities, landscape or theming works, themed concern pavements, hardscape soft landscaping, water and rockwork features, visual intrusion screens, area props and artwork etc. works for the attractions venues include: animal exhibits, marine animal, terrestrial animal, aviaries , bind exhibits, individual life support systems for animal , exhibits and non- animal related attractions, e.g. shipwreck play area, bamboo maze etc. installation of rides interactive rides , transportation rides etc. , works for venues include : event halls, outdoor live show area, cinema band stands, work for the merchandise / retail facilities include souvonir stores, novelty stores, games ascade, photo shops etc. in the ocean park.

Moreover, any ocean park also have works for the food and baverage facilities include: restaurants, ballery, food casrts as well as back of house facilities include: ocean park offices, break areas, warehouses , centralized facilities, operational facilities etc. , even the ocean park inside hotel development facilities. All of these may bring positive or negative leisure activities impacts to influence any one of this ocean park visitor individual emotion significantly, if he /she feel comfortable and enjoyable , when they enter this ocean park. This ocean park whole natural environment may influence they like to stay long time in this ocean park. So, when they can stay long time in this ocean park, they may spend money to live hotels, spend money to play any leisure machines and spend time to go to shopping, or buying tickets to see any movies in this ocean park. All of this ocean park natural environment facilities and leisure playing machines improvement may influence any one visitor individual emotion either negative or positive feeling.

On conclusion, any theme parks must need to implement FM strategy to improve their theme parks inside natural environment and leisure playing machines quality and hotel living facilities and theme park external transport tool stations facilities, e.g. taxi, bus , railway station distance to convenience any one visitor can catch any one kind of public transport tool to arrive this theme park in short time easily. Also, any theme parks need to impove environment facilities in order to let any one visitor feels comfortable and enhoyable feeling when they choose this theme park to play. Consequently, the theme park's visitors number may be influenced to increase by their positive playing emotion feeling.

CHAPTER EIGHT

Robots skill how raises organizational efficiency

Organization tangible and intangible resources function

Any organizations must have tangible and intangible resources. Tangible resources may include: Staffs, lands, equipment, producing machines, factory etc. They may help organizations to produce products or provide services to earn profit, e.g. one shop may be the firm's tangible assets if it can be designed to be the best and provide soft music to let customers to listen and provide clourful light design , they may influence they to bring happy consumption emotion in order to attract many customers to stay long time in the shop and increases shopping chance, the salespeople (staffs) to attract more customers , they may be influenced to feel enjoy to stay long long time by their services. Although, any customers visit any shops , it must not represent that they quarantee to buy any things before they leave the shop. However, I beleive that any business , their products functions and prices is one influential factor to persuade consumers to do shopping activities, their shop design attraction feeling may be also another main factor to persuade them to do shopping decision because when the consumer feels the shop is comfortable , it will cause he/she feels enjoyable to stay long time in the shop. Consequently, shop design attraction may be another influential intangible resource factor to encourage consumers to buy any things easily, if they can be influenced to stay long time in the shop by the ship design attraction. It is one kind of feeling factor to excite consumers to do shopping decision. SO, shop may be one important organization fixed asset resource to influence consumer individual purchase desire in any business environment. It is one good exmaple organizational tangible fixed asset redsource to help any organizations to create income.

The another kind of intangible resources, they are not seen by any customers and they can not be toughed by any customers. BUt they are organizational resources, they also may help any organizations to earn income. Why can intangible resource help organizations to earn income? I shall explain as below:

Customer services and staff skills, they may be organiztional intangible resources and they may help any organizations to create income. For example, when one shop has one kindly and friendly salespeople, when any one customer enters this shop, he will say" Good morning", " Good afternoon", "Good night" and when the customer leaves this shop, he will say " Goodby". Even, when the customer has not bought any thing till to leave this shop, this salesperson also speaks " Goodby". So, all of shop visitors, when the salesperson sees them, he must speaks above words, so any one must feel he is polite person and he can represents this shop's polite image also. Although, some shop visitors do not buy anything when they are staying in this shop, but they must feel that this salesperson's attitude is polite to let them to feel. THis salesperson can bring happy feeling to let all shop visitors feel. So, he must not be complainted easily, because when this salesperson discovers any one person is staying to close to any one producg shelf location in the shop, he will walk to the person to enquire him" DO you need I help you?" politely. Although, it is possible that this person won't need this salesperson to help him, but this salesperson can let this shop visitor to feel that he does not need find any one salesperson to enquire when he feels that he needs purchase help, e.g. whether the shirt has small size stock, or the shoe has organge colour etc. product information enquiries. SO, this salesperson can let this shop visitor feels he can take care to his purchase choice behavior and he can do and purchase help in this shop any time. So, this salesperson , his excellent service performance can let any one shop visitor feels service satisfaction, instead of his essential sale customer service performance. IN fact, this salesperson may let many shop visitors to feel that he does not only considerate whether whom is his real customer in order to enquire any purchase help. The non purchase plan shop visitors may also feel his kindly customer service help during they are staying in shop any time. So, this salesperson's polite and kindly customer service attitude may influence many non purchase planning shop visitors feel happy to see him in this shop. Consequently, it explains why salespeople excellent customer service performance which may help any businesses to increase customers number. It may be one kind of intangible organization resource to any organizations. I mean that when the shop can train many salespeople to raise customer service sale performance improvement.

Overall, these excellent customer service salespeople mus thelp this business to increase customer number easily, because this shop's all salespeople thier positive emotion may influence any one shop visitor feels enjoyment when they can feel they are taking care to their purchase choice need when they are staying in this shop any time. So, the minute, that the shop visitor does not plan to choose to buy any kinds of products, it does not represent that he does not plan to choose to buy any kinds of products next minute. So, any salespeople their excellent customer service performance may influence any one shop visitor to do purchase planning decision any minute. It seems that " salespeople customer service performance feeling" may be one kind of long time intangible resource to help any businesses to earn income in possible. Hence, it explains that any organizations must have tangible and intangible organizational resources to assist them to develop their businesses in long time success. They are essential elelments to influence whether the business's customers number can increase or decrease.

For computer sale business example, its tangible resource may be computer shop and intangible resource may be computer salespeople skills, because if any visitors feel this computer shop's computer desktop or laptop products can be putted in the right and easy seeking locations on any shelves, e.g. the low range price of laptops or desktops are putted on the lowest shelf position as well as the high range price of laptops or desktops are putted on the highest shelf position. So, when the planning purchase of desktop or laptop shop visitors may compare the different design of laptops or desktops their low range price or their high and low shelves locations easily. So, laptops and desktops putting on shelves position, they may influence any one desktop or laptop buyer individual final purchase choice decision. If the laptop planning purchase visitor, he plans to buy one low price of laptop, when he discovers there are all low range price of laptops are putting on the shelf loe position. Then , he may feel convenience to choose any one kind of low price of laptop design products from the lowest range shelf location easily. So, computer shops' computer putting shelves positions may be one kind tangible resource factor to influence any one computer buyer to choose any one kind of design of laptop or desktop priduct convenience. Their computer product choice time whether it is long or short may influence their final computer purchase decision. Hence, the shop's computers ' putting on shelves positions may be one essential tangible resources to influence any one computer visitor to do purchase decision.

The computer shop salespeople computer knowledge may be another intangible factor to influence any one computer buyer decision. For example, when one planning laptop purchaser wants to know whether the laptop's any function, if he enquiries to the computer salesperson, he ften let him to feel that his explanation can not satisfy his any enquiries about the design of laptop product function knowledge, e.g. how to set up password for this computer privacy. If the computer salesperson lets the planning computer buyer to feel that he is difficult to teach him how to set up the passwrod for the computer to use. Then, the computer salesperson's innocence of computer password set up knowledge which may influence the planning computer buyers makes final non purchase decision to this computer, because his innocence can let him to feel this computer is difficult to set up password , if he is one foolish computer user.

Hence, this computer shop's all computer salespeople their computer knowledge, they may influence any one computer buyer final purchase decision. They must need to be trained to learn how to use any one new design of desktop or latop computer products before they are employed to be salespeople in this computer shop。 SO, their computer knowledge may be this computer shop's intangible resource to influence this computer shop's customers number to increase or decrease every day. Hence, decision on any organizational tangible and intangible resources to the organization, they depend on whether what kind of the business needs to sell what kinds of products.

The organization is where resources come together . Organizations use different resources to accompolish goals, e.g. human resources, financial resources, physical resources, and information resources. SO, managers are responsible for managing the resources to accomplish goals. Organizational resources are all assets that are available to a firm for use during

the production process. The four basic types of organizational resources are human, monetary, raw material and capital. Managing organizational resources is the ability to understand and effectively manage organizational resources (e.e. people, materials assets , budget). This is demonstrated through measurement, planning and control of resources to maximize resources.

Company resources include tangible assets , such as its plant, equipment, finances, and location, human assets , in terms of the number of empllyees, their skills and motivation and intangible assets (such as technology, patents and copyrights, culture and reputation).

It brings this question: What makes organizational resource unique, in resource based view? Resources are available when they allow a firm to take advantage of opportunities or threats in its external environment. Many resources can either be immitated or substituted over time to any organizations. Hence, effectively managing resources helps companies more consistently deliver projects and services on time. This is because better resource management helps to improve insight into resources availability as well as improves timeline projections. Hence, the types of resources in management they may include: Human resource, natural resource, project resource, financial management, facility management, entertrise asset, public asset management.

ON conclusion, I believe that a company's most important resources may be human captial, such as talent employees, their technical knowledge may be intangible resource asset to help

the organization to develop its business in longf term success.

Internet will be intangible technology knowledge resource to e-commerce organization

New economy brings new way of resource management. The old loyalty and job security -based organization changes, organizations know that the assets are largely made up employees (HRM), but many new organizations begin to believe technology is important assets, such as Amazon is global ecommerce delivery service organization. It seems internet high technology is its important intangible resource to help it earn global e-buyers number increases . So , many organizations began to believe that technology will be important resource, such as internet can provide online business chance. With all the businesses are taking full advantage of internet, for example, the US department estimates that the value of retail e-commerce in 2000 year was about $25 billion, which represents less than 1% of US retail sales. Despite this, interest in e-business remains high.

Why internet may be main technology resource to organizations?

E-commere needs strategy in order to win competitors, questions include: What criteria do customers use to choose between our firms and competitors? How do the best employees decision whether to join? What business environment attracts and keeps the best suppliers making with our firms? What characteristics draw the most royal invesdtors to our firms? e.g. Amazon . com's web site and Wal-mart's can apply internet technology resource to create each e-store to let e-buyers to choose any kinds of products to buy athome conveniently. Hence, internet technology, even future other kinds of new technology may be main technology resources to organizations, when they can help organizations to raise sale competitive effort.

I mean that digital economy will be one kind new digital resource to future any organizations. The essential piece is the knowledge, it is what give it life and what makes it an interesting and fulifulling purchase and sale channel for people to spend their time , such as e-commerce virtual organization may be leaded to let purchase and ale transactions carry on easily from online websites. Hence, internet may be main knowledge management (intellectual capital) resource to any e-commerce organizations. It is about the storage, transfer knowledge.

For Amazon publish example, e-books will be knowledge as an object, like a book in library. Amazon can apply internet technology to help it to sell any author's ebooks from its book estores. So, ebooks are Amazon's knowledge resources to help it to create readers incomes. E-books is intangible knowledge resource to Amazon . Any authors' paper and ebooks will be sold cheap price to help Amazon to attract global readers to choose to buy its ebooks from its different countries e-webstores at home conveniently.

Hence, any e-commerce organizations also need HRM (emanagers) to help them to deliver a superior value (world class capabilities) in both te virtual and physical world. E-management will be another main human resources to e-commerce organizations. Why does e-management will be future main HRM resource to e-commerce organization? The reasons may include:

E-management demands in sort of managerial/e-commerce sale strategy effort, skills at positioning the firm within a networm of industries, e-management also demands the ability to see how the firm fits into a value creation-e-management is different because doing it work requires the e-engineering of business eco-systems, e-management demands the ability to be connected to thousands of inputs about specific changes among many industry participants , such as suppliers , customers, employees, competitors, media and shareholders.

Effective e-management requires the ability to monitor developments that can change with unusually high frequency. However, it is also essential that e-managers distinguish between the few meaningful inputs and the many inputs that have limited significance, ability to sustain organizational change, effectie e-managers monitor changes in their markets. So, instead of e-commerce organizations need to employ talent e-managment staffs to help them to manage overall e-commerce organizations. E-leading staffs (HRM) is another main HRM need. E-leaders need to know how to design online brochures, e.g. online brochures simply involved putting a company's market materials on the web. in order to attract or persuade online buyers visit its websites and choose the most right price of product to buy easily. E-leaders need to lead front-office transactions which involved putting customer facing customers , such as placing on order on the web when leaving back-office activities, such as order fulfillment unchanged.

E-leaders also need to integrate online online purchase transactions in which a firm actually linked its front -office and back -office systems and processes in a fashion, e.g. most companies have developed online brochures , in order to let online advertisement tool to attract e-buyer individual purchase choice from its webstores. Hence, future any e-commerce organizations must need (HRM (e-leaders and e-managers) to help them to bring innovation in order to achieve maximize profit aim. So, internet webstores, e-leaders , e-managers may be future e-commerce organization main resources. So, e-commerce organizations, manages are actors at three levels: In the front line , as entrepreneurs, in the middle , as facilitators, and integrators, at the top as institution builders.

Hence, future new economical society, it creates e-commerce organizations number increases, when consumers began to accept online purchase transaction activities. Hence, it causes e-commerce began to feel internet (e-webstores, e-leaders, e-managers), they will be the most influential resources (intangible knowledge managment and tangible URM both resourcees to influence their success or failure.

Why doe e-commerce organization believe (e-webstore design, e-leaders and e-managers) will be main organizational resources?

The most important question: It asks when e-buyers visit their webstores, wo are their target customers and shich needs of theirs are their trying to satisfy? For exap,e many airlines , e.g. American airlines, China airlines began to feel online e-tickets sale channel is more easily than paper ticket shop sale channel, because many air passengers began to accept e-ticket/online ticket purchase choice more than visiting airline shops . They feel that they do not want to waste time to visit airline shops. They like to pre-book to buy e-ticket to pay from the airline e-websote conveniently. Hence, e-webstore design knowledge management , e-leaders and e-management webstore management skill will be future any one e-commerce organizations their main tangible and intangible resources (assets) to help their e-commerce businesses development.

On conclusion, I believe that the current economy is not a high-tech economy or an internet economy, not an m-commerce economy , but instead customer econoomy. Customers need to gather with information and access, they are demanding, fair, global price, they are demanding that compares deal with them using the distribution channel , they choose manufacturing direct and through dealers and retailers. Base on those factors, they encourage future many e-commerce organizations cause organization change traditional resouce concept, such as land, capital equipment, tangible resource began to change to e-commerce organization's intangibel and tangible resource, such as knowledge management to e-online web store design skills, e-leaders and e-managers e-stores sale management strategy and e-buyer product research and brochure online advertisement design skill. All of these knowledge management skill will be future organizations' main resources to help them to create new economic competition effort.

In behavioral economic view , any organizations can attempt to apply behavioral economy method to use resources efficiently. Organizational excellence framework performance measurement takes a systematic approach . One of the most effective ways of using resources and minimizing that use of work. Calculating task cost in the most efficient economic method to help organizations to reduce cost and avoid resources waste, e.g. using resource management software, technology, planning and taking a systematic approach , which aims to manage the most efficient steps to follow to finish or implement each task in the most shor time as well as avoiding excess employees number.

Organizational resource efficiency means using the organization's limited resources in a sustainable manner when minimising impacts on the organization performance. It allows the organization to create more with less and to deliver greater value with less money. HR, raw material, technology input to carry on any organizational resources efficiently ? Management is the process of using organizational resources to achieve organizational goals of using organizational resources to achieve organizational goals effectively and efficiently through planning , organizing , leading and controlling. An efficient organization makes the most productive use of its resource in the most short time and the most eficiency and the least cost aspects.

What is efficient use of resources to any organizations in economics?

Economic efficiency implies an economic state in which every resource is optimially allocated to serve each individual or entity in the best way when minimizing waste and inefficiency. whan an economy is economically efficient, any changes made to assist one entity would harm another . Hence, budget how much spending on resources, e.g. employee saley, office and/or plant technological equipment facilities , before making resource expenditure spending decision. Budget is essnetial to help the organization to deduce resource using and excess purchase waste since budget and resource of organizations have interlock or interconnet relationship. If the organization can make exact udget, then it can avoid excess expenditure or waste resource to use. So, organizations need to acquire a talented resource pool , that can lead projects to success, when any kinds of resources are achieved to be supplied to use inn enough . For example, using an effective enterprise resource management system that delivers capabilities. Regardless of the approach and tools used, organizations must determine how to balance to use any kinds of resources efficiently. Thus, in organizational efficient resource using behavioral economy view, the organizational efficiency factor means that influences the efficiency of the organization's use if its resources can be both internal and external, e.g. how implementing strategic plans, they may include selecting what methods and resources to use, and leadning employees on guideline, working in coalitions with organizations around to deliver those needs in the most resource efficient way.

In organizational studies, resource managemetn is the efficient and one resource management technique of resource leveling, of finding the answers to the question, how to use available resource efficiently, effectively and economically ot organization resource expense. SO , resource management is the process of allocating resources and allocating.

What is meant by economic using of resource to organizations?

Economic resources are the factors used in producing goods or providing services. Economic resources can be divied into human resources, such as labors and management, and non humann resource, such as land, capital , goods, finished resources and technology , for example, natural resource is a key input in the production process that stimulates economic growth. Natural resources have limited direct economic use in satisfying human need, but transforming them into goods and services enhances their economic value to the socirty. So, if the country has many organizations know how to use their natural resources input in that production processes. Then, they can create themselves economic benefits directly and attribute economic benefit to society indirectly.

Thus, the types of economic organizations can be identified, there are subsistence recipreocal exchange with subsistence, peasant with primary reliance on self-produced food, but containing some exhange elements, market-commercial , redistribution or state socialist. Thus organizations need to learn hoe to use themselves organizational resources efficiently. Organizational resources are all assets that are to a firm for use during the production process. The four basic types of organizational resources are human, monetary, raw material and capital. Organizational resources are combined , used and transformed into finished products during the production process. So, a business that understands how to use resources efficiently. resource management is the process of allocating resources in order for a company to grow easily.

Organizational economic is used to study transactions within individual firms and determine management approach to managing resources. It is broken down into thee major subjects: agency theory, transaction cost economic and property rights theory. Agency theory is a priinciple that is used to explain and resolve issues in the relationship between business principles and their agents. Most commonly, that relationship is the one between shareholders as principles, and company executives as agents. Agency theory is used to understand the relationship between agents and principals. The agent represents the principal in a particular business transaction and is expected to represent the best interests of the principal without regard for seld interest. So, when the relationship between shreholders and company executives is kept the best.

Transaction cost economic is understood as alternative modes of organizing transactions (governance structure, such as markets, firms and bureaus) that mininize transactions costs. This, cost is the primary determinant of such as firm's decision whether it is the most right (the best) or the worst decision. It will influence the firm ho to spend resource behavior. The cost other than the money price that are incurred in trading good and service. SO, if the organization can often make the best decision to carry on any activites. It will avoid to waste resources efficiently. For example, if transaction cost influces the commission, paid to a stockbroker for completing a share deal and booking fee charges when purchase concert tickets. The cost of travel and time to complete an exhange , it means that transaction cost. So if the organization can make the best or the most reasonable decision to carry on any business activities. Then, its transaction cost can be influenced to reduce the most level in order to bring resources economic benefit. e.g. sunk costs are indpeendent of any event and should not resulting from economic trade in a market.

Property right theory means contracted choice, through ownership, property rights theour clarifies the firm's boundary choice. The maon egal property rights are the right of possession, the righ tof excession. So, for the efficiency of property rights al scarce resources are owned by someone. IN the right property rights approsed to the theory of the firm, I assume that in the case of sale ownership by party-property rights define the theoretical and legal ownership of resources and how resources can be used by organizatin. So, above three major organizational theories can assist organizations to know how to spend resources efficiently.

The relationship between organization resources using and social resources

Resources needers may include societies needers ,e.g. government house material householders , electricity , water , natural resources needers, schools, public houses , land number and area needs etc. as well as business organiztions , office building material, office, plant, land area, number need, equipment facilities limited number . So, when global office and plant business users need to buy more land, equipment materials etc. and electricity , water. Social resources number reduces to bring resourcee shortage challenge causes. Have they have shortage relationship (resource demand number is more than supply number) between social resources need and business resource need? I shall attempt to explain this question as below:

I assume global business organization number increases, they will need many natural resources, e.g. water, electricity, gas, land to supply for office, plant building , material and staff office electricity, gas, plant , office daily essential power need. So, when global business organizations number increases, they may need to use much raw material and natural resources for equipment facility, office plant building material, even day office, plant electricity , gas power, staff drinking water etc. basic office operational needs, when global business organizations number increase.

The question concerns whether they will cause natural resources shortage to supply to social need , when global business organizatins number increases. First, I shall explains what social resources needers mean as below:

Social resource are defined as any concrete or symbolic term that

can be used as an object of exchange among people (Foa & Foa, 1980), money, information, goods and services both tangible items , such as are ususally defined the assessment of social need is of central allocation between organization needers and social citizen needers both stakeholders. So, when global human birth rate and life time increases, population number will increase, then their social resources need are also increasing, if global organizaions and population number are increasing in the same time, due to earth natural resources has limit number to supply in order to satisfy organizations and families daily resources need, e.g. building material resources are used to build either to build offices, plants or private houses , public house, lands resources are used either to build private or public houses or offices , plants , water is supplied to either office staffs drinking or families drinking, electricity , gas resources are limited to supply either offices plants use or families private or public houses use. Hence, due to all of earth, but in the same time, global offices , plants, government organizations and families numbers both stakeholders number is continue increasing. They have possible to encounter natural resources shortage issue when natural resources are using much, but they can nt manufacturers to increase by human easily.

Can responding to resource scarcity help some kinds business grow?

Foe example, the food and agricultural business organizations, e.g. supermarkets, restaurants, they must send plactic material to manufacture plactic bags to supply to supermarket buyers to carry fruits, breads, mil, etc. foods when consumers need to buy the kinds of foods in any supermarkets, if plactic material supply number is decreasing, then a lot plactic bags can not supply to let buyers to carry their foods, due to plactic bags number is shortage , it will cause any supermarket buyers feel inconvenient when they need plactic bags to carry their foods, they choose to buy the kind of foods from supermarket to themselves homes.

So, if plactic bags manufacture material i shortage, it can not be manufactured to plactic bags to supply to global supermarket organizations. Then, the one supermarket can provide enough plactic bags to let them to carry their foods from supermarkets to themselves homes conveniently. The focus on plactic bag resource scareity is not impossible to occur to supermarket organization case. If families are often using plactic bag to carry rubbish daily at home. Then, plactic bags number can not increase to satisfy global supermarkets food plactic bags and families themselves homes rubbish plactic bags both stakeholders need. Plastic bags can not be manufactured to supply to manufacture lot plactic bags supply to satisfy global families rubbish plactic bags home users and supermarkets food plactic bas users needs. Consequently, plactic bags prices may be influenced to increases, when plactic bags demand increases, but supply decreases. It is one good exaple to explain why plactic bag manufacturered material supply decreases, it may influence plactic bags number decreases and price increases, because families home rubbish plactic bags and supermarket food plastic bags need both increase.

Consequence, supermarket cost may be influenced , due to plastic bags number also increase much, if one day shortage of plactic manufacturing material supply number is shortage. So, it seems that food plastis bags using number, they have close relationship to impact supermarket food plastic bags price, if supermarkets lack enough plastic bag number supplies, then they need to increase food price, even the supermarket may lose customers , if it can not supply plastic bags to let them to use the supermarket itself plastic bags to carry fruits, ,ilk, soft drinks conveniently. Hence, plastic bag material may be one kind of important natureal resource for supermarkets, because any one consumer may be influenced to choose another supermarket when he/she feels the another supermarket can supply plastic bags to let him/her to carry on fruits, milks, soft drinks conveniently.

Another kind of natureal resource , such as steel material for restaurants , steel material can help global restaurants to manufacture kniefs, glass sups for restaurants customers to eat food or drink , if much steels are used to manufactured cars product to satisfy car drivers‘ driving lesiure need , then it may also influence restaurants s’ knieves, glass cups price increases, due to cost increase, restaurants need to increase food price to compensate its knief, glass cups price. even, many families feel need to buy many gloass cups to drink water, then it may also influence global glass cups price increase. If one day steel material is shortage , this kind of natural resource must influence restaurants glass cups , knief cost increases. So, their general food price may be influenced to increase. It is not fair to global restaurants food consumers.

Hence, it explains resource shortage may influence some kinds of business cost increases, as well as consumer foods, products services price increases. It means that " resource shortage may influence some kinds of businesses cost increases".

In fact, in our societies, natural resource shortage may influence any kinds of business cost increases, w.g. car manufacturing industry, if one day stell manufacturing material is shortage. it will cause many car manufacturers can not buy enough steels to manufacture cars. When, global car buyers number increases, but global cars number can not increase rapidly, due to steel material can not supply enough. Then, cars prices may be influenced to raise. SO, it seems that steel resource shortage may bring reasonable chance to let global car manufacturers to raise cars prices. When , global car buyes ‘ new car purchase needs are increasing, hence, natural resource shortage may influence some kinds of business produce prices increase in possible, when the kind of product , such as many people begin to chose to buy new cars, more than second hand cars. The, when steel material supplies shortage, it may influence new car price increases in global can market.It means that any organizations ought not waste natural resource. Otherwise, it may influence their cost increases.

Environmental resource scarcity would likely have been adaptivve in the human evolitionary parst, resources in the environment and organization resource shortage problem might alsoo effect how satisfied they were. Hence, organizations in virtually every industry face the challenge of new managing resources effectively. The influence would run the other way instability as rival, such as big data platforms for e-commerce organizations, e.g. e-book publishers, online sellers. Big data platforms lift limitations on the size of computing resources that can be applied for data, in other words, data storage and e-commerce organizations can significantly influence computing efficiency.

Hence, organizational resources may also influence computer industry information gathering intangible resources, if the electronic books publish, or online electronic commerce product sellers can gather the most up-date consumer individual purchase behavioral data in short time daily rapidly. Then, they collect the most accurate electronic books readers or the kind of online product buyers past purchase choice in order to judge whether which topics of books are the most popular or which kinds of product to the most popular to let them to implement sale strategy, e.g. whether which topic of e-books prices need to be increased ot decreased, whether which kinds of products prices need to be increases or decreased. So, the big data gathering speed is the technology resource to e-commerce market organizations.

How to implement effective intangible resources management strategy to achieve performance improvement to Amazon e-commerce organization? Why does non intangible resources effective negligence management to Amazon organization, it will cause worse performance to Amazon e-commerce organization any one e-buyer?

One efficient organization must need have efficient and effective resources management strategy in order to provide enough resources for its organization overall different departments cooperation effectively and efficiently. How to implement effective resources management strategy to achieve performance improvement? Why does ersources shortage to organization, it will cause worse performance? I shall explain the reasons as below:

For Amazon e-commerce organization example, it is one global the most large goods transport delivery service moddleman role between global online customers and their product salespeople. Amazon owns its webstores, so global any one country buyer clicks to its different countries webstores , then he/she can choose any kinds of products to buy from Amazon any one country webstore. However, the product is owned the another seller. So, any products are not owned by from Amazon any one country webstores. However, the product is owned by the another seller. SO, any products are not owned by Amazon. It only provides webstores to let global any one e-buyer to buy the product after he/she has paid visa payment. So, Amazon's role is one middleman. It needs to provide goods transport service to help the product's seller to deliver the product to whose e-buyer individual hoime in the most short time, e.g. when one China e-buyer clicks to Amazon China webstore , after he chooses any brands of computers product from Amazon China webstore, he makes purchase of the brand of comouter decision. Then, he needs to pay visa to Amazon 's China webstore . When Amazon confirms that ie can accept payment by the China e-buyer's visa. Then, Amazon will deliver the product to the China e-buyer's home within one week or longer time, the delivery days time depends on how much delivery fee, the China's e-buyer , he can pay. So, Amazon only can receive commision infomr from the computer brand product seller. Because Amazon can build famous loyalty of rapid goods delivery service provider barnad and its different countries websites can provide above one million different kinds of brand products to let global different conuntries e0buyers to choose in order to make the most fair and the most reasonable purchase price decision from its different Amazon different countries webstores per day. So, Amazon can help its different countries sellers to apply Amazon itself unique different countries' websotes design to attract global many different countries e-buyers to click to Amazon's webstores to find any kinds of products to choose to buy conveniently.

So, such as Amazon e-commerce organization case, if it hopes to attract global different countries e-buyers prefer to click to Amazon itself any one webstore more than other firms themselves webstores . Then, it must need have enough resources (tangible and intangible) both in order to provide raoid goods delviery service and many different kinds of goods choice provision service and reasonable price consumption channel to let any one countrye-buyer feels confidence and safe payment transaction and enough product advertisement, photo, price, function information in order to make final purchase decision from Amazon itself different country webstores more easily.

Hence, the tangible and intangible resources are needed to supuply to Amazon e-commerce organization. They may include: Product photos, price information, product advertisement which are shown to Amazon's different countries webstores , enough online customer service enquiry employees number, enough computers number, enough computers number, different countries offices and warehouses number, computers, internnet technology etc. tangible resource as well as customer service enquiries feedbacks, global rapid goods delivery transport service to any one country e-buyer's home, safe e-payment channel, providing to buy global any one country sellers their products in the most reasonable and the most fair purchase transaction. All ot these issues are any one e-buyer individual purchase feeling to Amazon. SO, they are intangibel (non-tangible) resources to Amazon. It means that if Amazon can let global any one e-buyer feels it's e-purchase service provision can let they feel more satisfactory , then they will choose to buy Amazon webstores any kinds of products more than other sellers their webstores products, because Amazon webstores can provide the kind of product of different brands choice, it aims to compare whether which brand's price is unreasonable too high or which brand's product's quality is worse, or design is not very atrraction. So, Amazon's intangibale resource, such as rapid goods delivery service, online or phone customer enquiry service, webstores' products information whether e-buyers can feel satisfactory, e.g. reasonable price, clear product photo many different kinds of brands product choice. All of these intangible resources to Amazon, they may also influence Amazon's future e-buyer number absolutely.

How can Amazon raise intangible resource number to be effective?

SO, I explain that Amazon hadboth kinds of resources. They may include tangible and intangible resources. Internet speed, whether it is intangible resources. Internet speed, whether it is rapid or slow to satisfy global e-buyers online purchase speed and non online traffic jam accidents feeling. Amazon webstores any brands of products, photos, price information images whether they are clear to let any one global ebuyer to feel when they click to Amazon any one webstores. All of these internet technology resources to Amazon any one webstore will influence Amazon e-commerce organization's e-buyers number will increase or decrease . For example, if Amazon's China webstore can not let Chinese e-buyers to feel that it can not provide different kinds of brand products photos' clear image to let any one Chinese e-buyer to see the product photo clearly. When one Chinese e-buyer clicks to Amazon Chinese webstore to find any brands of laptop products to prepare to choose one to buy. But when he clicks to Amazon China webstore, he can not feel any one brand of laptop's photo is clear to let he feels. Then, theser unclear laptop photos may influence the Chinese e-buyer forgets his laptop purchase decision from Amazon 's China webstore easily. He may clcik to the another brand of laptop seller webstore to buy the brand of laptop from the laptop seller itself webstore. SO, Amazon's webstore design may be the important intangible resource to influence global any one e-buyer's visiting Amazon's any one webstore times or reducing to do to choose to visit Amazon's webstore behavior , due to they do not click to Amazon any one webstore websites again.

I recommend that Amazon ought consider how to design its any countries webstores in order to attract global e-buyers visiting Amazon itself webstores times number increase. So, global e-buyers' visiting Amazon different countries webstores times which will be Amazon's most important intangible resources to cause its future global e-buyers number. This kind of intangible resources may help Amazon e-commerce goods delivery service organization to raise its competitive effort,, because when one country's ebuyer feels Amazon can provide the most attraction and fair purchase channel from its different countries webstores. Then, the country's e-buyer will talk to his friends, families to prefer to choose Amazon if they have online purchase desire. Because Amazon's any one e-buyer , he .she will persduade his/her friends, families to choose Amazon's e-purchase channel., if he feels it can provide excellent e-purchase method to satisfy his online purchase need. Consequently, Amazon's e-buyers number may be influenced to increase.

ON conclusion, such as Amazon case, how to decide its whether which is the most important tangible and/or intangible resources in order to raise competition effort. It depends on whether how the seller sells its product, in order to concentrate on spending to increase the kind of resources number, such as Amazon e-commerce goods sale and delivery service organization case, internet webstores design intangible image dissatisfactory or satisfactory feeling which may be the most influential global e-buyers number increases or decreases. Moreover, Amazon's internet webstores design intangible satisfactory or dissatisfactory feeling resource may also influence e-buyer before or after e-purchase service requiry feedback feeling, safe visa card payment feeling, fair and reasonable brands of products price information and different brands of product photos image seeing satisfactory or dissatisfactory feeling , they are intangible resource asset to Amazon when global any one ebuyer must need to click to its any one webstore to find its any kinds of product to make purchase decision. So, any organizations must need to spend limit money to support its the most influential intangible resource , instead of tangible resources in order to increase clients number. On conclusion, we can increase organizational resources on these several aspects: Organizational resources are all assets that are available to a firm for use during the production process or service process, such as Amazon ecommerce organization case. The four basic types of organization resources are human, monetary, raw materials may be tangible, but internet technology may be another intangible resource to today any organizations. Improving organizational resources aim to improve efficiency, it means as the ability to accomplish something with the least amout of wasted time, money and effort or performance as well as effectiveness, such as improving internet speed, and none online traffic jam accidents occurrence easily. It means as trhe degree to which something is successful in producing a desired result success. However, we can improve resources by these way, they may include : Review who manages resources within the organization, build an-up-to date knowledge raise and company wide resource pool, manage the resource pool in line with the market, focus on education and talent employees growth, keep the customers in mind, work on quality services or products, learn to use technology , such as Amazon needs to learn how to raise high speed internet service for its webstores, and avoid online traffic jam frequent occurrent to its any one country webstore.

To sum up effective resource management strategy can help any organizations to increase resource number. Resource management is acquiring , allocating and managing the reosources, such as individuals, and their skills, finances, technology , material , machinery, and natural resources required for a project. Hence effective effective resource management strategy ensures that internal and external resources are used effectively on time and budget, resources may be obtained internally from the host organization or procured from external resources. SO, effective resource management can help organizations to save resources being wastes and finances being spend on the wrong things, a significant cost saving factor. Hence, such as Amazon e-commerce organization, it needs to know how to learn how to apply internet technology to improve its different countries webstores design, shorten goods transport delivery time, gathering more different brands of product prices, data and phoducts photos improving safe visa card transaction secret to increase e-buyer individual e-purchase confidence. When Amazon can concentrate on effective allocate limited resource to achiev ethese objectives. Then, its global e-buyer number may increase significantly.

Organization tangible and intangible resources function

Any organizations must have tangible and intangible resources. Tangible resources may include: Staffs, lands, equipment, producing machines, factory etc. They may help organizations to produce products or provide services to earn profit, e.g. one shop may be the firm's tangible assets if it can be designed to be the best and provide soft music to let customers to listen and provide clourful light design , they may influence they to bring happy consumption emotion in order to attract many customers to stay long time in the shop and increases shopping chance, the salespeople (staffs) to attract more customers , they may be influenced to feel enjoy to stay long long time by their services. Although, any customers visit any shops , it must not represent that they quarantee to buy any things before they leave the shop. However, I beleive that any business , their products functions and prices is one influential factor to persuade consumers to do shopping activities, their shop design attraction feeling may be also another main factor to persuade them to do shopping decision because when the consumer feels the shop is comfortable , it will cause he/she feels enjoyable to stay long time in the shop. Consequently, shop design attraction may be another influential intangible resource factor to encourage consumers to buy any things easily, if they can be influenced to stay long time in the shop by the ship design attraction. It is one kind of feeling factor to excite consumers to do shopping decision. SO, shop may be one important organization fixed asset resource to influence consumer individual purchase desire in any business environment. It is one good exmaple organizational tangible fixed asset redsource to help any organizations to create income.

The another kind of intangible resources, they are not seen by any customers and they can not be toughed by any customers. BUt they are organizational resources, they also may help any organizations to earn income. Why can intangible resource help organizations to earn income? I shall explain as below:
Customer services and staff skills, they may be organiztional intangible resources and they may help any organizations to create income. For example, when one shop has one kindly and friendly salespeople, when any one customer enters this shop, he will say" Good morning", " Good afternoon", "Good night" and when the customer leaves this shop, he will say " Goodby". Even, when the customer has not bought any thing till to leave this shop, this salesperson also speaks " Goodby". So, all of shop visitors, when the salesperson sees them, he must speaks above words, so any one must feel he is polite person and he can represents this shop's polite image also. Although, some shop visitors do not buy anything when they are staying in this shop, but they must feel that this salesperson's attitude is polite to let them to feel. THis salesperson can bring happy feeling to let all shop visitors feel. So, he must not be complainted easily, because when this salesperson discovers any one person is staying to close to any one producg shelf location in the shop, he will walk to the person to enquire him" DO you need I help you?" politely. Although, it is possible that this person won't need this salesperson to help him, but this salesperson can let this shop visitor to feel that he does not need find any one salesperson to enquire when he feels that he needs purchase help, e.g. whether the shirt has small size stock, or the shoe has organge colour etc. product information enquiries. SO, this salesperson can let this shop visitor feels he can take care to his purchase choice behavior and he can do and purchase help in this shop any time. So, this salesperson , his excellent service performance can let any one shop visitor feels service satisfaction, instead of his essential sale customer service performance. IN fact, this salesperson may let many shop visitors to feel that he does not only considerate whether whom is his real customer in order to enquire any purchase help. The non purchase plan shop visitors may also feel his kindly customer service help during they are staying in shop any time. So, this salesperson's polite and kindly customer service attitude may influence many non purchase planning shop visitors feel happy to see him in this shop. Consequently, it explains why salespeople excellent customer service performance which may help any businesses to increase customers number. It may be one kind of intangible organization resource to any organizations. I mean that when the shop can train many salespeople to raise customer service sale performance improvement.
Overall, these excellent customer service salespeople mus thelp this business to increase customer number easily, because this shop's all salespeople thier positive emotion may influence any one shop visitor feels enjoyment when they can feel they are taking care to their purchase choice need when they are staying in this shop any time. So, the minute, that the shop visitor does not plan to choose to buy any kinds of products, it does not represent that he does not plan to choose to buy any kinds of products next minute. So, any salespeople their excellent customer service performance may influence any one shop visitor to do purchase planning decision any minute. It seems that " salespeople customer service performance feeling" may be one kind of long time intangible resource to help any businesses to earn income in possible. Hence, it explains that any organizations must have tangible and intangible organizational resources to assist them to develop their businesses in long time success. They are essential elelments to influence whether the business's customers number can increase or decrease.
For computer sale business example, its tangible resource may be computer shop and intangible resource may be computer salespeople skills, because if any visitors feel this computer shop's computer desktop or laptop products can be putted in the right and easy seeking locations on any shelves, e.g. the low range price of laptops or desktops are putted on the lowest shelf position as well as the high range price of laptops or desktops are putted on the highest shelf position. So, when the planning purchase of desktop or laptop shop visitors may compare the different design of laptops or desktops their low range price or their high and low shelves locations easily. So, laptops and desktops putting on shelves position, they may influence any one desktop or laptop buyer individual final purchase choice decision. If the laptop planning purchase visitor, he plans to buy one low price of laptop, when he discovers there are all low range price of laptops are putting on the shelf loe position. Then , he may feel convenience to choose any one kind of low price of laptop design products from the lowest range shelf location easily. So, computer shops' computer putting shelves positions may be one kind tangible resource factor to influence any one computer buyer to choose any one kind of design of laptop or desktop priduct convenience. Their computer product choice time whether it is

long or short may influence their final computer purchase decision. Hence, the shop's computers ' putting on shelves positions may be one essential tangible resources to influence any one computer visitor to do purchase decision.

The computer shop salespeople computer knowledge may be another intangible factor to influence any one computer buyer decision. For example, when one planning laptop purchaser wants to know whether the laptop's any function, if he enquiries to the computer salesperson, he ften let him to feel that his explanation can not satisfy his any enquiries about the design of laptop product function knowledge, e.g. how to set up password for this computer privacy. If the computer salesperson lets the planning computer buyer to feel that he is difficult to teach him how to set up the passwrod for the computer to use. Then, the computer salesperson's innocence of computer password set up knowledge which may influence the planning computer buyers makes final non purchase decision to this computer, because his innocence can let him to feel this computer is difficult to set up password , if he is one foolish computer user.

Hence, this computer shop's all computer salespeople their computer knowledge, they may influence any one computer buyer final purchase decision. They must need to be trained to learn how to use any one new design of desktop or latop computer products before they are employed to be salespeople in this computer shop。 SO, their computer knowledge may be this computer shop's intangible resource to influence this computer shop's customers number to increase or decrease every day. Hence, decision on any organizational tangible and intangible resources to the organization, they depend on whether what kind of the business needs to sell what kinds of products.

The organization is where resources come together . Organizations use different resources to accompolish goals, e.g. human resources, financial resources, physical resources, and
information resources. SO, managers are responsible for managing the resources to accomplish goals. Organizational resources are all assets that are available to a firm for use during
the production process. The four basic types of organizational resources are human, monetary, raw material and capital. Managing organizational resources is the ability to understand and effectively manage organizational resources (e.e. people, materials assets , budget). This is demonstrated through measurement, planning and control of resources to maximize resources.

Company resources include tangible assets , such as its plant, equipment, finances, and location, human assets , in terms of the number of empllyees, their skills and motivation and intangible assets (such as technology, patents and copyrights, culture and reputation).

It brings this question: What makes organizational resource unique, in resource based view? Resources are available when they allow a firm to take advantage of opportunities or threats in its external environment. Many resources can either be immitated or substituted over time to any organizations. Hence, effectively managing resources helps companies more consistently deliver projects and services on time. This is because better resource management helps to improve insight into resources availability as well as improves timeline projections. Hence, the types of resources in management they may include: Human resource, natural resource, project resource, financial management, facility management, entertrise asset, public asset management.

ON conclusion, I believe that a company's most important resources may be human captial, such as talent employees, their technical knowledge may be intangible resource asset to help
the organization to develop its business in longf term success.

Internet will be intangible technology knowledge resource to e-commerce organization

New economy brings new way of resource management. The old loyalty and job security -based organization changes, organizations know that the assets are largely made up employees (HRM), but many new organizations begin to believe technology is important assets, such as Amazon is global ecommerce delivery service organization. It seems internet high technology is its important intangible resource to help it earn global e-buyers number increases . So , many organizations began to believe that technology will be important resource, such as internet can provide online business chance. With all the businesses are taking full advantage of internet, for example, the US department estimates that the value of retail e-commerce in 2000 year was about $25 billion, which represents less than 1% of US retail sales. Despite this, interest in e-business remains high.

Why internet may be main technology resource to organizations?

E-commere needs strategy in order to win competitors, questions include: What criteria do customers use to choose between our firms and competitors? How do the best employees decision whether to join? What business environment attracts and keeps the best suppliers making with our firms? What characteristics draw the most royal invesdtors to our firms? e.g. Amazon . com's web site and Wal-mart's can apply internet technology resource to create each e-store to let e-buyers to choose any kinds of products to buy athome conveniently. Hence, internet technology, even future other kinds of new technology may be main technology resources to organizations, when they can help organizations to raise sale competitive effort.

I mean that digital economy will be one kind new digital resource to future any organizations. The essential piece is the knowledge, it is what give it life and what makes it an interesting and fulifulling purchase and sale channel for people to spend their time , such as e-commerce virtual organization may be leaded to let purchase and ale transactions carry on easily from online websites. Hence, internet may be main knowledge management (intellectual capital) resource to any e-commerce organizations. It is about the storage, transfer knowledge.

For Amazon publish example, e-books will be knowledge as an object, like a book in library. Amazon can apply internet technology to help it to sell any author's ebooks from its book estores. So, ebooks are Amazon's knowledge resources to help it to create readers incomes. E-books is intangible knowledge resource to Amazon . Any authors' paper and ebooks will be sold cheap price to help Amazon to attract global readers to choose to buy its ebooks from its different countries e-webstores at home conveniently.

Hence, any e-commerce organizations also need HRM (emanagers) to help them to deliver a superior value (world class capabilities) in both te virtual and physical world. E-management will be another main human resources to e-commerce organizations. Why does e-management will be future main HRM resource to e-commerce organization? The reasons may include:

E-management demands in sort of managerial/e-commerce sale strategy effort, skills at positioning the firm within a networm of industries, e-management also demands the ability to see how the firm fits into a value creation-e-management is different because doing it work requires the e-engineering of business eco-systems, e-management demands the ability to be connected to thousands of inputs about specific changes among many industry participants , such as suppliers , customers, employees, competitors, media and shareholders.

Effective e-management requires the ability to monitor developments that can change with unusually high frequency. However, it is also essential that e-managers distinguish between the few meaningful inputs and the many inputs that have limited significance, ability to sustain organizational change, effectie e-managers monitor changes in their markets. So, instead of e-commerce organizations need to employ talent e-managment staffs to help them to manage overall e-commerce organizations. E-leading staffs (HRM) is another main HRM need. E-leaders need to know how to design online brochures, e.g. online brochures simply involved putting a company's market materials on the web. in order to attract or persuade online buyers visit its websites and choose the most right price of product to buy easily. E-leaders need to lead front-office transactions which involved putting customer facing customers , such as placing on order on the web when leaving back-office activities, such as order fulfillment unchanged.

E-leaders also need to integrate online online purchase transactions in which a firm actually linked its front -office and back -office systems and processes in a fashion, e.g. most companies have developed online brochures , in order to let online advertisement tool to attract e-buyer individual purchase choice from its webstores. Hence, future any e-commerce organizations must need (HRM (e-leaders and e-managers) to help them to bring innovation in order to achieve maximize profit aim. So, internet webstores, e-leaders , e-managers may be future e-commerce organization main resources. So, e-commerce organizations, manages are actors at three levels: In the front line , as entrepreneurs, in the middle , as facilitators, and integrators, at the top as institution builders.

Hence, future new economical society, it creates e-commerce organizations number increases, when consumers began to accept online purchase transaction activities. Hence, it causes e-commerce began to feel internet (e-webstores, e-leaders, e-managers), they will be the most influential resources (intangible knowledge managment and tangible URM both resourcees to influence their success or failure.

Why doe e-commerce organization believe (e-webstore design, e-leaders and e-managers) will be main organizational resources?

The most important question: It asks when e-buyers visit their webstores, wo are their target customers and shich needs of theirs are their trying to satisfy? For exap,e many airlines , e.g. American airlines, China airlines began to feel online e-tickets sale channel is more easily than paper ticket shop sale channel, because many air passengers began to accept e-ticket/online ticket purchase choice more than visiting airline shops . They feel that they do not want to waste time to visit airline shops. They like to pre-book to buy e-ticket to pay from the airline e-websote conveniently. Hence, e-webstore design knowledge management , e-leaders and e-management webstore management skill will be future any one e-commerce organizations their main tangible and intangible resources (assets) to help their e-commerce businesses development.

On conclusion, I believe that the current economy is not a high-tech economy or an internet economy, not an m-commerce economy , but instead customer econoomy. Customers need to gather with information and access, they are demanding, fair, global price, they are demanding that compares deal with them using the distribution channel , they choose manufacturing direct and through dealers and retailers. Base on those factors, they encourage future many e-commerce organizations cause organization change traditional resouce concept, such as land, capital equipment, tangible resource began to change to e-commerce organization's intangibel and tangible resource, such as knowledge management to e-online web store design skills, e-leaders and e-managers e-stores sale management strategy and e-buyer product research and brochure online advertisement design skill. All of these knowledge management skill will be future organizations' main resources to help them to create new economic competition effort.

In behavioral economic view , any organizations can attempt to apply behavioral economy method to use resources efficiently. Organizational excellence framework performance measurement takes a systematic approach . One of the most effective ways of using resources and minimizing that use of work. Calculating task cost in the most efficient economic method to help organizations to reduce cost and avoid resources waste, e.g. using resource management software, technology, planning and taking a systematic approach , which aims to manage the most efficient steps to follow to finish or implement each task in the most shor time as well as avoiding excess employees number.

Organizational resource efficiency means using the organization's limited resources in a sustainable manner when minimising impacts on the organization performance. It allows the organization to create more with less and to deliver greater value with less money. HR, raw material, technology input to carry on any organizational resources efficiently ? Management is the process of using organizational resources to achieve organizational goals of using organizational resources to achieve organizational goals effectively and efficiently through planning , organizing , leading and controlling. An efficient organization makes the most productive use of its resource in the most short time and the most eficiency and the least cost aspects.

What is efficient use of resources to any organizations in economics?

Economic efficiency implies an economic state in which every resource is optimially allocated to serve each individual or entity in the best way when minimizing waste and inefficiency. whan an economy is economically efficient, any changes made to assist one entity would harm another . Hence, budget how much spending on resources, e.g. employee saley, office and/or plant technological equipment facilities , before making resource expenditure spending decision. Budget is essnetial to help the organization to deduce resource using and excess purchase waste since budget and resource of organizations have interlock or interconnet relationship. If the organization can make exact udget, then it can avoid excess expenditure or waste resource to use. So, organizations need to acquire a talented resource pool , that can lead projects to success, when any kinds of resources are achieved to be supplied to use inn enough . For example, using an effective enterprise resource management system that delivers capabilities. Regardless of the approach and tools used, organizations must determine how to balance to use any kinds of resources efficiently. Thus, in organizational efficient resource using behavioral economy view, the organizational efficiency factor means that influences the efficiency of the organization's use if its resources can be both internal and external, e.g. how implementing strategic plans, they may include selecting what methods and resources to use, and leadning employees on guideline, working in coalitions with organizations around to deliver those needs in the most resource efficient way.

In organizational studies, resource managemetn is the efficient and one resource management technique of resource leveling, of finding the answers to the question, how to use available resource efficiently, effectively and economically ot organization resource expense. SO , resource management is the process of allocating resources and allocating.

What is meant by economic using of resource to organizations?

Economic resources are the factors used in producing goods or providing services. Economic resources can be divied into human resources, such as labors and management, and non humann resource, such as land, capital , goods, finished resources and technology , for example, natural resource is a key input in the production process that stimulates economic growth. Natural resources have limited direct economic use in satisfying human need, but transforming them into goods and services enhances their economic value to the socirty. So, if the country has many organizations know how to use their natural resources input in that production processes. Then, they can create themselves economic benefits directly and attribute economic benefit to society indirectly.

Thus, the types of economic organizations can be identified, there are subsistence recipreocal exchange with subsistence, peasant with primary reliance on self-produced food, but containing some exhange elements, market-commercial , redistribution or state socialist. Thus organizations need to learn hoe to use themselves organizational resources efficiently. Organizational resources are all assets that are to a firm for use during the production process. The four basic types of organizational resources are human, monetary, raw material and capital. Organizational resources are combined , used and transformed into finished products during the production process. So, a business that understands how to use resources efficiently. resource management is the process of allocating resources in order for a company to grow easily.

Organizational economic is used to study transactions within individual firms and determine management approach to managing resources. It is broken down into thee major subjects: agency theory, transaction cost economic and property rights theory. Agency theory is a priinciple that is used to explain and resolve issues in the relationship between business principles and their agents. Most commonly, that relationship is the one between shareholders as principles, and company executives as agents. Agency theory is used to understand the relationship between agents and principals. The agent represents the principal in a particular business transaction and is expected to represent the best interests of the principal without regard for seld interest. So, when the relationship between shreholders and company executives is kept the best.

Transaction cost economic is understood as alternative modes of organizing transactions (governance structure, such as markets, firms and bureaus) that mininize transactions costs. This, cost is the primary determinant of such as firm's decision whether it is the most right (the best) or the worst decision. It will influence the firm ho to spend resource behavior. The cost other than the money price that are incurred in trading good and service. SO, if the organization can often make the best decision to carry on any activites. It will avoid to waste resources efficiently. For example, if transaction cost influces the commission, paid to a stockbroker for completing a share deal and booking fee charges when purchase concert tickets. The cost of travel and time to complete an exhange , it means that transaction cost. So if the organization can make the best or the most reasonable decision to carry on any business activities. Then, its transaction cost can be influenced to reduce the most level in order to bring resources economic benefit. e.g. sunk costs are indpeendent of any event and should not resulting from economic trade in a market.

Property right theory means contracted choice, through ownership, property rights theour clarifies the firm's boundary choice. The maon egal property rights are the right of possession, the righ tof excession. So, for the efficiency of property rights al scarce resources are owned by someone. IN the right property rights approsed to the theory of the firm, I assume that in the case of sale ownership by party-property rights define the theoretical and legal ownership of resources and how resources can be used by organizatin. So, above three major organizational theories can assist organizations to know how to spend resources efficiently.

The relationship between organization resources using and social resources

Resources needers may include societies needers ,e.g. government house material householders , electricity , water , natural resources needers, schools, public houses , land number and area needs etc. as well as business organiztions , office building material, office, plant, land area, number need, equipment facilities limited number . So, when global office and plant business users need to buy more land, equipment materials etc. and electricity , water. Social resources number reduces to bring resourcee shortage challenge causes. Have they have shortage relationship (resource demand number is more than supply number) between social resources need and business resource need? I shall attempt to explain this question as below:

I assume global business organization number increases, they will need many natural resources, e.g. water, electricity, gas, land to supply for office, plant building , material and staff office electricity, gas, plant , office daily essential power need. So, when global business organizations number increases, they may need to use much raw material and natural resources for equipment facility, office plant building material, even day office, plant electricity , gas power, staff drinking water etc. basic office operational needs, when global business organizations number increase.

The question concerns whether they will cause natural resources shortage to supply to social need , when global business organizatins number increases. First, I shall explains what social resources needers mean as below:

Social resource are defined as any concrete or symbolic term that

can be used as an object of exchange among people (Foa & Foa, 1980), money, information, goods and services both tangible items , such as are ususally defined the assessment of social need is of central allocation between organization needers and social citizen needers both stakeholders. So, when global human birth rate and life time increases, population number will increase, then their social resources need are also increasing, if global organizaions and population number are increasing in the same time, due to earth natural resources has limit number to supply in order to satisfy organizations and families daily resources need, e.g. building material resources are used to build either to build offices, plants or private houses , public house, lands resources are used either to build private or public houses or offices , plants , water is supplied to either office staffs drinking or families drinking, electricity , gas resources are limited to supply either offices plants use or families private or public houses use. Hence, due to all of earth, but in the same time, global offices , plants, government organizations and families numbers both stakeholders number is continue increasing. They have possible to encounter natural resources shortage issue when natural resources are using much, but they can nt manufacturers to increase by human easily.

Can responding to resource scarcity help some kinds business grow?

Foe example, the food and agricultural business organizations, e.g. supermarkets, restaurants, they must send plactic material to manufacture plactic bags to supply to supermarket buyers to carry fruits, breads, mil, etc. foods when consumers need to buy the kinds of foods in any supermarkets, if plactic material supply number is decreasing, then a lot plactic bags can not supply to let buyers to carry their foods, due to plactic bags number is shortage , it will cause any supermarket buyers feel inconvenient when they need plactic bags to carry their foods, they choose to buy the kind of foods from supermarket to themselves homes.

So, if plactic bags manufacture material i shortage, it can not be manufactured to plactic bags to supply to global supermarket organizations. Then, the one supermarket can provide enough plactic bags to let them to carry their foods from supermarkets to themselves homes conveniently. The focus on plactic bag resource scareity is not impossible to occur to supermarket organization case. If families are often using plactic bag to carry rubbish daily at home. Then, plactic bags number can not increase to satisfy global supermarkets food plactic bags and families themselves homes rubbish plactic bags both stakeholders need. Plastic bags can not be manufactured to supply to manufacture lot plactic bags supply to satisfy global families rubbish plactic bags home users and supermarkets food plactic bas users needs. Consequently, plactic bags prices may be influenced to increases, when plactic bags demand increases, but supply decreases. It is one good exaple to explain why plactic bag manufacturered material supply decreases, it may influence plactic bags number decreases and price increases, because families home rubbish plactic bags and supermarket food plastic bags need both increase.

Consequence, supermarket cost may be influenced , due to plastic bags number also increase much, if one day shortage of plactic manufacturing material supply number is shortage. So, it seems that food plastis bags using number, they have close relationship to impact supermarket food plastic bags price, if supermarkets lack enough plastic bag number supplies, then they need to increase food price, even the supermarket may lose customers , if it can not supply plastic bags to let them to use the supermarket itself plastic bags to carry fruits, ,ilk, soft drinks conveniently. Hence, plastic bag material may be one kind of important natureal resource for supermarkets, because any one consumer may be influenced to choose another supermarket when he/she feels the another supermarket can supply plastic bags to let him/her to carry on fruits, milks, soft drinks conveniently.

Another kind of natureal resource , such as steel material for restaurants , steel material can help global restaurants to manufacture kniefs, glass sups for restaurants customers to eat food or drink , if much steels are used to manufactured cars product to satisfy car drivers' driving lesiure need , then it may also influence restaurants s' knieves, glass cups price increases, due to cost increase, restaurants need to increase food price to compensate its knief, glass cups price. even, many families feel need to buy many gloass cups to drink water, then it may also influence global glass cups price increase. If one day steel material is shortage , this kind of natural resource must influence restaurants glass cups , knief cost increases. So, their general food price may be influenced to increase. It is not fair to global restaurants food consumers.

Hence, it explains resource shortage may influence some kinds of business cost increases, as well as consumer foods, products services price increases. It means that " resource shortage may influence some kinds of businesses cost increases".

In fact, in our societies, natural resource shortage may influence any kinds of business cost increases, w.g. car manufacturing industry, if one day stell manufacturing material is shortage. it will cause many car manufacturers can not buy enough steels to manufacture cars. When, global car buyers number increases, but global cars number can not increase rapidly, due to steel material can not supply enough. Then, cars prices may be influenced to raise. SO, it seems that steel resource shortage may bring reasonable chance to let global car manufacturers to raise cars prices. When , global car buyes ' new car purchase needs are increasing, hence, natural resource shortage may influence some kinds of business produce prices increase in possible, when the kind of product , such as many people begin to chose to buy new cars, more than second hand cars. The, when steel material supplies shortage, it may influence new car price increases in global can market.It means that any organizations ought not waste natural resource. Otherwise, it may influence their cost increases.

Environmental resource scarcity would likely have been adaptivve in the human evolitionary parst, resources in the environment and organization resource shortage problem might alsoo effect how satisfied they were. Hence, organizations in virtually every industry face the challenge of new managing resources effectively. The influence would run the other way instability as rival, such as big data platforms for e-commerce organizations, e.g. e-book publishers, online sellers. Big data platforms lift limitations on the size of computing resources that can be applied for data, in other words, data storage and e-commerce organizations can significantly influence computing efficiency.

Hence, organizational resources may also influence computer industry information gathering intangible resources, if the electronic books publish, or online electronic commerce product sellers can gather the most up-date consumer individual purchase behavioral data in short time daily rapidly. Then, they collect the most accurate electronic books readers or the kind of online product buyers past purchase choice in order to judge whether which topics of books are the most popular or which kinds of product to the most popular to let them to implement sale strategy, e.g. whether which topic of e-books prices need to be increased ot decreased, whether which kinds of products prices need to be increases or decreased. So, the big data gathering speed is the technology resource to e-commerce market organizations.

How to implement effective intangible resources management strategy to achieve performance improvement to Amazon e-commerce organization? Why does non intangible resources effective negligence management to Amazon organization, it will cause worse performance to Amazon e-commerce organization any one e-buyer?

One efficient organization must need have efficient and effective resources management strategy in order to provide enough resources for its organization overall different departments cooperation effectively and efficiently. How to implement effective resources management strategy to achieve performance improvement? Why does ersources shortage to organization, it will cause worse performance? I shall explain the reasons as below:

For Amazon e-commerce organization example, it is one global the most large goods transport delivery service moddleman role between global online customers and their product salespeople. Amazon owns its webstores, so global any one country buyer clicks to its different countries webstores , then he/she can choose any kinds of products to buy from Amazon any one country webstore. However, the product is owned the another seller. So, any products are not owned by from Amazon any one country webstores. However, the product is owned by the another seller. SO, any products are not owned by Amazon. It only provides webstores to let global any one e-buyer to buy the product after he/she has paid visa payment. So, Amazon's role is one middleman. It needs to provide goods transport service to help the product's seller to deliver the product to whose e-buyer individual hoime in the most short time, e.g. when one China e-buyer clicks to Amazon China webstore , after he chooses any brands of computers product from Amazon China webstore, he makes purchase of the brand of comouter decision. Then, he needs to pay visa to Amazon 's China webstore . When Amazon confirms that ie can accept payment by the China e-buyer's visa. Then, Amazon will deliver the product to the China e-buyer's home within one week or longer time, the delivery days time depends on how much delivery fee, the China's e-buyer , he can pay. So, Amazon only can receive commision infomr from the computer brand product seller. Because Amazon can build famous loyalty of rapid goods delivery service provider barnad and its different countries websites can provide above one million different kinds of brand products to let global different conuntries e0buyers to choose in order to make the most fair and the most reasonable purchase price decision from its different Amazon different countries webstores per day. So, Amazon can help its different countries sellers to apply Amazon itself unique different countries' websotes design to attract global many different countries e-buyers to click to Amazon's webstores to find any kinds of products to choose to buy conveniently.

So, such as Amazon e-commerce organization case, if it hopes to attract global different countries e-buyers prefer to click to Amazon itself any one webstore more than other firms themselves webstores . Then, it must need have enough resources (tangible and intangible) both in order to provide raoid goods delviery service and many different kinds of goods choice provision service and reasonable price consumption channel to let any one countrye-buyer feels confidence and safe payment transaction and enough product advertisement, photo, price, function information in order to make final purchase decision from Amazon itself different country webstores more easily.

Hence, the tangible and intangible resources are needed to supuply to Amazon e-commerce organization. They may include: Product photos, price information, product advertisement which are shown to Amazon's different countries webstores , enough online customer service enquiry employees number, enough computers number, enough computers number, different countries offices and warehouses number, computers, internnet technology etc. tangible resource as well as customer service enquiries feedbacks, global rapid goods delivery transport service to any one country e-buyer's home, safe e-payment channel, providing to buy global any one country sellers their products in the most reasonable and the most fair purchase transaction. All ot these issues are any one e-buyer individual purchase feeling to Amazon. SO, they are intangibel (non-tangible) resources to Amazon. It means that if Amazon can let global any one e-buyer feels it's e-purchase service provision can let they feel more satisfactory , then they will choose to buy Amazon webstores any kinds of products more than other sellers their webstores products, because Amazon webstores can provide the kind of product of different brands choice, it aims to compare whether which brand's price is unreasonable too high or which brand's product's quality is worse, or design is not very atrraction. So, Amazon's intangibale resource, such as rapid goods delivery service, online or phone customer enquiry service, webstores' products information whether e-buyers can feel satisfactory, e.g. reasonable price, clear product photo many different kinds of brands product choice. All of these intangible resources to Amazon, they may also influence Amazon's future e-buyer number absolutely.

How can Amazon raise intangible resource number to be effective?

SO, I explain that Amazon hadboth kinds of resources. They may include tangible and intangible resources. Internet speed, whether it is intangible resources. Internet speed, whether it is rapid or slow to satisfy global e-buyers online purchase speed and non online traffic jam accidents feeling. Amazon webstores any brands of products, photos, price information images whether they are clear to let any one global ebuyer to feel when they click to Amazon any one webstores. All of these internet technology resources to Amazon any one webstore will influence Amazon e-commerce organization's e-buyers number will increase or decrease . For example, if Amazon's China webstore can not let Chinese e-buyers to feel that it can not provide different kinds of brand products photos' clear image to let any one Chinese e-buyer to see the product photo clearly. When one Chinese e-buyer clicks to Amazon Chinese webstore to find any brands of laptop products to prepare to choose one to buy. But when he clicks to Amazon China webstore, he can not feel any one brand of laptop's photo is clear to let he feels. Then, theser unclear laptop photos may influence the Chinese e-buyer forgets his laptop purchase decision from Amazon 's China webstore easily. He may clcik to the another brand of laptop seller webstore to buy the brand of laptop from the laptop seller itself webstore. SO, Amazon's webstore design may be the important intangible resource to influence global any one e-buyer's visiting Amazon's any one webstore times or reducing to do to choose to visit Amazon's webstore behavior , due to they do not click to Amazon any one webstore websites again.

I recommend that Amazon ought consider how to design its any countries webstores in order to attract global e-buyers visiting Amazon itself webstores times number increase. So, global e-buyers' visiting Amazon different countries webstores times which will be Amazon's most important intangible resources to cause its future global e-buyers number. This kind of intangible resources may help Amazon e-commerce goods delivery service organization to raise its competitive effort,, because when one country's ebuyer feels Amazon can provide the most attraction and fair purchase channel from its different countries webstores. Then, the country's e-buyer will talk to his friends, families to prefer to choose Amazon if they have online purchase desire. Because Amazon's any one e-buyer , he .she will persduade his/her friends, families to choose Amazon's e-purchase channel., if he feels it can provide excellent e-purchase method to satisfy his online purchase need. Consequently, Amazon's e-buyers number may be influenced to increase.

ON conclusion, such as Amazon case, how to decide its whether which is the most important tangible and/or intangible resources in order to raise competition effort. It depends on whether how the seller sells its product, in order to concentrate on spending to increase the kind of resources number, such as Amazon e-commerce goods sale and delivery service organization case, internet webstores design intangible image dissatisfactory or satisfactory feeling which may be the most influential global e-buyers number increases or decreases. Moreover, Amazon's internet webstores design intangible satisfactory or dissatisfactory feeling resource may also influence e-buyer before or after e-purchase service requiry feedback feeling, safe visa card payment feeling, fair and reasonable brands of products price information and different brands of product photos image seeing satisfactory or dissatisfactory feeling , they are intangible resource asset to Amazon when global any one ebuyer must need to click to its any one webstore to find its any kinds of product to make purchase decision. So, any organizations must need to spend limit money to support its the most influential intangible resource , instead of tangible resources in order to increase clients number.

On conclusion, we can increase organizational resources on these several aspects: Organizational resources are all assets that are available to a firm for use during the production process or service process, such as Amazon ecommerce organization case. The four basic types of organization resources are human, monetary, raw materials may be tangible, but internet technology may be another intangible resource to today any organizations. Improving organizational resources aim to improve efficiency, it means as the ability to accomplish something with the least amout of wasted time, money and effort or performance as well as effectiveness, such as improving internet speed, and none online traffic jam accidents occurrence easily. It means as trhe degree to which something is successful in producing a desired result success. However, we can improve resources by these way, they may include : Review who manages resources within the organization, build an-up-to date knowledge raise and company wide resource pool, manage the resource pool in line with the market, focus on education and talent employees growth, keep the customers in mind, work on quality services or products, learn to use technology , such as Amazon needs to learn how to raise high speed internet service for its webstores, and avoid online traffic jam frequent occurrent to its any one country webstore.

To sum up effective resource management strategy can help any organizations to increase resource number. Resource management is acquiring , allocating and managing the reosurces, such as individuals, and their skills, finances, technology , material , machinery, and natural resources required for a project. Hence effective effective resource management strategy ensures that internal and external resources are used effectively on time and budget, resources may be obtained internally from the host organization or procured from external resources. SO, effective resource management can help organizations to save resources being wastes and finances being spend on the wrong things, a significant cost saving factor. Hence, such as Amazon e-commerce organization, it needs to know how to learn how to apply internet technology to improve its different countries webstores design, shorten goods transport delivery time, gathering more different brands of product prices, data and phoducts photos improving safe visa card transaction secret to increase e-buyer individual e-purchase confidence. When Amazon can concentrate on effective allocate limited resource to achiev ethese objectives. Then, its global e-buyer number may increase significantly.

(AI) - driven automation industry development how to influence work nature change

On positive benefit hand, it is possible that (AI) -driven automation industry will create wealth and expand economy growth to any countries, but it will be accompanied by changed in the skills that workers need to learn, if the low skill workers expect to avoid unemployment threat when (AI) technology can replace their jobs in future one day. Thus, it is possible that (AI) technology will also bring negative influence to cause low skill worker unemployment challenge in the applied (AI) technology countries.

For the low skill worker unemploment reason, it is because that one of main ways that technology increases productivity is by decreasing the number of labor hours needed to create a unit of output. It implies (AI) technology will influence low educated and low skillful labor number to be decreased (reduction employment number).

Will (AI) bring benefits to the employers? In contrast, technological change tended to work in a different direction throughout the nowadays. The advance of computer and the internet raised the relative productivity of higher skilled workers. So, routine-intensive occupations that focused on predictable tasks disappearance, such as switch board, operators, filming checkers, travel agents and assembling line workers etc. were particularly replaced by new technologies. However, today, it may be challenging to predict exactly which jobs will be most immediately affected by (AI) driven-automation. The reason is because (AI) is not a single technology, but rather a collection of technologies that are felt unevenly through the economy to influence job changing both negatively and positively.

In positively view point, (AI) driven-automation will make many workers more productive and increase demand for certain skills. Consequently, new jobs are likely to be directly create in areas , such as the development and supervision of (AI) as well as indirectly created in a range of areas throughout the economy as higher incomes lead to expanded demand. So, (AI) will bring macro economy advantages in possible.

Otherwise, in negatively view point, many traditional human needed (demand) skillful jobs will be threatened by automation are highly concentrated among lower-paid, lower-skilled and less -educated workers. It means automation will cause pressure on demand for this group, pressure and employment, if (AI) can replace the low skilled and less educated workers‘ jobs. Thus, (AI) will have negative influence to impact on the labor market.

(AI) capabilities will enable automation of some tasks that have long required human labor. Can (AI) replace some simple human jobs? If (AI) can replace some simple human jobs, then it is possible to cause unemployment if employers applied (AI) machines to replace the low skill workers to do their simple jobs in future one day. For example, advances in robotics are expanding machines’ abilities to interact with and sharp the physical world. Combined , (AI) and robotics will give rise to smarter machines that can perform more sophisticated functions than ever before and brings more advantages that humans have exercised. This will permit automation of many tasks now performed by human workers and could change the shape of the labor market and human activity. It depends on whether employers choose to reduce all worker numbers to be replaced by (AI) machines or employers choose to apply (AI) machines to assist the low skillful workers to work more efficient or raise performance and productivities. If future employers apply (AI) machines to assist workers to raise performance and efficiency, then the unemployment challenge won’t cause, due to the number of worker won’t reduce. But if employers decide to unemploy all low skillful workers and they are replaced by (AI) machines, then the unemployment challenge will cause in possible.

How (AI) influences labor market

Today, it may be challenging to predict exactly which jobs will be most immediately affected by (AI)-driven automation. Because (AI) is not a single technology, but rather a collection of technologies that are applied to specific tasks.

Some specific predictions are possible based on the current (AI) technology. For example, driving jobs and house cleaning jobs, bank counter service jobs, telephone enquiry service operators. Restaurant cooking jobs, simple accounting record service jobs etc. that require relatively less education to perform. Advancements in computer vision and related technologies have made the feasibility of fully appear more likely, potentially displacing some workers in driving-dominant professions. Seemingly similar robot, for which the operational tasks is less specific of navigating to a specific destination when following a set of given rules and preserving safety.

In the future, the effects of (AI) on the labor market in the decade ahead will continue the trend toward skill-biased change that computerization and communication innovations have driven in recent decades. Thus, some human driving occupation will be disappeared or replaced by (AI) automation driven. For example, bus drivers, light truck or delivery services drivers, heavy and tractor-trailer truck drivers, school drivers, tax drivers, travel bus drivers.

However, (AI) technology could enable some workers to focus time on other job responsibilities, boosting their productivity, and actually raised wage growth among those still holding the reshaped jobs. For example, salespeople, who currently spend a considerable amount of time driving could find themselves able to do other work when a car drives them from place to place, or inspectors and appraisers could fill out paperwork, when their car drives itself. This (AI) -driven technology should make these workers more productive, with (AI) -driven technology serving as a complement, not a substitute. New jobs will also likely be created, both in existing occupations cheaper transportation costs with lower prices and increase demand for products and all the related occupations, such as service and fulfillment, and in new occupations not currently foreseeable.

What kind of jobs will be created by (AI) technology? Predicting future job growth is extremely difficult, due to it depends on technologies or substitute for existing today as well as they may complement or substitute for existing human skills and jobs. However, (AI) will also lead to substantial indirect job creation to the degree it raises productivity and wages, it may also lead to higher consumption that would support additional jobs from high-end draft production to restaurant and retail. The future(AI) " augmented intelligence", the technology's role is as assisting and expanding the productivity of individuals rather than replacing human work. Thus, based on the biased-technical change framework, demand for labor will likely increase the most in the areas where humans complement (AI) automation technologies. For example, (AI) technology , such as IBM's Watson may improve early detection of some cancers or other illnesses, but a human healthcare professional is needed to work with patients to understand and translate patients' symptoms, inform patients of treatment options, and guide patients through treatment plans. Shipping companies may also partner workers who pick up and deliver products over the last feet with (AI) enabled autonomous vehicles that move workers efficiently from site to site. In such cases, (AI) augments what a human is able to do and allows individuals to either be move effective in their specially task or to operate on a larger scale. Thus, it seems (AI) technology will also create new jobs, raise productivities and workers' efficiencies.

Redefining management in
the workforce of artificial intelligence

Change management

(AI) will influence office administrative efficieny to be raised. In the future, due to artificial intelligence influences to some kind of human jobs nature. So, the kind of human jobs of management methods will also need to change to adapt the artificial intelligence technology input to their organizations. It will cause challenges for every executive and manager if who won't have effort to manage their teams how to apply artificial intelligence technology to work efficiently and easily. For example, division of labor will change among humans and machines will increase. Thus, companies will have to adapt their training performance and talent strategies how to emphasize on work that how to make human judgment and skills and experimentation. Thus, (IA)'s greatest impact will be on administrative coordination and control tasks, such as scheduling , resource allocation.

In fact, mangers will encounter this challenges: How to apply human experience and expertise to judge critical business decisions and practices when the information available is insufficient to suggest a successful course of action? Due to this kind of work will require new skills and mindsets. I shall indicate these change management methods to adapt (AI) technology. Such as: administration and routine tasks, scheduling , allocation of resources and reporting will fall within the intelligence machines, responsibilities that have long been reserved for humans. For example, a typical store manager or a lead nurse at a nursing home most constantly arrange shift schedules, accounting for staff members' absences owing to illness, vacation time or sudden departures.

Thus, the managers need to learn how to arrange new division of labor within the organizations after (AI) technology had been implemented to the organization. Artificial intelligence is currently influencing into once considered exclusive to humans: assessing and acting on human emotions and personality traits. The influences to managers need to change their strategies to adapt (AI) technology implements include such as below:

Firstly, managers need to spend the bulk of their time on coordination and control tasks from intelligent system implements. Their time spending on these major three aspects from impact of intelligent system: coordinate and control, solve problems and collaborate and people and community , strategy and innovation three aspects. Thus (AI) will influence managers need to change their judgment method to teach whose teams how to adapt the (AI) system operations in any organizations.

Secondly, (AI) will influence top, middle and low level management needs to change to adapt the (AI) technology operations to any owned (AI) technology organizations in the future. Intelligent machines must be trained in context. Just like humans , on-the-job training is a requirement for such machines because they typically arrive with only very general capabilities. To get the most from (AI), managers at all levels must participate in the instructional experience and in the learning process and provides managers' familiarity with such systems on these aspects, e.g. How the system works and generate advice, how the system has a proven track record , how the system provides convincing explanations , how the system can make simple rule- based decisions.

Thirdly, managers need to learn how to make judgment more accurate (AI) systems assistance. Although (AI) will invariably take on more routine work and even augment human decision-making, it won't judgment work, the application of human experience and expertise to critical business decisions when the information available is insufficient to suggest a successful course of action or reliable enough to suggest an obvious course of action. For a sense of the nature of judgment work, consider big data marketing and sales analytics. Such analytics often provide insights that can inform promotional campaigns, including predicting which promotions will generate desired sales brand further into the future, marketing executives need use judgment, combining analytics with their own and others' insight and experience.

The application of experience and expertise to critical business decisions and practice represents the real value of human judgment. But, when artificial intelligent machines are implemented to any organizations to assist the low, middle and top level management to make any business judgment. These forms of judgment work that managers can gather data interpretation, idea development more absolute from (AI) machine assistance. Thus, why these level management executives need to learn how to apply (AI) machines to help them to make any business judgment more accurate.

How (AI) influences organizational change

Consequently creative and social intelligence will be in even greater demand as (AI) makes in management and the workforce. This development will represent a long term trend in labor markets , one characterized by intensifying demand and reward for social skills with a growing desire for creative capabilities, managers will seek to fashion of ideas and hypotheses from inside and outside of the enterprise to shape solutions to their most pressing business problems. Thus, (AI) will influence overall organizational team members who have chance to participate any decision to make more accurate business judgment.

Many managers mistakenly view judgment work as only an individual discipline, failing to appreciate that it can also involve decide interpersonal and organizational practices. In more complex settings, judgment is typically a collective outcome of individuals' and teams' diverse perspectives, insights and experiences. And often , the resulting choices are better informed than decisions that an individual would have arrived at on his or her own.

Thus, when any organizations apply (AI) technology to assist managers to gather data and ideas to make any judgment. In these cases, organizations can create the conditions for effective collective judgment by establishing structures , such as " shadow advisory boards" that prompt managers and employees to source and synthesize multiple perspectives. Thus, a traditional organization (firm) might freshen its thinking is t put together a shadow advisory board, comprised of young, digital people who can apply (AI) machine assistance to make judgment work more accurate whether related to people development, problem-solving or strategizing and innovating for considerable degrees of creative and social intelligence.

Thus, on the one hand, (AI) technology machine augmentation and automation can give these advantages to human

(organization managers) , e.g. developing people and community, solving problems and collaborating, coordinating and controlling work, shaping strategy and leading innovation. Besides, on the other hand, the next generation managers need have these individual attitude to treat intelligent machines to be as colleagues.
When, judgment is a human skill, intelligent machines can accelerate human learning that supports it, assisting in data -driven simulations, scenarios and search and discovery activities. Focuses on judgment work, some decisions require insight beyond what data can tell them. This is the sweet sport for human judgment, the application of experience and expertise to critical business decisions and practices. Thus, managers will also need to find ways to learn how to use digital (AI) technologies to tap into the knowledge and judgment of partners, customer external stakeholders and role models in other industries after the (AI) machine had been implemented to the organization.

Future works change: Automation, employment
and productivity
How (AI) influences employment

Human future " micro to macro" industry trends will be affected business strategy and public policy by (AI) technology. In the future (AI) technology will influence those six themes: productivity and growth, natural resources, labor markets, the evolution of global financial markets, the economic impact of technology and innovation and urbanization. However, (AI) technology will bring economic benefits of tackling gender inequality, a new global competition, Chinese innovation and digital globalization.
Nowadays, advances in robotics artificial intelligence, and machine learning are in a new age of automation, as machines match or outperform human performance in a development to any countries. For example, automation of activities can enable businesses to improve performance by reducing errors and improving quality and speed, and in some cases achieving outcomes that go beyond human capabilities. For example, some research indicated automation could raise productivity growth globally by 0.8 to 1.4 % annually; more than 2,000 work activities across 800 occupations. When less than 5% of all occupations can be automated using demonstrated technologies about 60% of all occupations have at least 30% of constituent activities that could be automated. Many occupations will change that will be automated away: Activities most susceptible to automation involve physical activities, in highly structured and predictable environments, as well as the collection and processing of data. They are most prevalent in manufacturing , accommodation and food service and retail trade and include some middle-skill jobs. For example, such as natural language processing is a key factor. Beyond technical feasibility, the cost of technology competition with labor including skills and supply and demand dynamics, performance benefits including and beyond labor cost savings, and social and regulatory acceptance will be affected by (AI) automation technology. Thus, (AI) automation will impact to influence global employment in those aspects as below:
Firstly, assuming that people are displaced by automation will find other employment. The anticipated shift in the activities in the labor force is of a similar order as the long-term shift away from agriculture and decreases in manufacturing share of employment. Both of manufacturing and agriculture industries which would be accompanied by the creation of new types of work not foreseen at the time.
Secondly, for business, the performance benefits of automation are relatively clear. Thus, the businessmen have opportunities for their micro economies to benefits from the productivity growth potential and macro economies to benefit to encourage continued progress and innovation , investment and market incentives. At the same time, employers must innovate policies to help workers and institutions adapt to the impact on employment.
This will likely include rethinking education and training, income support and safety nets , as well as support for those dislocated, when employees need to leave themselves homes to move to other cities to learn new (AI) automation works. Thus, individuals in the workplace will need to engage move comprehensively with machines as part of their everyday activities, and acquire new skills that will be in demand in the new automation age. Consequently , the scale of shifts in the labor force over many decades that automation technologies can be a similar order to the long -term technology -enables shifts in the developed countries' workforces away from agriculture in the 21 th century. Those shifts did not result in long-term mass unemployment because they were accompanied by the creation of new types of work not foreseen at the time. However, human will still be needed in the workforce

when the total productivity gains are caused by (AI) technology.

What occupations will be influenced by (AI) technology.

In the future, scientists predict that these occupations will be influenced by (AI) technology mostly. They include : retail salespeople, food and beverage service workers, language or translation teachers, health practitioners. Since these work activities have a more relevant occupations are made up of a range of activities with different potential for (AI) automation . For example, a retail salesperson will spend more time interacting with customers, stocking shelves , or ringing up sales. Each of these activities is distinct and requires different capabilities to perform successfully.
Thus, these job activities have similar simple control characteristics. Simple activities include greet customers, answer questions about products and services, clean and maintain work areas, demonstrate product feature process sales and transactions. All these activities can have similar simple activities in order to (AI) machines can be learn how to do these activities from (AI) technology . For example, the capability perception includes sensory perception, cognitive capabilities, such as retrieving automation, recognizing known patterns(supervised learning), logical reasoning problem solving.
Thus, (AI) machine is such human, which has feeling and emotion, such as social and emotional sensing, judgement reasoning methods, natural language understanding and physical capabilities, such as mobility , navigation, gross motor skill, fine motor skills. It seems that the future, (AI) human invents machines which will have these human characteristics to do human similar behavioral job duties more easily and efficiently. It implies these above human occupations will be replaced by (AI) human invention machines in the future. Due to (AI) creation, it is possible to cause unemployment number of these above workers will increase because (AI) machines can do their similar job behavioral activities.
Consequently, employers won't need to employ many of these skillful labor. Otherwise, they can buy less number (AI) machines to attempt to do whose job activities more easily and efficiently. So, it seems (AI) machines will have more high work performance to replace these occupation workers' work performance. Finally, these occupation worker unemployment number will only increase when the (AI) machines had been invented to achieve to do their work behavioral activities absolutely success in the future.

Whether (A) technology machine labor
will replace human worker more or assist
human worker more

There is no single agreed definition of a robot how outcome of a task that is completed without human intervention. When some definitions require the task to be completed by a physical machine moves and respond to its environment, other definitions use the term robot in connection with tasks completed by software , without physical embodiment.
However, to answer the question : Whether (AI) technology machine labor will replace human worker more or assist human worker more. I shall indicate some examples to let readers to judge whether (AI) technology can create new jobs or reduce old jobs.
Firstly, I shall explain what (AI) function is. (AI) is a service robot that performs useful tasks for humans or equipment excluding industrial automation application . Thus, the classification of a robot into industrial robot or service robot is done according to its intended application. It is also a personal service robot or a service robot for personal used for a non commercial task, usually by lay persons . Examples are domestic servant robot, and pet exercising robot. It is also a professional service robot or a service robot for professional used for a commercial task, usually operated by a properly trained operator. Examples, are cleaning robot for public places, delivery robot in offices or hospitals, fire-fighting robot, rehabilitation robot and surgery robot in hospitals. Thus, these functions will be future (AI) application to our daily life necessaries or business necessaries.
However, some authors agree (AI) will bring negative outcomes of automation, due to raise competiveness, reduce human job nature. Otherwise, other authors argue (AI) will bring positive outcomes of automation, due to raise

productivities, job creation, assist humans work.

On the positive outcome hand, robots can increase productivity . This is particularly important for small-to medium sized businesses both are in developed and developing countries economies. It also enables large companies to increase their competitiveness through faster product development and delivery. Increased use of robot is also enabling companies in high cost countries to re shore, or bring back to their domestic base parts of the supply chain that will have previously outsourced to sources of cheaper labor. Currently , the greater threat to employment is not a automation, but an inability to remain competitive. Automation has led overall to an increase in labor demand and positive impact on wages. The reason is that the middle-income/middle-skilled jobs have reduced as a proportion of overall contribution to employment and earnings leading to fears of increasing income inequality, the skills range within the middle income bracket is large. Thus, robots are driving an increase in demand for workers at the higher -skilled and with a positive impact on wages. This issue is how to enable middle-income earners in the lower-income range to unskilled or retain. Finally, the (AI) positive impact supporter who argue the future will be robots and humans can work together.

However, on the negative outcome hand, robots can substitute labor activities, but don't replace jobs. They believe that less than 10% of jobs are fully automatable. Increasingly , robots are used to complement and augment labor activities, the net impact on jobs and the quality of work is positive. Automation can provide the opportunity for humans to focus on higher-skilled, higher-quality and higher-paid tasks. Robots can improve productivity when they are applied to tasks that which perform more efficiently and to a higher and more consistent level of quality than humans. For example, increased productivity is enabling some firms, such as Whirlpool, Caterpillar and Ford Motors company in the US restructure their supply chains, bringing back parts of the manufacturing process to the country of origin. Thus, productivity gains due to robotics and automation are important not just at the company level, but also for build industry and nation competitiveness.

I suppose that productivity can be raised. What are the impacts of robots on employment? Firstly, the main focus of development has been on personal entertainment, which does not drive worker productivity (manufacturing production). When the internet (information and communication technology (ICT)) innovation. This is borne and by findings that manufacturing productivity, which has been driven by innovations in automation rather than consumer technologies, has government strongly than productivity in the services sectors of the economy in most nature economies. It seems (AI) automation will create many jobs in internet communication entertainment game industry. For example, many young people like to use internet to play any electronic games from computer or mobile at home or outside home conveniently. Thus, (AI) automation will increase demand to be invented to any new entertainment game from internet channel. It will need to employ many (AI) entertainment game inventors to create many automation entertainment games. Thus, (AI) automation in internet entertainment game industry will need human (AI) entertainment game inventors to invent the knowledge-based capital of (AI) automation entertainment games. The (AI) entertainment game inventors will need own research and development skills, form specific skills, organizational know-how skills, databased knowledge, design and various forms of intellectual property to do these (AI) automation entertainment game invention occupations in the future.

International Federation Of Robotics(2016) indicated that China will be as a major robotics manufacturer and user of robots, benefiting from jobs created by robot manufacturing and productivity gains from robot use. Chins had sold of robots to any one single market every year since 2017 year. The Chinese government has included a focus on robotics in its 10 year strategy. In order to achieve its target of a robot density of 150 units per 10, 000 workers by 2020 year. Thus, Chinese companies will have to install around 650,000 new industrial robots between 2016 to 2020 year, 2.5 times more than installed globally in 2015 year.

Hence, China (AI) manufacturing industry will need to employ many workers . It implies (AI) manufacturing industry will create many new occupations in China. Also, ministry of economy, trade and industry (2015) also showed that Japan currently has the largest stock of industrial robots in operations, primarily in the automation industry. Driven by a rapidly aging population and low productivity rates, the Japanese government has sights on a 20-fold increase in the use of robots in the non-manufacturing sector and a three-fold growth rate of labor productivity in the service sector both by 2020 year. Thus, it also implies Japan will need many robots to be provide to service industry. Due to robots will provide to serve any businessmen's clients. Thus, it is possible that the service workers won't be dismissed as well as it is depended on the serving job nature to decide whether Japan's service workers can still serve to their employer when the service (AI) robots are applied to whose employers.

Consequently, it seems that (AI) can create employment, Ministry of economy, trade and industry (2015) showed that such as China will develop the major (AI) automation manufacturing industry. The (AI) employers will need to employ many workers to manufacture any these different kinds of (AI) robots to satisfy China or overseas individual or business buyers needs. But, (AI) can also cause unemployment to the low skillful service workers. Such as if Japan some service businesses choose to buy any (AI) service robots to replace their service staffs to serve their clients. It is possible that the service staffs will be dismissed, due to (AI) robots can do such as their same service job duties to achieve better service performance.

Thus, today, it is increasingly common for people to use robots in various situations at home and in retail stores, hotels and hospitals these service industries. Robots are classified into server types based on their functionality (service and utility robots or those designed to communicate with humans) and appearance (humanoid robots or mechanical robots). The type of robot, to which each country allocated particular importance in the advance of robotics, reflects the sense of values and preferences of its population. Thus, if the country has high population needs to use robots, then they will influence either more new jobs creation or more old job loss in the country's (AI) manufacturing or (AI) service industries both. For example, Japan respondents often associate the term " robot " with humanoid robots that can communicate with human and they have a high level of familiarity with robot. The US has the highest level of robot utilization at home and in retail stores with its people being the most enthusiastic about the future use of robots. Germany shows a strong tendency to consider robots for industrial purposes and its people feel strong effort to the presence of robots in their households.

In conclusion, to judge whether how (AI) will influence the country's employment to be better or worse. It will depend on the country home buyers (users) or business buyers (users) how to use (AI) for their daily needs. If the country , such as US retail stores need to use (AI) , it will have possible to reduce some or many retail service workers. Even, if the country , such as Japan has many home users need to use (AI) , it will not influence the employment market. Otherwise, it will raise (AI) salespeople numbers. Even, if the country, such as Germany and China will have many (AI) manufacturers, then it will create many (AI) manufacturing occupations for these (AI) manufactory workers. Consequently, (AI) robots manufacturing and service needs will have positive or negative impact to any country's employment. It will depend on the (AI) service provision and service workers' job nature as well as the manufacturing workers of (AI) knowledge level to decide their employment chance in their country's employment market.

Reference

International Federation Of Robotics, 2016. IFR press release world robotics report. IFR, org . 29 Sept. Accessed Feb. 01, 2017. http://www.ifr.org/news/ifr-press-release/world-robitics report -2016-8321.

How robots help labor to reduce working time ?

- Developing countries labors abnormal long time working
- hours factor how influences
- long time low productive efficiency

This research is about Hong Kong employers need labors to work abnormal long time working hours whether it can assist Hong Kong economic growth and raise productivity both in the long term.

The outcome is either Hong Kong labors work long time working hours abnormally who can not rise Hong Kong economic growth or who can rise Hong Kong economic growth in long time. Generally, Hong Kong employers choose to pay less salary expenditure to need many extra labors to work abnormal working hours to help them to rise productivity, but who don't concern that long time working factor will influence unhealthy to current workers due to who need to work long time working hours abnormally in long time and it seems to cause their workers will reduce productivity and inefficiency in long time.

Although, it is possible that HK labors can be increased extra abnormal working hours to work to rise Hong Kong employers' productivity and assist HK social economy will be grown up in short term, but it is also possible that it can't rise Hong Kong economic growth due to their unhealthy or sick increasing to cause productivity declining and inefficiency in long time. Thus, I shall find evidence to analyze whether Hong kong labors need to work abnormal long time working hours. Otherwise, who will decline Hong Kong economic growth and reduce productivity and inefficiency in long time as well as I shall give suggestion to indicate whether either current workers work abnormal long time working hours or employers ought choose to employ more extra part time workers to assist current labors to rise their productivity to decide which is the best choice to raise HK economic growth and efficient productivity in long time.

1.1 What is abnormal working hours Economic Problem

Effects on Hong Kong employment of working time reduction is found to be difficult to predict. The results of Hong Kong macroeconomic simulations of the effects on employments of working time reduction rely heavily on certain basic assumptions, such as how many hours people will actually work or how productivity and pay levels will develop. Whether HK abnormal working hours will assist HK social economic growth or economic falling down in long term.

The reasons cause Hong Kong labours who need to work abnormal long time working hours. In fact, it isn't the reason that the Hong Kong high skilful labours market is shortage to supply for the nature of some occupations, e.g. hospital doctors and nurses, university teachers, law firm lawyers etc professional occupations. Hk has many high qualification university students graduation, it has enough labor supply to high labor market evey year. The reason is that employers don't like to spend more salary to increase to employ extra labors to share current workers workload, such as low skilful and hardworking labors, such as cleaners, securities, waiters and high skilful professionals, such as hospital doctors and nurses, university teachers, lawyers etc. However, the low and high skilful labor market can be enough supply in Hong Kong, but Hong Kong employers need the current high and low both skilful workers who need to work more than 10 to 12 hours or more per working day commonly. It is possible that HK high and low educational labours will be caused unhealthy and lack enough sleep if who still need to work abnormal working hours time in long time. Although, who can rise productivity and efficiency in the short time, but it is possible that who can't rise productivity and inefficiency in the long time. Moreover, it will cause many young or middle or old ages high educational or low educational knowledgeable hardworking workers who will lose many jobs provided and who will be hard to find any jobs in HK labor employment market if HK employers don't choose to pay extra salaries to employ extra full time workers to share current labors' workload in the high and low salary occupations, due to they only choose to increase abnormal additional extra working hours to current workers to achieve to reduce employment expenditure and raise productivity. Hence, it is possible to influence HK social economy grows up slowly, even it's economy can go down seriously in long time

Hypotheses Testing And Data Analysis

I shall assume that working wage or salary of every individual labors can not be increased, even can be decreased as well as whose normal working hours can be increased abnormally in generally. This means that the Hong Kong individual worker's income will be decreased and general productivity raising is not affected generally, due to HK employers need current labors to work abnormal extra working hours to attempt to raise productivity daily, but their salary or wage have not increased more. However, HK employers need many workers to accomplish the same amount of work, even who don't like to employ extra labors to assist current workers to achieve long term productivity rasing in their companies. These abnormal working hours labors will feel unfair treatment, due to they need to work abnormal working hours, but their salary or wage have not been increased.

In the first scenario of my hypothesis is about that HK labor employment market's general salary or wage has not been increased to the normal proportion of the increased extra abnomal working time(hours). Then, in HK labors market, due to the numbers of labors supply is more than the jobs supply because HK employers don't like to pay more salary or wage expenditure to employ extra labor, but they like to increase extra abnormal working hours to current workers to aim to achieve productivity. So it will cause many HK job seekers with adequate qualifications or with less qualifications who won't find any jobs easily, then the HK the numbers of unemployed people will be increased and their household incomes will decrease to cause many HK household do not like to spend easily. The result will cause a negative effect on HK social private consumption will be decreased and the businessmen' income will be decreased also. So, HK people private consumption decreasing will influence HK economy growth to be slow, even it will cause HK economy declining in the long time.

In the second scenario of my hypothesis is about that Hong Kong workers are fully compensated for the increasing extra abnormal working time(hours) by the abnormal additional working hours calculation. Although, Hong Kong companies' productivity will be raised, but which are not to the extent that it compensates Hong Kong enterprises for their increased wage or salary costs. In fact, Hong Kong enterprises, their costs are passed on to the clients, it causes Hong Kong's economic growth has an impact on international competitiveness to cause economic declining in possible when these enterprises need to raise their products' sale prices to balance their salary or wage cost rasing to win their import competitors. Another effect is that Hong Kong individual labor's incomes decrease, which means that Hong Kong private consumption also falls in this scenario to influence HK economic growth seriously. Thus, the HK economic growth problem will be caused, due to these factors lead to a fall in Hong Kong social household private consumption. Consequently, it will cause many HK employers hope to raise Hong Kong productivity and they will raise the total amount of Hong Kong labor actually worked hours will be risen to such as extent as the increasing in normal working time(hours) from 8 or 9 hours per normal working day to 10 or 11 or 12 hours, even more extra abnormal hours per working day to the current labors. But they do not like to spend more salary or wage expenditure to employ full time extra labors, instead of increasing extra abnormal working hours to current labors to achieve productivity of raising, due to the cost will be increased if they choose to employ extra full time labors if they want to raise productivity. However, I feel they will raise productivity in the short term, but they will not raise productivity in the long term when they choose to raise their current labors abnormal working hours per working day.

The assumption will be made regarding to the relationship between the HK labor market's abnormal long time working hours factor and whether it can influence Hong Kong economic growth in long time for this research economic problem. For example, how many hours Hong Kong labor would actually work or how much workers have efficient productivity and efficiency and how much salaries or wages would be affected as a result of the increasing in working time(hours) in Hong Kong employment market.

I shall apply endogenous growth theory to Hong Kong labor market. As this theory indicates that this model also incorporated a new concept of human capital, whose capital is increasing rates of return. Research done in this area has focused on what increases human capital (e.g. education) or technological change (e.g. innovation) to influence HK economic growth. In macro economic environment, it indicates that economic growth means the increase in the market value of the products and services produced by the country's economy over time. It is conventionally measured as the percent rate of increase in real growth domestic product or real GDP. The growth of the ratio of GDP to population (GDP per capital, per capita income). Thus, an increase in growth is caused by more efficient use of inputs is referred to as intensive growth. GDP growth is caused only be increased in such as capital, population or territory is called extensive growth. Thus, in economy growth theory, typically refers growth off potential output, i.e. production is at full employment. However, HK unemployment ratio is still high to compare other developed or developing countries, although the labors supply are enough to HK employment market.

The working time is the period of time that an individual spends at paid occupation labor. Many countries regulate the work week by law, such as minimum daily rest periods, annual holidays and a maximum number of working hours per week. Working time may vary from person to person often depending on location, cultural, lifestyle choice and the profitability of the individual's livelihood.

Generally, most Hong Kong employers need labours work long time working hours abnormally. For example, low educational workers, such as security occupations of labors need to work per working day is twelve hours or more, restaurant waiters and dish cleaners also need to work ten to twelve hours or more per working day, bank counter cashiers or audit firm staffs also need to work over time from 10 to 12 hours or more per working day and who have no extra salaries for over time salaries payment commonly. Standard working hours or normal working hours refers to the legislation to limit the working hours per day, per week, per month or per year. If an employee needs to work overtime, the employer will need to pay overtime payments to employees as required in the law. Generally speaking, standard working hours countries wordwide are around 40 to 44 hours per week (but not everywhere: such as France employers need labors work from 35 hours per week, North Korea employers need labors work up to 112 hours per week). Maximum working hours refers that the employee can't work than the level specified in the maximum working hours law. It seems that Hong Kong many employers had needed labors to work above standard working hours per week to compare to other developed countries, e.g. America, France, England, New Zealand etc. developed countries.

On the 20th century, work hours are declined by almost half, mostly due to rising wages are brought about by renewed economic growth with a supporting role from legislation human rights. The decline countined at a faster in Europe: For example, France adopted a 35 hours work week in 2000 year. In 1995, China adopted a 40 hours week, eliminating half day work on Saturday. Technology has also continued to improve worker productivity, permitting standards of living to rise as hours declined. In developed economies, as the time needed to manufacturing products has declined more working hours have become available to provide services. In fact, on the one hand, Hong Kong manufacturing industry has declined, such as clothing, shoes, toy etc. manufacturing industry. On the other hand, its service industry need many labors to supply in the labor market per day, e.g. banking, accounting, restaurant, security etc. service sectors. A reduction in Hong Kong working time can be accomplished in various ways, and that Hong Kong enterprise's production costs will be affected in different ways depending on what type of measured is used. Usually Hong Kong employers would be likely to ask those already employed to do more overtime or who will require part time workers to increase whose working hours, especially would pass salaries expense from them on to charge higher sale price to their clients. Then, which would increase the rate of inflation and weaken competitiveness to win overseas competitors' product import.

I shall use these methods to examine this research problem, e.g. statistical analysis and economic concepts, such as GDP, economic growth and labor participation rate. Aim to research whether HK abnormal long time working hours can raise productivity and influence HK economic growth in long term. As regards Hong Kong enterprises' productivity, my research will be discussed what factors that may lead to either an increase or a decrease in productivity and I shall conclude what the effects are very difficult to assess as conditions vary between and it will concern within different service industry sectors, e.g. hotel, bank, restaurant, security, professional service etc. service occupations. These service labors of numbers are more than manufacture labors of numbers in Hong Kong nowadays. Of vital importance for the effect on Hong Kong employment of a reduction of working time is the extent to which wages or salaries are adopted. If the occupations where there was a shortage of labors, Hong Kong employers were to try to contibute to higher pay claims to long time working labors. According to the 1961 year population census, the size of the economically active population was approximately 1.2 million during that year and who was also economically active population was seeking worker. The labor force had grown to 3.1 million by 1996 year (William. C & Wing. S, 1997).

In 1996 year, HK economy was industrialization process filled by a large supply of relativey unskilled but hardworking labor, many of them were refugees from China, the dominance of manufacturing has been largely displaced by commerce and service sector and the demand for unskilled labor is falling relative to the demand for skilled and educated workers in Hong Kong. According to the 1961 year population census, the size of the economically active population was approximately 1.2 million during that year and who was also economically active population or the active seeking worker. The labor force had grown to 3.1 million by 1996 year (William. C & Wing. S, 1997). William. C & Wing. S (1997) also indicated that HK Census and Statistics department (various years) reported specific labor participation rate and size of the Hong Kong force from 1961 year to 1996 year. "During this period the size of the labor force grew from 1.2 million to 2.5 million. The annual rate of increase was 3.7%. It implies labor supply increased so rapidly, so labor intensive industries were developed. However, Hong kong population had increased to 7 million till to 2015 year." Hence the size of the labor force had increased more and it implied labors would supply more than employers demand. But, HK employer job supply numbers are less than HK labor demand numbers in HK employment market. It seems that if HK employers did not like to spend more salaries expenditure to employ extra labors to rise productivity, it would cause many young single or married people unemployed.

Any countrie's economic growth are usually calculated in real terms. i.e. inflation adjusted terms to eliminate the effect of inflation on the price of products produced. Economic growth has the indirect potential to reduce poverty, as a result of an increase in employment opportunities and increased labor productivity. However, employment is no guarantee of escaping poverty. The international labor organization estimates that is as many as 40% of workers are poor, not earning enough to keep families above the $2 a day poverty line. For instance, in India, poor are wage earner in formal employment because jobs are insecure and low paid and offer no chance to accumulate wealth to avoid risk, other countries found bigger benefits from focusing more no productivity improvement than low skilled work. Thus, increase in employment without increase in productivity lead to rise in the number of working poor and these countries don't apply the creation of quality and not quantity in labor market policies. In Vietnam, for example, employment growth has slowed when productivity growth has continued. Furthermore, productivity increases don't always lead to increase wages, e.g. United States, the gap between productivity and wages was been rising since the 1980 year. The overseas Development Institute study showed that other sectors were just as important in reducing unemployment as manufacturing.

Nowadays, the services sector is most effective as translating productivity growth into employment growth in Hong Kong. The HK Government forecast (2012) indicated that "HK's economy has slowed, growing by 0.9% year-on year in the half of 2012 year, after expanding by 5% in 2011 year. For 2012 year, the economy is forecast to grow at 1-2%. Consumer prices increased by 5.3% in 2011 year and 4.7% year-on-year in the first half of 2012 year. The unemployment rate was 3.2% for April-June 2012 year, compared with 3.4% for 2011 year." Although, it seemed that unemployment rate decreased 0.2% for April to June 2012, but its unemployment was still existed. Moreover, HK's economy has slowed to grow by 0.9% only year-on-year in the first half of 2012 year and HK government forcast to grow at 1-2% for 2012. By United States Government statistic in 2006 year, the average man employed full time worked 8.4 hours mandatory minimum amount of paid time off for sickness or holiday. However, regular full time workers often have the opportunity to take about nine days off for various holiday. However, regular full time workers of skill leave and two weeks (10 business days) of paid holiday time with some workers receiving additional time after several years. Because of the pressure of working time with some workers receiving additional time after several years. It seems United States developed countries some workers still feel pressure of working shorten working hours can reduce the pressure of working. In fact, HK many professional workers put in longer hours than the forty hour standard per week. A forty hours work week is considered inadequate and may result in job loss or failure to be promoted. Although, these employers don't spend much salary expenditures to employ extra professional workers to share whose workload and who can perform to serve whose clients efficiently in the short time. But in the long time, it is possible that who will work pressure possibly due to who need to serve many clients every day, and whose working performance will become to be poor to cause inefficiently. Until now, HK has no legislations regarding maximum and normal working hours. The average weekly working hours of full time employees in HK is 49 hours. According to the Price and Earnings report (2012) conducted by UBS, when the global and regional average were 1,915 and 2,154 hours per year respectively, the average working hours in HK is 2,296 hours per year, which ranked the fifth longest yearly working hours among 72 countries under study. In addition, the survey is conducted by the public opinion study group of the University of HK, it showed 79% of the respondents agree that the problem of overtime work in HK is "serve" and 65% of the respondents agree that the legislation on the maximum working hours. In HK, 70% of surveyed don't receive any overtime remuneration. These show that people in HK concerns the working time issues. The equilibrium price for a certain types of labor is the wage rate. The model of labor market, even given all its assumption is logically. The criticism of application of the model of supply and demand generalizes particularly to all markets for factor of production, e.g. labor working hours. I assume HK employers don't like to employ many labors to assist current labors to raise service or productivity when their client numbers have increased. It is possible that who feel salaries expenditure can not be exceed to their reasonable budget. Hence, who need current labors to work long time hours to do too much work, even the HK labor supply is increasing and it will cause many people lose jobs. It seems HK service industry can influence its economic growth. If those service industry labors need to work long time, who will feel mental pressure to work unhealthly and who need have enough sleep. If who can't have enough sleep to face every day work in long term, whose working performance will be poor or reduce productivity to whose clients possibly in long time. I believe HK service industry labors work long time working hours per week that it will influence whose service performance to be poor. In fact, most developed countries labors working hours are less than HK seriously. For example, United States originating from the traditional American business hours of 9:00 AM to 5:00 PM. Monday to Friday, representing a workweek of five to eight hour per working day composing 40 hours in total. The actual time at work often varies between 35 and 48 hours in practice due to breakers. In many traditonal white collar positions, employees were required to be in the office during these hours to take orders from the bosses, workplace hours have become more flexible. Another example, South Korea has the fastest declining working time, which is the result of proactive more to lower working hours at all levels to increase leisure and than the 10 days of the united States and double that of the England's 8 days. Also, work hours in and 40 hour week (44 hours in specified workplaces). The overtime limits are: 15 hours a week, allowance should not be lower than 125% and not more than 150% of normal hourly rate. However, Hong Kong dish cleaners, bank cashiers occupations whose need to work over time often , due to client numbers are increasing every days and their employers do not plan to employ extra workers to share their work loading. Hence, it seems whose work over time are similar to work abnormal long time working hours in every week in HK.

Middison A.(2001) indicated that "the unemployment rate is a performance indicator of the economy." The purpose of economic activity is to transform productive resources into products and services. An economy that uses all or most of its labor force should clearly be considered as a better performing economy than one that lacks the ability to put all or most of its labor force into work and thus some labor productive respurces can not be used. In fact, in economy theory, labor demand is considered to be a derived demand, meaning that its demand is explained not by itself, but by the existence of demand for products and services that use labor as a factor production. If labor demand is a desired demand, then an assessment of the performance of the economy could certainly profit from an evaluation of how well a specific social system managers to transform labor input into products and services. It is convenient to distinguish between economic performance of an economic system and labor market performance. The former related with the ability of a social system to deliver products and services and the latter related with the important, but more specific issue, of how well the labor market managers to match supply and demand. Economic and Trade Information on HK (2012) key indicators of the labor market had finished sample simple average of 15 countries statistic analysis to show "the result was as for the role of work hours in explaining GDP per capital had negative relation between GDP and working hours, as if long working hours where used to compensate the low productivity. The historical downward trend of working time form the slightly less than 3000 annual hours per person employed of the 1870 year to the less than 1600 year of the late 1990 year could be taken as a confirmation of this hypothesis." Thus, this hypothesis could be supported by viewpoint. It was about HK long time working hours ought not increase HK GDP and long working hours where used to compensate the low productivity to HK employers in the long time.

What is the difference of benefits between normal working hours and abnormal working hours

These research will have these two questions to be answer:

1. Can Hong Kong this individual labour abnormal long time working hours factor gives welfare benefit to every labor in the long time?
2. Can Hong Kong this abnormal labor working hours factor grow HK society whole economy in the long time?

It seems that HK employers don't like to employ extra workers to share current worker's workload, even the supply of labours is enough. Due to who do not want to pay extra each worker's salaries to raise whose productivity. To explain relationship between the workers abnormal long time working hours factor and the other resources input factor to influence HK enterprises growth in an improved model in the long time. I shall develop a model is the selection of two variables to explore. These variables have a cause and effect relationship. I shall suppose HK employers believe that workers abnormal long time working hours which can raise their productivity efficiently and which can assist HK society overall economic growth in the long time. These variables have a cause and effect relationship. From this discussion to investigate HK society overall economic growth effect is caused by companies' variable factors. The variable factors include the raising of abnormal long time working hours factor or increasing capital and machinery and equipment and building assets factor or raising natural resources for production factor or taking risking of success or failure ability in an productive enterprise factor. Thus, these separate sets of variable have been indentifies and each set could be selected for a model. In fact, Hong Kong society overall economic growth disputes many occur because a variety of resources input factors can be considered to analyze an effect cause whether which kind of resources input factors which can cause HK society economy growth is fast or slow. In my viewpoint, my exploring reasons are for a slow growing economy in HK. Some economists focus on relationship between money supply and growth in society, some in society's spending growth and some on the price level. In fact, HK economic growth is slow in the long time. I shall focus on the relationship between the HK companies' workers abnormal long time working hours factor and the other resources input factor both to influence HK society overall economic growth. Hence, I shall give assupmtions and conditions are held to be true when exploring the relationship is between HK companies and resources input variables within a model. For example, the relationship is between HK economic growth is slow or fast and labor resources supply numbers are not shortage. But HK employers ususally employ their limited numbers of labors to cause current workers need to overtime work or work in abnormal long time working hours often. Understanding the factors behind labor participation decision is an important component of the understanding long time change in labor supply in Hong Kong society.

In my another viewpoint, discussing HK labor supply, it is important to distinguish between the supply economy. The supply of Hong Kong labor to particular firm, an industry can be highly responsive to wages or salaries as workers seek the most profitable employment in HK. The supply of labors to HK society economy. On the other hand, it is typically less elastic to the labors who often change new jobs because most HK employers who need workers who work long time working hours to cause most HK labors can't have much chance to change new jobs which can provide normal working hours. So, it seems that who won't choose to change new jobs often because many HK employers who need HK labors work abnormal working hours nowadays.

HK employees of large companies of public utilities sector and the HK Government both organizations which typically enjoy more benefits and have greater job security than employers of small firms in Hong Kong society. This has lead to cause a distinction between the small HK private companies and public HK Government and public utilities sector. In fact, nowadays, most HK jobs have changes to service job nature from manufacturing job nature. However, deregulation, downsizing and pressure factors have caused many HK large companies which choose change working hours from normal 7 to 8 hours per working day to adnormal 9 to 12 hours or more per working day. Specically, the occupations of service sector job nature include: restaurant waitors, banking counter servicers, professional lawyers, share agents, security servicers, accountants etc. different service sector occupation labors. The result will cause the labors who choose to leave whose employers if who could not accept to work abnormal working hours to their current employers. Even, it will also cause the current workers who feel nervous and tired and worry to work in pressure everyday, due to who need to increase many extra hours to work often and who will lose their private entertainment time with their family or friends often, even it will be unhealthy to them due to who lack sleeping. Although, HK business cycle was the short term economy in manufacturing macroeconomic environment in beginning from 1950 year. Then, HK economy growth had developed, so many the demanding of labor numbers had been caused to increase seriously till to nowadays. The economic and trade information on Hong Kong of HK Government statistic department (2012) reported " the HK economy was forecasted to grow at 1-2% for 2012 year and it's economy had slowed growing by 0.9% per year in the half of 2012 year after expanding by 5% in 2011 year." Although, it implied that HK labor market had enough labor numbers supply. Otherwise, many HK employers don't like to employ many labor numbers to share current workers' workload. It is possible that due to whose HK current workers need to spend adnormal working hours to raise their productivity per working day to save spending extra salaries or wages expenditures to pay to employ extra labors in HK current labor market. I feel that HK economy growth is slow or poor because the main reason is due to HK Government doesn't spend expenditures to assist HK employers to raise training to their current HK labors to provide human capital to achieve to raise whose service performance to improve their efficient productivity in HK service businesses sector only in the long time. Finally, the results were discovered and will be backed by these evidence

3.1 Whether quality of life of employee or abnormal working hours which is more chance to raise productivity and economic
growth in long term

My essay will truly be a qualitative and quantitative research, it is based on experimental fact and evidence. To research the long time employment influence relationship is between the labor abnormal long time working hours factor and the influence of HK economic growth in productive model factor both. This study suggests understanding of the relationship between economic growth influences and HK labors abnormal working hours need to be raised. In fact, the HK labor force participation rate will be fallen every year. Economic growth in HK was through phases that affects growth through changes in the labor force participation rate and the relative sizes of HK society service and manufacturing sectors. In fact, HK agricultural industry sector is not existed and manufacturing industry sector numbers are decreasing and it begins to enter service industry sector. The low knowledge level of jobs include security, banking, restaurant, cleaning, transportation etc. service nature of jobs as well as the high knowledge level of jobs include lawyer, accountant, medicine, doctor, computer technician etc. professonal service nature of jobs which both are providing service to HK society nowadays. The investment theory indicates that the education is as investment human capital to provide to any companies. The main difference is that human capital is incorporated in human beings and it can't be resold. When physical capital can be acquired at almost any desired amount in boom periods and be resold during recession on secondary markets, human capital can be acquired mostly in the beginning of individual behavior by firms. I shall recommend HK companies ought choose these methods to control labors whose working hours time efficiently.

Yasuhiro (2014) showed that "wage differentials based on age and length of service in-house training refers to a process whereby workers acquire skills through daily work and occasional of the job training. Whether or not they perceive it as "training" is irrelevant. Training is also included informal learning conducted independently by the worker without any feedback from an instructor. Conceptually, the skills acquired are divided into general skills that can be used in the company currently employing the worker. The process of acquiring the latter specific training." Generally, when companies minimizes personnel costs, the ratio of marginal productivity referred to below as productivity between workers are equal to wage ratios. Therefore, the coefficient of age in the wage function expresses the rate of productivity increases due to general training and the coefficient of length of service and the rate of wage increases due to special training reason. The sum of both coefficients will express the rate of productivity increase in current companies due to training is as an important causing factor.

In conclusion, in my viewpoint, HK employers need to provide on job training to current labors to aim to raise their efficiency to productivity in the long time. Because when their labors had been trained to let them to learn how to use special skill to finish their job duties easily, then they will not need to spend much time (additional working hours) to finish their job duties per working day. On the one hand, HK employers need to measure to compare what benefits are in favour of standard working hours to whose employees. The benefits include, such as promoting work life balance and enjoy family life, increasing time for leisure and rest, beneficial to health and employees can have more time to pursue further studies as well as employers do not need to pay higher salaries to longer working hours employees or overtime pay boost income as most HK companies pay time and a half to some employees only. On the other hand, HK employers need to measure to compare what benefits are against standard working hours to employers, such as employing many part time working hours employees to assist normal working hours full time employees rather than needing full time employees work abnormal hours daily, lowering or cancelling year and bonues etc. Moreover, HK employers may also use various measure to offset the increased cost of running businesses, such as lowering average hourly anual compensation. However, when HK employees are forced to work part time jobs, who may need to acquire additional employment to maintain their standard living. Even, HK employers only force employees to work overtime in some situations. Appropriate standard working hours can vary across different industries based on the type of work performed. Such as some HK certain professional positions are difficult to define in terms of appropriate working hours. Issues can arise with employers expecting exployees to work extra hours "off the clock" in order to keep costs down. Thus, I believe that HK labors abnormal working hours time issue ought be decreased and HK employers ought employ extra workers assistance to share current labors' workload to help them to raise productivity and efficiency and HK economy will grow fast in the long time. Finally, my research aims to find that the number of hours worked is a more responsive measure of the state of the labor market than employment in HK. Comparing the number of hours worked to indicators of the wider economy shows that it is likely to be demand from HK firms (employers) which is driving the numbers of hours, rather than individual job applicant supplys to HK employment market. My analysis also show that the HK appears to have developed a long working hours culture to compare other developed countries, such as America, England, Canada etc. In fact, in the presence of HK firms may even invest to find which are more profitable to able to reduce their every employee's abnormal working hours daily rather than normal number of working hours of their every employee.

Bibliography

Economic And Trade Information On Hong Kong, (14 Aug. 2012). Hong Kong Government Forecast for 2012, retrieved from the following URL: http://www.cepa.hktdc.com

Middison A. (2001). The World Economy. A Millennial Perspective, OECD, Paris.

Yasuhio, U. (2014). Japan Labor Review, vol.11 no.3, High Economic Growth And Human Capital: Conditions For Sustained Growth, Konan University.

William, C&Wing, S.(1997). The Hong Kong Economic Policy Studies Series, published by City University Of HK Press, Hong Kong

(AI) - driven automation industry development how to influence work nature change

On positive benefit hand, it is possible that (AI) -driven automation industry will create wealth and expand economy growth to any countries, but it will be accompanied by changed in the skills that workers need to learn, if the low skill workers expect to avoid unemployment threat when (AI) technology can replace their jobs in future one day. Thus, it is possible that (AI) technology will also bring negative influence to cause low skill worker unemployment challenge in the applied (AI) technology countries.

For the low skill worker unemploment reason, it is because that one of main ways that technology increases productivity is by decreasing the number of labor hours needed to create a unit of output. It implies (AI) technology will influence low educated and low skillful labor number to be decreased (reduction employment number).

Will (AI) bring benefits to the employers? In contrast, technological change tended to work in a different direction throughout the nowadays. The advance of computer and the internet raised the relative productivity of higher skilled workers. So, routine-intensive occupations that focused on predictable tasks disappearance, such as switch board, operators, filming checkers, travel agents and assembling line workers etc. were particularly replaced by new technologies. However, today, it may be challenging to predict exactly which jobs will be most immediately affected by (AI) driven-automation. The reason is because (AI) is not a single technology, but rather a collection of technologies that are felt unevenly through the economy to influence job changing both negatively and positively.

In positively view point, (AI) driven-automation will make many workers more productive and increase demand for certain skills. Consequently, new jobs are likely to be directly create in areas , such as the development and supervision of (AI) as well as indirectly created in a range of areas throughout the economy as higher incomes lead to expanded demand. So, (AI) will bring macro economy advantages in possible.

Otherwise, in negatively view point, many traditional human needed (demand) skillful jobs will be threatened by automation are highly concentrated among lower-paid, lower-skilled and less -educated workers. It means automation will cause pressure on demand for this group, pressure and employment, if (AI) can replace the low skilled and less educated workers' jobs. Thus, (AI) will have negative influence to impact on the labor market.

(AI) capabilities will enable automation of some tasks that have long required human labor. Can (AI) replace some simple human jobs? If (AI) can replace some simple human jobs, then it is possible to cause unemployment if employers applied (AI) machines to replace the low skill workers to do their simple jobs in future one day. For example, advances in robotics are expanding machines' abilities to interact with and sharp the physical world. Combined , (AI) and robotics will give rise to smarter machines that can perform more sophisticated functions than ever before and brings more advantages that humans have exercised. This will permit automation of many tasks now performed by human workers and could change the shape of the labor market and human activity. It depends on whether employers choose to reduce all worker numbers to be replaced by (AI) machines or employers choose to apply (AI) machines to assist the low skillful workers to work more efficient or raise performance and productivities. If future employers apply (AI) machines to assist workers to raise performance and efficiency, then the unemployment challenge won't cause, due to the number of worker won't reduce. But if employers decide to unemploy all low skillful workers and they are replaced by (AI) machines, then the unemployment challenge will cause in possible.

How (AI) influences labor market

Today, it may be challenging to predict exactly which jobs will be most immediately affected by (AI)-driven automation. Because (AI) is not a single technology, but rather a collection of technologies that are applied to specific tasks.

Some specific predictions are possible based on the current (AI) technology. For example, driving jobs and house cleaning jobs, bank counter service jobs, telephone enquiry service operators. Restaurant cooking jobs, simple accounting record service jobs etc. that require relatively less education to perform. Advancements in computer vision and related technologies have made the feasibility of fully appear more likely, potentially displacing some workers in driving-dominant professions. Seemingly similar robot, for which the operational tasks is less specific of navigating to a specific destination when following a set of given rules and preserving safety.

In the future, the effects of (AI) on the labor market in the decade ahead will continue the trend toward skill-biased change that computerization and communication innovations have driven in recent decades. Thus, some human driving occupation will be disappeared or replaced by (AI) automation driven. For example, bus drivers, light truck or delivery services drivers, heavy and tractor-trailer truck drivers, school drivers, tax drivers, travel bus drivers.

However, (AI) technology could enable some workers to focus time on other job responsibilities, boosting their productivity, and actually raised wage growth among those still holding the reshaped jobs. For example, salespeople, who currently spend a considerable amount of time driving could find themselves able to do other work when a car drives them from place to place, or inspectors and appraisers could fill out paperwork, when their car drives itself. This (AI) -driven technology should make these workers more productive, with (AI) -driven technology serving as a complement, not a substitute. New jobs will also likely be created, both in existing occupations cheaper transportation costs with lower prices and increase demand for products and all the related occupations, such as service and fulfillment, and in new occupations not currently foreseeable.

What kind of jobs will be created by (AI) technology? Predicting future job growth is extremely difficult, due to it depends on technologies or substitute for existing today as well as they may complement or substitute for existing human skills and jobs. However, (AI) will also lead to substantial indirect job creation to the degree it raises productivity and wages, it may also lead to higher consumption that would support additional jobs from high-end draft production to restaurant and retail. The future(AI) " augmented intelligence", the technology's role is as assisting and expanding the productivity of individuals rather than replacing human work. Thus, based on the biased-technical change framework, demand for labor will likely increase the most in the areas where humans complement (AI) automation technologies. For example, (AI) technology , such as IBM's Watson may improve early detection of some cancers or other illnesses, but a human healthcare professional is needed to work with patients to understand and translate patients' symptoms, inform patients of treatment options, and guide patients through treatment plans. Shipping companies may also partner workers who pick up and deliver products over the last feet with (AI) enabled autonomous vehicles that move workers efficiently from site to site. In such cases, (AI) augments what a human is able to do and allows individuals to either be move effective in their specially task or to operate on a larger scale. Thus, it seems (AI) technology will also create new jobs, raise productivities and workers' efficiencies.

Redefining management in
the workforce of artificial intelligence

Change management

(AI) will influence office administrative efficieny to be raised. In the future, due to artificial intelligence influences to some kind of human jobs nature. So, the kind of human jobs of management methods will also need to change to adapt the artificial intelligence technology input to their organizations. It will cause challenges for every executive and manager if who won't have effort to manage their teams how to apply artificial intelligence technology to work efficiently and easily. For example, division of labor will change among humans and machines will increase. Thus, companies will have to adapt their training performance and talent strategies how to emphasize on work that how to make human judgment and skills and experimentation. Thus, (IA)'s greatest impact will be on administrative coordination and control tasks, such as scheduling , resource allocation.

In fact, mangers will encounter this challenges: How to apply human experience and expertise to judge critical business decisions and practices when the information available is insufficient to suggest a successful course of action? Due to this kind of work will require new skills and mindsets. I shall indicate these change management methods to adapt (AI) technology. Such as: administration and routine tasks, scheduling , allocation of resources and reporting will fall within the intelligence machines, responsibilities that have long been reserved for humans. For example, a typical store manager or a lead nurse at a nursing home most constantly arrange shift schedules, accounting for staff members' absences owing to illness, vacation time or sudden departures.

Thus, the managers need to learn how to arrange new division of labor within the organizations after (AI) technology had been implemented to the organization. Artificial intelligence is currently influencing into once considered exclusive to humans: assessing and acting on human emotions and personality traits. The influences to managers need to change their strategies to adapt (AI) technology implements include such as below:

Firstly, managers need to spend the bulk of their time on coordination and control tasks from intelligent system implements. Their time spending on these major three aspects from impact of intelligent system: coordinate and control, solve problems and collaborate and people and community , strategy and innovation three aspects. Thus (AI) will influence managers need to change their judgment method to teach whose teams how to adapt the (AI) system operations in any organizations.

Secondly, (AI) will influence top, middle and low level management needs to change to adapt the (AI) technology operations to any owned (AI) technology organizations in the future. Intelligent machines must be trained in context. Just like humans , on-the-job training is a requirement for such machines because they typically arrive with only very general capabilities. To get the most from (AI), managers at all levels must participate in the instructional experience and in the learning process and provides managers' familiarity with such systems on these aspects, e.g. How the system works and generate advice, how the system has a proven track record , how the system provides convincing explanations , how the system can make simple rule- based decisions.

Thirdly, managers need to learn how to make judgment more accurate (AI) systems assistance. Although (AI) will invariably take on more routine work and even augment human decision-making, it won't judgment work, the application of human experience and expertise to critical business decisions when the information available is insufficient to suggest a successful course of action or reliable enough to suggest an obvious course of action. For a sense of the nature of judgment work, consider big data marketing and sales analytics. Such analytics often provide insights that can inform promotional campaigns, including predicting which promotions will generate desired sales brand further into the future, marketing executives need use judgment, combining analytics with their own and others' insight and experience.

The application of experience and expertise to critical business decisions and practice represents the real value of human judgment. But, when artificial intelligent machines are implemented to any organizations to assist the low, middle and top level management to make any business judgment. These forms of judgment work that managers can gather data interpretation, idea development more absolute from (AI) machine assistance. Thus, why these level management executives need to learn how to apply (AI) machines to help them to make any business judgment more accurate.

How (AI) influences organizational change

Consequently creative and social intelligence will be in even greater demand as (AI) makes in management and the workforce. This development will represent a long term trend in labor markets , one characterized by intensifying demand and reward for social skills with a growing desire for creative capabilities, managers will seek to fashion of ideas and hypotheses from inside and outside of the enterprise to shape solutions to their most pressing business problems. Thus, (AI) will influence overall organizational team members who have chance to participate any decision to make more accurate business judgment.

Many managers mistakenly view judgment work as only an individual discipline, failing to appreciate that it can also involve decide interpersonal and organizational practices. In more complex settings, judgment is typically a collective outcome of individuals' and teams' diverse perspectives, insights and experiences. And often , the resulting choices are better informed than decisions that an individual would have arrived at on his or her own.

Thus, when any organizations apply (AI) technology to assist managers to gather data and ideas to make any judgment. In these cases, organizations can create the conditions for effective collective judgment by establishing structures , such as " shadow advisory boards" that prompt managers and employees to source and synthesize multiple perspectives. Thus, a traditional organization (firm) might freshen its thinking is t put together a shadow advisory board, comprised of young, digital people who can apply (AI) machine assistance to make judgment work more accurate whether related to people development, problem-solving or strategizing and innovating for considerable degrees of creative and social intelligence.

Thus, on the one hand, (AI) technology machine augmentation and automation can give these advantages to human (organization managers) , e.g. developing people and community, solving problems and collaborating, coordinating and controlling work, shaping strategy and leading innovation. Besides, on the other hand, the next generation managers need have these individual attitude to treat intelligent machines to be as colleagues.

When, judgment is a human skill, intelligent machines can accelerate human learning that supports it, assisting in data -driven simulations, scenarios and search and discovery activities. Focuses on judgment work, some decisions require insight beyond what data can tell them. This is the sweet sport for human judgment, the application of experience and expertise to critical business decisions and practices. Thus, managers will also need to find ways to learn how to use digital (AI) technologies to tap into the knowledge and judgment of partners, customer external stakeholders and role models in other industries after the (AI) machine had been implemented to the organization.

Future works change: Automation, employment
and productivity

How (AI) influences employment

Human future " micro to macro" industry trends will be affected business strategy and public policy by (AI) technology. In the future (AI) technology will influence those six themes: productivity and growth, natural resources, labor markets, the evolution of global financial markets, the economic impact of technology and innovation and urbanization. However, (AI) technology will bring economic benefits of tackling gender inequality, a new global competition, Chinese innovation and digital globalization.

Nowadays, advances in robotics artificial intelligence, and machine learning are in a new age of automation, as machines match or outperform human performance in a development to any countries. For example, automation of activities can enable businesses to improve performance by reducing errors and improving quality and speed, and in some cases achieving outcomes that go beyond human capabilities. For example, some research indicated automation could raise productivity growth globally by 0.8 to 1.4 % annually; more than 2,000 work activities across 800 occupations. When less than 5% of all occupations can be automated using demonstrated technologies about 60% of all occupations have at least 30% of constituent activities that could be automated. Many occupations will change that will be automated away: Activities most susceptible to automation involve physical activities, in highly structured and predictable environments, as well as the collection and processing of data. They are most prevalent in manufacturing , accommodation and food service and retail trade and include some middle-skill jobs. For example, such as natural language processing is a key factor. Beyond technical feasibility, the cost of technology competition with labor including skills and supply and demand dynamics, performance benefits including and beyond labor cost savings, and social and regulatory acceptance will be affected by (AI) automation technology. Thus, (AI) automation will impact to influence global employment in those aspects as below:

Firstly, assuming that people are displaced by automation will find other employment. The anticipated shift in the activities in the labor force is of a similar order as the long-term shift away from agriculture and decreases in manufacturing share of employment. Both of manufacturing and agriculture industries which would be accompanied by the creation of new types of work not foreseen at the time.

Secondly, for business, the performance benefits of automation are relatively clear. Thus, the businessmen have opportunities for their micro economies to benefits from the productivity growth potential and macro economies to benefit to encourage continued progress and innovation , investment and market incentives. At the same time, employers must innovate policies to help workers and institutions adapt to the impact on employment.

This will likely include rethinking education and training, income support and safety nets , as well as support for those dislocated, when employees need to leave themselves homes to move to other cities to learn new (AI) automation works. Thus, individuals in the workplace will need to engage move comprehensively with machines as part of their everyday activities, and acquire new skills that will be in demand in the new automation age. Consequently , the scale of shifts in the labor force over many decades that automation technologies can be a similar order to the long -term technology -enables shifts in the developed countries‘ workforces away from agriculture in the 21 th century. Those shifts did not result in long-term mass unemployment because they were accompanied by the creation of new types of work not foreseen at the time. However, human will still be needed in the workforce when the total productivity gains are caused by (AI) technology.

What occupations will be influenced by (AI) technology.

In the future, scientists predict that these occupations will be influenced by (AI) technology mostly. They include : retail salespeople, food and beverage service workers, language or translation teachers, health practitioners. Since these work activities have a more relevant occupations are made up of a range of activities with different potential for (AI) automation . For example, a retail salesperson will spend more time interacting with customers, stocking shelves , or ringing up sales. Each of these activities is distinct and requires different capabilities to perform successfully.

Thus, these job activities have similar simple control characteristics. Simple activities include greet customers, answer questions about products and services, clean and maintain work areas, demonstrate product feature process sales and transactions. All these activities can have similar simple activities in order to (AI) machines can be learn how to do these activities from (AI) technology . For example, the capability perception includes sensory perception, cognitive capabilities, such as retrieving automation, recognizing known patterns(supervised learning), logical reasoning problem solving.

Thus, (AI) machine is such human, which has feeling and emotion, such as social and emotional sensing, judgement reasoning methods, natural language understanding and physical capabilities, such as mobility , navigation, gross motor skill, fine motor skills. It seems that the future, (AI) human invents machines which will have these human characteristics to do human similar behavioral job duties more easily and efficiently. It implies these above human occupations will be replaced by (AI) human invention machines in the future. Due to (AI) creation, it is possible to cause unemployment number of these above workers will increase because (AI) machines can do their similar job behavioral activities.

Consequently, employers won’t need to employ many of these skillful labor. Otherwise, they can buy less number (AI) machines to attempt to do whose job activities more easily and efficiently. So, it seems (AI) machines will have more high work performance to replace these occupation workers’ work performance. Finally, these occupation worker unemployment number will only increase when the (AI) machines had been invented to achieve to do their work behavioral activities absolutely success in the future.

Whether (A) technology machine labor
will replace human worker more or assist

human worker more

There is no single agreed definition of a robot how outcome of a task that is completed without human intervention. When some definitions require the task to be completed by a physical machine moves and respond to its environment, other definitions use the term robot in connection with tasks completed by software , without physical embodiment.

However, to answer the question : Whether (AI) technology machine labor will replace human worker more or assist human worker more. I shall indicate some examples to let readers to judge whether (AI) technology can create new jobs or reduce old jobs.

Firstly, I shall explain what (AI) function is. (AI) is a service robot that performs useful tasks for humans or equipment excluding industrial automation application . Thus, the classification of a robot into industrial robot or service robot is done according to its intended application. It is also a personal service robot or a service robot for personal used for a non commercial task, usually by lay persons . Examples are domestic servant robot, and pet exercising robot. It is also a professional service robot or a service robot for professional used for a commercial task, usually operated by a properly trained operator. Examples, are cleaning robot for public places, delivery robot in offices or hospitals, fire-fighting robot, rehabilitation robot and surgery robot in hospitals. Thus, these functions will be future (AI) application to our daily life necessaries or business necessaries.

However, some authors agree (AI) will bring negative outcomes of automation, due to raise competiveness, reduce human job nature. Otherwise, other authors argue (AI) will bring positive outcomes of automation, due to raise productivities, job creation, assist humans work.

On the positive outcome hand, robots can increase productivity . This is particularly important for small-to medium sized businesses both are in developed and developing countries economies. It also enables large companies to increase their competitiveness through faster product development and delivery. Increased use of robot is also enabling companies in high cost countries to re shore, or bring back to their domestic base parts of the supply chain that will have previously outsourced to sources of cheaper labor. Currently , the greater threat to employment is not a automation, but an inability to remain competitive. Automation has led overall to an increase in labor demand and positive impact on wages. The reason is that the middle-income/middle-skilled jobs have reduced as a proportion of overall contribution to employment and earnings leading to fears of increasing income inequality, the skills range within the middle income bracket is large. Thus, robots are driving an increase in demand for workers at the higher -skilled and with a positive impact on wages. This issue is how to enable middle-income earners in the lower-income range to unskilled or retain. Finally, the (AI) positive impact supporter who argue the future will be robots and humans can work together.

However, on the negative outcome hand, robots can substitute labor activities, but don't replace jobs. They believe that less than 10% of jobs are fully automatable. Increasingly , robots are used to complement and augment labor activities, the net impact on jobs and the quality of work is positive. Automation can provide the opportunity for humans to focus on higher-skilled, higher-quality and higher-paid tasks. Robots can improve productivity when they are applied to tasks that which perform more efficiently and to a higher and more consistent level of quality than humans. For example, increased productivity is enabling some firms, such as Whirlpool, Caterpillar and Ford Motors company in the US restructure their supply chains, bringing back parts of the manufacturing process to the country of origin. Thus, productivity gains due to robotics and automation are important not just at the company level, but also for build industry and nation competitiveness.

I suppose that productivity can be raised. What are the impacts of robots on employment? Firstly, the main focus of development has been on personal entertainment, which does not drive worker productivity (manufacturing production). When the internet (information and communication technology (ICT)) innovation. This is borne and by findings that manufacturing productivity, which has been driven by innovations in automation rather than consumer technologies, has government strongly than productivity in the services sectors of the economy in most nature economies. It seems (AI) automation will create many jobs in internet communication entertainment game industry. For example, many young people like to use internet to play any electronic games from computer or mobile at home or outside home conveniently. Thus, (AI) automation will increase demand to be invented to any new entertainment game from internet channel. It will need to employ many (AI) entertainment game inventors to create many automation entertainment games. Thus, (AI) automation in internet entertainment game industry will need human (AI) entertainment game inventors to invent the knowledge-based capital of (AI) automation entertainment games. The (AI) entertainment game inventors will need own research and development skills, form specific skills, organizational know-how skills, databased knowledge, design and various forms of intellectual property to do these (AI) automation entertainment game invention occupations in the future.

International Federation Of Robotics(2016) indicated that China will be as a major robotics manufacturer and user of robots, benefiting from jobs created by robot manufacturing and productivity gains from robot use. Chins had sold of robots to any one single market every year since 2017 year. The Chinese government has included a focus on robotics in its 10 year strategy. In order to achieve its target of a robot density of 150 units per 10, 000 workers by 2020 year. Thus, Chinese companies will have to install around 650,000 new industrial robots between 2016 to 2020 year, 2.5 times more than installed globally in 2015 year.

Hence, China (AI) manufacturing industry will need to employ many workers . It implies (AI) manufacturing industry will create many new occupations in China. Also, ministry of economy, trade and industry (2015) also showed that Japan currently has the largest stock of industrial robots in operations, primarily in the automation industry. Driven by a rapidly aging population and low productivity rates, the Japanese government has sights on a 20-fold increase in the use of robots in the non-manufacturing sector and a three-fold growth rate of labor productivity in the service sector both by 2020 year. Thus, it also implies Japan will need many robots to be provide to service industry. Due to robots will provide to serve any businessmen's clients. Thus, it is possible that the service workers won't be dismissed as well as it is depended on the serving job nature to decide whether Japan's service workers can still serve to their employer when the service (AI) robots are applied to whose employers.

Consequently, it seems that (AI) can create employment, Ministry of economy, trade and industry (2015) showed that such as China will develop the major (AI) automation manufacturing industry. The (AI) employers will need to employ many workers to manufacture any these different kinds of (AI) robots to satisfy China or overseas individual or business buyers needs. But, (AI) can also cause unemployment to the low skillful service workers. Such as if Japan some service businesses choose to buy any (AI) service robots to replace their service staffs to serve their clients. It is possible that the service staffs will be dismissed, due to (AI) robots can do such as their same service job duties to achieve better service performance.

Thus, today, it is increasingly common for people to use robots in various situations at home and in retail stores, hotels and hospitals these service industries. Robots are classified into server types based on their functionality (service and utility robots or those designed to communicate with humans) and appearance (humanoid robots or mechanical robots). The type of robot, to which each country allocated particular importance in the advance of robotics, reflects the sense of values and preferences of its population. Thus, if the country has high population needs to use robots, then they will influence either more new jobs creation or more old job loss in the country's (AI) manufacturing or (AI) service industries both. For example, Japan respondents often associate the term " robot " with humanoid robots that can communicate with human and they have a high level of familiarity with robot. The US has the highest level of robot utilization at home and in retail stores with its people being the most enthusiastic about the future use of robots. Germany shows a strong tendency to consider robots for industrial purposes and its people feel strong effort to the presence of robots in their households.

In conclusion, to judge whether how (AI) will influence the country's employment to be better or worse. It will depend on the country home buyers (users) or business buyers (users) how to use (AI) for their daily needs. If the country , such as US retail stores need to use (AI) , it will have possible to reduce some or many retail service workers. Even, if the country , such as Japan has many home users need to use (AI) , it will not influence the employment market. Otherwise, it will raise (AI) salespeople numbers. Even, if the country, such as Germany and China will have many (AI) manufacturers, then it will create many (AI) manufacturing occupations for these (AI) manufactory workers. Consequently, (AI) robots manufacturing and service needs will have positive or negative impact to any country's employment. It will depend on the (AI) service provision and service workers' job nature as well as the manufacturing workers of (AI) knowledge level to decide their employment chance in their country's employment market.

Reference
International Federation Of Robotics, 2016. IFR press release world robotics report. IFR, org . 29 Sept. Accessed Feb. 01, 2017. http://www.ifr.org/news/ifr-press-release/world-robitics report -2016-8321.

How robots help labor to reduce working time ?

- Developing countries labors abnormal long time working
- hours factor how influences
- long time low productive efficiency

This research is about Hong Kong employers need labors to work abnormal long time working hours whether it can assist Hong Kong economic growth and raise productivity both in the long term.

The outcome is either Hong Kong labors work long time working hours abnormally who can not rise Hong Kong economic growth or who can rise Hong Kong economic growth in long time. Generally, Hong Kong employers choose to pay less salary expenditure to need many extra labors to work abnormal working hours to help them to rise productivity, but who don't concern that long time working factor will influence unhealthy to current workers due to who need to work long time working hours abnormally in long time and it seems to cause their workers will reduce productivity and inefficiency in long time.

Although, it is possible that HK labors can be increased extra abnormal working hours to work to rise Hong Kong employers' productivity and assist HK social economy will be grown up in short term, but it is also possible that it can't rise Hong Kong economic growth due to their unhealthy or sick increasing to cause productivity declining and inefficiency in long time. Thus, I shall find evidence to analyze whether Hong kong labors need to work abnormal long time working hours. Otherwise, who will decline Hong Kong economic growth and reduce productivity and inefficiency in long time as well as I shall give suggestion to indicate whether either current workers work abnormal long time working hours or employers ought choose to employ more extra part time workers to assist current labors to rise their productivity to decide which is the best choice to raise HK economic growth and efficient productivity in long time.

1.1 What is abnormal working hours Economic Problem

Effects on Hong Kong employment of working time reduction is found to be difficult to predict. The results of Hong Kong macroeconomic simulations of the effects on employments of working time reduction rely heavily on certain basic assumptions, such as how many hours people will actually work or how productivity and pay levels will develop. Whether HK abnormal working hours will assist HK social economic growth or economic falling down in long term.

The reasons cause Hong Kong labours who need to work abnormal long time working hours. In fact, it isn't the reason that the Hong Kong high skilful labours market is shortage to supply for the nature of some occupations, e.g. hospital doctors and nurses, university teachers, law firm lawyers etc professional occupations. Hk has many high qualification university students graduation, it has enough labor supply to high labor market evey year. The reason is that employers don't like to spend more salary to increase to employ extra labors to share current workers workload, such as low skilful and hardworking labors, such as cleaners, securities, waiters and high skilful professionals, such as hospital doctors and nurses, university teachers, lawyers etc. However, the low and high skilful labor market can be enough supply in Hong Kong, but Hong Kong employers need the current high and low both skilful workers who need to work more than 10 to 12 hours or more per working day commonly. It is possible that HK high and low educational labours will be caused unhealthy and lack enough sleep if who still need to work abnormal working hours time in long time. Although, who can rise productivity and efficiency in the short time, but it is possible that who can't rise productivity and inefficiency in the long time. Moreover, it will cause many young or middle or old ages high educational or low educational knowledgeable hardworking workers who will lose many jobs provided and who will be hard to find any jobs in HK labor employment market if HK employers don't choose to pay extra salaries to employ extra full time workers to share current labors' workload in the high and low salary occupations, due to they only choose to increase abnormal additional extra working hours to current workers to achieve to reduce employment expenditure and raise productivity. Hence, it is possible to influence HK social economy grows up slowly, even it's economy can go down seriously in long time

Hypotheses Testing And Data Analysis

I shall assume that working wage or salary of every individual labors can not be increased, even can be decreased as well as whose normal working hours can be increased abnormally in generally. This means that the Hong Kong individual worker's income will be decreased and general productivity raising is not affected generally, due to HK employers need current labors to work abnormal extra working hours to attempt to raise productivity daily, but their salary or wage have not increased more. However, HK employers need many workers to accomplish the same amount of work, even who don't like to employ extra labors to assist current workers to achieve long term productivity rasing in their companies. These abnormal working hours labors will feel unfair treatment, due to they need to work abnormal working hours, but their salary or wage have not been increased.

In the first scenario of my hypothesis is about that HK labor employment market's general salary or wage has not been increased to the normal proportion of the increased extra abnomal working time(hours). Then, in HK labors market, due to the numbers of labors supply is more than the jobs supply because HK employers don't like to pay more salary or wage expenditure to employ extra labor, but they like to increase extra abnormal working hours to current workers to aim to achieve productivity. So it will cause many HK job seekers with adequate qualifications or with less qualifications who won't find any jobs easily, then the HK the numbers of unemployed people will be increased and their household incomes will decrease to cause many HK household do not like to spend easily. The result will cause a negative effect on HK social private consumption will be decreased and the businessmen' income will be decreased also. So, HK people private consumption decreasing will influence HK economy growth to be slow, even it will cause HK economy declining in the long time.

In the second scenario of my hypothesis is about that Hong Kong workers are fully compensated for the increasing extra abnormal working time(hours) by the abnormal additional working hours calculation. Although, Hong Kong companies' productivity will be raised, but which are not to the extent that it compensates Hong Kong enterprises for their increased wage or salary costs. In fact, Hong Kong enterprises, their costs are passed on to the clients, it causes Hong Kong's economic growth has an impact on international competitiveness to cause economic declining in possible when these enterprises need to raise their products' sale prices to balance their salary or wage cost rasing to win their import competitors. Another effect is that Hong Kong individual labor's incomes decrease, which means that Hong Kong private consumption also falls in this scenario to influence HK economic growth seriously. Thus, the HK economic growth problem will be caused, due to these factors lead to a fall in Hong Kong social household private consumption. Consequently, it will cause many HK employers hope to raise Hong Kong productivity and they will raise the total amount of Hong Kong labor actually worked hours will be risen to such as extent as the increasing in normal working time(hours) from 8 or 9 hours per normal working day to 10 or 11 or 12 hours, even more extra abnormal hours per working day to the current labors. But they do not like to spend more salary or wage expenditure to employ full time extra labors, instead of increasing extra abnormal working hours to current labors to achieve productivity of raising, due to the cost will be increased if they choose to employ extra full time labors if they want to raise productivity. However, I feel they will raise productivity in the short term, but they will not raise productivity in the long term when they choose to raise their current labors abnormal working hours per working day.

The assumption will be made regarding to the relationship between the HK labor market's abnormal long time working hours factor and whether it can influence Hong Kong economic growth in long time for this research economic problem. For example, how many hours Hong Kong labor would actually work or how much workers have efficient productivity and efficiency and how much salaries or wages would be affected as a result of the increasing in working time(hours) in Hong Kong employment market.

I shall apply endogenous growth theory to Hong Kong labor market. As this theory indicates that this model also incorporated a new concept of human capital, whose capital is increasing rates of return. Research done in this area has focused on what increases human capital (e.g. education) or technological change (e.g. innovation) to influence HK economic growth. In macro economic environment, it indicates that economic growth means the increase in the market value of the products and services produced by the country's economy over time. It is conventionally measured as the percent rate of increase in real growth domestic product or real GDP. The growth of the ratio of GDP to population (GDP per capital, per capita income). Thus, an increase in growth is caused by more efficient use of inputs is referred to as intensive growth. GDP growth is caused only be increased in such as capital, population or territory is called extensive growth. Thus, in economy growth theory, typically refers growth off potential output, i.e. production is at full employment. However, HK unemployment ratio is still high to compare other developed or developing countries, although the labors supply are enough to HK employment market.

The working time is the period of time that an individual spends at paid occupation labor. Many countries regulate the work week by law, such as minimum daily rest periods, annual holidays and a maximum number of working hours per week. Working time may vary from person to person often depending on location, cultural, lifestyle choice and the profitability of the individual's livelihood.

Generally, most Hong Kong employers need labours work long time working hours abnormally. For example, low educational workers, such as security occupations of labors need to work per working day is twelve hours or more, restaurant waiters and dish cleaners also need to work ten to twelve hours or more per working day, bank counter cashiers or audit firm staffs also need to work over time from 10 to 12 hours or more per working day and who have no extra salaries for over time salaries payment commonly. Standard working hours or normal working hours refers to the legislation to limit the working hours per day, per week, per month or per year. If an employee needs to work overtime, the employer will need to pay overtime payments to employees as required in the law. Generally speaking, standard working hours countries wordwide are around 40 to 44 hours per week (but not everywhere: such as France employers need labors work from 35 hours per week, North Korea employers need labors work up to 112 hours per week). Maximum working hours refers that the employee can't work than the level specified in the maximum working hours law. It seems that Hong Kong many employers had needed labors to work above standard working hours per week to compare to other developed countries, e.g. America, France, England, New Zealand etc. developed countries.

On the 20th century, work hours are declined by almost half, mostly due to rising wages are brought about by renewed economic growth with a supporting role from legislation human rights. The decline countined at a faster in Europe: For example, France adopted a 35 hours work week in 2000 year. In 1995, China adopted a 40 hours week, eliminating half day work on Saturday. Technology has also continued to improve worker productivity, permitting standards of living to rise as hours declined. In developed economies, as the time needed to manufacturing products has declined more working hours have become available to provide services. In fact, on the one hand, Hong Kong manufacturing industry has declined, such as clothing, shoes, toy etc. manufacturing industry. On the other hand, its service industry need many labors to supply in the labor market per day, e.g. banking, accounting, restaurant, security etc. service sectors. A reduction in Hong Kong working time can be accomplished in various ways, and that Hong Kong enterprise's production costs will be affected in different ways depending on what type of measured is used. Usually Hong Kong employers would be likely to ask those already employed to do more overtime or who will require part time workers to increase whose working hours, especially would pass salaries expense from them on to charge higher sale price to their clients. Then, which would increase the rate of inflation and weaken competitiveness to win overseas competitors' product import.

I shall use these methods to examine this research problem, e.g. statistical analysis and economic concepts, such as GDP, economic growth and labor participation rate. Aim to research whether HK abnormal long time working hours can raise productivity and influence HK economic growth in long term. As regards Hong Kong enterprises' productivity, my research will be discussed what factors that may lead to either an increase or a decrease in productivity and I shall conclude what the effects are very difficult to assess as conditions vary between and it will concern within different service industry sectors, e.g. hotel, bank, restaurant, security, professional service etc. service occupations. These service labors of numbers are more than manufacture labors of numbers in Hong Kong nowadays. Of vital importance for the effect on Hong Kong employment of a reduction of working time is the extent to which wages or salaries are adopted. If the occupations where there was a shortage of labors, Hong Kong employers were to try to contibute to higher pay claims to long time working labors. According to the 1961 year population census, the size of the economically active population was approximately 1.2 million during that year and who was also economically active population was seeking worker. The labor force had grown to 3.1 million by 1996 year (William. C & Wing. S, 1997).

In 1996 year, HK economy was industrialization process filled by a large supply of relativey unskilled but hardworking labor, many of them were refugees from China, the dominance of manufacturing has been largely displaced by commerce and service sector and the demand for unskilled labor is falling relative to the demand for skilled and educated workers in Hong Kong. According to the 1961 year population census, the size of the economically active population was approximately 1.2 million during that year and who was also economically active population or the active seeking worker. The labor force had grown to 3.1 million by 1996 year (William. C & Wing. S, 1997). William. C & Wing. S (1997) also indicated that HK Census and Statistics department (various years) reported specific labor participation rate and size of the Hong Kong force from 1961 year to 1996 year. "During this period the size of the labor force grew from 1.2 million to 2.5 million. The annual rate of increase was 3.7%. It implies labor supply increased so rapidly, so labor intensive industries were developed. However, Hong kong population had increased to 7 million till to 2015 year." Hence the size of the labor force had increased more and it implied labors would supply more than employers demand. But, HK employer job supply numbers are less than HK labor demand numbers in HK employment market. It seems that if HK employers did not like to spend more salaries expenditure to employ extra labors to rise productivity, it would cause many young single or married people unemployed.

Any countrie's economic growth are usually calculated in real terms. i.e. inflation adjusted terms to eliminate the effect of inflation on the price of products produced. Economic growth has the indirect potential to reduce poverty, as a result of an increase in employment opportunities and increased labor productivity. However, employment is no guarantee of escaping poverty. The international labor organization estimates that is as many as 40% of workers are poor, not earning enough to keep families above the $2 a day poverty line. For instance, in India, poor are wage earner in formal employment because jobs are insecure and low paid and offer no chance to accumulate wealth to avoid risk, other countries found bigger benefits from focusing more no productivity improvement than low skilled work. Thus, increase in employment without increase in productivity lead to rise in the number of working poor and these countries don't apply the creation of quality and not quantity in labor market policies. In Vietnam, for example, employment growth has slowed when productivity growth has continued. Furthermore, productivity increases don't always lead to increase wages, e.g. United States, the gap between productivity and wages was been rising since the 1980 year. The overseas Development Institute study showed that other sectors were just as important in reducing unemployment as manufacturing.

Nowadays, the services sector is most effective as translating productivity growth into employment growth in Hong Kong. The HK Government forecast (2012) indicated that "HK's economy has slowed, growing by 0.9% year-on year in the half of 2012 year, after expanding by 5% in 2011 year. For 2012 year, the economy is forecast to grow at 1-2%. Consumer prices increased by 5.3% in 2011 year and 4.7% year-on-year in the first half of 2012 year. The unemployment rate was 3.2% for April-June 2012 year, compared with 3.4% for 2011 year." Although, it seemed that unemployment rate decreased 0.2% for April to June 2012, but its unemployment was still existed. Moreover, HK's economy has slowed to grow by 0.9% only year-on-year in the first half of 2012 year and HK government forcast to grow at 1-2% for 2012. By United States Government statistic in 2006 year, the average man employed full time worked 8.4 hours mandatory minimum amount of paid time off for sickness or holiday. However, regular full time workers often have the opportunity to take about nine days off for various holiday. However, regular full time workers of skill leave and two weeks (10 business days) of paid holiday time with some workers receiving additional time after several years. Because of the pressure of working time with some workers receiving additional time after several years. It seems United States developed countries some workers still feel pressure of working shorten working hours can reduce the pressure of working. In fact, HK many professional workers put in longer hours than the forty hour standard per week. A forty hours work week is considered inadequate and may result in job loss or failure to be promoted. Although, these employers don't spend much salary expenditures to employ extra professional workers to share whose workload and who can perform to serve whose clients efficiently in the short time. But in the long time, it is possible that who will work pressure possibly due to who need to serve many clients every day, and whose working performance will become to be poor to cause inefficiently. Until now, HK has no legislations regarding maximum and normal working hours. The average weekly working hours of full time employees in HK is 49 hours. According to the Price and Earnings report (2012) conducted by UBS, when the global and regional average were 1,915 and 2,154 hours per year respectively, the average working hours in HK is 2,296 hours per year, which ranked the fifth longest yearly working hours among 72 countries under study. In addition, the survey is conducted by the public opinion study group of the University of HK, it showed 79% of the respondents agree that the problem of overtime work in HK is "serve" and 65% of the respondents agree that the legislation on the maximum working hours. In HK, 70% of surveyed don't receive any overtime remuneration. These show that people in HK concerns the working time issues. The equilibrium price for a certain types of labor is the wage rate. The model of labor market, even given all its assumption is logically. The criticism of application of the model of supply and demand generalizes particularly to all markets for factor of production, e.g. labor working hours. I assume HK employers don't like to employ many labors to assist current labors to raise service or productivity when their client numbers have increased. It is possible that who feel salaries expenditure can not be exceed to their reasonable budget. Hence, who need current labors to work long time hours to do too much work, even the HK labor supply is increasing and it will cause many people lose jobs. It seems HK service industry can influence its economic growth. If those service industry labors need to work long time, who will feel mental pressure to work unhealthly and who need have enough sleep. If who can't have enough sleep to face every day work in long term, whose working performance will be poor or reduce productivity to whose clients possibly in long time. I believe HK service industry labors work long time working hours per week that it will influence whose service performance to be poor. In fact, most developed countries labors working hours are less than HK seriously. For example, United States originating from the traditional American business hours of 9:00 AM to 5:00 PM. Monday to Friday, representing a workweek of five to eight hour per working day composing 40 hours in total. The actual time at work often varies between 35 and 48 hours in practice due to breakers. In many traditonal white collar positions, employees were required to be in the office during these hours to take orders from the bosses, workplace hours have become more flexible. Another example, South Korea has the fastest declining working time, which is the result of proactive more to lower working hours at all levels to increase leisure and than the 10 days of the united States and double that of the England's 8 days. Also, work hours in and 40 hour week (44 hours in specified workplaces). The overtime limits are: 15 hours a week, allowance should not be lower than 125% and not more than 150% of normal hourly rate. However, Hong Kong dish cleaners, bank cashiers occupations whose need to work over time often , due to client numbers are increasing every days and their employers do not plan to employ extra workers to share their work loading. Hence, it seems whose work over time are similar to work abnormal long time working hours in every week in HK.

Middison A.(2001) indicated that "the unemployment rate is a performance indicator of the economy." The purpose of economic activity is to transform productive resources into products and services. An economy that uses all or most of its labor force should clearly be considered as a better performing economy than one that lacks the ability to put all or most of its labor force into work and thus some labor productive respurces can not be used. In fact, in economy theory, labor demand is considered to be a derived demand, meaning that its demand is explained not by itself, but by the existence of demand for products and services that use labor as a factor production. If labor demand is a desired demand, then an assessment of the performance of the economy could certainly profit from an evaluation of how well a specific social system managers to transform labor input into products and services. It is convenient to distinguish between economic performance of an economic system and labor market performance. The former related with the ability of a social system to deliver products and services and the latter related with the important, but more specific issue, of how well the labor market managers to match supply and demand. Economic and Trade Information on HK (2012) key indicators of the labor market had finished sample simple average of 15 countries statistic analysis to show "the result was as for the role of work hours in explaining GDP per capital had negative relation between GDP and working hours, as if long working hours where used to compensate the low productivity.

The historical downward trend of working time form the slightly less than 3000 annual hours per person employed of the 1870 year to the less than 1600 year of the late 1990 year could be taken as a confirmation of this hypothesis." Thus, this hypothesis could be supported by viewpoint. It was about HK long time working hours ought not increase HK GDP and long working hours where used to compensate the low productivity to HK employers in the long time.

What is the difference of benefits between normal working hours and abnormal working hours

These research will have these two questions to be answer:

1. Can Hong Kong this individual labour abnormal long time working hours factor gives welfare benefit to every labor in the long time?
2. Can Hong Kong this abnormal labor working hours factor grow HK society whole economy in the long time?

It seems that HK employers don't like to employ extra workers to share current worker's workload, even the supply of labours is enough. Due to who do not want to pay extra each worker's salaries to raise whose productivity. To explain relationship between the workers abnormal long time working hours factor and the other resources input factor to influence HK enterprises growth in an improved model in the long time. I shall develop a model is the selection of two variables to explore. These variables have a cause and effect relationship. I shall suppose HK employers believe that workers abnormal long time working hours which can raise their productivity efficiently and which can assist HK society overall economic growth in the long time. These variables have a cause and effect relationship. From this discussion to investigate HK society overall economic growth effect is caused by companies' variable factors. The variable factors include the raising of abnormal long time working hours factor or increasing capital and machinery and equipment and building assets factor or raising natural resources for production factor or taking risking of success or failure ability in an productive enterprise factor. Thus, these separate sets of variable have been indentifies and each set could be selected for a model. In fact, Hong Kong society overall economic growth disputes many occur because a variety of resources input factors can be considered to analyze an effect cause whether which kind of resources input factors which can cause HK society economy growth is fast or slow. In my viewpoint, my exploring reasons are for a slow growing economy in HK. Some economists focus on relationship between money supply and growth in society, some in society's spending growth and some on the price level. In fact, HK economic growth is slow in the long time. I shall focus on the relationship between the HK companies' workers abnormal long time working hours factor and the other resources input factor both to influence HK society overall economic growth. Hence, I shall give assupmtions and conditions are held to be true when exploring the relationship is between HK companies and resources input variables within a model. For example, the relationship is between HK economic growth is slow or fast and labor resources supply numbers are not shortage. But HK employers ususally employ their limited numbers of labors to cause current workers need to overtime work or work in abnormal long time working hours often. Understanding the factors behind labor participation decision is an important component of the understanding long time change in labor supply in Hong Kong society.

In my another viewpoint, discussing HK labor supply, it is important to distinguish between the supply economy. The supply of Hong Kong labor to particular firm, an industry can be highly responsive to wages or salaries as workers seek the most profitable employment in HK. The supply of labors to HK society economy. On the other hand, it is typically less elastic to the labors who often change new jobs because most HK employers who need workers who work long time working hours to cause most HK labors can't have much chance to change new jobs which can provide normal working hours. So, it seems that who won't choose to change new jobs often because many HK employers who need HK labors work abnormal working hours nowadays.

HK employees of large companies of public utilities sector and the HK Government both organizations which typically enjoy more benefits and have greater job security than employers of small firms in Hong Kong society. This has lead to cause a distinction between the small HK private companies and public HK Government and public utilities sector. In fact, nowadays, most HK jobs have changes to service job nature from manufacturing job nature. However, deregulation, downsizing and pressure factors have caused many HK large companies which choose change working hours from normal 7 to 8 hours per working day to adnormal 9 to 12 hours or more per working day. Specically, the occupations of service sector job nature include: restaurant waitors, banking counter servicers, professional lawyers, share agents, security servicers, accountants etc. different service sector occupation labors. The result will cause the labors who choose to leave whose employers if who could not accept to work abnormal working hours to their current employers. Even, it will also cause the current workers who feel nervous and tired and worry to work in pressure everyday, due to who need to increase many extra hours to work often and who will lose their private entertainment time with their family or friends often, even it will be unhealthy to them due to who lack sleeping. Although, HK business cycle was the short term economy in manufacturing macroeconomic environment in beginning from 1950 year. Then, HK economy growth had developed, so many the demanding of labor numbers had been caused to increase seriously till to nowadays. The economic and trade information on Hong Kong of HK Government statistic department (2012) reported " the HK economy was forecasted to grow at 1-2% for 2012 year and it's economy had slowed growing by 0.9% per year in the half of 2012 year after expanding by 5% in 2011 year." Although, it implied that HK labor market had enough labor numbers supply. Otherwise, many HK employers don't like to employ many labor numbers to share current workers' workload. It is possible that due to whose HK current workers need to spend adnormal working hours to raise their productivity per working day to save spending extra salaries or wages expenditures to pay to employ extra labors in HK current labor market. I feel that HK economy growth is slow or poor because the main reason is due to HK Government doesn't spend expenditures to assist HK employers to raise training to their current HK labors to provide human capital to achieve to raise whose service performance to improve their efficient productivity in HK service businesses sector only in the long time. Finally, the results were discovered and will be backed by these evidence

3.1 Whether quality of life of employee or abnormal working hours which is more chance to raise productivity and economic
growth in long term

My essay will truly be a qualitative and quantitative research, it is based on experimental fact and evidence. To research the long time employment influence relationship is between the labor abnormal long time working hours factor and the influence of HK economic growth in productive model factor both. This study suggests understanding of the relationship between economic growth influences and HK labors abnormal working hours need to be raised. In fact, the HK labor force participation rate will be fallen every year. Economic growth in HK was through phases that affects growth through changes in the labor force participation rate and the relative sizes of HK society service and manufacturing sectors. In fact, HK agricultural industry sector is not existed and manufacturing industry sector numbers are decreasing and it begins to enter service industry sector. The low knowledge level of jobs include security, banking, restaurant, cleaning, transportation etc. service nature of jobs as well as the high knowledge level of jobs include lawyer, accountant, medicine, doctor, computer technician etc. professonal service nature of jobs which both are providing service to HK society nowadays. The investment theory indicates that the education is as investment human capital to provide to any companies. The main difference is that human capital is incorporated in human beings and it can't be resold. When physical capital can be acquired at almost any desired amount in boom periods and be resold during recession on secondary markets, human capital can be acquired mostly in the beginning of individual behavior by firms. I shall recommend HK companies ought choose these methods to control labors whose working hours time efficiently.

Yasuhiro (2014) showed that "wage differentials based on age and length of service in-house training refers to a process whereby workers acquire skills through daily work and occasional of the job training. Whether or not they perceive it as "training" is irrelevant. Training is also included informal learning conducted independently by the worker without any feedback from an instructor. Conceptually, the skills acquired are divided into general skills that can be used in the company currently employing the worker. The process of acquiring the latter specific training." Generally, when companies minimizes personnel costs, the ratio of marginal productivity referred to below as productivity between workers are equal to wage ratios. Therefore, the coefficient of age in the wage function expresses the rate of productivity increases due to general training and the coefficient of length of service and the rate of wage increases due to special training reason. The sum of both coefficients will express the rate of productivity increase in current companies due to training is as an important causing factor.

In conclusion, in my viewpoint, HK employers need to provide on job training to current labors to aim to raise their efficiency to productivity in the long time. Because when their labors had been trained to let them to learn how to use special skill to finish their job duties easily, then they will not need to spend much time (additional working hours) to finish their job duties per working day. On the one hand, HK employers need to measure to compare what benefits are in favour of standard working hours to whose employees. The benefits include, such as promoting work life balance and enjoy family life, increasing time for leisure and rest, beneficial to health and employees can have more time to pursue further studies as well as employers do not need to pay higher salaries to longer working hours employees or overtime pay boost income as most HK companies pay time and a half to some employees only. On the other hand, HK employers need to measure to compare what benefits are against standard working hours to employers, such as employing many part time working hours employees to assist normal working hours full time employees rather than needing full time employees work abnormal hours daily, lowering or cancelling year and bonues etc. Moreover, HK employers may also use various measure to offset the increased cost of running businesses, such as lowering average hourly anual compensation. However, when HK employees are forced to work part time jobs, who may need to acquire additional employment to maintain their standard living. Even, HK employers only force employees to work overtime in some situations. Appropriate standard working hours can vary across different industries based on the type of work performed. Such as some HK certain professional positions are difficult to define in terms of appropriate working hours. Issues can arise with employers expecting exployees to work extra hours "off the clock" in order to keep costs down. Thus, I believe that HK labors abnormal working hours time issue ought be decreased and HK employers ought employ extra workers assistance to share current labors' workload to help them to raise productivity and efficiency and HK economy will grow fast in the long time. Finally, my research aims to find that the number of hours worked is a more responsive measure of the state of the labor market than employment in HK. Comparing the number of hours worked to indicators of the wider economy shows that it is likely to be demand from HK firms (employers) which is driving the numbers of hours, rather than individual job applicant supplys to HK employment market. My analysis also show that the HK appears to have developed a long working hours culture to compare other developed countries, such as America, England, Canada etc. In fact, in the presence of HK firms may even invest to find which are more profitable to able to reduce their every employee's abnormal working hours daily rather than normal number of working hours of their every employee.

Bibliography

Economic And Trade Information On Hong Kong, (14 Aug. 2012). Hong Kong Government Forecast for 2012, retrieved from the following URL: http://www.cepa.hktdc.com

Middison A. (2001). The World Economy. A Millennial Perspective, OECD, Paris.

Yasuhio, U. (2014). Japan Labor Review, vol.11 no.3, High Economic Growth And Human Capital: Conditions For Sustained Growth, Konan University.

William, C&Wing, S.(1997). The Hong Kong Economic Policy Studies Series, published by City University Of HK Press, Hong Kong

CHAPTER NINE

Airlines service innovation strategy

Quality of traveler individual leisure need reducing

For environmental quality concept, it concerns with health, safety, wellbeing, residential satisfaction and the physical sustainability can be considered to result from an when live ability can be considered to represent the interaction between the physical and the social domains. As with expenditure on the environment, investment in social capital contributes to quality of life. However, the benefits will again vary amongst individuals, depending largely on the security of their individual circumstance. As with the environment, the government can certainly adopt strategies that provide for public security by taking measures to reduce crime, a measure likely to be appreciated by everybody (except criminal) , at least to one degree or another. In other necessary to enhance social interaction, namely community centers or sports facilities. Furthermore, the creation of social capital has an statement which responds to general social trends to raise Ireland citizen's quality of life.

I shall indicate Ireland to explain whether environmental factor is the main factor to influence our quality of life and economic growth. Is environmental quality higher in the Ireland west regions? And if so, does this compensate for lower incomes in these regions? Is it bad that rural areas are characterized by higher costs of living in areas other than housing by environmental factor? In fact, in Ireland , UK country, population increase has a direct impact on the environment by placing demands on local natural resources, particularly open space and water. It also leads to a sense of crowding that reduces the utility associated with access to the environment. How can environment factor influence economy growth in Ireland? In Ireland, agriculture has gone through a period of significant change that has been accelerated reductions in the amount of mixed cropping and traditional land management. Indeed, changes in the expectations of young farmers will ensure that further change is likely to be characterized by increases in farm size and greater specialization with implications for landscape and wildlife. These characteristics of farm holdings are more familiar in the east regions of Ireland , UK country. As with likely to extend to the west regions as the older generation of farmers retires, although this will probably be accompanied by a trend to more farming of production needs to young farmers. So, good natural environment can provide Ireland young farmers to produce more agriculture to earn income, even who can export more rice, fruits, vegetable etc. agriculture foods to overseas. Hence, Ireland GDP will be raise if it can have good natural resource environment to provide Ireland young farmers to grow foods to sell to domestic and /or foreign agricultural market. Given the rate of economic growth, and its concentration in the east of the Ireland, UK country, it would be easy to presume that the quality of the environment is higher the further away from the mid east one goes. Thus, good natural environment is an important factor to influence the farming industry development in Ireland , UK county to satisfy their needs and to raise their quality of life nowadays.

I shall indicate New Zealand and America two developed countries to explain why which are facing environmental pollution challenge to influence their citizen's quality of life and economic growth nowadays. The first country is NZ, although, New Zealand is a developed and natural environmental country, but it had been envountering air pollution annouance and noise annoyance to influence it's citizen's health-related quality of life. I shall indicate why which has this relationship between of them in New Zealand. Nowadays, New zealand population growth is an increasing demand for consumer products and urbanization have lead to concerns over the lived environments in many of the world's cities, such as Auckland, wellington cities in New Zealand. However, environmental quality is an important determinant of health, such as the bad influence of traffic-related air and noise pollution on health outcomes, specially with respect to at risk groups, both in relation to long term exposure as well as acute effect, from brief exposures. For example, cholesterol levels and in relation to myocardial infaction. Nowadays, New Zealand is encountering the high degree of air pollution and noise annoyance to influence it's citizen's quality of life. Air pollutants can be detected either visually, such as witnessing smoke emanating from a vehicles's exhaust, or by smell, such as when odorants stimulate olfactory receptors. The evidence linking air pollution to adverse impacts on human health.

Many air impacts on human health. Many air pollution health studies have focused specifically on urban area, and vehicle generated pollution in particular, as road vehicles are one of the major sources of pollution across much of the world. Elemental carbon, Nox and ultrafine particles an considered to be pollutants most strongly associated with road traffic emissions. In Auckland and Wellington cities, New Zealand , it has been estimated that 71% of summer and 21% of winter concentrations of fine particulate matter is attributable to motor vehicles. Moreover, poor town planning decisions in Auckland (and in New Zealand in general) over many decedes has meant that may people live in very close proximity to busy road and motorways within " road corridors" and so are the adverse effects of road traffic, including noise and air pollution as well as experiencing on potential for degradation in their quality of life. Such as, New Zealand is highly suitable for studies investigating the impact of roads on the health of its residents. For example, NZ, road traffic noise and aviation noist has been linked to cardiovascular disease, hypertension and ischemic heart disease. It influences NZ resident personal psychological and physical both health challenges. In fact, NZ noise increases morbidity and mortality independently of air pollution exposure, though air pollution constituted a greater burden of disease when arise exposure had a greater impac on quality of life, e.g. NZ road traffic noise and air pollution will be caused from drivers in busy time. Specially in Auckland and Wellington cities. It will influence urban and rural environmental pollution. Some retired old people who will feel annoyance when this road traffic occurs in Auckland or Wellington cities to close to their houses in transportation busy time every day.

Next developed country is America, this country's air pollution is also serious nowadays. Because traffic jam often occurs in New York, Washington, Boston etc. big cities in US. So, U.S. cities' parks and its trees have significant influence to produce fresh air to provide U.S. residents who are living in cities to breach for their body health. David J. & Gordon , M. (2016) indicated " In U.S. these urban parks are estimated to contain about 370 million trees with a structural value of approximately $300 billion." The number of park trees varies by region of the country, but which can produce significant air quality effects in and near parks, related to air temperatures, air pollution, ultraviolet indication and carbon dioxide (a dominant greenhouse gas related to global climate change). Additional open space and other vacant lands in cities, which may contain trees and other vegatation. Contribute significant additional benefits, effects of parks and open space at the city scale can vary significantly depending on the amount of parkland and amount of tree cover within the parkland.

The reasons why parks can reduce air pollution. Parks generally have lower air temperature than surrounding areas. Temperatures are usually cooler toward the center of a park than around its edges. At night, the center of a large park may be 13 degree cooler than surrounding city areas. The cooler air from parks often moves out into adjacent developed neighborhoods. This cooling of surrounding areas tends to increase with park size and percentage of the park covered by trees. So, cooler air temperature is provided by urban parks can have significant impacts on human health. During heat wave events, which can kill hundreds of people, park areas may provide city dwellers with some respite from high air tempertture, particularly in the evening, during hot, sunny days tree shade can greatly increase human comfort. Because park influences on air temperature extend to developed areas outside of parks, local energy use for heating and cooling buildings is also effected. Although, the net around effect of parks on energy costs has been by reducing temperature is difficult to estimate at least in the southern United States the effect will usually be a net annual benefit. Futhermore, large park trees will reduce winds and may provide a benefit of winter heating of buildings near the park. Although, the overall economic effect of urban trees and parks on air temperature reduction is not fully billions of dollars annually at the national scale in terms of improved environmental quality and human health.

In fact, trees and vegetation in parks can help reduce air pollution both by directly removing pollutants and by reducing air temperatures and building energy use in and near parks. There tree effects can reduce pollutant emissions and formation. However, park vegetation can increase some pollutants by either directly emitting volatile orgnic compounds that can contribute to ocone and carbon monoxide formation or indirectly by the emission of air pollutants through vegetation maintenance practices, such as operation of chain and use of transportation fuels. David J. & Gordon , M. (2016) showed "Annual pollution removal and economic benefits by U.S. urbank park trees is estimated at about 75,000 tones ($500 million) or 80 pounds per acre of tree cover ($300 per acre of tree cover). Carton storage and annual removal by urban park trees and soils in the United States is estimated at about: carton storage trees: 75 million tons ($1.6 billion), carton storage (soils) : $102 million tons of carbon removal (trees): 2.4 million tons ($50 million)". Park management is recommended by U.S. environment protection department: considering that most of the effects of trees on microclimate and air quality are beneficial for park users and nearby residents; park designs that include a variety of land cover, areas of dense trees, scattered trees and lawn are likely to provide the greatest opportunities for optimum physical comfort of visitors; increase the number of healthy trees (increase pollution removal and carbon storage); sustain existing tree cover (maintains pollution removal levels) and (carbon storage); maximize use of low volatile organic compound emitting trees reduces ozove and carbon monoxide formation; sustain large, healthy trees (large trees have greatest per tree effcts on pollution and carbon removal); using long-lived trees (reduces long term pollutant emissions from removal; reducing fossil fuel in maintaining vegetation reduces pollutant ans carbon emissions)." So, if US had many green parks, then which can reduce air pollution, also it can assist many travellers who prefer to travel to US to raise GDP travelling income growth generally.

(i) Why environmental pollution and human right abuses has close relationship to influence quality of life and economic growth?

In fact, environment pollution and human right abuses has close relationship. It is clear that poverty situations and human rights abuses are worsened by environmental degradation. The result can influence poor human quality of life to the developing countries' people unfairly. There are these several abvious reasons: firstly, the exhaustion of natural resources leads to unemployment and emigration to cities; secondly, this affects the enjoyment and exercise of basic human rights. Environmental conditions contribute to a large extents to the spread of infections diseases. From the 4,400 million of people who live in developing countries, almost 60% lack basis health care services, a almost a third of these people have no access to safe water supply; thirdly, degradation poses new problems, such as environmental refugees. Environmental refugees suffer from significant economic, socio-cultural and political consequences. And fourthly, environmental degradation worsens existing problems suffered by developing and developed countries. David J. Nowak & Gordon M. Melsler (2016) showed" Air pollution , for example, accounts for 2.7 million to 3.0 million of deaths annually and of these 90% are from developing countries. " Hence, our societies need to concern human right law to protect unfair treatment to developing countries people. Firstly, both disciplines have deep social root, even though human rights law is more rooted within the collective consciousness, the accelerated process of environmental degradation is generating a new " environmental consciousness". Secondly, both disciplines have become internationalized . The international community has assumed the commitment to observe the realization at human rights and respect for the environment. Thirdly, both areas of law tend to universalize their object of protection. Human rights are presented as universal and the protection of the environment appears as everyone is responsibility.

Human right and environment law can raise our quality of life because the first approach is one where environmental protection is described as a possible means of fulfulling human rights standards. Here, environmental law is conceptualized as giving a protection that would help ensure the well-being of future generations as well as the survival of those who depend immediately upon natural resources for their livelihood. So, the end is fulfulling human rights, and the route is though environmental law, the second approach places the two sphere in inverted positions, it states that the legal protection of human rights is an effective means to achieving the ends of conservation and environmental protection. Therefore, the presently existing human right is as a route to environmental protection. The focus is on the connection to influence any economy: health, food supply , housing, fresh natural air supply etc. aspects of quality of life issues. Hence, human right and environment law and human quality of life and economic growth has close relationship . We can not neglect to concern how to achieve human right law to protect our nature environment existing in our societies.

What are environmental factors affect human health in important way, both positive and negative? On positive environmental factor aspect, which can sustain health, and promoting them is preventive medicine. They include : sources of nutrition (farming, oil quality, water availability, bio diversity/bio integrity, genetically modified organisms ; hurting, fishing: wildlife, fish populations; water (drinking, cooking, cleaning,sanitation); air quality; ozone layer (protection from cancers disease etc).; space for exercise and recreation, sanitation/waste recycling and disposal. On negative environmental factors aspect, which are threats to health, and controlling them is public environmental health. They include: environmental conditions favouring disease sectors (endemic and exotic sectors); invasive biota (visuses, bacteria etc.), their hosts and sectors; environmental disruptions: floods, droughts, storms, fires earthquakes, volcanoes; air quality: pollution landing to respiratory disease or cancers; water quality: biotic and abiotic contaminants ; integrity of water transport and intrastructure; monitoring and management of municipal, agricutural, industrial outflows to the environment (gases, liquids, solid waste), human changes of the environment that: create conditions that favour disease; disturb and release noxious levels of previously bound chemicals (e.g. mercury released becomes poison) or bioto (e.g. methane released from thawed peat contributes to climate changes, create temporary, intense, life threatening heat islands (e.g. urban heat waves exacerbated by climate change); result from nuclear; biological or chemical welfare or terrorism, disruption cased by other war and violense.

(ii) What is space and environmental technology?

For example, Cananda is a developed country and it begins to concern environmental pollution challenge to announced $3 million to support the initiative strengthening health and environment linkages: from knowledge to action. The initiative will bring together scientific, technical and socio-economic information on environment and health linkages, and transfer that knowledge to inform decision-making at the local, regional and national levels. Also, Canada is principally concerned with the health of Canadians. This involves health factors in Canada and in biologically shared health regions (shared geography or exposure through trade and travel). Supports international health initiatives, such as determining health risks throught environmental analysis of disease vectors in Africa or Asia.

How can the space and environmental factors affecting health? Environmental information and environmental management contribution to the maintenance and restoration of health. Space based environmental management factors and communications can play roles in: Environmental information is for optimising use of health resources; distribution of and access to health advice and treatment (i.e. to health staff treatment facilities; short range environmental prediction for avoidance of high risk, situations and to guide immediate health system responses. Managing acute risks, adopting to them (e.g. temporary moving of vulnerable elderly monitored; modeling of health impact of environmental parameters; prediction of long term health resource needs and environmental planning and mitigation and adaptation to global changes. Large benefits are possible from attention to environmental factors, e.g. asthma prevention, disease and epidemiology. Benefits need to be quantified. This is of particular interest and relevance to pandemics , such as malasia in underdeveloped countries, potentially saving thousands of lives.

What is space and environmental technology? It can contribute to and keep abreast of environmental health forecasts (using existing models and known parameters); prepare and deliver prospectuses for what space can do in anticipation or response; steer space programs according to real risks and real accumulative health benefits, as long technical investment, don't focus primarily on threats that may have high emotional impact , but are of low actual risk; position space technology and the canadian space program in people's winds, aggressively and realistically, as a first line contributor to foresight and preduction, long term maintenance of well-being and prevention of factors of ill-health ; ongoing delivery of health services and management of current health factors and potentially capable and ready to respond in health emergencies. Finally, making the full business case for investment in space technology and space program contributions relative to the full and public and private cost of health programs. This connects not only to GDP raising, but to indicators of quality of life to any countries.

● Reference

Cornelia, B.F. (1999) Rural development news, the North Central Regional Center For Rural Development vol. no 24 , IOWA.

David J. Nowak & Gordon M. Melsler (2016) " Air quality effects of urban trees and parks." National recreation and park association, USA.

De Hollander, A. E. M., J.M. Melse, Elebret & P. G.N. Kramers (1999), " An Aggregate public health indicator to represent the impact of multiple environmental exposures" Epidemiology: 606-617.

Felce, D. and Perry, J. (1995). Quality of life: A contribution to its definition and measurement, vol. 16, no.1 pp: 51-74.

Los Angeles Country Department Of public Health (2016), Country Health Ranking Model, Retrieved From www.countryhealthrankgings.org/our-approach. USA.

Melse, J.M. & A.E. M. De Hollander (2001). " Human Health And The Environment", background document for the OECD Environmental Outlook, OECD, Paris.

McGregor, S.L. T., & Goldsmith, E.B. (1998). Expanding our understanding of quality of life, standard of living and well-being. Journal of family and consumer science, 90(2), 2-6, 22.

McMichael, A.J. M. Mckee, J. Shkolnikov and T. Valkanen (2004), " Morality trends and setbacks, global convergence or divergence?", Lancet 363, 1155-1159.

Yale Center For Environmental Law And Policy (2006). Environmental Performance Index. Data available on-line at http://epi.yale.edu

Future of sustainable resources
scarcity economic and social loss to oil industry

In economic theory, it indicates two major factors are responsible for the emergence of economic problems. They are (i) the existence of unlimited human wants and (ii) the scarcity of available resources, such as limited numbers of food and natural resource shortage. I feel that human need to solve these two problems before 2050 years. How to balance an optimization approach for human and ecological flow needs ? How to solve climate change environment problem and welfare is for the centrality of human need? Because natural environment factor and natural resource and food shortage and our social economic growth which will have close connection relationship. If natural environment is bad, it will influence a lot of crops numbers can't be grown in farms. The reason of crops shortage will be caused, due to numbers of crops supply to be reduced because bad weather can not grow much crops and overpopulation numbers will increase largely at the same time before 2050 year. It will cause the numbers of demand is more than supply seriously. The result of the prices of foods will be increased by overpopulation and food shortage, so that it will cause every country inflation will be risen, it will occur in developing countries urban areas due to which have , such as India , China, Africa etc. countries have no many farms to provide to farmers to grow foods because air and water pollution and factories are built on farm land , so which need to pay higher price to import crops and foods to provide whose overpopulation to eat from overseas developed countries. Experience of developing countries that have succeeded in the reducing hunger and malnutrition shows that economic growth doesn't automatically ensure success, the source of growth matters too. This isn't surprising since 75% of the poor in developing countries live in rural areas and their incomes are directly or indirectly linked to agriculture. Many countries will continue depending on international trade to ensure their food security. It is estimated that by 2050 year developing countries net import of rice will were than double from 135 million tones in 2008/2009 to 300 million in 2050 year. It seems overpopulation will cause developing countries foods shortages in 2050 years.

Climate change and increased biofuel production represent major risks for long term food security. Studies estimate that the aggregate negative impact of climate change on African agricultural output up to 2080 year to 2100 year could be between 15% and 30%. Agriculture will have to adapt to climate change, but it can also help mitigate the effects of climate change. A recent study estimates that continued rapid expansion of biofuel production up to 2050 year would lead to the number of pre-school children in Africa and South Asia being 3 and 1.7 million higher. Thus, policies promoting the use of food based biofuels need to be reconsidered with the aim of reducing the competition between food and fuel for scare resources. The sharp increases in food price that occurred in global and national markets in recent years, and the resulting increases in the number of hungry have sharpened the awareness of policy makers and of the general public. Hence, different countries governments need to concern safe agricultural system to avoid any foods shortage to supply after 2050 year.

The perspective for 2050 year raises a number of important questions. Are current public and private investments sufficient to ensure adequate agricultural production potential, sustainable use of natural resources, information and communication research for technological breakthroughs to avoid foods shortage for the future? What needs to be undertaken to help agricultural meet the challenges of climate change and growing energy scarcity? What can be done to ensure food security in Africa, India , China etc. developing countries. The facing highest population growth rates,. The severest impacts from climate change and the heaviest burden of HIV/AIDS etc. diseases threats.

Finally, on the changing socio-economic environment hand, the main socio-economic factors that drive increasing food demand are population growth, increasing urbanization and rising incomes. In 2007 year, the USA dept. of Economic and Social affairs indicated that in fact, the developed countries population growth is slower than developing countries. However, all of the growth in the world's population will take place in urban areas. By 2050 year, more than 70% of the world's population is expected to be urban. Thus, scientists need to concern to predict developing countries urban area people foods demand and supply both numbers whether global foods can provide enough supply to urban area people in developing countries after 2050 year. On the other side, human will concern whether there be enough natural resource base of land, water and genetic diversity to meet developing countries needs after 2050 year.

What factors cause the resources scarcity and why human need to solve the resources scarcity before 2050 year

In comparison to the past 50 years, the rate at which pressure are building up on natural resources-land, water, bio-diversity will be increasing during the coming 50 years. An expanded use of agricultural feedstock for biofuels and ongoing environment degradation would work in the opposite direction. Much of the natural resource base already in use worldwide shows degradation . These include capture fisheries and water supply . In addition, actions to other ecosystem services, such as the ecosystem service, food production often cause the degradation of others, soil nutrient depletion, erosion, desertification, deflection of freshwater reserves, loss of tropical forest and biodiversity are clear indicators.

Whether natural resource base should be adequate to meet the future demand at global level. Whether any developing countries should still limit commercial natural resource import capacity to let rural area population to use to protect whose domestic natural industry development when rural area population will be increasing seriously in 2050 year. Biodiversity, another essential resource for agricultural and food production is threatened by urbanization , deforestation, pollution and the conversion of wetlands. As a result of agricultural modernization, changes in diets and population density, humankind increasingly depends on a reduced amount to agricultural biological diversity for its food supplies.Thus major reforms and investments are needed in all regions to cope with rising scarcity and degradation of land, water and biodiversity and with the added pressures resulting form rising incomes, climate change and energy demands.

There is a need to establish the right incentives to protect agriculture's environmental services to protect biodiversity and to ensure food production using new agricultural technologies before 2050 year. For the developing countries, in order to ensure that resources are available in the required quantity and quality and in the urban locations where they are needed, large additional investments need to be made in order to avoid rural people of hunger coincides with resource scarcity before 2050 year. Increased investment incentives and provided stable production growth incentives : land, water and biodiversity of three natural resources. The aim should be to stop over-exploitation, degradation and pollution, promote efficiency gains and expand overall capacities as appropriate .

To provide the rural population engaging in ecosystem services with win-win solution to improve the sustainability of ecosystems, mitigate climate change and improve rural incomes. Whether and under what conditions the estimated future food demand can be met and how food security can be achieved. Hence, every country needs to have an effective economy system to attempt to solve the basic economic problems. The function of the economy is to allocate scarce resources among unlimited wants. Moreover, every country needs to have effective economic system to study of its citizen behavior in relation to how scarce resources to allocated and how choices are made between alternative uses of the country government's limited expenditure. Due to our earth has scarce resources, it implies human will scarce natural resources to provide us to use. Our governments need to predict whether what our earth's limited natural resources will be all used in order to solve our natural resources to be used in the short time quickly as well as our governments need to apply effective economic system to design soluble methods to avoid our earth will be not to provide any natural resources to satisfy our daily essential needs in one day.

The average U.S. resident , in a year, consumes 275 pounds of meats, uses 635 pounds of paper and uses energy equivalent to 7.8 metric tons of oil. Before, long years ago, the average American ate 197 pounds of meat, used 366 pounds of paper and used energy equivalent to 5.5 metric tons of oil. In the U.S. there is about one passenger car for every two people. Otherwise, Europeans have about one passenger car for every 3.1 people. On the other side, Developing countries have on average, about one passenger car for every 49 people. What does economics have to tell us about these differences in consumption?

Consume sovereignty means the idea that consumer's needs and wants determine the shape of all economic activities. Is this belief valid? That is are the final goals of economic activity all to be found in the act of consumption. Hence, if one day, our earth scarce any kinds of natural resources to be caused shortage, e.g. water, air, oil, land , gas, solar, gas , unclear , wind energy resources as well as foods e.g. vegetables and meats etc. eating resources. Due to human numbers are increasing, such as China, India and Africa etc. developing countries‘ people numbers are increasing much than the USA, UK etc. developed countries 's people numbers every year. But, our earth's vegetables and pigs, cows, sheet etc. meats foods numbers are decreasing every year. I believe that our foods and vegetables and natural energy resources prices will be influenced to be rose too much due to human demands (wants) are excessive to compare to our earth natural energy resources and meats and vegetables foods supply numbers. On the other side ,if every country's inflation will be increasing , but our salaries will be decreasing, or our salaries will be kept to stable and no changing, even employers will decide to dismiss employees to cause unemployment ratio rising. In result, global consumers' shopping ability will be falling down and crime numbers will be rising by poor, such as developing countries, e.g. Africa, China, India etc. will have many people feel hungry, or who feel diseases , even who will be sick to die from diseases or will be kill to die by crimes. Also , these other factors include foods scarcity, foods and natural energy prices rising, working and home environment pollution etc. factors , these factors can then cause global economic poor , serious inflation ,unbalance incomes reallocation between rich and poor people, discrimination and unfair threat will be caused between countries, even , the war between countries will be caused. Hence, our governments need to concern how to solve our earth natural energy resources and foods and vegetables scarcity challenge , due to which will be caused shortage to supply to human to consume to use or eat in the future on day occurrence. Thus, above reasons can be concluded that as below:

Nowadays, the numbers of human (every country people) are increasing more than just the increasing numbers of consumers‘ consumption activities , such as our daily essential consumption include meats and vegetables etc. foods and natural energy resources, such as lands, water, gas, oil, wind, water, nuclear, electricity etc. energy . Moreover, natural resources and foods numbers are decreasing due to overpopulation are increasing in developing countries and the numbers of emigration are rising to developing countries, such as UK, USA, France, Germany poor people numbers are increasing due to war or poor issues occur in the developing countries. Moreover, due to the provision consumption activities are most directly address living standard (or lifestyle) goals, which have to do with satisfying basic needs and getting pleasure through the use of natural resources energy provision service demand and vegetables and foods tasty demand by the developed countries' people needs . Also, these poor issues will occur in the developing countries possibly in the future. Due to these factors, I predict our essential consumption , such as foods, vegetables and natural energy resources service provision price will be increasing in global competitive market due to foods and vegetables and energy shortage will be caused by the overpopulation demands rising up and foods and natural energy resources supply numbers falling down factors. Hence, our governments must need to find methods to solve the problem of our essential natural resources shortage and foods scarcity issues occurrence in the future.

Suggestions to solve resources scarcity methods

● Estimation of growth of rural population and income and expected changes of natural resources supply numbers

I recommend developing countries need to estimate growth of rural population and incomes numbers and expected changes numbers in consumption patterns . Taking into account developing countries‘ known resource capacities and projected development of yields, input use and technologies and making assumptions about their future trading capacity, estimates are also make of future food production level, land use and natural resource numbers import trade demand of developing countries estimation before 2050 year.

Estimation of water natural resources, such as water scarcity agreement on key definitions, the conceptualization of water scarcity in ways that are meaningful for policy development and decision making, the quantification of water scarcity, policy and technical response options available to ensure food security in conditions of water scarcity, criteria and principles that should be used to establish priorities for action to response to water scarcity in agriculture and ensure effective and efficient water scarcity copying strategies. Thus, developing countries will concern to reduce water resources shortage risk. Why is predict water supply important?

During the twentieth century, large multi-purpose dams have served the needs of agriculture, energy and growing cities, and helped protect population from flood hazards. On farm water conservation, particularly the adoption of agricultural practices that reduce runoff to increase the infiltration and storage of water in the soil in rained agriculture is the most relevant local supply enhancement option that farmers have to increase foods production by increasing water availability and decentralized water harvesting conveniently in rural areas for farmers needs. For example, ground water exploitation has grown or in scale. Ground water's capability to provide flexible, on demand water in support of irrigation has been as a major advantage by farmers in rural areas. Thus, farmers need to learn how to reduce water losses increase water productivity and water re-allocation to avoid natural resource of water shortage after 2050 year.

● Renewable natural resources and foods planting sustainability development

The concept of sustainability has become the current answer to absolving our earth of its environment and economic crises in the 21 ST. century. On the one side, the pessimists, usually ecologists and other scientists, who are convinced the earth can't forever support the different countries' demand of renewable and non renewable resources. On the other side, are the optimists, the economists, who are equally convinced that the earth, with market incentives, appropriate public policies, material substitution, recycling and new technology can satisfy the needs and improve the quality of human welfare. Both views are supporting arguments are explored used and sustainable development. Thus, renewable old energy natural resource can keep old energy natural resource to renew to use or research other new energy resource to substitute old natural resource, it will reduce the risk of energy resource shortage if the other new natural resource can be substituted to the old natural energy resource to use in our daily life , such as inventing one kind of new energy resource can be used to substitute gas to drive cars or drive boats or plans or the old gas can be renewed or cycled to use to drive cars or boats or the oil can be renewed or cycled to use to cook. Also, our earth foods, e.g. fruits, vegetables or meats etc. foods if which can be recopied to grow many numbers planting foods from any one kind food or many kinds of foods, such as one meat can be copied to manufacture two to three same kind tasty meats or unlimited same kind tasty meats. I believe the renewable natural resource energy or recopied foods can reduce our foods or energy shortage after 2050 year.

The application of sustainable strategy
between local and national and regional

of international countries

A redefined concept is of the society as whole system, made up of three concentric circles: the economy is found within the society, and both the economy and society exist within the environment. Sustainability indicators are therefore said to attempt to measure the extent to which these boundaries are respected.

I think sustainability measure as a whole concept environment, society and economy. At the bottom of the triangle is the environment or the ultimate means which represents natural resources as a precondition for decent human life. The economy (which includes technology, politics and ethics) is on the next, is not independent but serves as a vehicle for achieving ultimate ends. At the top is equity or society or ultimate end which refers to the wellbeing of the human being.

According to Daly(1990) who indicated "that the economy therefore succeeds to the extent that it conserves and restores ultimate means the environment, and enables the achievement of ultimate ends society equity. This is the application of sustainable strategies to local, national and regional issues, as well as the role of international agencies in local /national strategies." Our earth occurs issues of overpopulation, diseases and political conflict, developed countries also have to deal with problems, such as pollution and unlimited urban expansion with limited resources. Sustainability is the process suggested to improve the quality of human life within the limitations of global environment. It involves solutions for improving human welfare that doesn't result in regarding the environment. We(human) need to concern living within certain limits of the earth's capacity to maintain life, understanding the interconnections among economy, society and environment and maintaining a fair distribution of foods and vegetables and natural energy resources and opportunity for this generation and the next. Thus, on the one side, our governments need to concern three categories: Social/ political, environmental and economic issues are interconnection. Social issues include poverty, consultation, empowerment and culture. Environmental issues include pollution, natural resources and biodiversity/ resilience and economic issues include efficiency, growth and stability. It seems our governments need to considerate social and environment and economic issues to reduce our natural energy resources and foods and vegetables to allocate to let every country people to use fairly.

Reducing global warming and biodiversity
issue occurrence

It seems that we need to know our society will influence our natural environment good or bad. If our society damaged our natural environment, then it will be possible to influence our foods supply of decreasing numbers. e.g. fishes, pigs, cows, sheep and vegetables and fruits etc. foods . Due to bad climate and air and lands and ocean pollution can influence foods can not be grown easily and successfully in farms or fishes can not be lived healthy in ocean. Then, it will cause our meats, fruits and vegetables etc. foods supply shortage. Even, our gas , oil, water etc., natural resources will cause our oceans and lands pollution if human pollute our oceans and lands. In result, our natural resources used numbers will be reduced due to clean lands and oceans are polluted for long time. Finally, natural resources and meats and vegetables and fruits , rice etc. foods prices will be risen due to which are shortage to supply and developing countries' population numbers are increasing which will cause more demand.

Finally, it shall cause many developing countries' poor people who can't eat enough meats, fruits, rice vegetables etc. foods as well as who can't use enough natural resources to attempt to adapt whose past normal daily life, such as lacking enough oil to help them to cook foods to be heat to eat at home or lacked enough water to be boiled to drink. Even, whose health will be poor , then who get diseases to cause die easily when there is no enough oil to buy or enough water to drink. Hence, these developing countries governments need to concern foods and natural resource scarcity problems which will be occurred if who do not find methods to reduce this issue to be occurred after 2050 year.

As Erekson et. al.(1999) concerns about" loss of resources, such as biodiversity or global weather (climate) warming are pacified with the potential of new technology which will lead to greater investments to the future generations for alternative resources and welfare."

Hence, I recommend our governments need to concern global warming or biodiversity issue because of our foods and vegetables and natural resources, such as water, air will be possible polluted to be caused shortage quickly if our earth's global warming or biodiversity issue occurrence to cause our earth's large oceans or lands areas to be polluted. Our governments can attempt to control natural resources , such as oil, gas, water supply into the market and not though the political special conditions to keep them, without considering the political and social standings, which rule the control power and the use of those resources. Such as developed countries can be able to minimize the impact of foods or/and natural resources production and consumption over the natural resources, they are only mechanisms built within an economic rationality, which should be possible to control its people's demand of natural resources, e.g. oil, gas, water and supply of natural resources get more balance. Then these natural resources sale price won't be raised more every year. When there developed countries' people , such as American and Britain who can control to reduce to spend to use the excessive natural resources too much in any time and any place habitually. Then , I believe the developing countries‘ governments e.g. Africa, China, India, which can buy those developed countries governments' excessive natural resources to raise those developed countries‘ natural resources supply numbers to provide to whose people to use as well as the most important benefit is that developed countries can gain foreign income from excessive natural resources expectation. Then, these governments will raise GDP economic growth. Hence, if developed countries could control whose people consume natural resource numbers and they could also control to produce natural resource supply numbers . Then, they can gain more excessive natural resources export chance to achieve to raise GDP economic growth aim for long term. As Kirkby et al., (1995)explained "the complexity of sustainable development our natural environment. If our governments can let our earth natural environment gets creation to maintenance, then our natural environment will be reduced the time to degradation. In the long time result, our society rural and urban economy will be growth , then our different countries‘ global growth will be caused diversity." Hence, it seems different countries' governments need to concern sustainable development to our natural environment .

How to apply agricultural green bio-economy concept to solve control sustainable food consumption and production in a resource-constrained world

Nowadays, challenges for the global food supply have never been so complex. Between now and 2050 year, it has been predicted that growth in the global population and changing diets in developing countries, special in India and China and Africa etc. developing countries which may lead to an increase of around 70% in food demand. At the same time, depletion of fossil hydrocarbons will increase the demand for biomass for biofuels and industrial materials. Hence, developed and developing countries‘ governments ought need to coordinated to reduce air and water pollution and approached to lands use planning and oceans use planning to supply enough farms to grow potatoes, vegetables, tomatoes, fruits and let cows, pigs, sheep etc. animals can have comfortable and clean farm to live to produce good tasty meats to provide human to eat as well as to reduce pollution to supply fresh and clean water to let fishes to be lived and provides to human to drink clean water. Due to overpopulation will be predicted by scientists after 2050 year, so it will be caused foods and energy shortage possibly. Hence, different countries' governments need have long term perspectives to prepare to have enough foods and energy supply to provide us to eat and use for our earth with resource constraints and environmental limits, and which includes guideline on agricultural research to achieve foods supply aim.

On the one hand, I believe the knowledge-based bio-economy can play in realizing there challenges in particular the balance demand between foods, feed and fuel and the strategic role new technologies can have upon developing a sustainable an green bio-economy. On the other hand, I also think production of the presently high resource dependence and to build more environmentally begin sustainable agriculture system able to feed 9 billion people by 2050 year. I recommend global governments need to concern all aspects of food security including the total food chain and impacts of other land-use and management as well as non food areas, research areas which can be closed to free resources for new priorities, research to manufacture more new unique natural resources, due to gas, oil etc. resources will be used all in one day. On the energy shortage aspect, Substitution of these oil, gas etc. natural resources are needed . For example, nuclear energy is a kind of new natural resource, it can be used to push machines of rockets to be moved in space. In the future, I hope that nuclear energy can be used to drive cars or ships or trains etc. transportation tools in land. Hence, new natural resource research is essential and valid investment to be improved by scientists in the future.

On the global food supply interconnected challenges hand, including climate changes, energy and water supply are further encountered by the financial and economic changes in an increasingly globalized world. As a result, it is unclear how the growing demand for food and bioenergy (both biomass and biofuels) within a wider bio-economy can be met without further compromising ecosystem services on which all economic activities and social depend. I shall emphasizes the interaction of the economic, social and ecological components of our food systems at various levels, with feed backs increasingly the uncertainty and risks relating to future developments.

We need to face the food requirements of a growing world population have to be satisfied and we also need to the face of increasing resource scarcities, such as water, energy and land and foods etc. with the situation further exacerbated by climate change. Thus, we need to focus on our reducing demand through food consumption behavioral changes and structural changes in food systems and food chains change. Due to some developed countries people often to choose to buy these foods to eat excessively e.g. cow meat and pig meat and drink excessive soft drinks, e.g. man-made color juice. So, these developed countries consumers will feel these excessive foods and soft drinks can be rubbish if these developed countries consumers often drink these man-made color juice and eat pig and cow meats often excessively. It seems who ought to change their diet behavior and food consumption to avoid to spend too much money to buy excessive foods and drinks and who often shall not decide to eat and drink them when who feel not hungry habitually . Hence, changing human diet habit is one important psychology factor to reduce water and foods shortage, due to the meats and juices can be reduced to be rubbish if human can learn how to control their diet habit to reduce to consume excessive meats and vegetables and rice and soft drinks etc. kind of foods and drinks. Then, I believe that food and water drinking numbers will be reduced too much in the future. Hence, different countries‘ governments need to educate whose people to know that why who will face foods and water scarcity possibly and to let who to know how the issue can be avoided to cause by the changing of their diet habit and consumption behavior. Teaching includes, such as let who to learn why resources scarcities are expected to reduce and defining food security concept, the need is for a better understanding of complexity of vegetable systems, the need to improve the diversity and response capacity of food systems to enhance resilience, the need to address both food consumption and production, knowledge generation and innovation through cross-sector approaches is essential and the need for agricultural knowledge and innovation systems that are fit for farming purpose. After developed countries' people are educated to let who to know why who need to reduce to consume excessive foods and soft drinks habitually to aim to avoid the chance of foods and water supply shortage will be occurred after 2050 year.

On the other side, in the case of biodiversity, the loss of functional biodiversity destabilizes ecosystems and weakens their ability to deal with natural disasters or human induced stresses, such as pollution and climate change. Hence, scientists need to research how to reduce new diseases to cause foods and water pollution, even new diseases cause to influence human health. Due to unpredictable new diseases will be caused foods, fruits, vegetables etc. can't be grow easily , even cows, pigs, sheep etc. animals are not health to cause diseases to be died easily. Then, those new diseases will be decreases our foods supply numbers seriously.

Resources scarcities are expected to define future food security. The predominant form of agriculture, food processing and retailing relies heavily on cheap inputs and the potential impact on this of long term resource scarcity trends has been largely overlooked. Scarcities are either biophysical limits, such as resource supply and availability or environment limits relating to pollution and its impacts on ecosystems and the global climate system. Hence, every country's government ought to educate to let whose citizen to discuss how to protect future food security topic to avoid resource scarcities occurrence after 2050 year. We need to know we are facing pollution (e.g. land, water, energy) and related to environmental limits e.g. climate change, ocean acidification and biodiversity loss. They represent a real threat, not only to future food supplies, but also to global stability and prosperity, through increasing poverty to developing countries and impacts on international trade, finance and investments.

Hence, pollution and environmental limits will have direct relationship to influence every countries' foods supply numbers , then it will influence every country's gross domestic product income if the consumption is reduced by foods inflation. For example, the combined effect of climate change and bio-diversity which makes the food production systems poorly due to a reduced resilience to shocks and changes over the long term , such as the limited availability of ore resources, soil degradation to loss of biodiversity. Both of these require a long term strategic approach to research and an openness to new research directions. These will need to help provide solutions towards more sustainable food consumption and production, some of which will need to break with current farmers or food manufacturers way of producing food methods. For example, research into ecological approaches: foods nutrient and water clean management and replacement of energy intensive inputs are priorities. Research to support energy efficient technologies for use in the food chain is also needed. Industry should assist in tackling the forthcoming challenges with new business models that can support the decoupling of resource use and changing consumption excessive foods behaviors and improving health foods production methods. For instance, changing the foods supply chains) e.g. more local purchasing) may have huge impacts on costs and also on creating closer links and confidence between producers and consumers.

In conclusion, different countries need find methods to solve foods and energy scarcity problem before 2050 year. I recommend that who can attempt to solve earth warm climate, innovate agricultural production and supply system, change human diet habit and food consumption of behavior, co-operate the trade of foods and energy demand and supply between countries fairly and reasonably, reduce food and natural resource waste, renew and recopy new kind of foods, research new natural resource substitution etc. different methods. However, if every country government can attempt to find any one or more of these methods to solve food scarcity to avoid to occur before 2050 year. I believe that the food scarcity challenge won't be occur after 2050 year in the future.

Reference

Erekson, O.H., Loucks, O.L. Strafford, N.C. 1999.
The context of sustainability . In: Sustainability
perspectives for resources and business
USA, p. 3-21.

Daly, H.E. 1990, Towards some operational
principles of sustainable development,
ecological economics, 2(1), 1-6.

Kirkby, J; O' Keefe P., Timberlake, L. (eds.) 1995.
The earthscan reader in sustainable development.
Earthscan Publications Ltd., London, 1-14p.

4.1 Suggestions to solve resources scarcity methods to oil supply

I. Estimation of growth of rural population and income and expected changes of natural resources supply numbers

I recommend developing countries need to estimate growth of rural population and incomes numbers and expected changes numbers in consumption patterns . Taking into account developing countries' known resource capacities and projected development of yields, input use and technologies and making assumptions about their future trading capacity, estimates are also make of future food production level, land use and natural resource numbers import trade demand of developing countries estimation before 2050 year.

Estimation of water natural resources, such as water scarcity agreement on key definitions, the conceptualization of water scarcity in ways that are meaningful for policy development and decision making, the quantification of water scarcity, policy and technical response options available to ensure food security in conditions of water scarcity, criteria and principles that should be used to establish priorities for action to response to water scarcity in agriculture and ensure effective and efficient water scarcity copying strategies. Thus, developing countries will concern to reduce water resources shortage risk. Why is predict water supply important? During the twentieth century, large multi-purpose dams have served the needs of agriculture, energy and growing cities, and helped protect population from flood hazards. On farm water conservation, particularly the adoption of agricultural practices that reduce runoff to increase the infiltration and storage of water in the soil in rained agriculture is the most relevant local supply enhancement option that farmers have to increase foods production by increasing water availability and decentralized water harvesting conveniently in rural areas for farmers needs. For example, ground water exploitation has grown or in scale. Ground water's capability to provide flexible, on demand water in support of irrigation has been as a major advantage by farmers in rural areas. Thus, farmers need to learn how to reduce water losses increase water productivity and water re-allocation to avoid natural resource of water shortage after 2050 year.

II. Renewable natural resources and foods planting sustainability development

The concept of sustainability has become the current answer to absolving our earth of its environment and economic crises in the 21 ST. century. On the one side,
the pessimists, usually ecologists and other scientists, who are convinced the earth can't forever support the different countries' demand of renewable and non renewable resources. On the other side, are the optimists, the economists, who are equally convinced that the earth, with market incentives, appropriate public policies, material substitution, recycling and new technology can satisfy the needs and improve the quality of human welfare. Both views are supporting arguments are explored used and sustainable development. Thus, renewable old energy natural resource can keep old energy natural resource to renew to use or research other new energy resource to substitute old natural resource, it will reduce the risk of energy resource shortage if the other new natural resource can be substituted to the old natural energy resource to use in our daily life , such as inventing one kind of new energy resource can be used to substitute gas to drive cars or drive boats or plans or the old gas can be renewed or cycled to use to drive cars or boats or the oil can be renewed or cycled to use to cook. Also, our earth foods, e.g. fruits, vegetables or meats etc. foods if which can be recopied to grow many numbers planting foods from any one kind food or many kinds of foods, such as one meat can be copied to manufacture two to three same kind tasty meats or unlimited same kind tasty meats. I believe the renewable natural resource energy or recopied foods can reduce our foods or energy shortage after 2050 year.

III. The application of sustainable strategy
between local and national and regional
of international countries

A redefined concept is of the society as whole system, made up of three concentric circles: the economy is found within the society, and both the economy and society exist within the environment. Sustainability indicators are therefore said to attempt to measure the extent to which these boundaries are respected.

I think sustainability measure as a whole concept environment, society and economy. At the bottom of the triangle is the environment or the ultimate means which represents natural resources as a precondition for decent human life. The economy (which includes technology, politics and ethics) is on the next, is not independent but serves as a vehicle for achieving ultimate ends. At the top is equity or society or ultimate end which refers to the wellbeing of the human being. According to Daly(1990) who indicated "that the economy therefore succeeds to the extent that it conserves and restores ultimate means the environment, and enables the achievement of ultimate ends society equity. This is the application of sustainable strategies to local, national and regional issues, as well as the role of international agencies in local /national strategies." Our earth occurs issues of overpopulation, diseases and political conflict, developed countries also have to deal with problems, such as pollution and unlimited urban expansion with limited resources. Sustainability is the process suggested to improve the quality of human life within the limitations of global environment. It involves solutions for improving human welfare that doesn't result in regarding the environment. We(human) need to concern living within certain limits of the earth's capacity to maintain life, understanding the interconnections among economy, society and environment and maintaining a fair distribution of foods and vegetables and natural energy resources and opportunity for this generation and the next. Thus, on the one side, our governments need to concern three categories: Social/ political, environmental and economic issues are interconnection. Social issues include poverty, consultation, empowerment and culture. Environmental issues include pollution, natural resources and biodiversity/ resilience and economic issues include efficiency, growth and stability. It seems our governments need to considerate social and environment and economic issues to reduce our natural energy resources and foods and vegetables to allocate to let every country people to use fairly.

IV. Reducing global warming and biodiversity
issue occurrence

It seems that we need to know our society will influence our natural environment good or bad. If our society damaged our natural environment, then it will be possible to influence our foods supply of decreasing numbers. e.g. fishes, pigs, cows, sheep and vegetables and fruits etc. foods . Due to bad climate and air and lands and ocean pollution can influence foods can not be grown easily and successfully in farms or fishes can not be lived healthy in ocean. Then, it will cause our meats, fruits and vegetables etc. foods supply shortage. Even, our gas , oil, water etc., natural resources will cause our oceans and lands pollution if human pollute our oceans and lands. In result, our natural resources used numbers will be reduced due to clean lands and oceans are polluted for long time. Finally, natural resources and meats and vegetables and fruits , rice etc. foods prices will be risen due to which are shortage to supply and developing countries' population numbers are increasing which will cause more demand. Finally, it shall cause many developing countries' poor people who can't eat enough meats, fruits, rice vegetables etc. foods as well as who can't use enough natural resources to attempt to adapt whose past normal daily life, such as lacking enough oil to help them to cook foods to be heat to eat at home or lacked enough water to be boiled to drink. Even, whose health will be poor , then who get diseases to cause die easily when there is no enough oil to buy or enough water to drink. Hence, these developing countries governments need to concern foods and natural resource scarcity problems which will be occurred if who do not find methods to reduce this issue to be occurred after 2050 year.

As Erekson et. al.(1999) concerns about" loss of resources, such as biodiversity or global weather (climate) warming are pacified with the potential of new technology which will lead to greater investments to the future generations for alternative resources and welfare." Hence, I recommend our governments need to concern global warming or biodiversity issue because of our foods and vegetables and natural resources, such as water, air will be possible polluted to be caused shortage quickly if our earth's global warming or biodiversity issue occurrence to cause our earth's large oceans or lands areas to be polluted. Our governments can attempt to control natural resources , such as oil, gas, water supply into the market and not though the political special conditions to keep them, without considering the political and social standings, which rule the control power and the use of those resources. Such as developed countries can be able to minimize the impact of foods or/and natural resources production and consumption over the natural resources, they are only mechanisms built within an economic rationality, which should be possible to control its people's demand of natural resources, e.g. oil, gas, water and supply of natural resources get more balance. Then these natural resources sale price won't be raised more every year. When there developed countries' people , such as American and Britain who can control to reduce to spend to use the excessive natural resources too much in any time and any place habitually. Then , I believe the developing countries' governments e.g. Africa, China, India, which can buy those developed countries governments' excessive natural resources to raise those developed countries' natural resources supply numbers to provide to whose people to use as well as the most important benefit is that developed countries can gain foreign income from excessive natural resources expectation. Then, these governments will raise GDP economic growth. Hence, if developed countries could control whose people consume natural resource numbers and they could also control to produce natural resource supply numbers . Then, they can gain more excessive natural resources export chance to achieve to raise GDP economic growth aim for long term. As Kirkby et al., (1995)explained "the complexity of sustainable development our natural environment. If our governments can let our earth natural environment gets creation to maintenance, then our natural environment will be reduced the time to degradation. In the long time result, our society rural and urban economy will be growth , then our different countries' global growth will be caused diversity." Hence, it seems different countries' governments need to concern sustainable development to our natural environment .

V. How to apply agricultural green bio-economy concept to solve control sustainable food consumption and production in a resource-constrained world

Nowadays, challenges for the global food supply have never been so complex. Between now and 2050 year, it has been predicted that growth in the global population and changing diets in developing countries, special in India and China and Africa etc. developing countries which may lead to an increase of around 70% in food demand. At the same time, depletion of fossil hydrocarbons will increase the demand for biomass for biofuels and industrial materials. Hence, developed and developing countries' governments ought need to coordinated to reduce air and water pollution and approached to lands use planning and oceans use planning to supply enough farms to grow potatoes, vegetables, tomatoes, fruits and let cows, pigs, sheep etc. animals can have comfortable and clean farm to live to produce good tasty meats to provide human to eat as well as to reduce pollution to supply fresh and clean water to let fishes to be lived and provides to human to drink clean water. Due to overpopulation will be predicted by scientists after 2050 year, so it will be caused foods and energy shortage possibly. Hence, different countries' governments need have long term perspectives to prepare to have enough foods and energy supply to provide us to eat and use for our earth with resource constraints and environmental limits, and which includes guideline on agricultural research to achieve foods supply aim.

On the one hand, I believe the knowledge-based bio-economy can play in realizing there challenges in particular the balance demand between foods, feed and fuel and the strategic role new technologies can have upon developing a sustainable an green bio-economy. On the other hand, I also think production of the presently high resource dependence and to build more environmentally begin sustainable agriculture system able to feed 9 billion people by 2050 year. I recommend global governments need to concern all aspects of food security including the total food chain and impacts of other land-use and management as well as non food areas, research areas which can be closed to free resources for new priorities, research to manufacture more new unique natural resources, due to gas, oil etc. resources will be used all in one day. On the energy shortage aspect, Substitution of these oil, gas etc. natural resources are needed . For example, nuclear energy is a kind of new natural resource, it can be used to push machines of rockets to be moved in space. In the future, I hope that nuclear energy can be used to drive cars or ships or trains etc. transportation tools in land. Hence, new natural resource research is essential and valid investment to be improved by scientists in the future.

On the global food supply interconnected challenges hand, including climate changes, energy and water supply are further encountered by the financial and economic changes in an increasingly globalized world. As a result, it is unclear how the growing demand for food and bioenergy (both biomass and biofuels) within a wider bio-economy can be met without further compromising ecosystem services on which all economic activities and social depend. I shall emphasizes the interaction of the economic, social and ecological components of our food systems at various levels, with feed backs increasingly the uncertainty and risks relating to future developments.

We need to face the food requirements of a growing world population have to be satisfied and we also need to the face of increasing resource scarcities, such as water, energy and land and foods etc. with the situation further exacerbated by climate change. Thus, we need to focus on our reducing demand through food consumption behavioral changes and structural changes in food systems and food chains change. Due to some developed countries people often to choose to buy these foods to eat excessively e.g. cow meat and pig meat and drink excessive soft drinks, e.g. man-made color juice. So, these developed countries consumers will feel these excessive foods and soft drinks can be rubbish if these developed countries consumers often drink these man-made color juice and eat pig and cow meats often excessively. It seems who ought to change their diet behavior and food consumption to avoid to spend too much money to buy excessive foods and drinks and who often shall not decide to eat and drink them when who feel not hungry habitually . Hence, changing human diet habit is one important psychology factor to reduce water and foods shortage, due to the meats and juices can be reduced to be rubbish if human can learn how to control their diet habit to reduce to consume excessive meats and vegetables and rice and soft drinks etc. kind of foods and drinks. Then, I believe that food and water drinking numbers will be reduced too much in the future. Hence, different countries' governments need to educate whose people to know that why who will face foods and water scarcity possibly and to let who to know how the issue can be avoided to cause by the changing of their diet habit and consumption behavior. Teaching includes, such as let who to learn why resources scarcities are expected to reduce and defining food security concept, the need is for a better understanding of complexity of vegetable systems, the need to improve the diversity and response capacity of food systems to enhance resilience, the need to address both food consumption and production, knowledge generation and innovation through cross-sector approaches is essential and the need for agricultural knowledge and innovation systems that are fit for farming purpose. After developed countries' people are educated to let who to know why who need to reduce to consume excessive foods and soft drinks habitually to aim to avoid the chance of foods and water supply shortage will be occurred after 2050 year. On the other side, in the case of biodiversity, the loss of functional biodiversity destabilizes ecosystems and weakens their ability to deal with natural disasters or human induced stresses, such as pollution and climate change. Hence, scientists need to research how to reduce new diseases to cause foods and water pollution, even new diseases cause to influence human health. Due to unpredictable new diseases will be caused foods, fruits, vegetables etc. can't be grow easily , even cows, pigs, sheep etc. animals are not health to cause diseases to be died easily. Then, those new diseases will be decreases our foods supply numbers seriously.

Resources scarcities are expected to define future food security. The predominant form of agriculture, food processing and retailing relies heavily on cheap inputs and the potential impact on this of long term resource scarcity trends has been largely overlooked. Scarcities are either biophysical limits, such as resource supply and availability or environment limits relating to pollution and its impacts on ecosystems and the global climate system. Hence, every country's government ought to educate to let whose citizen to discuss how to protect future food security topic to avoid resource scarcities occurrence after 2050 year. We need to know we are facing pollution (e.g. land, water, energy) and related to environmental limits e.g. climate change, ocean acidification and biodiversity loss. They represent a real threat, not only to future food supplies, but also to global stability and prosperity, through increasing poverty to developing countries and impacts on international trade, finance and investments. Hence, pollution and environmental limits will have direct relationship to influence every countries' foods supply numbers , then it will influence every country's gross domestic product income if the consumption is reduced by foods inflation.
For example, the combined effect of climate change and bio-diversity which makes the food production systems poorly due to a reduced resilience to shocks and changes over the long term , such as the limited availability of ore resources, soil degradation to loss of biodiversity. Both of these require a long term strategic approach to research and an openness to new research directions. These will need to help provide solutions towards more sustainable food consumption and production, some of which will need to break with current farmers or food manufacturers way of producing food methods. For example, research into ecological approaches: foods nutrient and water clean management and replacement of energy intensive inputs are priorities. Research to support energy efficient technologies for use in the food chain is also needed. Industry should assist in tackling the forthcoming challenges with new business models that can support the decoupling of resource use and changing consumption excessive foods behaviors and improving health foods production methods. For instance, changing the foods supply chains) e.g. more local purchasing) may have huge impacts on costs and also on creating closer links and confidence between producers and consumers.

In conclusion, different countries need find methods to solve foods and energy scarcity problem before 2050 year. I recommend that who can attempt to solve earth warm climate, innovate agricultural production and supply system, change human diet habit and food consumption of behavior, co-operate the trade of foods and energy demand and supply between countries fairly and reasonably, reduce food and natural resource waste, renew and recopy new kind of foods, research new natural resource substitution etc. different methods. However, if every country government can attempt to find any one or more of these methods to solve food scarcity to avoid to occur before 2050 year. I believe that the food scarcity challenge won't be occur after 2050 year in the future.

Environment Economy-Pollution and illness influences oil consumer behavior

How the economic consequences of outdoor air pollution influences consumer behaviors ? Air pollution can increase number of respiratory and cardiovas cular diseases. How they can impact economic growth, e.g. on human health, mortality and morbidity and agriculture aspects ? Whether when this diseases are caused from outdoor air pollution, why it can influence consumer behavior or brings negative consumpton emotion?

The macroeconomic costs of these impacts of outdoor air pollution that are linked to economic activity, and it raises welfare costs related to activity morality and pain and suffering from illness to consumers. For example, market costs are those that are associated with biophysical impacts that directly affect economic activity, e.g. lower crop yields affect agricultural production . Non market costs may also include the monetised welfare costs of morality (premature deaths) , and of the disutility of illness (pain and suffering).

Raising emissions reflect the assumptions on economic growth with increasing GDP and energy demand, especially in fast growing economies, such as the high population countries, India and China. These large changes are due to the increase in the demand for agricultural products and energy (include transport and power generation). For continuousing increase in energy demand to China and India car drivers, when they need to drive their cars to go to anywhere often. The higher emission will bring serious pollution. The environment protecting householders will decrease to use emissions from energy demand for, with reflects technology improvement in energy efficiency, the use of cleaner fuels, and biomass in open fire to cleaner energy sources including LPG, ethanol or enhanced cooking stoves. Hence, when many people get the diseases from air pollution. It will increase the medical (healthcare) cost to governments or when government needs to give welfare assistance to patients.

The three different market impacts of air pollution may include: reduced labor productivity, increased health expenditures and crop yield losses. They may reduce the GDP pollution feedback on the economy. At the global level, the consequences of labor productivity and health expenditure may impact to market cost increases,because increases expenditure to labor productivity, health expenditure and value added generated in agriculture from low productivity changes in crop yields.

What is the welfare costs of mortality and illness ? It is possible to attribute a cost to non-market impacts, such as the premature deaths and the costs of pain and suffering from illness . The welfares cost of the premature deaths caused by air pollution are calculated using the value of a statistical life to any one. Large costs can also associated with the pain and suffering from illness. So, pollution causes diseases to bring welfare cost increases, they include hospital living day to every patient when he is caused illnesses from air pollution. Moreover, it will impact government pollution expenditure to raise welfare cost to assist the low income level pollution illness patients' hospital living welfacre cost when they need to live long days in hospitals.

How does air pollutin impact on consumer automobile choices ? Air pollution levels can bring negatively affect the sales of fuel inefficient cars to China or India car drivers. They will choose to buy electronic cars to drive to replace fuel cars, because electronic cars only need to charge battery and it can reduce air pollution. When China or India their big city people's income level is rising, they will have more money to buy electronic cars to drive to reduce air pollution. Moreover, they believe that electronic cars can have better car quality and reduced air pollution need to charge battery fuel efficiency to compare fuel cars, when they need to often drive cars on roads. Som electronic cars demand will be the preference choice battery fuel efficiency or green driving tools to compare general fuel cars to satisfy China and India car purchasers when they are living in serious air pollution environment cities.

When the high environment protection awareness car buyers number is increasing in the countries, environment protection awareness will influence their car choice decison on which car to buy , when they are living in more heavily polluted cities tend to buy less fuel-inefficient cars. So, the electronic cars number need will increase in China and India both car market, because these two countries have similar characteristics, they have high population and gardens and farms number is less and there are many people are living in cities and many people are high income level , they usually have one car at least. So, they must feel cities are serious polluted by their diving behaviors. So, their environment protection awareness are ususally higher to compare other countries , they have less cities. So high air pollution to cities can excite the environment protection awareness to China and India car purchasers as well as they will prefer to choose to buy electronic cars to replace fuel cars to drive in possible, because they do not hope to live a high car dirty cities to cause their poor health when they have high income level. Also, it implies that it has direct relationship between China and India cities have high income level people number increases and air pollution level increases and electronic car demand number increases and fuel car demand number decreases in China and India car market in micro economic China and India electronic car and fuel car demand and supply market.

I assume that each China and India car consumer makes a relatively fuel or electronic car choice among possible car transmissions, between the option of buying no car and buy car or between the option of buying electronic car and fuel car. However, air pollution will be one major factor to influence China and India car purchase demand number on electronic and fuel car supply number. If china and India's air pollution can reduce, then car purchase number will increase, as well as the fuel car demand number will also increase ,because China and India have many cities are polluted serious. It can influence car purchase buyers how to decide car choice to make car or no car purchase decision, even purchase either fuel car or electronic car decison.

● How consumer decisions are impacted on environment?

Environmental impacts may occur on households, when they need to buy food, mobility, house, household goods and appliances for home use in household consumer behavior view. It can bring direct impacts, that occue because of the use of householder products and services during householders are staying at home. When householders feel need to raise living quality, they will considerate how they use services and related household products. When minimizing the use of natural resources and toxic materials as well as the emissions of waste and pollutants over the life cycle of the service or household product, e.g. using electricity or fuel time at home, cooling time and bathing time at home activities. So, for on householder who has high environment protection awareness and energy protection awareness, he will reduce long time to use electricity or fuel use time for cooking, bathing, watching television, listening radio time activities at homes, because he does not hope energy waste and protect air fresh at homes.

So, consumption is concerned by environment factors, such as demographics, technology, income and prices, psychological, social , cultural environments, e.g. consumers economic behavior is influenced by habt, routines, conventions etc. different environment factors influence. So, economic assumptions of rational and regular behavior is based on long-established principles, such as utility maximization. For example, when one country is encountering serious air or water pollution, then consumers will spend long time to search any data (marketing research activities) when they need to make purchase decision on pollution environment as well as pollution environment is dependent on (e.g. attitude, intention to the consumers).

Because when pollution environment will influence consumption behavior, such as behavioral and experimental economic to consumers. It implies on pollution environment's psychological assumptions on individual consumption motives, such as on the role of mental habits, loss confidence. So, consumers usually feel to spend long time to make purchase choice or decison on pollution environment, exaggerated optimism, expectatons, avoiding miscalculation,short-sightedness more enjoyment etc. psychological factors. When they need to make purchase decision on pollution environment, e.g. when one car consumer will need to make choice to buy one car, when he is living in China city, city is polluted serious. So, he will need to spend long time to gather any car model and brand and quality and fuel quality air polluted level to achieve to choose to buy the most clean fuel and the most least air polluton car to avoid to cause air polluton when he is driving the car in the China's city. So, air pollution way causes the China environment protection awareness car consumers to spend long time to gather any less use fuel car information to avoid to cause air pollution when he needs often to drive the car on the city roads in the China cities. Hence , air pollution may cause the China car purchasers feel need to spend more time to gather car information in order to decide whether he ought to buy one car or no car purchase choice on the air pollution environment. So, the car must use less fuel to avoid air pollution easily when he drives the car on the China's cities' roads.

Reference

Erekson, O.H., Loucks, O.L. Strafford, N.C. 1999. The context of sustainability . In: Sustainability perspectives for resources and business USA, p. 3-21.

Daly, H.E. 1990, Towards some operational principles of sustainable development, ecological economics, 2(1), 1-6.

Kirkby, J; O' Keefe P., Timberlake, L. (eds.) 1995.
The earthscan reader in sustainable development.
Earthscan Publications Ltd., London, 1-14p.

Nowaday, airline industry is entering global competition. So, any some less positive or negative social environment changing which will influence any airlines' passenger behavioral consumption change. For example, air ticket price rises or fuel price rises or the country's season is bad or the global economy is bad or the country has terrible death threat etc. different negative social environment change fastors which will influence any country passenger individual travel consumption desires.

In Special, business class airline transportation demands are also increasing, due to many business travelers need to catch planes to go to any different countries to do business as well as many cargoes need to be carried from planes to transport to different countries to sell. So, business class traveler target group behavioral consumption is difficult to influence travelling consumotion desires from external environmental factors because business class traveler target group concerns to need to catch planes to go to another country to discuss business co-operation with the country's businessmen. So, their business travel desires won't easy to be influenced more than individual entertainment travel consumer's desire.

It seems cargo and business aim of aviation transportation industry has less chance to be influenced to reduce businessmen traveler or cargo transportation numbers to compare to entertainment traveler numbers by external environment change influences, due to the business travelers and cargo transportation travelling desires is difficult to reduce travelling or transportation needs to reduce the " doing businesses to earn profit chance with another country's businessmen". However, ignorance of internal or external market dynamics, catching entertainment travelers business can be detrimental to airline profitability more than carrying cargoes or business travelers business. Because the demands of travelling different countries' travelers' consumption are still more than the demands of businessmen carrying cargoes in any countries every year. So, the global GDP of travelling income sector is still have the important position to any country nowadays.

How can positive or negative social environment change influence any airlines' air ticket prices to be risen or fallen as well as how can these social environment change influence passenger consumption desires ? For example: What is the petroleum price change influence ?In fact, the increase in petroleum price can have chance to affect every airlines passenger has a negative manner to reduce travel consumption because increased oil prices have resulted in the reduction of airline services operations, the number of airline schedules flights, even airline bankruptcies. Whether global economic inflation or deflation, terrorism threats to the country, oil shortage or oil price rising or fallening, bank interest rate increasing or decreasing etc. external factors which have the most influential causes to bring the bad or good effects to cause airline industry share price reducing or increasing or increasing or reducing air ticket price. In result, these external environmental changes will influence the global traveler numbers to be increased or decreased at the time.

To support this hypotheses, this are my research first question, such as : Does a combination of terrorism and price of petroleum significantly influence airline profit changing mostly? The alternative hypothesis was my research second question, such as: Whether a significant relationship exists between terrorism, price of petroleum and airline profitability more than other factors, such as inflation, bank interest rate or air ticket price changing of these factors to influence passenger consumption desires change. I shall indicate that the first assumption was that terrorism has a negative effect on airline profitability and another assumption was that only external factors as oil prices or terrorism affect airline profitability. Finally, the terrorism and oil shortage and oil rising price factors can influence every passenger travel consumption desire to be reduced mainly.

Terrorism attack influences traveller need

However the effects of oil price and terrorism on airline profitability was limited to a regional perspective, so oil price and terrorism external environmental change will only influence some countries' airline traveler numbers to be decreased, e.g. the terrorism attack of plane crash event to USA on 11 Sept. After the terrorism attack happened on USA 11 Sept. incident of terrorism attack was restricted to events of skyjacking, attacks on oil production, refinery and distribution. Then, due oil shortage will be caused due to reducing oil production, refinery and distribution as well as it will influence oil price is risen and airline ticket price is also risen. It will reduce travel consumption desire to some countries if their airlines' ticket prices are also increasing. Other types of terrorist activities, such as attacks on financial targets or senior government officials could have an adverse effect on the petroleum and airline industry. I think the disruption of the production or distribution of petroleum because of incidents of terrorism was costly in terms of loss of business and the inflationary effect on fuel dependent products or services.

In fact, some airlines have adopted more fuel saving technology, so whose fuel consumption would not use more than other non fuel saving technology airlines. It seems fuel price increasing will not be the only factor to influence the airline industry's traveler numbers decreasing due, the owning more fuel saving technologic airlines which air tickets prices won't influence to be risen , due to reducing oil production and shortage influences . However, due to some airlines which have fuel saving technology, so which can avoid to use more fuel to provide planes to use and which fuel costs will be reduced, then which can provide cheaper air ticket fare prices to compare the non fuel saving technology airlines. The result will cause some not owning fuel saving technological airlines which will lose travelling customers in this global airline travelling market, also the not fuel saving technological airlines need to renew their fuel technology if which want to keep their competitive abilities to avoid to close down their businesses. So, what factors will influence the not owning fuel saving technological airlines profitability to be reduce if the oil shortage factor can not influence their planes energy supply to be reduced to cause air ticket prices to be increased? To answer this question, I shall indicate another financial risk factor how it influences airline industry behavioral change.

Also, I shall indicate the financial risk of airline industry evidence from Cathay Pacific airways and China airlines against key determinants of which include interest rate, exchange rate and fuel price risk for the period of January 1996 year to December 2011 year. During this period, these key external factors which were the most serious influence to cause these two airlines choose to change their strategic behaviors. Due to any these financial risks is difficult to predict and it was also changing often, these factors will also affect any airlines stock returns which arise from changing economic conditions, e.g. fuel price movements and fluctuations in exchange rates. These external unpredicted changing factors will attribute to the air tickets cyclical demand, capital investment, fixed costs of labor and landing rights to this global airline industry. Finally, it will cause some airlines need to rise air ticket prices to reduce expenditures increasing.

However, the relationship between fuel price and stock prices varies across economies which will influence travel passenger consumption of desires. For example, the effects of oil price changes in sub-sector indices, such as wood, paper and printing, insurance and electricity. In the past, on global stock exchange market was positively significant in 2011 year. Otherwise, with respect to the U.S.A. aviation industry, some economists suggested that global airlines stock returns were negatively to percentage change in fuel prices related to any airline firm value, e.g. Qantas and Air New Zealand were negatively share price growth to fuel price risk in the short term in the 2011 year. Thus, due to these two airlines share price went down, it will influence investors who loss confidence to buy their shares as well as it will influence travelling passengers who choose to buy other airlines' air tickets to go to travel because they will feel these two airlines have business challenges, e.g. bad service quality and food quality and uncomfortable airline seat environment and poor management style. etc different bad feeling. So, these two airlines' share prices went down, it will influence every travel passenger's confidence to choose to buy their air tickets to sit their planes to go to travel.

Airlines fuel manufacturing supply strategy

However, there are some airlines which are the characteristic of self organization . It means that they are present in that both of oil fuel production and providing flights service in airline industry. So, these self organization airlines can control the oil fuel price by themselves. However, any self supply airline organization is also evident in efforts by businesses acts of terrorism against economic targets by adopting proactive steps, such as airline and airport security. So, it seems any self suply airline organization can reduce the risk to avoid oil price raising and terrorism attacks in airline industry risk management sector because oil shortage won't influence their air ticket prices need to be raised.

Beside, these self supply airline organizations which have high technology of fuel efficient aircrafts, the use of one aircraft model, the adoption of direct routes versus customer loyalty programs and other operational cost reductions are strategies for increased profitability.

To solve oil price, terrorism etc. external risk to airline industry. Instead of high technology of fuel efficient aircrafts and self supply airline organization methods can solve terrorism attacks and oil price rising risks. However, I believe that there are other risks will threaten to airline industry. This risks concern traveller individual psychological factors influence, so it means that any airlines can apply psychological methods to predict which airline passengers' travel consumption desires. The risks include such as (1) user factor, such as : the travel country culture and tradition difference will influence the traveler chooses to prefer to go to the country to travel , the traveler's education level is high , who will choose to go to developed countries to travel, e.g. USA, UK. Otherwise, if the traveler's education level is low, who will choose to go to developing countries to travel, e.g. China, India etc. (2) economic factor, such as air tickets and airline fuel costs, (3) human resources and macro economic factor, such as political stability, economic development, educational policy, health policy, environmental policy. However, these risks occurrences are resulting in the relationship of cause and effect events. These events are not directly observable.

Such as, the complexity of relationship between terrorism and airline profitability. Hence, if global airline industry can predict when those risks occur to do protective strategic behavior. It is possible that which can understand why these risk events will occur and their protective strategic behaviors also influence their outcomes to be positive to avoid any external risk threats on the long term. However, I think hierarchy, self supply airline organization efficiency methods which are as possible predictors of user preferences to avoid risk threat events to cause whose airline businesses failure occurrences in airline industry because it can reduce oil shortage factor which causes their air ticket prices need to be rised to keep their planes can have enough fuel supply.

- Why tourism and airline industries have close relationship to influence their profitability between of them.

In my study, I suppose terrorism, profitability and the price of petroleum which had properties of distinct and interrelated close relationship. Moreover, these variables (terrorism, profitability and the price of petroleum) displayed differentiation, self replication, efficiency and hierarchy which can cause risk events to airline industry. However, I also think the other internal and external threat factors of airline industry, such as inflation, bank interest rate, business model, service quality, airline fuel or plane engine technology, air ticket pricing, brand loyalty, airline strategic management, government policy and fuel hedging of these factors which can also raise the risks to threaten any airlines existence in airline industry.

There are two basic business models in airline industry. They are network (full service) and low cost (discount) carriers. The network carrier model employs diversification strategy by increased domestic destinations, serving international routes, providing diverse seating arrangements (business, economy and first class), maintaining a complex system of offering high quality service. Otherwise, low cost (discount) airlines focus on lower air fares. To keep operating costs down, discount airlines offer shorter routes and provide point-to-point destinations rather than through sophisticated flights are primarily in domestic destinations. So, discount airlines operate a common model aircraft fleet, offer a single seating arrangement and cheaper flight services offered to compare network airlines. However, these two basic business models have their unique competitive abilities to provide any airlines existence in airline industry nowadays.

In fact, natural resource of oil is decreasing in our earth. But as the same time, human demand is increasing and oil supply is decreasing, so it also causes the oil fuel price is increasing to supply to airline industry. It influences not only to airline industry, it also impacts of higher oil fuel price to tourism, such as expansion of airports are made based on expected demand increase.

Tourism has been proven to many adverse events, including terrorism, flight disruptions. Beside, the bad natural climate change influences, such as the volcanic ash cloud event occurred in April 2010 year. So, airline industry need to concern climate change because it will cause high fuel prices indirectly. For example, the event occurred the extreme increase in operating costs for airlines in 2008 year, due to unprecedented prices for aviation fuel also meant, that despite the introduction of fuel charges, so this event causes the global airline industry recorded losses seriously. Even if alternative fuels become commercially available for airlines which are still likely to be more expensive than present aviation fuel. Thus, it seems that poor tourism will influence poor travel consumption and low airline tickets sale.

Higher airfares in the future are likely to lead to reduction in travel and cause tourists to shift from more distant to closer destination. When some of the economic responses to higher oil prices are obvious assessing the overall economic impacts on tourism is difficult. However, long term changes in global oil price rises will be similar to global changes in other commodity prices, exchange rates and income. It is therefore important to consider the impact of high oil prices on tourism from a general equilibrium perspective rather than relying only on bottom partial equilibrium. However, I believe tourism and airline industries have close relationship, such as tourism and airline industries are likely to suffer in an environment of high oil prices. Given that tourism destinations receive tourists from a range of origins, it would be useful to understand of some countries are increasing oil prices than others. Such as the net oil importing countries are selling higher oil prices than oil exporting countries generally. For example, New Zealand is an oil import country to provide planes for international visitor arrivals, so its oil fuel price is usually higher to charge to NZ airlines because any NZ airlines need to pay to foreign countries to buy any oil more expensive price. So, NZ airlines usually charge higher airfares to its visitors to compare the other exporting oil countries' airlines.

In economic theory, on income effects indicate negative impacts on tourism demand, the exact effects of higher oil fuel prices for specific destinations are far from clear. However, airline industry's different market segments show different sensitivities to air ticket fares changes. On the first hand, if the visitors are long destinations generally wealthier than average and therefore potentially less affected, as energy costs would be a smaller proportion of their income compared will be those from less wealthy groups. On the second hand, oil prices don't translate into higher transport costs especially not on air routes that are highly competitive and that are maintained for strategic reasons. On the third hand, many other factors shape tourists‘ decision making, including emotion drivers or those related to images, fashions and perceptions.

Increasing environmental protection awareness of tourists could also be an important factor to influence tourism consumption, instead of oil fuel price raising causes air ticket fares raising factor to reduce traveler numbers. However, oil price raising reason causes also due to high use of cars, vans and domestic air transport in some countries, e.g. Hong Kong, China countries, there are many people like to buy cars to drive. So, the private driver numbers are increasing demand to cause these countries' oil fuel prices raise in the short time suddenly. It will influence HK and China air tickets prices need to be risen , due to there are many cars, vans and domestic air transport tools need to use oil to supply energy to cause oil import numbers will increase to HK and China and HK and China airlines need to pay higher price to buy oil to use. In the result, HK and China airlines air ticket prices will also need to rise and it will influence HK and China travel consumption desire.

Fuel raising price solve methods

- Why oil fuel raising price factor can cause risk to airline.

In long run, implications of changes to supply and demand side conditions of oil fuel energy may differ qualitatively. For example, due to investment responses of producers, consumers and governments in alternative energy sources and more energy efficient plants, vehicles are supplied in order to achieve oil fuel price can't be risen seriously.

However, I believe oil fuel rising charge will be an important factor to influence global airline ticket fares to be also increased. Firstly, on the bank interest changing factor, e.g. bank interest rate rising which only attract more bank saving. But it can not influence the bank savers who choose to reduce relax time to go to other countries travelling. Otherwise, when the bank savers can save more money to earn higher interest in banks, who will prefer to choose to use their saving to consume travelling. Due to who can earn higher interest rate after a period of saving time. So, I believe whose behavioral travelling consumption will be raised when the banks will raise interest rate, then the bank savers won't choose to save more money in banks. So it is possible that who will withdraw more money to consume to go to travelling from their bank saving. It seems bank interest rate changing won't influence bank savers‘ behavioral travelling consumption to be reduced. Secondly, on the exchange rate changing factor, although any country's exchange changing will cause other countries' money value to be fallen down or risen up. However, it won't influence any travelers' behavioral consumption to be reduced seriously. Although, it is possible that the traveler won't spend too much to go to shopping when who travel to the another country and arrive the country. But, it is not possible to influence the traveler decides to reduce consumption to buy any air ticket to go to travelling. Thirdly, any country inflation also can not reduce travelers' travelling consumption easily because inflation can influence consumers who choose to buy cheaper foods and clothing and reduce entertainments in their every day life. But, one country's inflation can not influence it's citizen do not spend much travelling expenditure because travelers only spend one time or two times of travelling every year usually. So, the travelling expenditure rate of any households is not too much to compare daily essential expenditure. So, it seems that bank interest rate and exchange rate changing and inflation factors won't influence any travelers' travelling consumption of decisions to be reduced easily. Otherwise, if the oil fuel price raises too much, then global airlines' cost will be raised. So, the airlines only choose to increase their air fare prices to aim to avoid loss possibly. It seems that oil fuel price has direct influence airline income.

● Methods to solve rising air fare prices demand.

I. Why will biofuels energy be demanded ?

I suggest these methods how to avoid the oil raising price factor to cause airline air fare prices to be risen to lead the risk of traveler numbers to be reduced.

The first method: Whether aviation fuel markets will have what benefits from biofuels supply to planes. I shall refer the scope includes trends in jet fuel price, airline response to fuel price, increases and volatility and environmental goals for aviation. The aviation fuel supply industry includes production, distribution and consumption of aviation fuel and it outlines players in the aviation fuel supply chain. For example, at each airport, fuel supply chain organization and fuel sourcing could differ with regard to the role of oil companies, airlines, airport owners and operators and airport service companies. However, major jet fuel purchasers are airlines, general aviation operators, corporate aviation and the military, with most of the jet fuel in global different countries demanders being used for domestic commercial and civilian flights carrying passengers, cargos or both. Commercial aviation fuel efficiency has improved dramatically over time, largely due to aircraft and engine upgrades and operational and air traffic control improvements. So, it seems that fuel supply factor can influence airline fare prices majorly.

However, jet fuel prices generally correlate with prices of crude oil and other refined petroleum products, such as diesel. So, increasing prices and the persistent price volatility of jet fuel markets import airline industry finances in any countries. However, airlines use various strategies to manage aviation fuel price certainty, including financial hedges, increased vertical integration and adjustments in aircraft utilization and size to avoid the jet fuel raising price risk. Investments in alternative aviation fuel could be a mechanism to diversity expose to the price of petroleum. It seems the use of alternative aviation fuel would serve to diversify the fuel mix to reduce the risk of jet fuel monopoly raising price threat. If a diversified fuel mix were to avoid either fuel raising price in short term or to avoid fuel raising price in long term. Potential benefits include reduced actual fuel costs from only choice of jet fuel supply increased price certainty and lessened fuel costs. This diversify could allow airlines to become more consistently profitable and to make other investments in their businesses.

So, biofuels have potential to meet aviation industry needs, possibly including managing risks of upward fuel price trends and fuel price volatility and avoid risks with greenhouse gas emissions. So, the aviation fuels market could use biofuels to reduce greenhouse gas emission and mitigate long-term upward price trends, fuel price volatility or both.

What are the challenges of high priced oil for aviation? In fact, nowadays not the resources of oil as such, but much more the insecurity of supply, due to geopolitical instability in combination with a tight oil market makes a scenario with much higher oil prices than the world is currently experiencing not unlikely. Aviation is completely dependent upon oil as its fuel source. Since no practical energy substitute is readily available for commercial aviation, a scarcity of petroleum relative to demand will present a major aviation policy. In addition, efficiency gains, due to operational measures and new aircraft medium term. In particular, it has been demonstrated that the annual reduction rate in fuel consumption traffic unit is not a constant, but is itself also falling, in contrast to past estimates.

So, a high-priced oil scenario will have severe consequences for demand, airline revenues, the competitive position of airports and eventually airline networks, strategies and fleet development. In particular, transfer demand, short-haul and leisure traffic can be expected to be heavily affected by high oil prices, due to their relative high price sensitivity. So, different countries‘ governments or/and airlines are valuable to research another new and potential biofuel energy to substitute oil energy to supply our planes to reduce the threat of oil monopoly supply to influence the cause of air fare raising prices. Because the elasticity is very high to travelers, when the travelers feel air fares are rising high or even low level to influence travelers who will choose not to buy the air tickets to go to travel easily.

Will the fuel (oil based inputs) risk be higher to compare other costs to cause air ticket prices to be increased?, e.g. engineering maintenance, employees salaries, general cleaning, security office expenses etc. expenditures to airlines? If the probability-weighted upside effect on firm value when a risk is resolved favorably is greater the risk than the probability-weighted downside effect if the risk is resolved badly, then expected value work not be enhanced by hedging. So, the risk will be resolved badly to any commercial airlines. Airlines are an interesting case because the direct effect of source of risk resides squarely within the no offset in revenue functions (unlike for oil producers, for example), so value effects from costs feed directly into equity value. Most directly, the risk source is fuel costs to commercial airlines. Jet fuel is of course, a mix product of crude oil, so airlines indirectly face oil price risk. There are reasons to expect that airlines' fuel costs might to convex in oil price (i.e. absent any hedging). For example, oil prices, being generally pro-cyclical in recent times, tend to be highest when airline demand is strong. Airlines are therefore apt to use more high priced fuel than low-priced fuel over time. Airlines can raise air fare benefit is limited by the elasticity of demand. Also, cost functions could be influenced from fuel cost corresponds to upturns in economic activity overall (due to demand pressures on oil related prices), so it causes that airline's capacity delivers their services given their level of fixed capital. The essence of airlines basis risk in the case of jet fuel is essentially the time profile of the refining margin between crude and jet fuel, or the time profile of the price differential between other refined distillates and jet fuel. Thus, it is far from clear that risk management with oil is sure to add value to any airlines. It seems the impact of airline energy and any countries‘ domestic or foreign airline passenger travel numbers which have direct close relationship.

II. Whether the relationship between terrorism and oil prices has close relationship.

Whether the relationship between terrorism and oil prices has close relationship. It needs to judge to determine if a combination of terrorism and the price of petroleum significantly predicted airline profitability and which variable whether the further period was the most significant between the terrorism occurrence and the price of petroleum influence. So, different countries' governments or airlines need to collect samples of financial records from which country's any airline commercial passengers and cargo airlines on costs of fuel and any airline profitability. Also, gathering the terrorism data were comparison of terrorist attacks on petroleum in oil-producing nations, and incidents of high jacking aboard any country's aircraft. When any countries‘ airlines or governments can judge whether the impact of airline energy and terrorism risk level is high or middle or low level. Then, which can use this sample data to measure how to do positive social change to whether to increase or reduce employment in commercial aviation industry, or ought need to invest other higher commercial activity in tourist and other travel related service businesses and when is the most right time to adopt of green technologies by the civil aviation manufacturing industry after the terrorism attacks occurrence to any country. It seems that any countries' governments or airlines which ought concern that the event of when the terrorism attacks will occur and gather past sample data to predict when the next time terrorism attacks event will be occurred and the risk will be high or middle or low level to influence global airline industry development.

III. What factors will influence airline industry's price elasticity of supply and demand?

In fact, the airline industry is largely dependent on the supply of the oil industry. Otherwise, the oil industry is inelastic. However, the increase or decrease of the price of airfare is directly related to the increase or decrease of the oil's price to fuel the aircrafts because there has no any new energy which can be substituted to oil fuel to airline industry. So, it seems oil fuel producers are monopolies to control its sale price to be raised easily.

Another factor that can affect airline industry to be directly targeted by a tragedy brought about by terrorism. The past four years, from 2001 year to 2005 year, there had been at least $40 billion worth of losses in the airline industry because of the September 11 date terrorism attacks in 2000 year. There had been an expected and significant decrease in the demand for the airline industry services because of the attacks that involved planes hijacking and crashing into key locations like the World Trade Center and the Pentagon in USA. Although, terrorism attacks can bring risk to influence fuel price rising in airline industry. However, this risk occurrence to airline industry is only that after the terrorism attacks occurred. It is possible that terrorism attacks won't occur again in the future.

Otherwise, our concerning ought be the greenhouse emissions and how it affects global warming. The air quality would be better once this new regulations are adopted. However, it would affect large airlines. So, it would increase the price of airfares because of economic fees that airline companies have to cover. Air pollution can give a negative impact on the domestic or oversea owned airline companies for long term. If airlines' planes can use clean fuel to fly, e.g. biofuel, then it will bring benefits to global airlines for long term. On the positive side, the environment would be healthier as the earth's temperature would rise, and greenhouse effect would be dramatically reduced. This positive effect can come at a cost that is greater than most people perceive. So, the environment protection travellers who will reduce travelling times to avoid air pollution is caused to influence human health. It seems that airlines need to concern to apply psychological method to predict whose travelling consumption of behavior which is more suitable than behavioral economy method.

On the psychology view point on travelers, who will be more preferable to catch planes to go to different countries to travel, due to the chance of air pollution and global environmental warm issues will be reduced to low risk to influence our health if planes can use biofuel to be energy to fly in the future one day. It seems that spending expenditure to research other non polluted biofuel new energy is one solvable method to global airline industry in the future. To solve, any airlines or countries' governments or oil producers ought choose to spend more time to research new biofuel. Otherwise, the predicting when terrorism attacks event will be occurred, it is more difficult to predict the time more than researching to produce new biofuel energy method in the future.

So, I recommend that researching the new biofuel energy or other kinds of energy to substitute the oil energy and air pollution risk these two factors are the urgent behavioral economy method is used to solve this challenge which the airlines or oil producers or different countries' governments which need to concern nowadays. Because these two negative environment factors are the most influential to cause traveller individual travelling consumption desire to be fallen among of other negative environment factors.

The main cost related factors to offline or online travel agents

Nowadays,many online or offline travel agents have interest to find what the main factors that can affect their strategies to reduce airline costs. The main factors include route structure, type and characteristics of the aircracft, cost of labor and management quality, which will influence whether which airline routes are the most suitable to let online travel agents or offline travel agents to help them to sell paper air tickets or electronic air tickets to attract travel consumption more easily.

Thus, a cost-related strategy is the main important factors to influence travel consumption choice between online or offline travel agents. For example, considering that advantages in costs is an important strategy for carriers to remain in travel transportation market.

The deregulation process of travel markets and increasing opportunities for competition have created excess capacity in many markets that causes lower rates, even with its rising costs. Thus, the travel strategic costs management as well as travel consumers that their behavior under different influences can bring competitive advantages over travel players.

Cost reduction in the travel market -based industry is a very important way of being competitive between offline and online travel agents, when facing travel air ticket prices decreasing for every trip. So reduce to total travel cost, e.g. fuel, maintenance, labor etc. is relevant, but the influence of each component on every total trip cost depends on factors that are related or not to airline operation. For example, some airline can adopt the lowest cost model to sell air tickets from offline or online travel agents which compete for travel passengers with traditional modes as self driving road transport trip in large areas of countries domestic travel market, such as US, UK domestic travel market. However, the decision about the relevance of one cost is not a simple matter. The effectiveness of reduction of each item that comprises the total cost of airline can change over time, depending on both the business model and the scope of the airline company or online /offline travel agent company as well as external factors.

However, there are three types of competition advantage between online and offline travel market: They are such as agility, differentiation cost and the differentiation may be related to a product of superior quality, higher value f the brand or the company's positive reputation. Such as the online travel agent's providing the different airline cheap air ticket price and kind of trips to provide to travel consumer consumer comparison or the offline travel agent's famous brand or positive reputation to let travel consumers feel travel agents can provide many actual trip package to let them to compare by oral clearly. Thus, the online travel agent's weakness is lack of travel agent individual exploration to let every travel consumer to understand every trip package more clearly.

But online travel agent's strength is it can provdide one website to let travel consumer attempt to compare different trip air ticket and/or hotel price to make personal travel pre-booking decision at home. The another advantage is related to techniques that reduce production cost, making it is possible to offer cheaper air ticket, or hotel room rents, or cheap trip package, than the competition. Such as online travel agent can sell more cheape electronic air ticket price to compare traditional offline travel agent's paper air ticket price.

Finally, agility refers to the speed which the company responds to market demands. For example, if the online travel agent can make statistics to analyze how many online travel consumers to choose to buy which airlines' electronic or paper air tickets, e.g. which airline trip destinations and trips and hotels choices are the most popular attraction to them. Then, the online airline has possible to respond to provide to the most popular airline trips choices, electronic air ticket price comparison choices and hotel rooms prices choices to attract many online travel consumers to enter their online travel websites to choose different airline electronic tickets to buy or pre-book hotel rooms from travel agent websites. Also, if the traditional offline travel agents can attempt to gather every travel consumer's destination trips, hotels , airline paper or electronic ticket prices enquires to make statistics to make which travel trip journeys or destinations and airline paper travel ticket prices are the most popular. Then, it is possible that they can respond to every travel consumer individual demand more to attract whose travel agent choice more easily.

Airline travel agency AirAsia in the domestic airline low cost strategy

There are three major characteristics of the airline industry namely is product nature, its expenditure structure and its market entry conditions. Airline agent's product is homogeneous or undifferentiated , causing significant competition in airline domestic travel or foreign travel both markets, which are free from regulations and economic barriers. However, high capital and operating expenditure is another important characteristic of the airline industry. Aircrafts, airlines' major capital expenditure are very costly to acquire . For operating expenditures, aviation fuel and labor make up the two major costs in the industry.

Another important characteristic of the airline industry is the conditions for market entry, which differs between international and domestic airline markets . In the international travel market, airline travel agency entry is very difficult as international flights and routes are the results of regotiations between governments . On the other hand, in the domestic and regional travel market, travel agency entry depends on the level of deregulation or liberalisation.

More and more countries, however are opening up their domestic travel markets for more competition. In addition, government plays an important role to regulate the travel markets and existing players may significant influence over now travel agent entrants.

In fact, the mjor factors influence to international or domestic travel consumption increasing numbers are the global economy and safety issues, instead of other different economic factors, such as travel destination choice, electronic air ticket or paper air ticket price, hotel price , the country's political change, e.g. war occurrence, bad weather , e.g. very cold or very hot etc. different factors infuence. Because generally , the world or any region of it is in an economic crisis or depression , the demand for airline services will fall. The late 1990 year Asian financial crisis for example, resulted in minimal increase in the number of worldwide airline passengers incrased only minimally from 1997 to 1998 year. Another factor of influencing the travel passenger number to be decreased, it concerns safety issues are also an important driver of the travel industry, which is subject to very safety standards to influence travel passengers' travel choice to the country. In addition, they are also unexpected safety related events, such as the 11

Sept. 2001 year tragedy in the US, which caused reduction in passengers . The increasing popularity of low cost airlines is the newest trend in the airline industry if which hope many passengers choose to buy whose electronic air ticket or paper air ticket to catch which planes to fly from online travel agent or offline travel agent channels.

The rise of low cost airlines, such as AmericaWest, JetBlue and Airtran in US, Ryanair and EasyJet in Europe and Vigin Blue in Australia. The share of low cost airline strategy is popular in the US and European airline market. For example, the Southwest airline low cost strategy is the basis of most low cost airlines operations. The key of the strategy is to reduce costs when at the same time offering low prices to passengers. History showed that the low cost airline strategy is easy to replicate , but difficult to implement successfully.

However, I suggest airlines need to know what functions which can attract passengers to chose to catch their planes to fly if they expect to rise passenger numbers. For example, the critical function of the Malaysia airline travel is to connect the major towns and remote interior areas within East Malaysia, which has poor road systems and limited availability of other significant means of transportation . In contrast, West Malaysia has more developed and extensive rod and railway systems.

Therefore, airline travel is not the main mode of long distance transportation. It implies Malaysis airline ought concentrate on focusing short distance transportation strategy for passenger beneficial choice function. For example, a new small Malaysia airline serving one or two routes may enter easily. Otherwise, a larger airline servicing multiple routes may be harder to enter Malaysis airline market. It also means access to capital and labor are the major obstacles for new airline entrants to Malaysia airline market. Thus, small airlines into a larger airline is probably more likely to be successful as in Air Asia's case to Malaysia airline market.

Thus, the airline low cost strategy competition positions include very low or minimal pressive from other airline similar service substitute products, low or medium power of airline similar input suppliers. In conclusion, low cost airline strategy is a god method to be attempted to win competitors in airline market.

How consumers select travel service between online and offline mode in travel industry

Nowadays, the travel industry is operating through two different modes, online and offline respectively. It involves the identification of the competitive strategies adopted by the tour operators. For example, it was found that e-retil travel is platform that is bringing two market forced the demand and supply tour operators and the customers together, and both parties and more inclined towards online mode in near future. Tour operators are gaining by operating at low cost and increasing their business reach when customers get what they desire as per their convenience. For example, many tour operators had promoted tourism destination through website that allow user to use interface for booking transporttion, foreign exchange etc. However, the role of travel operators (agents) should be assisted any airlines to promote their travel package service by internet more easily , such as tourism destination , arrangement of hospitality, restaurants, transportation tools during their trips.

The reasons why consumers choose online travel service include:

Firstly, it is online researching hospitality service. Online travel websites can provide many different accommodation furniture, such as seeking hotel locations, rooms prices comparison, prepaid hotel rooms by visa card payment transaction method, range from luxury five stars deluxe category hotels to small guest houses. The primary need of tourist is to find a place for residing in foreign country or domestic country to ensure whose safety and relaxing needs. Online travel website channel can help whom to find a place , according to his/her needs and paying capacity in the most shorten times.

Secondly, it is online restaurant (food and beverages researching) service. Full service restaurants are divided into two categories, fine dining and casual dining restaurants . Fine dining restaurants are usually located in the premises of luxury hotels, provide high quality food at premium price with good ambience and highly trained professionals. Thus, travel consumers can also compare the different restaurant food price and seek where is the restaurant and find.

What food taste of food supply from the travel agency or travel operator website easily 250 + tour operators are registered with the ministry of tourism (website of tourism ministry) , and the major players in the industry are dealing online and are dominating the travel industry. The major online travel players are Thomas cook, Cox and Kings, make any trips, clear trip, gatra.com and Expedia.

The tour operators whether online or offline offers a large number of services to the tourists including customized package where the customer selects each element of the tour package, specialized tourism package and complete tour guide package.

Nowadays, the tour operational travel (agents) are working through two different modes: offline online . Big brands with luge investment are dealing online and enjoying low cost benefits and huge profit margins. When the small tour operators have their market niche and managing have their market niche and managing their profits by dealing offline.

It is generally prefer offline mode that is the opportunity for small capital investment or employee number for tour operators. But the large scenario is changing as with the usage of internet by the tour operations have given convenience to the customers and now the customers of modern age have started developing preference for online modern. Thus, internet technology change any countries‘ travel agents or tour operators' air ticket sale method. So, it brings electronic ticket sale method is more popular to compare to traditional travel paper air ticket sale method.

However, online electronic ticket sale method has its disadvantages such as online transaction is unsafe, if the consumer 's name and address and visa card number is stolen to let any internet users to know to be used to buy any products from internet channel easily. Otherwise, traditional walk in offline travel paper ticket sale method is more safe, because the travel consumers can pay cash to the travel agents directly.

However, offline travel agent disadvantages include that the research identified that information communication and technology has very crucial role for tourism industry. Tourist can access any kind of information about tourism destination and tourism products from any part of the world. Tourism comprehends with social media. For example, it was found that (ICT) is bosting up tourism industry. (ICT) helps in searching the location, search for information on tourism products, and e-booking of airline tickets and hotel reservation.

The online travel sale service attraction is that the recent development in the field of information communication and technology and its practical application in tourism and hospitality industry. Generally , online travel sale service must have consumer side and the supplier side.

The decision making prcess of consumer was analyzed and it was found that travel information search and traveller individual electronic ticker pre paid to prebook any plane seat, hotel rooms and restaurants prices comparison to prebook service of traveler individual purchase behavior are corresponding with the usae of (ICT).

What is the online travel sale service strategy?

The two most important things for travel operators (agents) are online travel marketing and strategic management. Former can enhance business operations. Use of (ICT) develops financial capabilities , however, it depends on management choice, financial condition and position. Some researchers recommended that the usage of IT should not be restricted at operational level, however it should be extended up to senior level and should be used for decision making. Social media is regarded as a platform where the tourists and travel operators/agents (suppliers) of tourism industry cross each other. Thus, the role of social media has been directed for future research in tourism industry. Hence, it seems online travel sale service has these features to attract travel consumers to choose to use this online mode to buy electronic air ticket. Such as, airline electronic air ticket price comparison, pre-booking plan seats to avoid full seats flights to delay consumer individual trip plan, pre-booking hotel rooms and prices comparison as well as prebooking restaurant seats and food price and taste comparison, travel destination easy search. Otherwise, these features to attract travel consumers to choose to walk in to travel agents to buy paper air ticket directly. They include: safe cash or visa card payment to avoid personal information is stolen by website payment channel, e.g. via card number, address, name , birth date personal information. Also the travel consumer can enquire any questions from the travel agent and gets individual feedback from the travel agent by oral before who ensure to choose to buy which kind of travel package for whose travel destination. In special, when the travel consumer has much time to spend to enquire any travel trip question, walk in travel agent is the best enquire methods to let the travel consumer to know the trip information clearly.

- Online/offline travel operators (agents) maketing strategies

Offline walk in travel unique segment service strategy

Nowadays, online and offlce travel operators competitions are serious. In fact, tourism marketing , there will be more need for online travel operators in the future, due to online travel sale service is popular to be accepted by online travel consumers. Thus, I recommend walk in offline travel agents need to concentrate on focusing some unique travel service to attract new or old travel consumers if who hope to survive.

I recommend that they can focus on specific specialized services, such as travel consultation (specialization) hypothesizing that systematic differences exist between the usage of travel agents for different travel contexts and travel agents can survive if they focus on specific segments of the market, such as older travelers (segmentation; hypothesizing that systematic differences exist between the usage of travel agents depending on the personal characteristics of travellers). The unique travel needs include: specific services related to package holidays, transport services, beach on city holidays, as well as destinations travellers are not familiar with.

I shall give my opinions to provide insight into alternative strategies for travel agencies in a matured travel market with a high internet penetration as below:

The internet online travel sale service is a reality of popular to let travel consumers to feel convenient to pre-book air seat, hotel rooms , air electronic ticket prices comparison. In order to make final purchase decision very easily in the shortest time. Consequently , it has penetrated the decision making process of travel to attract them to choose to buy electronic air ticket, prebooking hotel rooms or restaurant seats from online travel agent channel more than walk in offline travel agent channel. This is especially true in the tourism business where consumption to consume (booking) and the purchase-related information search (Bieger & Lasesser 2004; Crotts 1998).

In fact , apply website to provide travel sale method has these good consequence. From travel operator (agent) supplier's perspective, the success potential derived from operating a website consist of lower distribution costs, higher revenues and a larger potential market share (due to the ubiquitous access). From traverler's perspective, the internet allows direct communication with tourism suppliers facilitatinf requests for information and allowing services and travel related products, e.g. prebooking hotel rooms, restaurant seats , electronic or paper air tickets, travel trip arrangement package products to be purchased at any time and any place from online travel agents /operators conveniently.

Offline / online travel agency (operator) business depends on earn commissions on behalf of airlines. Thus, offline walk in travel agency (operator) business model that would extend existence as a booking agency (thus focusing on consultation and interpersonal contact) strategy.

As a matter of fact, commission -cutting , which began in the US well ahed of Europe, has had a profound effect specially on business travel agents . Consequently , many of them have re-invented themselves as " travel managers", instead of selling tickets and making arrangements, they charge consultancy fees for reducing the amounts client companies spend on travel (Daneshku, 1999).

- Systematic differences strategy applies to offline walk in travel agent

Thus, I recommend systematic differences strategy can be applied offline walk in travel agent (operator). It means that walk in travel agents could reorient their offline walk in travel agent business to focus on contexts that are less substitutable by other channels and media . Factors hypothetically attributing to the delineation of travel contexts include: helping travellers to choose best travel destinations, helping travellers to attempt to find the number of previous trips (indicating the familiarity with a destination) for their travel reference, helping them to find the cheapest, the most convenient and the most close transportation to ctch during their trips, helping them to find the different types of accommodation and rooms price comparison , nature/type of the trip comparison , arrangement of time of booking (as indicator of spontneous / planned travel) nd helping them to budget overall travel expenditure .

Systematic differences in travel agent use exist in dependence of personal (characteristics with with tourists. Walk in offline travel agents could benefit from a travelling client segmentation strategy and customize and target their services to those travellers that are most likely to be and remain their customers.

Factors hypotheticlly attributing to the traveller segment include: travel expenditure per day, useful travel information as indicator for perceived risk and socio-demographic (age, gender, highest completed and education, professional positions) . Generally, the role of walk in offline travel agent with regard to the travel infrormation search and booking behavior have take an incoming perspective. Such as looking at visitors from different travel markets at a similar destinations. The comparison of central importance in determining whether specialization of travel contexts or market segments is the more promising strategy for walk in offline travel agents.

However, travel package tours strategy must b offline walk in travel attraction . Due to some walk in travellers target segmentation market has still needs. Generally, this travel package tours of travel segmentation consumer who like to enquire the travel agents to concern what the hotel rooms price are the cheapest to provide to them to live, what transportation tools the travel agent can arrange to them to catch anywhere the country destination, the travel agent can provide them to visit during their tour journey. Thus, the travel trip package service is still popular need to offline walk in travel agent (operator). This market is only belonged to offline walk in travel agents (operators) nowadays.

Service fees and commission cuts strategy

The reduction or removal of airline commission continues to challenge travel agencies‘ profitability It is crucial to understand what trends travel agencies need to be aware of to ensure how to profitability and increase travel agencies' revenues with service-fee models.

Service fees are not only a way to compensate for the loss of airline commission but also a way to generate new revenue sources for travel agencies that guarantee their long term profitability. Many travel agencies are expanding their service fee models, both in terms of the mounts changed and the number of service to airline.

However, if travel agent charge too much service fee to exceed the general airline travel market service fee reasonable or standard level. It will influence many airlines do not choose to find the travel agent to help them to sell air tickets. Travel agents apply fees most often for airline related services. They charge differentiated fees depending on the destination, type of reservation (e.g. frequent flyer), number of tickets sold or type of airline (e.g. full service versus).

However, service fee increases can raise customer loyalty and satisfaction. It won't reduce client numbers or result in a lose in clients.. The reason is that service fees can be tailored to suit individual customer. This helps travel agencies target their clients, with tailored services based on their past purchasing patterns and identity services for which clients‘ willingness to pay is greater , such as trip planning identity service for which pay , such as hotel only or special promotion.

To revenue mix for travel agencies is increasingly shifting to service fes as airlines have lowered or cut commissions. Successful travel agencies in many European countries are fast adopting, and constantly upgrading , their service fee schemes. Thus, it seems reasonable service fee level is one important factor to influence travel agents and airlines good relationship. In fact, even travel agents raise service fee, it won't influence travel consumer number to be reduced , even they raise air ticket price. It they can provide the informations concerning the reasonable hotel rooms prices and food quality comparison to satisfy travel consumers' living arrangement or helping them to find the reasonable restaurants‘ food prices and where are their location arrangement or providing the reasonable airlines' electronic air tickets or paper air tickets sale service, even arrangement any high entertainment quality of travel destination trips to let travel consumers to feel satisfactory.

However, I believe the raise air ticket price factor won't influence the travel consumer number to be decreased. Any offline or online travel agents will encounter this crisis. By cutting travel agents‘ commission. Airlines decreased their dependence on travel agencies as a distribution channel. In fact, three key variable factors will influence travel agents' commission income to be decreased. They include below:

- The unsustainable or no change financial losses by airlines , due to the growth of low cost carriers, leading to an increase in the number of bankruptcies.
- No negative consequences from previous commission cuts: airline had progressively lowed the commission payments.
- No effective resource for travel agencies to satisfy airlines needs.
- The appearance of now airlines and air routes to provide to travel agencies to fall down air ticket price to attract consumers‘ choices, due to who don't feel to spend much money to go to this new air routes or catch new airline

plans , whether these new air routes are excite to entertainment or whether they are safe planes to catch.

- An increase in the number of bankruptcies to cause travel comsumption desire to be reduced.
- New competition forced down air fares.
- The necessity to cut production costs, especially with low cost meaning low production costs and low fares, even if the two are closely linked.

Internet negative influences to travel agents

Although, on the one hand, internet creates offline travel agents to use websites to help them to sell electronic air ticket or travel related products, such as prebooking hotel rooms , restaurants, transportation tools etc. travel service. However, on the other hand, internet also brings travel agencies competitive disadvantage with regad to suppliers' direct websites , when airlines are able to control seat availability and prices. Indeed internet cause the decision is made by the airlines to reduce and/or eliminate travel agency commission has led them to use technology that many of their distrust or are not inclined to use, and to compare prices and travel schedules constantly.

As a result of this travel sale service environment, traditional offline travel agencies are at a competitive disadvantage with regard to online travel agencie and to airline carriers, which have developed their own direct websites where they are able to control seat availability and prices.

Nevertheless, travel agents' pay programmes remain. From some airlines, travel agents receive negotiated incentive commission closely linked to their performance as incentive . However, airlines still need travel agents' assistance to help them to promote air tickets to sell, due to travel agents can provide trip packages, transportation tools, prebooking hotel rooms, restaurants and air tickets arrangement and they can give any enquiries to every individual travel consumer. It is free charge travel professional enquiry service for travel agency's competitive features.

Consequently, how agencies can reduce their reliance on airline commission payments. I recommend these following strategic options to them to apply as below:

- Streamlining operations, controlling staff costs, when ensuring the client feels as little impact as possible.
- Expanding or moving into the leisure business, where commissions on ono-air products remain high (cruise, hotel, railway travel)
- Specializing in geographic areas or becoming niche players for specific leisure products, e.g. destination weddings, student travel group cultural travel, cruises only, cruise and railway travel etc.
- (d) establishing a service fee driven business model.

Concentrating on business travel marketing strategy

The certain characteristics to the business travel market allowed this sector to adapt more easily to the disappearance of commission. Business travel systems have always had different relationship with different customers. They usually have long term buyer relationships, set up long before the commission cap. Some of them quickly renegotiated their contracts to include a transaction or management fee, knowing that the majority of these fee arrangements are specific the need of the client.

The reasons why airlines reduce commission to paid to travel agents. They include petrol costs increasing, e.g. indirect and by pass the established distribution chain by developing airlines' their own websites; reducing or removing commission paid to travel agencies. Consequently, the decision to cut travel agencies' commission clearly shows that airlines wanted to decrease their reliance and dependence on travel agencies as a distribution channel. Thus, the internet appears to be an efficient and cost-effective distribution channel. Also, by creating airlines' own websites and setting directly to their clients, airlines are also to control seat availability to their clients and prices to their websites.

What an e-commerce strategy is used by internet travel websites?

Nowadays, the commercial use of electronic travel ticket travel is common, the most purchased online products include, for example, the name brands in online travel Epedia.travel .com and cheap tickets have been or are being integrated in large online travel firms.

Generally, online travel websites apply these strategies to attract travel consumers as below:

Firstly, shopping mall strategy, means to conduct a comprehensive factors for e-commerce. The online service provider needs to organize catalogs of services, take orders through their websites, accept payments securely, send service or related document, such as airline tickets to consumers and manage client data , such as client profiles.

Secondly, portal strategy, portal websites , such as yahoo give visitors the chance to find almost everything , they are working for in one place. Websites , such as Altavista.com and yahoo.com provide users with a shopping page that links them to many sites carrying a variety of products. Once a client is familiar with a website, who will be more likely to use the online service.

Thirdly, pricing strategy, low price is as a major competitive weapon. It includes a comparison pricing on discount price or price negotiation to let online travel consumers to get the best electronic travel ticket price choice to buy any airline tickets.

Travel agents vs online booking: Tackling the shortcomings and strengths

Consequently, however, one travel consumer who chooses either online booking sale service or traditional walk in offline travel agent to enquire travel service. These both of travel sale methods have shortcomings also. Such as it is possible that online electronic travel ticket purchase has personal data ,e.g. visa card, name, birth data, address, which will be stolen by online crime internet users more easily, who can not enquire any travel questions to get clear travel information concern whose travel destination package service choice or hotel room choice or transportation tool or restaurant choice and airline choice by travel agent. Also, it is possible that walk in travel agent paper travel ticket purchase shortcomings include that the travel consumer can not check any airlines' seat and pre book hotel room or transport tool or restaurant in the shorten time if who needs to fly immediately. Thus, it seems that online travel agent's client group is business travel intention, who does not need to enquire travel agent and has desire to per book airline seat in the short time. Otherwise, the offline walk in agent's client group is entertainment intention , who need to walk in to travel agent to enquire whose travel package and has no desire to pre book airline seat in the short time. Thus, online travel agent ought concentrate on design good travel package for the business travel consumers. Otherwise, offline travel agent ought concentrate on design good travel package for the entertainment travel consumers. Thus, they can have themselves unique travel target package to adopt to their different travel need. Such as business travel consumers need to live cheap and comfortable hotels, catching cheap and fast transportation tools in their business trips, eating in cheap and good taste food in restaurant and spending the less time to catch the airline plan to arrive the destination and cheap and comfortable business class plan seat. Such as entertainment travel consumers need the travel agent can help them to design cheap and enjoyable travel package, includes living comfortable hotel room, exciting and enjoyable trip, good taste food and
railway, travel bus, cruise and plane provision in trip.

In conclusion, In fact, tourism is a quite unique area of business in a sense that is a travel sale service product and it can't be observed or manipulated through direct experience prior to purchase . Instead clients have to purely rely on indirect or virtual experience. Thus, every online or offline travel agent ought attempt to design different travel package to attract every business traveler or entertainment traveller trip need because every traveler will have personal unique trip need in this competitive travel sale service market in the future.

Reference

Bieger. Th., and Ch. Laesser (2004). " Information sources for travel decisions: Toward a source process model," Journal of travel reserch, 42(4): 357-371.

Daneshku, S. (1999). " Unwived travel agents unworried bi internet, " Financial Times , London. June 16, 1999:10.

Foucault, B. Lery, N. Rifkin, A. & Silfies , 2000.
" Comparision of textbook prices by retailer and by college" working paper. Cornell University, Ithaca, Ney.

What factors can influence travel behavioural consumption

Prediction travel behavioral consumption from traditional human's mind of tourism market research method

How to predict travel consumption? It is one question to any travel agents concern to use what methods which can predict how many numbers of travelers where who will choose to go to travel more accurately. I think that who can consider how to predict travel behavioral consumption from psychology view and computer science view both.

On the psychology view, It has evidence to support the relationship between self-identify threat and resistance to change travel behavior to any travelers, controlling for whose past travelling behavior, resistance to change if a psychological phenomenon of long standing interest in many applied branches of psychology. Past travelling behavior has been acknowledged as a predictor of future action. Such as travelling behavior that is experienced as successful is likely to be repeated and may lead to habitual patterns. Some psychologists differentiate habit between two concepts, such as goal oriented and automatic oriented both. Although repeated past travelling behavior is addition goal oriented and automatic oriented. Further non-deliberative nature of habit may make appeals to judge and to predict future individual traveler's behaviour accrately. However, repeated travelling behavior without a necessary constraint of goal orientation and automatic oriented both. So, it seems that psychological factor can influence any individual traveler why and how who choose to decide whose travelling behaviour.

On the computer statistic view, structural equation modeling is an extremely flexible linear-in-parameters multivariate statistical modeling technique. It has been used in modeling travel behavior and values since about 1980 year. It is a software method to handle a large number of variables, as well as unobserved variables specified as linear combinations (weighted averages) of the observed variable.

Whether climate change can influence travelling behaviours.

The flexibility of human travelling behavior is at least the result of one such mechanism, our ability to travel mentally in time and entertain potential future. Understanding of the impacts is holidays, particularly those involving travel. Using focus groups research to explores tourists' awareness of the impacts of travel own climate change, examines the extent to which climate change features in holiday travel decisions and identifies some of the barriers to the adoption of less carbon intensive tourism practices. The findings suggest many tourists don't consider climate change when planning their holidays. The failure of tourists to engage with the climate change to impact of holidays, combined with significant barriers to behavioral change, presents a considerable challenge in the tourism industry.

Tourism is a highly energy intensive industry and has only recently attracted attention as an important contributions to climate change through greenhouse gas emissions. It has been estimated that tourism contributes 5% of global carbon dioxide emissions. There have been a number of potential changes proposed for reducing the impact of air travel on climate change. These include technological changes, market based changes and behavioral changes. However, the role that climate change plays in the holiday and travel decisions of global tourists. How the global tourists of the impacts travel has on climate change to establish the extent to which climate change, considerations features in holiday travel decision making processes and to investigate the major barriers to global tourists adopting less carbon intensive travel practices. Whether tourists will aware the impacts that their holidays and travel have on climate changes.

When, it comes to understand indvidual traveler's behavioral change, wide range of conceptual theories have been developed, utilizing various social, psychological, subjective and objective variables in order to model travel consumption behavior. These theories of travel behavioral change operate at a number of different levels, including the individual level, the interpersonal level and community level. Whether pro-environmental behavior can be used to predict travel consumption behavior in a climate change. However, the question of what determines pro-environmental behavior in such a complex one that it can not be visualized through one single framework or diagram. Despite the potentially high risk scenario for the tourism industry and the global environment, the tourism and climate change ought have close relationship. Whether what are the important factors and variables which can limit tourism? e.g. money, time, family problem, extreme hot or cold weather change, air ticket price, journey attraction etc. variable factors. Mention of holidays and travel were deliberately avoided in the recruitment process, so as not to create a connection factor to influence traveler's individual mind. However, the dismissal of alternative transportation modes can be conceived as either a structural barrier, in the sense that flying is perhaps the only realistic option to reach long-haul holiday destination, or a perceived behavioral control barriers in that an individual perceives flying as the only option open to whom. The transportation tool factor will be depend to extent on the distance to the destination. This can also be interpreted in a social perspective as an intention with the resources available where much international tourism is structured around flying. To increase the availability of different transportation modes, tourists could choose holiday destination closer to home.

Finally, also how to predict future travel behavioural consumption. I feel that travel agents need to predict whether any country's random daily variation of weather factor is also important to influence travel behaviour. e.g. in weather, temperature, rainfall adn snowfall with traffic accidents factors will have relationship to cause travel demand. Some scientists estimate suggest that when warmed temperatures and reduced snowfall are associated with a moderate decline in non-fatal accidents, they are also associated with a significant increase in fatal accidents. Thus increase in fatalities and temperature. Half of the estimated effect of temperature on fatalities is due to changes in the exposure to pedestrians, bicyclists and motorcyclists as temperature increase. So, if any countries have rainfall, snowfall and low temperature to cause traffic accidents, whether this accident occurrence will influence the travelers who liking climb snow hills, riding bicycle, running sports who will avoid to travel to these countries' bad weather after occurs. So, why I feel that this natural climate factor will also be one serious factor to influence travel behavioral consumption.

Market method predicts future travel consumption behavior

Whether individual habitual behaviour can influence travelling behaviour : e.g. renting travel transportation tools

Whether habit can be intended to predict of future travel behavior to people are creatures of habits. Many of human's everyday goal-directed behaviors are performed in a habitual fashion, the transportation made and route one takes to work, one's choice of breakfast. Habits are formed when using the some behavior frequently and a similar consistency in a similar context for the some purpose whether the individual past travel consumption model will be caused a habit to whom. e.g. choosing whom travel agent to buy air ticket or traveling package; choosing the same or similar countries' destinations to go to travel ; choosing the business class or normal (general) class of quality airlines to catch planes. Does habitual rent traveling car tools use not lead to more resistance to change of travel mode? It has been argued that past behavior is the best predictor of future behavior to travel consumption. If individual traveler's past consumption behavior was always reasoned, then frequency of prior travel consumption behavior should only have an indirect link to the individual traveler's behavior. It seems that renting travel car tools to use is a habit example. So, a strong rent traveling car tools useful habit makes traveling mode choice. People with a strong renting of traveling car tools of habit should have low motivation to attend to gather any information about public transportation in their choice of travelling country for individual or family or friends members during their traveling journeys.

Even when persuasive communication changes the traveler whose attitudes and intention, in the case of individual traveler or family travelers with a strong renting travel car tools habit. It is difficult to change whose travel behaviors to choose to catch public transportation in whose any trips in any countries. However, understanding of travel behavior and the reasons for choosing one mode of transportation over another. The arguments for rent traveling car tools to use, including convenience, speed, comfort and individual freedom and well known. Increasingly, psychological factors include such as, perceptions, identity, social norms and habit are being used to understand travel mode choice. Whether how many travel consumers will choose to rent traveling car tools during their trips in any countries. It is difficult to estimate the numbers. As the average level of renting travel car tools of dependence or attitudes to certain travel package policies from travel agents. Instead different people must be treated in different ways because who are motivated in different ways and who are motivated by different travel package policies ways from travel agents.

In conclusion, the factors influence whose traveler's individual behavior either who chooses to rent traveling car tools or who chooses to catch public transportation when who individual goes to travel in alone trip or family trip. It include influence mode choice factors, such as social psychology factor and marketing on segmentation factor both to influence whose transportation choice of behavior in whose trip.

How to determine future travel behavior from past travel experience and perceptions of risk and safety for the benefits to travel consumers?

How to determine future travel behavior from past travel experience and perceptions of risk and safety for the benefits to travel consumers? Why does individual traveler avoid certain destination(s) is(are) as relevant to tourist decision making as why who chooses to travel to others. Perceptions of risk and safety and travel experience are likely to influence travel decisions. If travel agents had efforts to predict future travel behavior to guess whether travelers will feel where is(are) risk and unsafe to cause who does not choose to go to the country to travel. Then, the travel agents will avoid to choose to spend much time to design the different traveling package to attract their potential travel consumers to choose to travel. The reason is because in the case of individual traveler's tourism experience, the traveler whose past disappointment travel experience (psychological risk) will be a serious threat to the traveler's health or life (health, physical or terrorism risk). The past safety or unhealthy risk to the country(countries) will influence the traveler decides to choose not to go to the countries(country) to travel again in the future.

What is push and pull factors to influence any
traveler who chooses where is whose preferable travelling destination

How to predict individual traveler's behavioral intention of choosing a travel destination. Understanding why people travel and what factors influence their behavioral intention of choosing a travel destination is beneficial to tourism planning and marketing. In general, an individual's choice of a travel destination into two forces. The first force is the push factor that pushes an individual away from home and attempt to develop a general desire to go somewhere, without specifying where that may be. The other force is the pull factor that pull an individual toward in destination, due to a region-specific or perceived attractiveness of a destination. The respective push and pull factors illustrate that people travel because who are pushed by whose internal motives and pulled by external forced of a destination. However, the decision making process leading to the choice of a travel destination is a very complex process. For example, a Taiwanese traveler who might either choose new travel destination of Hong Kong or another old travel Asia destinations again or who also might choose any one of Western country, as a new travel destination. The travel agents can predict where who will have intention to choose to travel from whose past behavior and attitude, subjective and perceived behavioral control model.

The factors influence where is the traveler choice, include personal safety, scenic beauty, cultural interest, climate changing, transportation tools, friendliness of local people, price of trip, trip package service in hotels and restaurants, quality and variety of food and shopping facilities and services etc. needs. So, whose factors will influence where is the individual travel's choice. It seems every traveler whose choice of travel process, will include past behavior. e.g. travelling experience, travelling habit, then to choose the best seasoned travelling action to satisfy whose travel needs. This process is the individual traveler's psychological choice process, who must need time to gather information to compare concerning of different travel packages, destination scene, climate change, transportation tools available to the destination, air ticket price etc. these factors, then to judge where is the best right destination to travel in the right time.

Why expectation, motivation and attitude factor can influence travelling behaviour.

Social psychology is concerned with gaining insight into the psychological of socially relevant behaviors and the processes. For instance, on a global level bad influence to global warming, it influences some countries extreme cold or hot bad climate changing occurrence, then it ought influence some travelers' behavioral decision to change their mind to choose some countries to go to travel at the moment which do not occur extreme hot or cold climate (temperature). e.g. above than 40 degree in summer or below than 0 degree in winter. Due to the extreme climate changing environment in the countries, it will cause them to feel uncomfortable to play during their trips. So, the global warming causes to climate changing factor will influence the numbers of travel consumption to be reduced possibly. This is global climate changing environment factor influences to bad or uncomfortable social psychological feeling to global travelers' mind of traveling decision. What is individual traveler expectation, motivation and attitude? Tourism sector includes inbound (domestic) tourism and outbound (overseas) tourism both incomes to any countries. According to recent article, a tourist behavior model has been developed, called the expectation, motivation and attitude (EMA) model (Hsu et al., 2010).

This model focuses on the pre-visit stage of tourists by modeling the behavioral process by incorporating expectation, motivation and attitude. Travel motivation is considered as an essential component of the behavioral process, which has been increasing attention from the travel; industry. The economic approach defines "tourism" is an identifiable nationally important industry. It includes the component activities of transportation, accommodation, recreation, food and related service. So, tourism behavioral consumption is concerned the individual tourist's usual habituate of the industry which responds to whose needs, and of the impacts that both the tourist and the tourism industry have on the socio-cultural, economic and physical environment.

However, travel motivation means how to understand and predict factors that influence travel decision making. According to Backman and others (1995, p.15), motivation is conceptually viewed as " a state of need, a condition that services as a driving force to display different kind of behavior toward certain types of activities, developing preferences, arriving at some expected satisfactory outcome." So, motivation and expectancy which has close relationship to any tourist before who decided to do any tourism of behavior. Some economists confirmed motivation and expectancy which has relations, such as expectation of visiting an outbound destination has a direct effect on motivation to visit the destination; motivation has a direct effect on attitude toward visiting the destination; expectation of visiting the outbound destination has a direct affect on attitude toward visiting the destination and motivation has a mediating effect on the relationship in between expectation and attitude.

What methods can predict future travel behavioural consumption

How to use qualitative of travel behavioural method to predict future travel consumption?

I also suggest to use qualitative of travel behavioural method to predict future travel consumption. Methods such as focus groups interviews and participant observer techniques can be used with quantitative approaches on their own to fill the gaps left by quantitative techniques. These insights have contributed to the development of increasingly sophisticated models to forecast travel behavior and predict changes in behavior in response to change in the transportation system. First, survey methods restrict not only the question frame but the answer frame as well, anticipating the important issues and questions and the responses. However, these surveys methods are not well suited to exploratory areas of research where issues remain unidentified and the researched seek to answer the question "why?". Second, data collection methods using traditional travel diaries or telephone recruitment can under represent certain segments of the population, particularly the older persons with little education, minorities and the poor. Before the survey, focus group for example can be used to identify what socio-demographic variables to include in the survey, how best to structure the diary, even what incentives will be most effective in increasing the response rate. After the survey, focus, focus groups can be used to build explanations for the survey results to identify the "why" of the results as well as the implications. One Asia Pacific survey research result was made by tourism market investigation before. It indicated the travel in Asia Pacific market in the past, had often been undertaken in large groups through leisure package sold in bulk, or in large organized business groups, future travelers will be in smaller groups or alone, and for a much wider range of reasons. Significant new traveler segments, such as female business traveler. The small business traveler and the senior traveler, all of which have different aspirations and requirements from the travel experience.

Moreover, Asia tourism market will start to exist behaviors in the adoption of newer technologies, a giving the traveler new ways to manage the travel experience, creating new behaviors. This with provide new opportunities for travel providers. The use of mobile devices, smartphones, tablets etc. and social media are the obvious findings to become an integral part of the travel experience. Thus, quality method can attempt to predict Asia Pacific tourism market development in the future.

However, improving the predictive power of travel behavior models and to increase understanding travel behavior which lies in the use of panel data(repeated measures from the same individuals). Whereas, cross-sectional data only reveal inter-individual differences at one moment in time, panel data can reveal intra-individual changes over time. In effect, panel data are generally better suited to understand and predict (changes in) travel behavior. However, a substantial proportion was also observed to transition between very different activity/travel patterns over time, indicating that from one year to the next, many people renegotiated their activity/travel patterns.

How to apply advanced traveler information systems (ATIS) to predict future travelling behaviour?

Nowadays, information can impact on traveler behavior and network performance. For example, when steadily growing levels of vehicle ownership and vehicle miles traveled information has been identified as a potential strategy towards man aging travel demand, optimizing transportation networks and better utilizing available capacity. Toward, this goal to predict further tourist behavioral consumption. Many countries, government tourism development institutes has applied advanced traveler information systems (ATIS) which travel behavior models and high-fidelity network performance models made increasingly feasible through the rapid advances in computer power. Crucial components of this problem domain are the modeling of individual tourist drivers' response to travel information and the development accurate guidance of relevance to real would trip makers. So, this advanced traveler information systems (ATIS) can assist the tourist who like to rent travelling car tools to travel in any countries own free traveler information systems service conveniently. Also, this travel information system can be intended to assist travelers to make better travel choices. e.g. this system can improve the decision making of individual traveler rather than improvements of network performance overall. So, we need to understand how tourists make their travel plans. Also, understanding decision process that lead to booking of the trip is equally important, as it allows of a potential behavior.

How does online tourism sale channel can influence traveling consumption of behaviour?

Nowadays, internet is popular, it seems that booking air ticket behavior of using internet is predicted to influence overall tourism air tickets payment method. Tourism industry has grown in the previous several decades. Despite its global impact, questions related to better understanding of tourists and whose habits. Using online travel air ticket booking benefits include booking electronic air tickets can be made from entering any electronic travel agents websites in the short time and electronic travel ticket payers do not need leave home, who can pay visa card to pre booking any electronic travel ticket from online channel conveniently.

How to analyze activity based travel demand ? Nowadays, human are concerning the traffic congestion and air quality deterioration, the supply oriented focus of transportation planning has expanded to include how to manage travel demand within the available transportation supply. Consequently, there has been an increasing interest in travel demand management strategies, such as congestion pricing that attempts to change aggregate travel demand. The prediction aggregate level, long term travel demand to understanding disaggregate level (i.e. individual levels) behavioral responses to short term demand policies, such as ride sharing incentives, congestion pricing and employer based demand management schemes, alternate work schedules, telecommuting limitation of travel agent traditionally work nature shall influence oriented trip based travel modelling passenger travel demand indirectly.

Finally, online travel purchase will be popular to influence the number of travel behavioural consumption nowadays. Any travel package products can be sold from websites to attract travellers to choose to prebook air ticket for any trips conveniently. In the past ten years, the internet has become the predominant carrier of all types of information and transactions. Regarding travel decisions, internet has also become an important sales channels for the travel industry, because it is associated with comparably lower distribution and sales costs, but also because ir adapts to hign supply and demand dynamics in this industry. Consequently, the travel and tourism industry tries to increase the internet sale specific share of sales volumes. So, internet sale channel has changed travel consumption behavioural pattern and characteristics and travel experience. For example, Switzerland has one of the highest population-to-computer ratio in Europe. It is also one of the most highly internet penetrated countries in terms of use of the WWW on a day-to-day basis, with more than 75 percent of the population older than 14 years using the WWW daily (ICT, 2005).

The reason of booking online tourism may include: convenience, fast transaction, finding traveling package choice easily, more airline seats available. So, online booking tourism will influence the traditional tourism agents visiting of sales and air tickets and travelling package numbers to be decreased. Finally, the online booking tourism market shares will be expanded to more than traditional tourism agents visits sale market in the future one day. So, the travel agents who still use the traditional tourism visiting sale channel which ought raise whose features to compare to differ to online tourism sale channel if these traditional touriam agents want to keep competitive ability in tourism industry for long term.

Actively based patterns of urban population of travel behavioural prediction method.

Actively based patterns of urban population. It is a method of motivational framework means in which societal constraints and inherent individual motivations interact to shape activity participation patterns. It can be used to predict one city or urban the numbers of travel demand in the year. It has two elements: First, capability constraints refer to constraints are imposed by biological needs, such as eating and sleeping and/or resources, such as income, availability of cars etc. to undertake the urban or city's family activities in the year. Second, coupling constraints define where, when and the duration of planning activities that are to be pursued with other individuals. So, this method needs to gather information (data) to get the relationship between activities, travel and spending work time and space time to evaluate whether there are how many families who have real needs to spend time to go to travel in the year.

What is trip based versus activity based approaches?

What is trip based versus activity based approaches? The fundamental difference between the trip-based and activity based approaches is that the former approach directly focuses on trips without explicit recognition of the motivation or reason for the trips and travel. The activity based approach , on the other hand, views travel as a demand derived from the need to pursue travel activities. So, it is better understand the individual or family behavior basis for individual or family travelling decision regarding participation in travelling activities in certain places or cities or countries at given times and hence the resulting travel needs. This behavioral basis includes all the factors that influence the why, how, when and where of performed activities and resulting individuals and household, the cultural/social norms of the community and the travel surrounding environment.

Another difference between the two approaches is in the way travel is represented. The trip based approach represents travel as a collection of trips. Each trip is considered as independent of other trips, without considering the inter-relationship in the choice attributes , such as time, destination and mode of different trips. As tours are chains of trips beginning and ending at a same location , say home or work. The tour based representation helps maintain the consistency across and capture the interdependency and consistency of the modeled choice attributed among the trips of the same tour.

In addition to the tour based representation of travel, the activity based approach focuses on sequences or patterns of activity participation and travel behavior, using the whole day or longer periods of time is the unit of analysis. Such as approach can address travel demand management issues through an examination of how people modify their activity participation, for example, will individuals substitute more out-of-home activities for in home activities in the evening of who arrived early form work due-to a work schedule change?

The major difference between trip based and the activity based approaches is in the way, the time dimension of activities and travel is considered. In the trip based approach, time is reduced to being simply a cost making a trip and a day's viewed as a combination, defined peak and off peak time periods. On the other hand, activity based approach views individuals' activity travel patterns are a result of their time use decisions with a continuous time domain. As individuals have 24 hours in a day or multiples of 24 hours for longer periods of time and decide how to use that travel among or allocate that time to activities and travel and with who, subject to their socio-demographic, transportation system and other and scheduling of trips. So, determining the impact of travel demand management policies on time use behavior is an important step to assessing the impact of such policies on individual travel behavior. The final major difference between this two approaches relates to the level of aggregation. In the trip based approach, most aspect of travel, e.g. number of trips etc. are analyzed at an aggregate level.

Consequently, trip based methods accommodate the effect of socio-demographic attributes of households and individuals in a very limited fashion, which limits the activity of the method to evaluate travel impacts of long term socio-demographic characteristics of the individuals who actually make the activity travel choices and the travel service characteristics of the surrounding environment. So, the activity based models are better equipped to forecast the longer term changes in travel demand in response composition and the travel environment of urban areas. Also, using activity based models, the impact of policies can be assessed by predicting individual level behavioral responses instead of employing trip based statistical averages that are aggregated over defined demographic segments.

Why senior age will be main travelling target?

In the past, Germany government had established tourism survey analysis to analyze survey data in order to arrive at reliable conclusions on future trends in travel behavior. To aim to find how demographic change will influence the tourism market and how the industry can adapt to those changes. The travel analysis provided data on tourism consumer behavior, including attitudes, motives and intentions. Since, 1970 year, it is based on a random sample, representative for the population in private households aged 14 years or older. Then, a continuous high scientific standard combined with a national and international users makes the travel analysis a useful tool and reliable source for tourism industry and policy decisions. It aimed to gather statistical data. e.g. on the age structure and on demographic trends, quantitative and qualitative analysis with time series data from the travel analysis. It shows e.g. not only the future volume , quite different from today's seniors, or how who will travel of family holidays will change, e.g. single parents of low, but grandparents of growing significance for tourism.

Demographic change is said to be one of the important drivers for new trends in consumer traveling change behavior in most European countries (e.g. Lind 2001). Because the growing number of senior citizens in the European Union and other industralised countries, such as the USA and Japan, looks to become one of the major marketing challenges for the tourism industry. United Nations statistics predict that the share of people being 60 age or older will grow dramatically in the coming future, and is expected to rise from 10 percent of the world population in 2000 year to more than 20 percent in 2050 year (United Nations Population Division, 2001). From its statistic, some data showed that travel propensity increased throughout life until the age of about 50 years of age and was then kept stable until very late in life 75 age. The most important results is that the travel propensity when getting older is not going down between 65 and 75 age of course, the overall development of this variable is influenced by a lot of other factors which are rsponsible for quite a variation over time. It is now possible to suggest that the general pattern of travel propensity is one of the key indicators for holiday life cycle travel behaviour, includes three stages. The growth stage tends to increase from early aduithood until 45 age old or when reaching some 80%. The next stage is stabilisation from the ages of around 50 age,until 75 age old, starting with a lower increase. Finally, the decrease stage is a slight decrease occurs once people reach the more advanced age of 75 age to 85 age old (Lohmann & Danielsson 2001).

So, it seems Germany government tourism prediction to future travellers' behaviour indicated these findings, such as on how future senior generations will travel, who had used survey data to examine the patterns of travel behaviour of a generation getting older and applied the findings to draw conclusions on the future. Also, it predicted that on the future of family trips, family semgmentation will be the travel behaviour patterns in the future. These findings together with the statistical data on demographic change allowed for a better understanding of the coming tends in family holidays. It's aim developed in consumer behaviour related to demographic change and predicted what will happen future of tourism one had to consider other influences and drivers as well, for example, trends on the supply side. e.g. low cost airlines or in travelling consumption behaviour in general whether how the past may provide a key to predict travel patterns of senior sitizens to the future.

Given the projected growth of the senior citizens market, designing specific marketing strategies to meet the prospective needs of elderly tourists will become increasingly important. It has been an implict assumption that it will be a close relationship between the travel behaviour of today's senior citizens and the those of future ones. The growing number of senior citizens in the world. e.g. China, Hong Kong, Japan, USA etc. countries. Global senior citizen tourism market will be based solely on demographic predictions about the future of the population's age structure. However, many of these seniors won't only live longer but will be fitter and more active until later in life. Many of the will also have plenty in life. Many of them will also have plenty of time and money to spend on travel. So, will these new seniors behave like today's senior citizens? Will they adopt the same travel behaviour as the previous generation or become a new market of oldies for the leisure and tourism indudtry? However, to determine the actual number of senior citizens who will be travelling and to sought to evaluate and specify certain difficult to predict the actual numbers of senior citizen to any country. However, they can be based on the implicit assumption that there is a close relationship between the travel behaviour of past, present and future seniors. But is this a valid assumption? As the reiseanalyse travel analysis survey, which was conducted in Germany every year, offered some interesting data possibiltieis. It was designed to monitor the holiday travel behaviour, opinions and attitudes of Germans and has been carried out since 1970 year, questions in the questionnaire. Data are based on face to face interviews, with a representative sample of more than 7,500 repondents, the interviews being carried out in January each year. All results refer to the average for the defined generated, which ranges generally over ten years. The group of people then at the age of 60 to 69 age is described. This corresponds to the same generation ten years ago, when they had an age of 50 to 59 age. When this methodological approach is not necessarily very sophisticated, it does have the important advantages of being cost effective.

Psychological method to predict travel behavioural consumption.

On the psychological view point, I think individual traveler's character will have those kind of personal characteristics. First, simplicity searchers value above everything ease not transparency in their travel planning and holiday making, and are willing to avoid having to go through extensive research. Second, cultural purists use their travel as an opportunity to immerse themselves in an unfamiliar looking to break themselves entirely from their home lives and engage. Sincerely with a different way of living. Third, social capital seekers understand that to be well travelled is a personal quality, and their choices are shaped by their desire to take maximum of social reward from their travel. They will exploit the potential of digital media to enrich and inform their experiences, and structure their adventures always keeping in mind they are being watched by online audiences. Finally, reward hunters seek a return on the investment who make in their busy , high-achieving lives. Linked in part to the growing trend of wellness, including both physical and mental self improvement who seek truly extraordinary and often indulgent or luxurious' must have experiences.

Why needs to know the personal character of individual traveler's characteristics? Because if travel agents could feel which kinds of individual traveler's character, then who can predict which kind of travel package to design to them more easily. For example, how to determine future travel behaviour from past travel experience and perceptions of risk and safety? We need to concern that the influences of past international travel experience, types of risk associated with international travel and the overall degree of safety feeling during international travel on individual's travelling experiences likelihood of travelling to various geographic regions on their next international vacation trip or avoidance of those regions, due to perceived risk. Because individual traveler's experience of safety risk degree to the countries, it will influence who chooses to go to the countries/country to travel again.

Why do travellers avoid certain destinations are as relevant decision making? Why do they choose to go to the country(countries) to travel? Perceptions of risk and safety and travel experiences are likely to influence travel decisions; efforts to predict future travel behaviour can benefit to individual tourist's decision making. As Weber & Bottorn (1989) defined risky decision is as "choices among alternatives that can be described by prodability distributions over possible outcomes" (p.114). Some psychologists judge subjective perceptions of physical reality, i.e. image of a particular tourist destination, whereas value judgement refers to the way individual rank destinations according to whose attributes. i.e. attractiveness, safety, risk etc. factors to form on overall image. So, if the individual traveler had unhappy and worried and unsafe experiences to go to where the place(country) to travel during whose vacation time before. Then, this negative travel experience will influence who is afraid to go to the place (country) to travel again. Risk of place, country, destination or region means the danger is relatively high to the place, ie. increasing in airplane accidents, crime or terrorist activity targeting citizens of potential traveler's nationality or the probability of occurrence is great , ie. recent occurrences involving travel regions/destinations under consideration or effective actions to control consequences exist. i.e. selecting safe regions and destinations, taking extra precautions when traveling to risky destinations. These risk factors will influence the individual traveler who chooses to cancel travel plan to go to the country again.

Another interesting research, how to predict behavioural intention of choosing a travel destination, which has focus of toursm research for years, but the complex decision making process leading to the choice of a travel destination has not been well researched. The planned behaviour model using its core constructs, attitude, subjective norm and perceived behavioural control, with the addition of the past behavioural variable on behavioural intention of choosing a travel destination.

Understanding why people travel and what factors influence their behavioural intention of choosing a travel destination is beneficial to tourism planning and marketing. Understanding travel motivation is the push and pull model. The idea of the push and pull model is the decomposition of an individual's choice of a travel destination into two forces. The first force is the push factor that pushes an indvidual away home and attempts to develop a general desire to go somewhere else, without specifying where that may be. The second force is the pull factor, that pulls on individual toward a destination, due to a region specific travel location or perceived attractiveness of a destination. The respective push and pull factors illustrate that people travel because who are pushed by their internal motives and pulled by external forces of a destination. Nevertheless, how push and pull factors guide people's attitude and how these attributes lead to behavioural intentions of choosing a travel destination have rarely been investigated. The decision making process leading to the choice of a travel destination is a very complex process. The planned behaviour model is as a research framework to predict the behavioural intention of choosing a travel destination. The model based on the three constructs of attitude, subjective norm, and perceived behavioural control (Fishbein & Ajzen, 1975).

In conclusion, the factors can influence travelers who decide to choose to travel the country, which include personal safety was perceived to the highest motivation factors among the important factors which include, scenic beauty, cultural interests, friendliness of local people, price of trip, services in hotels and restaurants, quality and variety of food and shopping facilities and services. The factors include both push and pull. Push factors include knowledge, prestige, and enhancement of human relationship etc., whereas, the most significant pull factors include high technologic image, expenditure and accessibility etc. For example, Japanese travelers visiting Hong Kong. Push factors are such as exploration dream fulfillment and pull factors are such as benefits sought, attractions and good climate city. It will be the factor of future travel patterns and motivations of sub-cultural and ethic groups for Japanese choice to go to Hong Kong travelling.

Bibliography

Backman, K., Backman, S., Uysal, M. And Sunshine, K. (1995). Event Tourism : An Examination Of Motivations And Activities. Festival Management And Event Tourism, 3(1), 15-24.

Fishbein, M., & Ajzen, Z. (1975). Belief, Attitude, Intention And Behaviour: An Introduction To Theory And Research, Boston: Addison Wesley.

Hsu, C.H.C., Cai , L.A., Li, M(2010). Expectation, Motivation And Attitude: A Tourist Behavioral Model. Journal Of Travel Research, 49(3), 282-296. http://dx.doi, org/10.1177/004728750 9349266.

ICT Information And Communication Technology Switzerland, 2005. ICT Fakten (ICT facts). Available from http://www.ictswitzerland.ch/de/ict%2fakten/factsfigures.asp(retrieved Dec.12, 2005) in German.

Lind, (2001): Befolkningen, Familjen, Livscykeln- Och Ekonomisk Tillvaxt. Institutet For Tillvaxtpo-litiska studier/ Vinnova/Nutek.

Lohmann, Martin (2001): The 31 st. Reiseanalyse-RA 2001. Tourism: vol. 49, no.1/2001;pp.65-67, Zagreb.

United Nations Population Division (2001). World Population Prospects: The 2000 year Revision, New York.

Weber E.U., & W, P.Bottom (1989). "Axiomatic Measures Of Perceived Risk: Some Tests And extensions." journal of behavioral decision making, 2 (2): 113-31.

Oil price changes influences tourism industry experiences growth life cycle stage or decline life cycle stage

New economic development in Tourism and oil industries

● How to develop new economic tourism industry

How to develop tourism industry in new economic environment? Any examination of the new economic development of travel and tourism requires definitions of the subject and its components, which are suitable for economic analysis. However, in new economic development to tourism industry, it is also important to look at tourism conceptually, in order to set the scene for a deeper understanding of the future new tourism industry development.

Tourism is neither a phenomenon nor a simple set if industries, however, in new or old economic development environment. It is a human activity which encompasses human behavior, use of resources, and interaction with other people, economies and leisure enjoyment environment. It is also involved physical movement of tourists to locales other than their normal living places.

In future new economic environment, traditional travel needs to include these element in order to satisfy traveler enjoyment and leisure feeling: They may include: Tourist needs and motivations, tourism selection and behavior and constraints , travel away from home , market interactions between tourists and those supplying products to satisfy tourist needs and impacts on tourists , hosts, economies and environments.

In new economic environment, the tourism products may include: carriers, in any forms of transport for tourist travel accommodation, man-made attractions, which could also include the managed areas of natural attractions, private sector and public sector support services, middlemen, such as tour wholesalers and travel agents.

The tourism resources may also include: Natural resources, lands , minerals, water and biological; labor resources, human work, and enterprise; capital resources, manmade enhancement and other resources. The travel and tourism resources problems may include: As there is frequently a mismatch between producer and consumer perception of what constitutes the tourism product , there may be conflict in ideas of which resources are properly involved as well as many of the resources likely to be in demand for tourism are public goods , or even free resources.

In new economic development to tourism industry view, we need to consider that tourism and travel has the reputation of being a relatively clean and pleasant industry in which to work or invest in order to attract a greater number of resource suppliers than as less well-perceived industry, which therefore keeps rewards prices down by competition, how to attract those retiring from or travel business for example, if their finances are already sound, income from travel is not expected to be optimal , travel and tourism is frequently highly seasonal , offering rewards that are competitive with other industries only some of the time, destination products are often in locations which are of little use to other industries, so that competition for resource use if minimal and hence rewards are low.

In general, tourist purpose may include: recreational purpose : holiday, health and sport and religion as well as business purpose: company business , e.g. conventions and sales trips. So, in new economic tourism development aim, tourism industry need consider hoe to achieve incentive trips to let these both tourists to feel. For example, the overall type of tourism required, destination arrangement, travel mode, accommodation and attraction visiting and purchasing method or distribution channel. The purchasing method choices may include: whether to buy an inclusive package or separate service, whether to buy direct from suppliers, such as airlines or hotels or use an agent , which tour wholesaler or operate or agent to use.

I predict the tourism development in new economic view, it may have these characteristics: Few enterprises in travel and tourism are large, highly cashed-up and have a large asset base, enterprises within travel and tourism that are not in a financial position to diversify, and those do well success to the above –average growth obtainable in travel and tourism compared with many other industries, they would therefore tend to expand within the sector. The result of individual enterprise growth and integration within travel and tourism is an increase in the concentration of that industry. The degree to which output is produced of fewer and fewer enterprises. This can be only be accounted for realistically with the context of an individual economy, Levels of concentration in any part of travel and tourism in the future are likely to depend on two opposing factors: The constant demand by many tourist market segments for new experiences and products, which encourages the development and survival of more and diverse enterprises, and therefore leads to the reduction of concentration as well as technology, which in travel and tourism frequently calls for large capital outlays and requires mass markets for efficient use, promotes integrations and large scale enterprise, especially in air travel and non-personal services (marketing and information communication, travel insurance , tourism payment methods). IN these areas, concentration will undoubtedly increase in future new economic development environment.

● How new economic development in oil industry

The future global economic growth, it will influence personal incomes and GDP rise. They would carry different weight in different countries at different times. Starting from low levels of incomer and economic development. Household consumption will change from being dominated by basic heat to rapidly rising energy use for higher levels of comfort in space heating and cooling (and large dwellings), and greater use of electrical appliances, finally to a degree of saturation influenced by the income distribution patterns of the country concerned. Income distribution typically changes very slowly, so that the technical market for heart will never be saturated because there will always be a proportion of poor people living in small spaces less comfortably than the average. Industrial energy consumption will be influenced by technical efficiency within each sector, and by changes in the structures of the economy, e.g. changing proportions of agriculture, heavy and light industry, and services. One may eventually see evidence of diminishing marginal returns to additional energy inputs compared to other inputs. Energy consumption in the energy transformation sector may be influenced by income, which drives the demand for electricity to influenced by income, which drives the demand for electricity to grow faster than the demand for heat, but is also subject to the chosen technology of transformation, which is influenced by the cost and availability of primary energy inputs (fuels) in new economic development environment.

IN new economic development environment, it will influences that fuels do not compete in all sectors; for example, the transport sector is dominated by oil. Nuclear and hydroelectric power (and most renewables) reach the user through electricity; electricity itself competes with the direct burning of fossil fuels. Electricity provides the means by which other fuels can compete with oil and gas in sectors, such as space heating and process heat. It also is the only means of powering applications such as motors, computers and lighting: these subsectors are difficult to analyze. However, there is strong evidence that higher incomes do not weaken the demand for electricity so much as the demand for energy in total (in contrast to the effect on the demand for non-electric energy forms).

Econometricians look at the historical record of change in fuel prices and quantities to distinguish several factors between the new economic development and old economic development to oil industry in the future. An income effect. Increasing (reducing) fuel prices reduces (increases) the purchasing power of consumers' income: higher incomes caused by lower prices will increase energy consumption; the consumers' allocation of the increased income to energy purchases may reduce as income rises. Thus income may be heading in a different direction from fuel prices that the effect of fuel price changes when incomes are rising means simply that rising incomes have increased demand. Reducing the cost of using energy through win-win efficiency measures causes a similar problem . On the consequence, in future new economic development environment, it may influence in both cases demand will be less than if the future oil price or efficiency has not changed. The other effect is that an efficiency or substitution effect. An increase in fuel prices may cause consumers to spend more on new equipment, building materials and management operations, which will reduce the amount of fuel required to give the same energy result to the user. The extent of the efficiency effect depends on what happens to the price of the new equipment or building: if those price s rise in line with the fuel price, changes in the balances between fuel and capital or management will not occur. A new user technology , such as the development of the combined cycle gas turbine generator may increase efficiency and thus greatly reduce the quantity of primary fuel needed to produce the required output in this case electricity. If electricity prices had remained sticky, and the electricity and gas markets were not competitive, some of this advantages could have accrued to the gas suppliers in the form of an increase in price, because th4 unit of gas produces more output of electricity, it would have a higher value. In reality, the development of new economic competitive environment in both gas and electricity has tended to ensure that the benefits of such technical advanced accrue to the consumer through lower final prices. The same many apply in the case of improved efficiency in future non-manual driving auto vehicle development: the consumer's cost of motoring is reduced in new economic non-manual driven auto vehicle (Artificial intelligent vehicle) can replace manual driven vehicle , even electricity battery can replace oil energy to be used in vehicles. So, oil price may be influenced to reduce in future new economic development environment.

New and old economic theories explain oil is not main factor to influence tourism income

● Can economic theory explain old price change to influence tourism income?

I shall attempt to apply old and new economic theory to explain whether oil changing price has direct relationship to influence global tourism indusry development or tourism income as below:

Is oil changing price the main to influence tourism income or tourism development or economic growth ? If oil price rises ar falls, it will or won't cause tourism income decreases or increases? If they have cause and effect relationship, what are the main factors to influence tourism income changes by oil price rises or falls ?

I aim to investigate how any why among oil price shocks will influence tourism income variables. We may distinguish between these oil price shocks: Supply-side , aggregate demand and oil specific demand shocks. I assume that oil specific demand shocks affect inflation and the tourism sector equity index. By constrast, I also believe that aggregate demand oil price shock exercisr an effect, either directly and indirectly tourism generated income and economic growth. So, in old economic theory, supply-side , aggregate demand view to oil specific demand shocks will influence tourism income varies. So, governments ought implement strategies against future oil price movements or plan for economic policy development.

In fact, instead of oil price changes will influence tourism income, it could also harm economic growth and tourism activities, due to the effect they expert on transporation, production cost, economic uncertainty.Because tourism activities is one important sector to influence any country's leisure consumption GDP income source. So, sudden fluctations in oil prices may also influence economic growth. It is based a hyphthesis known as the tourism led economic growth. So, it seems that they have direct or indirect relationship to case effect between oil price and tourism activities and development. So, increase on tourism income, the called " economic-driven tourism growth". In addition, high oil prices are affecting certain tourism industry segments , e.g. airlines, cruises lines, hotel, rent travelling car services etc. for oil, importing countries example, with reference to macro economic effects, higher oil prices generally lead to higher inflation, when they negatively influence to country's income.

Hence, from a micro-economic perspective, positive oil price shocks lead to a decline in disposable income. for low income people, it will bring an immediate and negative impact on tourism, mainly due to they feel tourism leisure is regarded as a luxury good, when oil price shocks to rise suddenly . It influences any airline or cruise entertainment service providers' costs are influenced to raise. Then, they need to increase air ticket or cruise ticket price. It will bring on negative tourism leisure demands-side the oil price increases low income group, potential tourism leisure consumers. Hence, it seems that oil price may have indirect relationship to influence tourism leisure consumers' needs.

● How the price of oil changes influences global tourism industry growth or recession?

In macro-economic view, sudden mid and long term oil price shock can influence global torusim industry growth or recession. For example, a oil price of US$180 per barrel was considered only a few years ago, now this has a realistic scenario to which all plaers in the T&T sector have to adapt. At such a high level, the price of oil will become even more critical to almost every part of the tourism value chain. Although, weak global demand, caused by global economic recesson, resulted in a steep oil price decline to US$45 per barrel by the fourth quarter of 2008 in the past low oil price occurrence history, this won't change the mid to long -term oil forecast.

In fact, the past oil price occurrence history of the dramatic structural had changed a high price imposed on airlines, travelers, and destination countries, all of which will have to navigate through times of shifting or even declining travel demand. I assume that a high oil price scenario is assumed in the long term in order to highlight the changes , such a senario would mean for consumer behavior and the competitiveness of several destinations.

Low oil price in the 1970 and early 1980 did not bring significant growth of international air travel, but its growth has been strongest between 1980 and 2004, a period with stable and relatively moderate oil prices. Also, the rapid development of the low-cost carrier business model in the 1990s further fueled air travel growth by capturing tourism leisure demand , such as weekend leisure travel to cities using mostly secondary airports in any big area countries, such as UK, US . However, the tourism growth is whole influenced by high oil prices, due to oil price had been continue rising in possible.

Basis of oil is shortage supply product, oil is assumed to be the main energy source for the aviation sector for the nest 30 years. Although, second-generation biofuels seem to be on the horizon, the economics as well as the production scalability and aviation biofuel shortage will be a main challenge to airline industry. So, I assume that oil price will continue rise up, if there have none any aviation biofuel can be reflected to oil to use for air plane energy.

Until 2004, the only factors to have affected air travel growth, negatively were in external shocks , such as 9/ 11, causes catching air plane crisis or US regional geopolitical conflicts. It brings some travelers feel fear to go to US travel, as well as until recently 2019, human mouth disease can influence air to have disease to anyone from mouth. So, global travelers number had been continue decreasing, because they are fear to get disease by air when many themselves every stranger travelers are sitting on the without windows air planes. Although, mouth human and air disease and US 9/11 air attack both matters may influence oil price falls effect, because air planes flying times will reduce. They won't need frequent to fly, to cause aviation oil energy need reduce. Consequently, oil price will decrease, due to travelers number reduces and air planes flying times are also influenced to reduce. (oil demand decreases cause oil price decrease). Although, air lines ' cost will also be influenced reduce, but oil price decrease can not bring travelers number increase , when air ticket price reduce because global many leisure and business trip travelers feel fear to catch air planes frequently when human mouth air disease occured in 2019. So, oil price decreases can not grow up tourism industry growth or rise tourism income.

However, the obvious impact of a high oil price is an increase in the operating costs of airline. Moreover, fuel cost as a percentage of airline operating costs vary significantly based on the length of the flight. The longer the flight, the higher the fuel costs as a percentage of the airline operating cost. So, from an online's perspective, long -hauel flights represent the most criticial challenge to profitable operation because the share of fuel on these flights, compared with other cost items, is largest, because of the unfacorable fuel economics, due to fuel costs even at high-load factors. For example, Thai airways dropped its non-stop Bongkok to US flights in the summer of 2008 for commercial reasons, because fuel reached operating cost levels of 55 percent on this route, a cost burden that could not be passed on to their customers. So, the estimated price elacticity of passengers demand at this Bongkok to US flights route is high, if Thai Airways rises less air ticket price, it will influence many travelers to choose other airlines to catch air plan to fly. Hence, due to Thai Airways can not make decision to rise air ticket price, because it believes that it will lose many travelers, so it only chooses to drop this non-stop Bongkok to US flights to avoid fuel cost rising economic loss.

However, although micro and macro economic theories may also that oil price variable or change, it may influence global tourism income. But, recently, on 2019, human mouth and air diseases, it can influence global individual leisure and business trip travelers feel fear to catch air plans to avoid their bodies get this kind of death sickness when they sit in the no fresh air supplying air planes. They feel that they reduce leisure travelling flying times or business trip flying times with strange travelers to sit in crowd air planes together. Then, they must many avoid human moth and air disease to avoid death crisis. Hence, in this global human mouth and air diseases threat environment occurrence, even oil price sudden reduces to low price, it brings airline's cost reduces and air ticke price reduces. However, when air ticket price reduce to be very cheaper, it can not still attract global many leisure or business trip travelers to buy air tickets to fly frequently. Why does air ticket reduction, it can not attract many leisure or businee trip travelers to buy air ticket to fly ? The main reason is because human mouth and air disease influences global many travelers feel fear to catch air planes frequently. In psychological view, this kind of human mouth and air sickness will bring long time negative influence to global traveles do not want to catch air planes for business trips or travelling leisure frequently. So, it implies that oil price changing to influence air ticket price reduction factor ought not main factor to influence tourism income. It may include traveler individual negative emotion psychological factor, such as human mouth and air disease or 2019 9/11 attack both cases, they can influence global travelers feel fear to catch air planes to fly to avoid death threat. So, oil changing price ought not be only one absolute main factor to influence global tourism income significantly.

On conclusion, in economic view, it seems that oil chang price may have indirect or direct relationship to influence tourism income, instead of some unpredicted external environment factors influence, such as US 9/11 attack crisis and human mouth and air disease factors, they may be main factors to influence travellers number to reduce in non-economic external unpredicted environment view.

Bibliography

Stam , A. C. 1996, Win, Lose or Draw: Domestic politics and the crucible of war . Ann Arbor: University of Michigan Press.

Economic recession or boom how influences consumer behavior when the business had been experiencing decline life cycle stage

● COVID -19 disease how influence businesses may experience either growing life cycle stage or decline life cycle stage.

Nowadays, we are facing global economic recession period, since COVID 19 human mouth disease effect can bring economic crisis. Can it influence businesses feel difficult to adapt how global economic recession change after their decline life cycle stage? However, the effects of COVID 19 spreading will have wider implication , not just on how economies function, but also on how consumers behave, across china, Asia-pacific and around the world. Another effect of China;s economic rise is its influence in the adoption and adaption to new technological invention to manufacture , e.g. manufacturing robotic products had sold to China factories to replace workers to manufacturer products. It also will influence many China manufacturing workers lose jobs, when many China factories apply manufacture robotics to replace them in nowadays economic recession period.

Considering the adoption of online-offline shopping and home online office tasks, they are influenced by COVID-19 human disease influence, it also influences on regional travel in China, even global travel income is also reducing, because many travelers feel afraid to catch air planes to avoid to get COVID 19 human disease when they are sitting in close window airplanes by air . HOwever, COVID 19 also influences global consumer behavior changes to online shopping, because many people are afraid to enter crowd shops to avoid get COVID 19 human disease easily. So global shops will lose many visiting shop consumers, if they do not decide to attempt to open online stores to let customers to apply internet to buy their products. So, COVID 19 human mouth disease induced changes in consumer behavior. Shop online will be one new trend to influence young and old consumers make shopping from online stores. They will enquire whether the kind of product is worth to choose to buy by social media, e.g. facebook, online post . Hence, COVID19 human mouth disease may influence global economic recession, but it also brings e-commerce boom chance, when many consumers are fear to enter any crowd shops , when they need to stay long time in any shops. Then, they get COVID 19 human mouth disease chance will increase. Hence, it will influence many customers reduce to visit shops times, but it also creates online-shopping new business model . For example, China families are renewing their joy in home cooking. Onlins cooking videos are helping with the discovery od new recipes, new ways to create dishes , and new influences. So, opportunities are opening for more cleaning products, new ways to clean and new home hacks from online videos will bring global home consumers spend more time on their wellness or beauty routines ? So, COVID-19 disease also influences many families choose to cook dinner at homes at nght. Restaurants will lose many eating clients, because they are fear to enter restaurants to eat together to avoid to get COVID19 human mouth disease. But, it also creates home cooking products sale chance, e.g. rice cookers, dishes or any cooking tools because many families choose to cool at home. Hence, in some situation, economic recession will create new business chance , such as online store or rice cooker sale increases, they may be influenced in this COVID 19 human mouth disease occurrence environment.

Economic recession also influences business strategy changes. Many companies seem to be applying many aspects of a retrenchment approach , e.g. reduced fixed costs, narrower product offering, reduced staffs, but also there are some aspects of an investment approach which can be observed , because customers number will be influenced to reduce in economic recession environment. Companies have felt the robustness and quality of the approaches being applied had been allowed to decline. As a consequence of the challenges of a recession, urgent improvement have needed to be made because factories will reduce workers number to avoid salary expenditure spending more , but customers umber reduced in recession environment .

Hence, they will choose to buy manufacturing robotics to replace workers. If robotics can be improved to be proficient manufacture. Then, they won't need to buy many robotics to help them to replace to replace many workers to manufacture any products efficiently. So, manufacturing and improvement to robotics number demand may increase to any factories , e.g. vehicle manufacture, electronic products, e.g. computer hime cooking electronic products , e.g. rice cookers, heaters etc. products may be manufactured by manufacturing robotics. It creates the manufacturing robotic sale improvement quality chance in recession environment. It may impact on medium, or long term, it depends on how long time of recession. So, economic recession may bring robotic manufacture industry boom , when electronic products manufacturers need many improved robotics to replace workers in factries in order to reduce spending too much salaries expenditure in recession.

It is one external environmental factor to influence sudden manufacture robotic industry boom absolutely ,because electronic manufacturer's manufacturing robotic needs increases in recession environment. So, robotic manufacturers' strategy need to change , such as how to improve any manufacturers' needs in recession, e.g. manufacturing robotic product categories, market segments, geographic areas, core technologies, reliability , price, customisation, robotic manufacturing efficiency how to be improved of business.Change strategy to any manufacturing robotics manufacturers. So, recession may influence some kinds of manufacturing robotics' needs raise in robotic manufacturing market.

● How recession influences the role of advertising changes?

Advertising plays a key role in a dynamic economy. It may provide valuable information about products and services in an efficient manner, communicates client value, builds brand awareness and creates demand. However, when one country is experiencing recession, how it influences the country's businessmen spending on advertisement behaviors? Due to clients number reduces, a company usualy cuts come from the advertising budget than companies begin to cut back on advertiseing during an economic recession, they become less visible to the public because they predict clients number ought reduce next three months, even half year or one year. It depends on how long economt recession occurs. So, economic recession many impact any companies' advertising budget expenditure to be reduce . How much on the reduction on advertising budget expenditure, it depends on the company predicts how many clients number will reduce.However, due to advertising number reduces, it can influence consumer behavior changes indirectly.

In economic boom environment, consumers can watch to different kinds advertisement from television. Advertisement may bring positive alternative evaluation phase of biying decision-making process is bring exposed to buy several communication messages. In such an economic boom environment, any organizations may be clearly heard by the consumers, after any advertisement programs are broadcasted on television. Therefore, advertisemtn can persuade clients to choose to buy the kind of product after the kind of product advertisement is broadcasted from television absolutely.

However, when recession occurs, any companies; advertisement time is shortened , even number is reduced . Hence, they can not receive any client's positive or negative feedback immediately in short time afer advertisements are broadcasted from television . So, recession may influence advertisement time is shortened and number is rediced . On consequence, companies can not have any repsonse to know whether how market or customers' demand is changing to themselves products in shor time.

However, recession may bring worse advertisement effect to influence any businesses . On one hand, there is a negative economic recession environment because of the negative media reporting, these would be a decline in demand for the products and services and eventually companies would want to save more than they spend , But in the other hand, when the companies cut back advertiseing expenditures, they become less visible to public. Hence recession may influence many companies brand image will be lost, due to spending on advertisement expenditure wil reduce. Then, clients number may be influenced to reduce, because they can not watch the kind of product advertisment from television home often.

When one country is encountering recession, how are the various components of household consumption affected ?

How is the impact of the recesion distributed across socio-demographic group? How does the recession compare to previous recessions? When book will boom? In fact, any country's recession may impact consumer behavior changes, it depends on these factors: age, race, education and wealth groups resulted in a decline in consumption inequality. The rich group is the " wealth effect influence group" when recession comes, it may influence their wealth reduces, so their enjoyment dsires will be influenced to reduce, e.g. purchase expensive cars driving enjoyment desires, purchase expensive house living enjoyment desires. If one rich person loses jobs , it may influence him to spend less time to drive themselves cars, so consumption of gasline will be influenced to reduce.
Economic theory (e.g. consumer behavioral economic theory) predicts that when economic recession occurs, it will cause many businesses may experience decline cycle life stage rapidly, that link between income shocks and consumption has close relationship, such as rich person consumer group, if his income reduces, then he will buy less gas to drive himself car, even if he loses his job in recession environment, he will choose to sell his car to exchange cash. Hence, consumption may fall as a direct consequence of a fall in income induced by job loss, reduced hours or productivity and negative returns from assets, if there are long term changes to a household's econmic resource in recession environment. Hence, in recession environment, job loss or income reduction factors that may affect consumers and their shopping attitudes in the recession period. Otherwise, for low income group, recession may influence food consumption to low income consumer behavior changes to worse. Because low income person may reduce income ot lose job, then cheap food consumption will be influenced to worse to low income consumer group.

In recession period, if the food price is raised , due to the cost increase of food, it will lead to change in the reductin on quantity and type of food being purchase to low income food buyers. This may lead to a reduction in the quantity of food consumed and/or the substitution of high-priced food for cheaper food, which is often less nutritous and of worse quality. Hence in recession perios, low income food consumers will consider whether the kind of food price has how much increase or decrease. They won't consider the quantity of food consumed for maintaining energy balance and the quality of food consumed for maintaining ample intakes of protains, fats and micronutrients, such as vitamins, minerals and trace elements on food issue. So, if the kind of food price reduced in recession period, it ought may attract many low income food consumers number, even its food nutritious is worse. Hence, if the kind of meat price can be reduced in recession , the cheap types of meat consumption to low income consumer may be increased, even its nutritious is worse to compare the recession occurs before period.
On conclusion, in either economic recession or boom period, in general, consumer behavior will be influenced to change. Some products may be influenced to have higher sale in recession period, e.g. home electronic rice cookers , due to COVID 19 human mouth disease influenced many households choose to cook dinner at home at ight. Otherwise, some products may be influenced to have lowr sale., e.g. expensive cars sale in recession period, many high income people may lose jobs or reduce salaries , then it will influence their car purchase desires to be reduced. But if COVID 19 human mouth disease has medicine to kill this kind of disease. Then, economy will boom, many households will choose to go to restaurants to eat dinner. The, the electronic rice cookers sale number may reduce, when they reduce time to cook at home at night. Hence, it explains why economic recession or boom period may have impact to influence consumer behavior in behavioral economic view.

Tourism industry service innovation strategy

Our global tourism development had been developed from birth cycle stage to decline life cycle stage nowadays. From 1960 beginning, when airplanes were popular to be increased need to global travelers. Hence, from 1960 to 1970 is whole global tourism industry birth cycle stage. Till to 1971 beginning, many Asia, e.g. Singapore, Japan, China and Western, e.g. UK, UK etc. countries people, they have jobs to do ,and they have more extra money to prepare to choose any leisure activities. From 1971 to 1980, it is growth life cycle stage to global tourism industry. Many airplane manufacturers had been beginning to manufacturer many airplanes because they felt global traveler number would increase. In fact, in this ten years, global traveler number had been increasing every year. Then, from 1981 to 2019 this fourty years, it is global tourism industry nature life cycle stage. It means that every year travel number had been increasing more significantly to compare past. Also, many travelers feel need to travel every year. So, global travel tourism industry may reach the most top travel clients level in this fourty years. However, till to 2020

, due to COVD19 human mouth and disease occurrence, it influences global travelers feel fear to catch air planes to travel because this kind COVD 19 human mouth disease may cause lung disease from air. When many travelers are sitting in the close window air plane, if one person has ths kind COVD19 human mouth disease. The sick person may contact air to let the persons to breath to cause lung disease in possible in airplane. So, global travelers number is decreasing after 2019 . Also, it implies that tourism industry is facing decline life cysle stage.

It brings these questions: IS it right time to develop space tourism? Can space tourism help future tourism industry to re-grow its life cycle stage from nowadays decline life cycle stage? Can space tourism develop to nature stage from birth life cycle stage ? I shall attempt to give evidence to explain whether space tourism may be developed to let human has more one kind tourism . It may be future leisure new trend for travelers, instead of earth travel. Because one day earth tourism destination may not bring leisure interesting to global traveler, then space tourism may be attempted to replace this kind of travelling activity . So, space tourism is birth life cycle stage. However, our earth tourism may define moral tourism, nature tourism, green tourism, responsible tourism in future new travelling leisure trend.

It bring these questions: Can our future tourism industry meet the expectations with the terms " ecological tourist"? Which factors affect the product life cycle of eco tourism? Nature and green tourism may be our earth new kind of travel activities, when many young and old age travelers like to climb mountains, they feel life nature scene more than non-man made) nature scene in their journeys, they do not like to visit cities to travel. It is possible that they often work in offices, this office working factor may influence many travelers like green tourism in the future. So, green or nature tourism will be our future popular tourism leisure activities. It may influence nowadays our tourism decline life stage to re-grown to nature life cycle stage in possible in this COVD19 people mouth disease influential environment.

New economic development in Tourism and oil industries

● How to develop new economic tourism industry

How to develop tourism industry in new economic environment? Any examination of the new economic development of travel and tourism requires definitions of the subject and its components, which are suitable for economic analysis. However, in new economic development to tourism industry, it is also important to look at tourism conceptually, in order to set the scene for a deeper understanding of the future new tourism industry development.

Tourism is neither a phenomenon nor a simple set if industries, however, in new or old economic development environment. It is a human activity which encompasses human behavior, use of resources, and interaction with other people, economies and leisure enjoyment environment. It is also involved physical movement of tourists to locales other than their normal living places.

In future new economic environment, traditional travel needs to include these element in order to satisfy traveler enjoyment and leisure feeling: They may include: Tourist needs and motivations, tourism selection and behavior and constraints , travel away from home , market interactions between tourists and those supplying products to satisfy tourist needs and impacts on tourists , hosts, economies and environments.

In new economic environment, the tourism products may include: carriers, in any forms of transport for tourist travel accommodation, man-made attractions, which could also include the managed areas of natural attractions, private sector and public sector support services, middlemen, such as tour wholesalers and travel agents.

The tourism resources may also include: Natural resources, lands , minerals, water and biological; labor resources, human work, and enterprise; capital resources, manmade enhancement and other resources. The travel and tourism resources problems may include: As there is frequently a mismatch between producer and consumer perception of what constitutes the tourism product , there may be conflict in ideas of which resources are properly involved as well as many of the resources likely to be in demand for tourism are public goods , or even free resources.

In new economic development to tourism industry view, we need to consider that tourism and travel has the reputation of being a relatively clean and pleasant industry in which to work or invest in order to attract a greater number of resource suppliers than as less well-perceived industry, which therefore keeps rewards prices down by competition, how to attract those retiring from or travel business for example, if their finances are already sound, income from travel is not expected to be optimal , travel and tourism is frequently highly seasonal , offering rewards that are competitive with other industries only some of the time, destination products are often in locations which are of little use to other industries, so that competition for resource use if minimal and hence rewards are low.

In general, tourist purpose may include: recreational purpose : holiday, health and sport and religion as well as business purpose: company business , e.g. conventions and sales trips. So, in new economic tourism development aim, tourism industry need consider hoe to achieve incentive trips to let these both tourists to feel. For example, the overall type of tourism required, destination arrangement, travel mode, accommodation and attraction visiting and purchasing method or distribution channel. The purchasing method choices may include: whether to buy an inclusive package or separate service, whether to buy direct from suppliers, such as airlines or hotels or use an agent , which tour wholesaler or operate or agent to use.

I predict the tourism development in new economic view, it may have these characteristics: Few enterprises in travel and tourism are large, highly cashed-up and have a large asset base, enterprises within travel and tourism that are not in a financial position to diversify, and those do well success to the above –average growth obtainable in travel and tourism compared with many other industries, they would therefore tend to expand within the sector. The result of individual enterprise growth and integration within travel and tourism is an increase in the concentration of that industry. The degree to which output is produced of fewer and fewer enterprises. This can be only be accounted for realistically with the context of an individual economy, Levels of concentration in any part of travel and tourism in the future are likely to depend on two opposing factors: The constant demand by many tourist market segments for new experiences and products, which encourages the development and survival of more and diverse enterprises, and therefore leads to the reduction of concentration as well as technology, which in travel and tourism frequently calls for large capital outlays and requires mass markets for efficient use, promotes integrations and large scale enterprise, especially in air travel and non-personal services (marketing and information communication, travel insurance , tourism payment methods). IN these areas, concentration will undoubtedly increase in future new economic development environment.

HOW TO PROLONG TOURISM LEISURE MATURE LIFE CYCLE STAGE AS WELL AS AVOID DECLINE AND DEATH LIFE CYCLE STAGE OCCURENCE FROM COVID 19 HUMAN DISEASE

Any businesses expect to reach the mature life service cycle stage and they also hope to prolong to stay in this stage and avoid to have chance experience decline life service cycle stage, even death stage in future whole business life cycle stages. However, in fact, there are many businesses need to spend long time to have effort to reach mature life cycle stage from birth and growth both stages, even when they have effort to experience this the topest level stage, many can not stay to prolong time in this stage, then they will reach next stage, such as decline life cycle stage, even final death life cycle stage possibly. Hence , research whether how can reach the mature life cycle stage in short time and prolong to say in this stage. It is one common researching value question to any businesses. Such as COVID 19 human disease had been occurrence in 2019 end , it bring global tourism industry traveller number began to reduce. I shall attempt to explain how airline organizations implement strategies to avoid to enter decline service life cycle stage as below:

- How to avoid to reach the decline service life stage rapidly to global airlines tourism service industry due to COVID 19 human disease occurred

Strategies for growing and maturity a product or raise service performance, and increasing profit margins and prolonging to stay on the mature service life stage. I believe that it is any service businesses final aim. However, in any service life cycle stages, when the service , e.g. airline tourism leisure service industry will experience the decline service life stage , due to the COVID19 human disease influences to global travelers began to feel fear to catch airplanes to avoid air contact to give this kind of disease from 2020. So, nowadays, airlines ought have the suitable or right strategies to help them to solve travelers reducing number to influence their profit growth to encounter decline life service cycle stage later.

Life cycle strategy is based on product or service life cycle thinking from marketing, the factors may influence when the business can reach the mature life cycle stage, but some unpredicted factors may influence their clients number reduce, such as this airlines organizations traveler number reduces is due to COVID 19 human disease influences they feel fear to catch airplanes to travel case, their strategies may include: market growth rate, market growth potential, breach of service lines, number of competitor, distribution of market, share among competitors, customer loyalty , barriers to entry and technology improvement etc. factors to influence the global airlines tourism service industry can continue develop or expand to future overseas tourism market, when COVID 19 human disease may be killed by new medicine later.

Such as this COVID 19 human disease influences travelers feel fear to catch airplanes to avoid get this kind of disease and it influences global travelers number is decreasing in 2020 case, when the airline organization reaches the growth life service cycle stage from the birth stage, if it expects to spend short time to reach the mature life service cycle stage. Before COVID 19 human disease had not been killed by new medicine, if they hope to attract many travelers to choose to catch their airplanes to fly , the extension strategies that any airline organization can attempt to achieve, they may include, rebranding, establishing airline service in order to differentiate the other airline competitors tourism service , ticket price discounting and seeking new marketers, rebranding is the creation od a new look and feel for an established airline tourism service from the airline's competitors.

The airline service life cycle extension strategies also may include these methods to help the airline organization to grow or grow up or develop its airline tourism market rapidly, e.g. repackaging and new sizes, the appearance of airline tourism service can be crucial gaining a passenger's attention and developing tourism interest , new formulas or additional airline tourism features to the tourism country, lower ticket prices to maintain interest or liquidate surplus stock new airline tourism service advertising campaign, altering the new airline channel of destination, such as online ticket purchase.

Hence, after COVID 19 human disease had been skilled by new medicine , any airline organizations need to consider how to choose the most suitable strategy from different kinds of key strategies to expand their airline new tourism channels throughout the different airline tourism service life stages, in these four distinct stages: introduction, growth, maturity and decline or possible death stage, when this COVID 19 human disease had occurred from 2019 end, it may influence global travelers number had significant been reducing to bring any airline organizations may enter the decline life service cycle stage rapidly, even death life service cycle stage comes consequently.

Any airline organizations can use various marketing strategies in each stage to try to prolong the life cycle or attempt to reach the mature life cycle stage in short time. Avoiding to experience decline life service cycle stage, such as the COVID 19 human disease occurrence causes global travelers number began to reduce. It is ensure that any airline organizations do not expect to experience or reach the decline service life stage due to this COVID 19 human disease influences. The question is that how the airline organizations can maintain a strategy in the decline stage , such as COVID19 human disease influences global travelers number reduced and it brings many airlines income began to reduce, for example, reducing the airline promotional expenditure in this COVID 19 human disease occurrence period, reducing the number of airline distribution outlets , e.g. Hong Kong to New York airline flight channel reduces implementing ticket price cuts to get passengers to but the maintaining the airline tourism service and waiting for airline competitors to withdraw from the global airline tourism market.

Thus, following the initial growth, in this COVID human disease occurrence period, when the new airline organization enterprise enters the expansion stage during which the routing operation succeeds. The new airline organization can either reach the mature life service cycle stage either it can prolong to stay in this stage or it can not prolong to stay and enters to decline service life cycle stage , even death service life cycle stage. So , how to avoid the decline service life cycle stage comes to the new airline organization in this COVID 19 human disease occurrence period. It is any airline organizations concerning question when they are experiencing in the mature life cycle stage, but when COVID 19 human disease occurs to influence global travelers number began to reduce. May the airline organization experience the decline service life cycle stage rapidly when the COVID 19 human disease occurs ? It depends on whether it's strategies implementation are effective , its' strategies are effective, it may avoid to reach the decline life service cycle stage in short time easily due to COVID 19 human disease influences.

For this COVID 19 human mouth disease case , since 2019 had occurred, it brought serious tourism industry economic loss to any countries, many people loss jobs, many people feel fear to enter any shops when they are in crowd shop environment, e.g. restaurants can not permit to allow many people to sit closely, because when one person has COVID 19 human mouth disease, he can bring this disease to another person from air. So, many restaurants lose many clients in morning, lunch and night busy eating time, even ships also can not permit many people to enter their ships, because they avoid many people may contact, if one or some people has/have COVID 19 mouth disease, when he/she talks to the salespeople in the shop. It has high chance to cause many people get COVID human disease by mouth. So, any shops can not allow crowd in themselves shops to avoid any people have COVID 19 human disease occurrence. So, this COVID 19 human mouth disease may influence many businesses are experiencing decline life cycle stage, because clients number is continue decreasing, unless drug invention succeeds to fill this kind human mouth disease. Otherwise, on the consequence, many businesses will face death life cycle stage in short time possible. So, it is good example to explain unpredicted external environmental factor to bring global businesses will face decline life cycle in 2020 or next year, even after two years latter. So, COVID -19 human mouth disease may also influence any businesses had been experiencing long time in the mature life cycle to change to decline life cycle stage in possible.

Instead of the businesses are experiencing in either birth or growth life cycle stage. for example, UK Cathay airline had been experiencing long time in the mature life cycle stage from 2000, when its clients number had been increasing, but when the end of 2019, COVID-19 human mouth and air contact disease had occurred in global to influence any people feel fear to catch airplanes to travel or business travel frequently, due to airplanes have none windows, its none window environment will bring COVID-19 disease to any passengers when the airplane has many passengers are sitting together closely, if anyone has COVID-19 disease, he will cause any one airplane service waiter, passenger , even pilot to have COVID-19 disease easily.

So, global airline industry is experiencing decline life cycle stage. even Cathay airline is one big UK developed airline , it's passengers number is large in the past, but when COVID-19 disease occurs to cause travelers number had been decreasing. Hence, Cathay airline is experiencing decline life cycle stage from mature life cycle stage. It needs to implement dismissing staffs to keep salaries expenditure reducing strategy in global, e.g. HK will have 4,000 front line airline service staffs or airport check in service staffs , they will be dismisses in HK Cathay airline market. Although, HK government had given money to support it to continue to alive in order to avoid dismissing employees decision . But, Cathay airline had made decision that it will dismiss many airline service staffs in different countries. In fact, if Cathay airline expects it would not reach to the decline life cycle stage later, this dismissing employees strategy aims to avoid spending much salaries expenditure , it may be one good method to avoid decline , even death life cycle stage occurs in this year or latter.

On conclusion, it is difficult to predict what factors may cause the business itself will face decline life cycle stage occurrence in any time. Hence, any businesses ought to spend time to research whether which methods or strategies can help them to continue to expand their market or fight any kinds of threats in those four identified business life cycle stages. To avoid business can not continue develop or die, when the business is experiencing in the decline life cycle stage, the strategy is that , the organization needs to spend time to observe or learn how and why its market environment is changing in order to make the most accurate or effective strategies decisions to solve any challenges in any one of these four life cycle stages successfully.

● How new economic development in oil industry

The future global economic growth, it will influence personal incomes and GDP rise. They would carry different weight in different countries at different times. Starting from low levels of incomer and economic development. Household consumption will change from being dominated by basic heat to rapidly rising energy use for higher levels of comfort in space heating and cooling (and large dwellings), and greater use of electrical appliances, finally to a degree of saturation influenced by the income distribution patterns of the country concerned. Income distribution typically changes very slowly, so that the technical market for heart will never be saturated because there will always be a proportion of poor people living in small spaces less comfortably than the average. Industrial energy consumption will be influenced by technical efficiency within each sector, and by changes in the structures of the economy, e.g. changing proportions of agriculture, heavy and light industry, and services. One may eventually see evidence of diminishing marginal returns to additional energy inputs compared to other inputs. Energy consumption in the energy transformation sector may be influenced by income, which drives the demand for electricity to influenced by income, which drives the demand for electricity to grow faster than the demand for heat, but is also subject to the chosen technology of transformation, which is influenced by the cost and availability of primary energy inputs (fuels) in new economic development environment.

IN new economic development environment, it will influences that fuels do not compete in all sectors; for example, the transport sector is dominated by oil. Nuclear and hydroelectric power (and most renewables) reach the user through electricity; electricity itself competes with the direct burning of fossil fuels. Electricity provides the means by which other fuels can compete with oil and gas in sectors, such as space heating and process heat. It also is the only means of powering applications such as motors, computers and lighting: these subsectors are difficult to analyze. However, there is strong evidence that higher incomes do not weaken the demand for electricity so much as the demand for energy in total (in contrast to the effect on the demand for non-electric energy forms).

Econometricians look at the historical record of change in fuel prices and quantities to distinguish several factors between the new economic development and old economic development to oil industry in the future. An income effect. Increasing (reducing) fuel prices reduces (increases) the purchasing power of consumers' income: higher incomes caused by lower prices will increase energy consumption; the consumers' allocation of the increased income to energy purchases may reduce as income rises. Thus income may be heading in a different direction from fuel prices that the effect of fuel price changes when incomes are rising means simply that rising incomes have increased demand. Reducing the cost of using energy through win-win efficiency measures causes a similar problem . On the consequence, in future new economic development environment, it may influence in both cases demand will be less than if the future oil price or efficiency has not changed. The other effect is that an efficiency or substitution effect. An increase in fuel prices may cause consumers to spend more on new equipment, building materials and management operations, which will reduce the amount of fuel required to give the same energy result to the user. The extent of the efficiency effect depends on what happens to the price of the new equipment or building: if those price s rise in line with the fuel price, changes in the balances between fuel and capital or management will not occur. A new user technology , such as the development of the combined cycle gas turbine generator may increase efficiency and thus greatly reduce the quantity of primary fuel needed to produce the required output in this case electricity. If electricity prices had remained sticky, and the electricity and gas markets were not competitive, some of this advantages could have accrued to the gas suppliers in the form of an increase in price, because th4 unit of gas produces more output of electricity, it would have a higher value. In reality, the development of new economic competitive environment in both gas and electricity has tended to ensure that the benefits of such technical advanced accrue to the consumer through lower final prices. The same many apply in the case of improved efficiency in future non-manual driving auto vehicle development: the consumer's cost of motoring is reduced in new economic non-manual driven auto vehicle (Artificial intelligent vehicle) can replace manual driven vehicle , even electricity battery can replace oil energy to be used in vehicles. So, oil price may be influenced to reduce in future new economic development environment.

New and old economic theories explain oil is not main factor to influence tourism income

- Can economic theory explain old price change to influence tourism income?

I shall attempt to apply old and new economic theory to explain whether oil changing price has direct relationship to influence global tourism indusry development or tourism income as below:

Is oil changing price the main to influence tourism income or tourism development or economic growth ? If oil price rises ar falls, it will or won't cause tourism income decreases or increases? If they have cause and effect relationship, what are the main factors to influence tourism income changes by oil price rises or falls ?

I aim to investigate how any why among oil price shocks will influence tourism income variables. We may distinguish between these oil price shocks: Supply-side , aggregate demand and oil specific demand shocks. I assume that oil specific demand shocks affect inflation and the tourism sector equity index. By constrast, I also believe that aggregate demand oil price shock exercisr an effect, either directly and indirectly tourism generated income and economic growth. So, in old economic theory, supply-side , aggregate demand view to oil specific demand shocks will influence tourism income varies. So, governments ought implement strategies against future oil price movements or plan for economic policy development.

In fact, instead of oil price changes will influence tourism income, it could also harm economic growth and tourism activities, due to the effect they expert on transporation, production cost, economic uncertainty.Because tourism activities is one important sector to influence any country's leisure consumption GDP income source. So, sudden fluctations in oil prices may also influence economic growth. It is based a hyphthesis known as the tourism led economic growth. So, it seems that they have direct or indirect relationship to case effect between oil price and tourism activities and development. So, increase on tourism income, the called " economic-driven tourism growth". In addition, high oil prices are affecting certain tourism industry segments , e.g. airlines, cruises lines, hotel, rent travelling car services etc. for oil, importing countries example, with reference to macro economic effects, higher oil prices generally lead to higher inflation, when they negatively influence to country's income.

Hence, from a micro-economic perspective, positive oil price shocks lead to a decline in disposable income. for low income people, it will bring an immediate and negative impact on tourism, mainly due to they feel tourism leisure is regarded as a luxury good, when oil price shocks to rise suddenly . It influences any airline or cruise entertainment service providers' costs are influenced to raise. Then, they need to increase air ticket or cruise ticket price. It will bring on negative tourism leisure demands-side the oil price increases low income group, potential tourism leisure consumers. Hence, it seems that oil price may have indirect relationship to influence tourism leisure consumers' needs.

- How the price of oil changes influences global tourism industry growth or recession?

In macro-economic view, sudden mid and long term oil price shock can influence global torusim industry growth or recession. For example, a oil price of US$180 per barrel was considered only a few years ago, now this has a realistic scenario to which all plaers in the T&T sector have to adapt. At such a high level, the price of oil will become even more critical to almost every part of the tourism value chain. Although, weak global demand, caused by global economic recesson, resulted in a steep oil price decline to US$45 per barrel by the fourth quarter of 2008 in the past low oil price occurrence history, this won't change the mid to long -term oil forecast.

In fact, the past oil price occurrence history of the dramatic structural had changed a high price imposed on airlines, travelers, and destination countries, all of which will have to navigate through times of shifting or even declining travel demand. I assume that a high oil price scenario is assumed in the long term in order to highlight the changes , such a senario would mean for consumer behavior and the competitiveness of several destinations.

Low oil price in the 1970 and early 1980 did not bring significant growth of international air travel, but its growth has been strongest between 1980 and 2004, a period with stable and relatively moderate oil prices. Also, the rapid development of the low-cost carrier business model in the 1990s further fueled air travel growth by capturing tourism leisure demand , such as weekend leisure travel to cities using mostly secondary airports in any big area countries, such as UK, US . However, the tourism growth is whole influenced by high oil prices, due to oil price had been continue rising in possible.

Basis of oil is shortage supply product, oil is assumed to be the main energy source for the aviation sector for the nest 30 years. Although, second-generation biofuels seem to be on the horizon, the economics as well as the production scalability and aviation biofuel shortage will be a main challenge to airline industry. So, I assume that oil price will continue rise up, if there have none any aviation biofuel can be reflected to oil to use for air plane energy.

Until 2004, the only factors to have affected air travel growth, negatively were in external shocks , such as 9/11, causes catching air plane crisis or US regional geopolitical conflicts. It brings some travelers feel fear to go to US travel, as well as until recently 2019, human mouth disease can influence air to have disease to anyone from mouth. So, global travelers number had been continue decreasing, because they are fear to get disease by air when many themselves every stranger travelers are sitting on the without windows air planes. Although, mouth human and air disease and US 9/11 air attack both matters may influence oil price falls effect, because air planes flying times will reduce. They won't need frequent to fly, to cause aviation oil energy need reduce. Consequently, oil price will decrease, due to travelers number reduces and air planes flying times are also influenced to reduce. (oil demand decreases cause oil price decrease). Although, air lines ' cost will also be influenced reduce, but oil price decrease can not bring travelers number increase , when air ticket price reduce because global many leisure and business trip travelers feel fear to catch air planes frequently when human mouth air disease occured in 2019. So, oil price decreases can not grow up tourism industry growth or rise tourism income.

However, the obvious impact of a high oil price is an increase in the operating costs of airline. Moreover, fuel cost as a percentage of airline operating costs vary significantly based on the length of the flight. The longer the flight, the higher the fuel costs as a percentage of the airline operating cost. So, from an online's perspective, long -hauel flights represent the most critinal challenge to profitable operation because the share of fuel on these flights, compared with other cost items, is largest, because of the unfacorable fuel economics, due to fuel costs even at high-load factors. For example, Thai airways dropped its non-stop Bongkok to US flights in the summer of 2008 for commercial reasons, because fuel reached operating cost levels of 55 percent on this route, a cost burden that could not be passed on to their customers. So, the estimated price elacticity of passengers demand at this Bongkok to US flights route is high, if Thai Airways rises less air ticket price, it will influence many travelers to choose other airlines to catch air plan to fly. Hence, due to Thai Airways can not make decision to rise air ticket price, because it believes that it will lose many travelers, so it only chooses to drop this non-stop Bongkok to US flights to avoid fuel cost rising economic loss.

However, although micro and macro economic theories may also that oil price variable or change, it may influence global tourism income. But, recently, on 2019, human mouth and air diseases, it can influence global individual leisure and business trip travelers feel fear to catch air plans to avoid their bodies get this kind of death sickness when they sit in the no fresh air supplying air planes. They feel that they reduce leisure travelling flying times or business trip flying times with strange travelers to sit in crowd air planes together. Then, they must many avoid human moth and air disease to avoid death crisis. Hence, in this global human mouth and air diseases threat environment occurrence, even oil price sudden reduces to low price, it brings airline's cost reduces and air ticke price reduces. However, when air ticket price reduce to be very cheaper, it can not still attract global many leisure or business trip travelers to buy air tickets to fly frequently. Why does air ticket reduction, it can not attract many leisure or businee trip travelers to buy air ticket to fly ? The main reason is because human mouth and air disease influences global many travelers feel fear to catch air planes frequently. In psychological view, this kind of human mouth and air sickness will bring long time negative influence to global traveles do not want to catch air planes for business trips or travelling leisure frequently. So, it implies that oil price changing to influence air ticket price reduction factor ought not main factor to influence tourism income. It may include traveler individual negative emotion psychological factor, such as human mouth and air disease or 2019 9/11 attack both cases, they can influence global travelers feel fear to catch air planes to fly to avoid death threat. So, oil changing price ought not be only one absolute main factor to influence global tourism income significantly.

On conclusion, in economic view, it seems that oil chang price may have indirect or direct relationship to influence tourism income, instead of some unpredicted external environment factors influence, such as US 9/11 attack crisis and human mouth and air disease factors, they may be main factors to influence travellers number to reduce in non-economic external unpredicted environment view.

How can artificial intelligent tools predict travelling consumer behavior in airline and air agent travelling market

I believe that applying (AI) big data tool to predict vehicle buyer consumption choice behavior, it is similar to predict traveler consumption choice behavior. In this chapter, I shall indicate how to apply (AI) big data gathering tool to predict vehicle buyer consumption choice behavior. Then, I shall its what its similar points to be applied to predict traveler consumption choice behavior.

Nowadays, many vehicle manufacturers hope their vehicles can attract to vehicle buyers to choose to buy their vehicles. However, there are many different brands of vehicles to provide to them to choose, so the vehicle market competition is very serious.

How to judge their different kinds of vehicle price which is reasonable acceptance to attract vehicle buyers to choose to buy the brand of vehicle manufacturers' any kinds of vehicles, e.g. fast speed sport style vehicles, comfortable and slow speed common cars, for four passengers common small size or more than four passengers common large car size?

How to evaluate the vehicle prices issue is important factor to influence vehicle buyers' choices. Either if the brand of vehicle price is too high to compare other brands of similar vehicle price, it will influence many vehicle buyers choose to buy other brands‘ vehicles or if the brand of vehicle price is too low, it will influence vehicle buyers feel this brand's vehicle machine quality or safe driving level or manufacturing steel material or speed or not comfortable sitting etc. different factors is worse to compare to other vehicle brands' similar vehicle products.

Thus, if the brand of vehicle manufacturers can predict how to design vehicles which can attract many vehicle buyers to choose to buy whose any vehicle products. What are future vehicle buyers‘ favorable vehicle styles? Then, the vehicle manufacturer can concentrate on manufacturing the kind style of vehicle products to sell already. It will reduce its vehicle manufacturing investment risk.

How to apply (AI) tools to predict vehicle buyers' behavioral consumption model? Whether artificial intelligent tools can predict automotive buyers‘ behavioral consumption model and predict future vehicle design trend. In fact, automotive brands and dealerships are facing an increasingly competition when attempting to manually gathering the vast quantities of data required to create customer focused programs that increase retention, ultimately new sales and service automotive business.

Building a based on that client's intrinsic needs and interests to any kinds of automotive vehicles at any given time. This is especially true in the automotive industry where the time span between purchases is measured in years. Because vehicle buyers would not like often to change their old vehicle to another new one. So, their decisions to buying another new vehicle, the time is usually after one year, even longer time. Hence, it seems any vehicles won't be frequent consumption products to the owned at least one vehicle family consumers (vehicle buyers). It implies that why vehicle manufacturers ought need to spend time to predict future vehicle buyer design choice for whole year vehicle buyer number growth because they won't often change preferable vehicle design to change another new vehicle more easily.

Hence, how to predict vehicle consumers' taste or preferable which styles of vehicle choices issues is very important. If the vehicle manufacturers can not manufacture any attractive vehicles to sell easily in this year. Then, it will lose time, money in this year because it won't know when the owned least one vehicle users or non-owned any vehicle users who will decide to buy one new vehicle or change another new vehicle ensure. The different brand vehicle dealers will possible wait more than one year to attract them to buy their vehicles if their styles are not attractive to compare other brands of vehicle competitors.

However, artificial intelligence and machine learning can help any vehicle manufacturers to find solution to solve patterns in highly to solve patterns in highly complex data-sets that are beyond the capability of a human brain, and then building and automatically acting on the customer insights it generates.

Given the automotive customer need for individualized communications, this technology is positioned to become a critical component of any successful vehicle retailer's domestic or/and overseas vehicle markets. How can vehicle manufacturers and retailers use (AI) to enhance their vehicle marketing campaigns? How will (AI) affect their vehicle sale marketing strategy? What criteria would they use when selecting on (AI) solution?

Vehicle consumers today are able to quickly access different brands of vehicle information, research vehicle products and reviews, negotiate prices and compare one vehicle brand or retailer to another resulting of the brands of vehicle customers. At the same time, the rise of " big -data mining", wearable devices that track user's every move and preference and greater contextualization in advertising and social media has resulted in consumer expectations of individualized. Thus, it seems that (AI) tools can be used to gather " big-data" and then they can make human's mind to analyze how to design kinds of vehicles to satisfy vehicle buyers‘ needs.

As automotive vehicle marketers can apply (AI) tools to achieve messaging strategies to meet the needs of this new generation of informed vehicle consumers, using data from a variety of sources to move from a variety of sources to move from mass- messaging to more personalized messages aimed at particular vehicle buyer segments, e.g. fast speed sport vehicle buyer segment, slow speed comfortable small size or large size of buyer segment. However, when 90% of vehicle marketers believe having a single vehicle buyer view is important, only 6% have achieved it.

However, one of the main issues vehicle marketers are facing the lack of capacity to efficiently sift through and analyze the massive vehicle buyer amounts of data required to create vehicle buyer individualized vehicle customer experiences easily. This is especially difficult for automotive dealers, the long periods between purchase cycles, and the highly considered nature of the vehicle purchase means that each vehicle dealer needs to not only track a large number of potential vehicle customers for an extremely long period of time, but each of those vehicle customers will generate a huge amount of different kinds of vehicle behavioral consumption data as they research their next vehicle purchase. However, by choosing the right (AI) technological tools and programs , vehicle dealers can solve this big data gathering challenge into a major advantage.

For Forrester vehicle brand example, vehicle consumers have more power over the Forrester vehicle brand's reputation than ever before. Mayne, L. (2014) indicated that Forrester calls this new (AI) tools is the " age of the vehicle customer", a 20 year business cycle in which the most successful vehicle enterprises will reinvent themselves to systematically understand and serve increasingly powerful vehicle consumers. To win in this new age, Forrester declares companies must become vehicle customer obsessed and the only sustainable competitive advantage is knowledge and engagement with customers, such as (AI) gathering data knowledge.

Thus, the biggest challenge vehicle businesses currently face is not the collection of a large quantity of vehicle consumer data, but what to do with that data once they have it. Even at a large vehicle data research firm, the data sets are often too big for a single analyze, or even a team of analysts to sort through and draw conclusion from. However, enter artificial intelligence and machine learning , an efficient technology solution that can continuously find patterns in highly complex data sets that are way beyond the capacity of a human brain and then automatic drive action based on the customer insights is generated.

What is (AI) machine learning tool? Machine learning is a type of (AI) that learns from data and is not explicitly program. Think Amazon, face book. Machine learning serves up relevant content based on an individual vehicle purchase behavior and experiences. More simply, machine learning is a computer program that can learn relationships between data, subject those learnings to errors functions, and then learn from its errors. The program in effect, trains itself.

Lee, T. (2016) explained that "Thus, (AI) tools can learn deep a more advanced branch of machine learning inspired by how our brain's nervous function, has also been found to be especial effective in identifying patterns from data."

When this way sound is complicated from a vehicle dealer perspective, the implementation of a marketing program driven by artificial intelligence can take care of these tasks in an automatic vehicle fashion with little to no manual intervention required from the staff at time vehicle stores.

In practice at a vehicle dealership, the program will continue track vehicle customer behavior online, merging that data with any offline source (like CRM or DMS data) and then analyze this aggregated vehicle buyer data set to predict what vehicle customer may be shopping for and what information they might like to relevance from different kinds style of vehicle design photos.

Why does travelling market seem to similar to vehicle market which can apply (AI) learning tool to predict travellingconsumer behaviors?

Artificial intelligence refers to complex in vehicle market and travelling entertainment market which is very seem to be applied to predict consumer behaviors.

(AI) machine learning that posses the same characteristics of human intelligence and that have all our sense, all our reason and think just like human vehicle buyer who prefer vehicle purchase choice or travelling consumer who prefer travelling package or travelling destination and airline choice. Besides, machine learning is the practice of using algorithms to collect and examine data, learn from it, and then make a determination or prediction about something in the world.

So, it can be attempted to gather data concerns that travelling consumer past travelling destination choice and air ticket price choice and different travelling package, e.g. high, middle, or low class hotel and foods supply and entertainment places choice in their past travelling journeys.

The machine is " trained" using large amounts of data and algorithms that give it the ability to learn how to automatically perform a task with increasing accuracy. Otherwise, deep learning is primarily based on artificial neural networks inspired by our understanding of the biology of human's brains.

Thus, (AI) big data can gather all these past traveler consumption behavioral choice data to make reference to analyze whether how many travelers will choose to go to the specific travelling destination in any time by the past traveler number record to different travelling destinations, then it can gather the past air ticket sale price to different destinations and past travelling package design to different destinations in order to analyze whether it is the cheap airline ticket price factor or attractive travelling package factor or attractive travelling entertainment etc. in order to predict which factor is the most potential influential factor to they choose to go to the destination to travel in different time within one year. Then, traveler agent or airline can collect these big data to judge how to design their package to attract travelers to go to anywhere to travel or what the main factor influence most of them to choose to visit the destination to travel.

For example, travel agents or airlines can apply "Deep learning" breaks down tasks in ways that enables machines to assist them to predict when travelling consumer choice will be changed and why their travelling choice will change and how their travelling choice will change with increasingly complex tasks.

So, such as why (AI) technology can be applied to predict how travelling consumer behavior changes to bring to judge whether anywhere will be many travelling consumers who will prefer to choose travelling hot destinations next year or next month.

Then, travel agents and airlines can gather overall past travelling consumer data to analyze and conclude the more accurate prediction of different travelling destinations to the number of traveler. Then, they can choose how much air ticket price is more reasonable to charge to the travelling destination or how to design the travelling package which can bring more attractive to the prediction number of different travelling destination travelers in order to achieve to raise the different travelling destination number next year.

Thus, (AI) big data machine learning can help airlines or travel agents to solve how to design any attractive travelling package challenge. A travelling package is both one of the most important and carefully considered travelling entertainment consumption the majority of travelling people will ever make in their lifetime at least one travelling time.

It is also a prediction how travelling package will be designed that tends to be fundamentally tied to a travelling person's travelling destination choice identify and travelling package view of themselves. As the same time, travelling consumers' travelling choice changing lifestyles result in changing travelling destination needs, e.g. the country's young travelers can choose to change non-extreme exciting travelling entertainment package from past extreme exciting travelling entertainment package. Due to personal feeling factor in general. However, I believe that (AI) big data can also be attempted to predict when the country's young travelers will choose to change non-extreme exciting travelling behavior.

It is similar to automotive dealers need to remember that vehicle customers and prospects are individual human beings with risk, complex and ever-changing lives factors, these factors will influence every vehicle consumer why who feels has vehicle purchase need, and how who choose to buy the first vehicle if who decided to buy the first vehicle.

It seems that travelling agents or airlines need to remember that travelling consumers and different features or designs are very traveler beings with risk, complex and ever-travelling package attitude personal changing factors in different travel season, these factor will influence every individual traveler why who feels has travel entertainment need, and how who choose to buy different feature or design travelling package if who decide to travel.

The (AI) big data technological travelling customer behavioral prediction tool seems to be the best travelling behavioral prediction tool in the world are those that know every one of different country's traveler need. Their likes and dislikes which style of travelling package, preferences and travel destination changing tastes to travelling destination choices.

The capacity of the human brain, however, limits us from achieving these different type of travel package sales. In this competitive travelling destination choice entertainment environment, (AI) big data machine learning enables platforms to assist the air ticket and travel package sales team by tracking the travelling consumer behaviors of each travelling customer, learning and memorizing their preferences and predicting their future travelling destination choice and travelling package design needs.

Finally, I recommend that for a travel agent or airline travelling marketing platform to make their travelling customer engagement efficient and fully-functional, I should be able to: applying (AI) tools to track every travelling customer behavior across the web, connecting to a society of data sources, CRM, DMS, third-party, web travelling brands, social traveler email, click etc., aggregating and accurately cross-reference data from a variety of sources, leveraging this data to drive insights on a mass scale, as well as on an individualized basis, driving actions and automatically direct travelling customer engagement via multiple channels based on where each customer is in their travelling individual lifecycle.

Why is (AI) big data gathering tool better than psychological and survey methods to predict traveler individual travel choice behavior?

Prediction travel behavioral consumption from psychology and survey methods.

How to predict travel consumption? It is one question to any travel agents concern to use what methods which can predict how many numbers of travelers where who will choose to go to travel more accurately. I think that who can consider how to predict travel behavioral consumption from psychology and survey travel choice prediction method, but it is better to apply (AI) big data gathering method to predict travel consumer's destination choice more accurate. The reason is as below:

The first reason is that traveller individual travel psychological desire is difficult to predict accurate more than (AI) big data gathering method, it is due that the data is past traveler's destination choice and travel package and ticket price actual data from (AI) big data gathering method. Otherwise, survey investigation is only traveler psychological thinking method. It lacks enough past actual traveler data gathering.

The second reason is that on the weakness of traveler individual psychological thinking view of survey investigation. It has evidence to support the relationship between self-identify threat and resistance to change travel behavior to any travelers, controlling for whose past travelling behavior, resistance to change if a psychological phenomenon of long standing interest in many applied branches of psychology.

Past travelling behavior has been acknowledged as a predictor of future action. Such as travelling behavior that is experienced as successful is likely to be repeated and may lead to habitual patterns. Some psychologists differentiate habit between two concepts, such as goal oriented and automatic oriented both. Although repeated past travelling behavior is addition goal oriented and automatic oriented. Further non-deliberative nature of habit may make appeals to judge and to predict future individual traveler's behavior accurately.

However, repeated one traveler will choose the destination to repeat to travel without a necessary constraint of goal orientation and automatic oriented both. So, it seems that psychological factor can influence any individual traveler why and how who choose to decide to repeat to choose the destination to travel.

So, survey investigation is only the traveler's thinking to answer the travel firm. It is not sure that the traveler's past travel experience is real answer. Otherwise, (AI) big data gathering method is computer gathering method which gather past traveler consumption actual data to analyze and conclude future traveler possible repeated travel destination choice and travel package choice more accurate.

The third reason is that on the strength of (AI) big data gathering method computer statistic view to predict future traveller consumer's destination and travel package choice. It is structural equation modeling is an extremely flexible linear-in-parameters multivariate statistical modeling technique. It has been used in modeling travel behavior and values since about 1980 year. It is a software method to handle a large number of variables, as well as unobserved variables specified as linear combinations (weighted averages) of the observed variable.

Can (AI) big data gather data to predict when climate will change to influence poor travelling behaviours?

(AI) big data tool can predict the flexibility of human travelling behavioral change is at least the result of one such mechanism, our ability to travel mentally in time and entertain potential future. Understanding of the impacts is holidays, particularly those involving travel.

Using focus groups research to explores tourists' awareness of the impacts of travel own climate change, examines the extent to which climate change features in holiday travel decisions and identifies some of the barriers to the adoption of less carbon intensive tourism practices.

The findings suggest many tourists don't consider climate change when planning their holidays. The failure of tourists to engage with the climate change to impact of holidays, combined with significant barriers to behavioral change, presents a considerable challenge in the tourism industry. In the future, computer (AI) big data tool can attempt to predict when the country's climate change to influence travelers to choose to go to the country to travel, e.g. next month or next half year or next year hot travelling destinations.

Tourism is a highly energy intensive industry and has only recently attracted attention as an important contributions to climate change through greenhouse gas emissions. It has been estimated that tourism contributes 5% of global carbon dioxide emissions. There have been a number of potential changes proposed for reducing the impact of air travel on climate change. These include technological changes, market based changes and behavioral changes.

However, the role that climate change plays in the holiday and travel decisions of global tourists. How the global tourists of the impacts travel has on climate change to establish the extent to which climate change, considerations features in holiday travel decision making processes and to investigate the major barriers to global tourists adopting less carbon intensive travel practices.

It will bring this question: Will tourists aware the impacts that their holidays and travel have on climate changes to influence their travelling decision?

When, it comes to understand individual traveler's behavioral change, wide range of conceptual theories have been developed, utilizing various social, psychological, subjective and objective variables in order to model travel consumption behavior. These theories of travel behavioral change operate at a number of different levels, including the individual level, the interpersonal level and community level. Whether pro-environmental behavior can be used to predict travel consumption behavior in a climate change. However, the question of what determines pro-environmental behavior in such a complex one that it can not be visualized through one single framework or diagram.

Despite the potentially high risk scenario for the tourism industry and the global environment, the tourism and climate change ought have close relationship.

However, (AI) big data tool can be applied to find what factors to influence the time of travelers' travelling choices. What are the important factors and variables which can limit tourism? e.g. money, time, family problem, extreme hot or cold weather change, air ticket price, journey attraction etc. variable factors.

Mention of holidays and travel were deliberately avoided in the recruitment process, so as not to create a connection factor to influence traveler's individual mind. However, the dismissal of alternative transportation modes can be conceived as either a structural barrier, in the sense that flying is perhaps the only realistic option to reach long-haul holiday destination, or a perceived behavioral control barriers in that an individual perceives flying as the only option open to whom.

The transportation tool factor will be depend to extent on the distance to the destination. This can also be interpreted in a social perspective as an intention with the resources available where much international tourism is structured around flying. To increase the availability of different transportation modes, tourists could choose holiday destination closer to home.

Finally, also how to predict future travel behavioral consumption. I feel that travel agents need to predict whether any country's random daily variation of weather factor is also important to influence travel behavior. e.g. in weather, temperature, rainfall and snowfall with traffic accidents factors will have relationship to cause travel demand.

Some scientists estimate suggest that when warmed temperatures and reduced snowfall are associated with a moderate decline in non-fatal accidents, they are also associated with a significant increase in fatal accidents. Thus increase in fatalities and temperature. Half of the estimated effect of temperature on fatalities is due to changes in the exposure to pedestrians, bicyclists and motorcyclists as temperature increase.

So, if any countries have rainfall, snowfall and low temperature to cause traffic accidents, whether this accident occurrence will influence the travelers who liking climb snow hills, riding bicycle, running sports who will avoid to travel to these countries' bad weather after occurs. So, why I feel that this natural climate factor will also be one serious factor to influence travel behavioral consumption. However, (AI) big data tool can predict more accurate than survey method when climate change to influence the country's climate to be poor, then it can predict when which countries are not popular acceptable to global country consumers' travel choice next month.

How can apply (AI) to provide travelling businesses with better-informed decisions ?

I shall explain how (AI) big data gathering technology can provide travelling businesses with better-informed decisions to drive top-line growth, deliver meaningful experience for travelling customers and smooth their path along the travelling consumer journey. The widely understood definition of (AI) involves the ability of machines or computers to learn human thinking, reasoning and decision-making abilities.

So, such as (AI) learning machine system can attempt to learn travelling consumer's travel destination or travel package thinking, judgement of their reasons why they choose to go to the destination to travel or why they choose to buy the travel package and learn how and why they make their past travelling decisions from their past travel big data gathering.

A Narrative science study in 2015 year identified that (AI) was being used primarily in voice recognition, machine learning virtual assistants and decision support. This study also highlighted the many branches of (AI) and that techniques and their definition are used interchangeably. It is possible that (AI) can be used to gather big data , then to analyze to help travel businesses to predict travelling consumer travel destination and travel package choice behaviors. For example, one of the most common techniques is traveler machine learning, where algorithms are used to perform tasks by learning from the airline or travel agent whose past all travelers' travelling destination choice and travel package choice historical data.

However, during 2017 year, search engines will begin to find what additional factors can influence past traveler personal travelling destination and travelling package travelling behavioral data into prediction of future travelling customer behavioral results, such as the online traveler (user's) history of travelling data searches, such as anywhere are the most popular travelling locations or travelling destinations and previously captures conservations.

Artificial intelligence will use this past travelling destinations and travelling package information to power predictive search results, e.g. predictive future travelling consumer's choice behavioral processing for where will be their preferable travelling destination choice and how to design travelling package to satisfy future travelling clients' needs. Predictive search will improve the quality of online travelling search results, and provide new insights into travelling consumers' travelling destination and package behavior and the moments which matter to them. Search will give recommendation into tailored how travelling consumer individual travelling destination choice in travelling decision making process. Several of the largest online platforms already use (AI) travelling machine learning to improve predictive travelling consumer behavioral search results.

For example, Google's rank brain technology adds research by understanding the context in which the travelling consumer has entered it. Over time, rank brain will learn further from user behaviors Amazon's DSSTNE (pronouned destiny) learns from shoppers' purchasing habits and consumption behavior to offer better product recommend actions, which Amazon can offer before a consumer has entered anything into the search bar.

Such as (AI) big data can gather past online travelers' e-ticket purchase transactions to conclude that online traveler's travelling choice habits and online traveler consumption behavior to offer better travelling destinations and travelling package opinions to travel agents or airlines. However, this technology is not independent of human input. For example, Google engineers will periodically retain the rank brain system to improve the models it uses.

For another example, in 2016 year , Apple computer revamped its travelling scene photos app to allow travelling consumers to search for specific travelling destinations in the travelling scene phots, they want to find anywhere travelling destination photos, not just dates and locations. Each travelling photo that an intelligent phone or intelligent pad user takes goes through 11 billion computations, so that travelling scene photos can understand exactly where is the travelling destination photography to let online travelling consumer to feel anywhere they plan to go to the location to travel. So, (AI) learning machine can make online travelling photos more attractive to influence potential travelers choose to the destination to travel after they see the travelling destination scene photos from internet.

It seems that in future, (AI) machine learning will allow online travelling search to evolve even further. Search engineers will deliver refined recommendations to airlines' online traveler e-ticket search users and use less human input to predict travelling consumers' needs from internet channel. For IBM computer example, it indicated 90% of the data that exists today has been created in the last two years.

This huge explosion of past traveler's e-ticket consumption data gives the opportunity to quickly spot and react to the latest trends, fashion and fads among its travelling clients and potential clients. This will allow airline or travel agent companies to better engage with younger travelling consumers, who gain influence access to the latest travelling destination and package trends.

They associate with to help define who they are as individuals. Thus, travelling company brands have to identify and make use of them before travelling consumers move on, but the vast quantity of past e-ticket purchase data available makes from internet channel. This a resource-intensive task. For next example, Lesara, a based online clothes store, uses this machine learning to inform its product decision often gathering information from internal and external sources.

When its trends -spotting shoes. Lesara has a range of over 20 styles and sells hundreds of pairs a day. It focus on giving consumers, the very latest trends allow Lesara to develop on average of 50,000 new items each year. It compared to 11,000 old items each year. Thus, travelling agents or airlines can attempt to apply (AI) big data gathering method to gather all past e-ticket purchase data, concerns where they prefer to choose to go to the destinations to travel and what travelling packages are the most attractive to the travelers to choose to buy. It aims to help them to predict where future travelers will prefer to choose to go to travel or what travelling package they will prefer to choose to buy next year.

For another (AI) big data prediction example, Lesara is one online clothes store, uses machine learning decisions after gathering information from internal and external sources. One of its most popular products, shoes with LED started life when its trend spotting software flagged up a blogger wearing similar shoes. Now Lesara has a range of over 20 styles and sells hundreds of pairs a day. Its focus on giving consumers the very latest trends allows Lesara to develop an average of 50,000 new items each year, compared to 11,000 for its competitor Lara.

It seems (AI) big data gathering machine learning can help Lesara business to predict what kinds of shoes design or style that shoe consumers will prefer choose to buy in future shoe market trend. Thus, Lesara can predict shoe consumers' taste successfully and it can manufacture many attractive style of shoes.

(AI) machine learning can gather global past shoe consumer's shoe shopping experiences, then analyzes to make conclusion to give lesara recommendation successfully. This will make the experience more enjoyable for shoe consumers and allow Lesara to advert whose different new style or design of shoes to deliver them move relevant messages by understanding the context of the experience.

So, online travel agents or online airline can also attempt to apply (AI) big data gathering method to predict where travelers will prefer to go to travel and how they ought design travelling packages to attract them to choose to buy next year. Hence, (AI) big data gathering technology can conclude how to design traveler agents' travelling package products to be the most attractive to excite many travelers choose to buy their travelling package, due to it has more accurate to predict travelling consumer destination and travelling package choice behaviors to compare human themselves prediction judgement effort, e.g. travelling survey or marketing research, or telephone enquire. It seems that (AI) machine judgement effort is more accurate to compare to human judgment effort in travelling industry.

Future travel consumption behavior

Can (AI) big data gathering tool predict traveler individual habitual behavior , e.g. renting travel transportation tools ?

Can (AI) big data gathering tool can predict past traveler destination and travelling package choice habit and it can be intended to predict of future traveler behavior to people are creatures of habits judgement of future anywhere travelling destination choice next year or next month or next half year destination prediction ?

Many of human's everyday goal-directed behaviors are performed in a habitual fashion, the transportation made and route one takes to work, one's choice of breakfast. Habits are formed when using the some behavior frequently and a similar consistency in a similar context for the some purpose whether the individual past travel consumption model will be caused a habit to whom. e.g. choosing whom travel agent to buy air ticket or traveling package; choosing the same or similar countries' destinations to go to travel ; choosing the business class or normal (general) class of quality airlines to catch planes.

Does habitual rent traveling car tools use not lead to more resistance to change of travel mode? It has been argued that past behavior is the best predictor of future behavior to travel consumption. If individual traveler's past consumption behavior was always reasoned, then frequency of prior travel consumption behavior should only have an indirect link to the individual traveler's behavior. It seems that renting travel car tools to use is a habit example. So, a strong rent traveling car tools useful habit makes traveling mode choice. People with a strong renting of traveling car tools of habit should have low motivation to attend to gather any information about public transportation in their choice of travelling country for individual or family or friends members during their traveling journeys.

Even when persuasive communication changes the traveler whose attitudes and intention, in the case of individual traveler or family travelers with a strong renting travel car tools habit. It is difficult to change whose travel behaviors to choose to catch public transportation in whose any trips in any countries. However, understanding of travel behavior and the reasons for choosing one mode of transportation over another. The arguments for rent traveling car tools to use, including convenience, speed, comfort and individual freedom and well known.

Increasingly, psychological factors include such as, perceptions, identity, social norms and habit are being used to understand travel mode choice. Whether how many travel consumers will choose to rent traveling car tools during their trips in any countries. It is difficult to estimate the numbers. As the average level of renting travel car tools of dependence or attitudes to certain travel package policies from travel agents. Instead different people must be treated in different ways because who are motivated in different ways and who are motivated by different travel package policies ways from travel agents.

In conclusion, the factors influence whose traveler's individual traveler destination choice behavior The factors include either who chooses to rent traveling car tools or who chooses to catch public transportation when who individual goes to travel in alone trip or family trip. It include influence mode choice factors, such as social psychology factor and marketing on segmentation factor both to influence whose transportation choice of behavior in whose trip. So, (AI) big data can be attempted to gather past traveler transportation tool choice, rent travelling car tools choice or catching public transportation tools choice to predict where destination can provide what kind of transportation tool to attract many travelers to choose to go to the place to travel.

How (AI) big data determine future travel behavior from past travel experience and perceptions of risk and safety for the benefits to travel consumers?

How (AI) big data determine future travel behavior from past travel experience and perceptions of risk and safety for the benefits to travel consumers? Why does individual traveler avoid certain destination(s) is(are) as relevant to tourist decision making as why who chooses to travel to others?

Perceptions of risk and safety and travel experience are likely to influence travel decisions. If travel agents had efforts to predict future travel behavior to guess whether travelers will feel where is(are) risk and unsafe to cause who does not choose to go to the country to travel. Then, the travel agents will avoid to choose to spend much time to design the different traveling package to attract their potential travel consumers to choose to travel. The reason is because in the case of individual traveler's tourism experience, the traveler whose past disappointment travel experience (psychological risk) will be a serious threat to the traveler's health or life (health, physical or terrorism risk). The past safety or unhealthy risk to the country(countries) will influence the traveler decides to choose not to go to the countries(country) to travel again in the future.

What is push and pull factors to influence any traveler who chooses where is whose preferable travelling destination ?

How to apply (AI) big data to predict individual traveler's behavioral intention of choosing a travel destination? Understanding why people travel and what factors influence their behavioral intention of choosing a travel destination is beneficial to tourism planning and marketing. In general, an individual's choice of a travel destination into two forces.

The first force is the push factor that pushes an individual away from home and attempt to develop a general desire to go somewhere, without specifying where that may be.

The other force is the pull factor that pull an individual toward in destination, due to a region-specific or perceived attractiveness of a destination. The respective push and pull factors illustrate that people travel because who are pushed by whose internal motives and pulled by external forced of a destination. However, the decision making process leading to the choice of a travel destination is a very complex process.

For example, a Taiwanese traveler who might either choose new travel destination of Hong Kong or another old travel Asia destinations again or who also might choose any one of Western country, as a new travel destination. The travel agents can predict where who will have intention to choose to travel from whose past behavior and attitude, subjective and perceived behavioral control model. When (AI) big data gather past every country traveler number who chose to go to which countries to travel in order to judge where destinations will be the country travelers' travelling choice destinations in the future.

The factors influence where is the traveler choice, include personal safety, scenic beauty, cultural interest, climate changing, transportation tools, friendliness of local people, price of trip, trip package service in hotels and restaurants, quality and variety of food and shopping facilities and services etc. needs. So, whose factors will influence where is the individual travel's choice. It seems every traveler whose choice of travel process, will include past behavior. e.g. travelling experience, travelling habit, then to choose the best seasoned travelling action to satisfy whose travel needs. This process is the individual traveler's psychological choice process, who must need time to gather information to compare concerning of different travel packages, destination scene, climate change, transportation tools available to the destination, air ticket price etc. these factors, then to judge where is the best right destination to travel in the right time.

Hence, (AI) big data can gather past different countries' climate changing data, transportation tool changing data, destination scene environment changing etc. different data to give opinions to travelling businesses whether any country's these above factors will influence about how many traveler number will be increase or decrease in the future.

Why can expectation, motivation and attitude factor influence travelling behavior?

Social psychology is concerned with gaining insight into the psychological of socially relevant behaviors and the processes. For instance, on a global level bad influence to global warming, it influences some countries extreme cold or hot bad climate changing occurrence, then it ought influence some travelers' behavioral decision to change their mind to choose some countries to go to travel at the moment which do not occur extreme hot or cold climate (temperature). e.g. above than 40 degree in summer or below than 0 degree in winter. Due to the extreme climate changing environment in the countries, it will cause them to feel uncomfortable to play during their trips. So, the global warming causes to climate changing factor will influence the numbers of travel consumption to be reduced possibly. This is global climate changing environment factor influences to bad or uncomfortable social psychological feeling to global travelers' mind of traveling decision. What is individual traveler expectation, motivation and attitude? Tourism sector includes inbound (domestic) tourism and outbound (overseas) tourism both incomes to any countries. According to recent article, a tourist behavior model has been developed, called the expectation, motivation and attitude (EMA) model (Hsu et al., 2010).

This model focuses on the pre-visit stage of tourists by modeling the behavioral process by incorporating expectation, motivation and attitude. Travel motivation is considered as an essential component of the behavioral process, which has been increasing attention from the travel; industry. The economic approach defines "tourism" is an identifiable nationally important industry. It includes the component activities of transportation, accommodation, recreation, food and related service. So, tourism behavioral consumption is concerned the individual tourist's usual habituate of the industry which responds to whose needs, and of the impacts that both the tourist and the tourism industry have on the socio-cultural, economic and physical environment.

However, travel motivation means how to understand and predict factors that influence travel decision making. According to Backman and others (1995, p.15), motivation is conceptually viewed as " a state of need, a condition that services as a driving force to display different kind of behavior toward certain types of activities, developing preferences, arriving at some expected satisfactory outcome." So, motivation and expectancy which has close relationship to any tourist before who decided to do any tourism of behavior.

Some economists confirmed motivation and expectancy which has relations, such as expectation of visiting an outbound destination has a direct effect on motivation to visit the destination; motivation has a direct effect on attitude toward visiting the destination; expectation of visiting the outbound destination has a direct affection on attitude toward visiting the destination and motivation has a mediating effect on the relationship in between expectation and attitude.

Hence, (AI) big data can gather all the country's climate environment change, transportation tool change, entertainment scene change, hotel price and restaurant price change etc. data to give opinions whether the country will attract how many traveler to choose to go to travel in the year.

Reference

Backman and others "motivation is conceptually viewed as " a state of need, a condition that services as a driving force to display different kind of behavior toward certain types of activities, developing preferences, arriving at some expected satisfactory outcome.", 1995, p.15.

Fishbein & Ajzen, "The model based on the three constructs of attitude, subjective norm, and perceived behavioral control". 1975.

Hsu et al. "A tourist behavior model has been developed, called the expectation, motivation and attitude " (EMA) model ,2010.

ICT,WWW . "Switzerland has one of the highest population-to-computer ratio in Europe." Switzerland, 2005.

Jorea Ministry of Environment, " For South Korea environmental attitude is a major factor in decision making vis-a-vis the consumption of " green" food and services", Korea, 2015.

Korea Ministry Of Environment. Public Organizations spend 2.2 Trillon Korean Won To
Purchase green Products in 2014; Ministry Of Environment: Sejoung, Korea, 2015.

Lind , Lohmann & Danielsson , United Nations Population Division, "Demographic change is said to be one of the important drivers for new trends in consumer traveling change behavior in most European countries". 2001.

Mayne, Lonnie. " Evolve of die in the age of the consumer". Entrepreneur, N.P. , 16 Apr. 2014. web of Oct. 2016.

Lee, D.; Kim, M. ; Lee, J. adoption of green electricity policies: Investigating the role of environmental attitudes via big data-driven search-queries. Energy policy 2016. 90, 187-201.

Lee, Terrence, " Tech in Asia-connecting Asia's startup system " Tech. in Asia- connecting Asia's startup ecosystem, N.p.,4 July 2016.

Weber & Bottorn "risky decision is as choices among alternatives that can be described by probability distributions over possible outcomes" , 1989, p.114.

Airport service life cycle stage improvement strategy

Any organizations will have life cycle stage from birth, growth , mature to decline. In airport service organizations have theis life cycle stages in service aspect. Airports organizatins aim to provide safe, comfortable , even shopping environment to let passengers to stay and to wait to transfer another air planes to visit another destination or arrive the country's airport to check out or check in to enter the airport to leave. If airports have life cycle stages, what the characteristics to every stage? How to improve airport service in order to reach mature life cycle stage rapidly? How to implement airport service strategy in order to reach mature life cycle stage to the aorport organization rapidly?I shall explain as below:

Any airports need to be planned in order to raise excellent service to let passengers to let any travelers choose to travel the country whether the country can provide excellent service and facilities. It will bring indirect emotion impact to influence the travelers chooce to revisit the country to travel again. However, soft or hard element or) staff service performance or airport facility), they will influence whether the different countries travelers to choose to travel to re-visit the country again. So, learning how to keep the mature or airport service life cycle stage to stay long time, it will be one important factor to influence any airport business in success.

In the birth life style stage to airport, airport organizations must maintain the capability to provide expert advice to airport owners an matters including operational safety, during construction, environmental compatibility, and airport development standards. No other private or public organization can be expected maintain this level of proficiency. These value-added services enhance public trust when assuring consistant application of standards for the nation's airport system. So, it seems that when the new airport is built if it hopes its passenger customers can consider themselves emotion need. So, it ought concentrate on nowadays airplane landing cunways or airport transfer free service transport etc. facilities can let them to feel safe when they were walking in any airport places. If they feel anywhere are dangerous when they are walking or staying in the ne sirport, then new airport non safe or dangerous factor may influence travelers to choose the country to travel again.

Any new airports will need have good new national airport plan in order to it might operate in the near future with respect to safety areas. The plan elements may include as below:

Achieving zero accidents aim, establish standard safety areas at all commercial service airports , achieving the most minimum 85% of all passenger flights operate on runways with safe feeling, increase measure to 100% of all passenger flight operating on runways with standard safety areas after three months. Within 5 years, 95% of all passenger flights begin and end on runways with standard safety areas.

On benefits aspect, aims to mobilize work force to improve safety area performance describes realistic investment benefits. So, in any new airports birth life cycle stage, they must need to consider safety and expenditure for repair aspect in order to keep its service performance to avoid passengers have dissatisfactory feeling when they are staying in their new airports.

When the country has many travelers travel to the country , then the country's new airport passengers number must increase. It is its the new airport growth life cycle stage. These are critical success factors influence the airport, whether it can improve service performance in order to excite different countries travelers visiting the country's airport desire or grow up the visitors number successfully. The critical success factors may include: Having necessary support from internal and externa stakeholders to implement and willing to share information and identify anywhere the total airport facilities of repair needs that are both reliable and feasible projections to let passengers to feel more safe feeling when they are staying in the airport, understand its future service vision and mission, set strategic direction and goals to process/product specific objectives and decision-making across and doen the organization, define, model and prioritize planning prcesses critical for mission performance, practice hand-on sernior management ownership of planning process and allow field, personnel flexiblity in performing jobs, adjust organizational structures , an essessment program to evaluate planning process and product management , e.g. national airport system performance, create organizational understanding of the value management to customer and stakeholder current and future expectations developing human resources management strategies to support new process that solves needs planners and engineers, building information resources strategies change, especially for entering data at the source and maintains data integrity and timeliness.,establish central support group to support reengineering efforts, outreach and training efforts across the organization, phase in short-and long-term results that achieve set goals and objectives over the next two years.

Thus, when one new airport begins to feel passengers number is increasing. It ought experience the growth life cycle stage to the new airport , if it hopes that it can reach mature life cycle stage rapidly as well as keeps its mature life cycle stage to stay in this stage long time or reachs the airport service performance to the most satisfactory level in this mature life cycle stage. It must need to attempt to plan these strategies to implement in order to avoid decline life cycle stage occurs in short time. So, it explains why some new airport can experience the development to mature life cycle stage from grow life cycle stage in short time,even when it reachs mature life cycle stage. It can keep to stay in this stage long time. The reason is that it had prepared effective strategies to achieve how to improve its airport service performance aim in order to satisfy passenger needs. When they are staying in the country's airport any time. Hence, every year revising service performance is needed to any airports.

Any airports must have development processes. The question is that whether the airport needs how long time to reach growth or mature life cycle stage from birth stage or decline life cycle stage will be delayed how long to occur. The development processes may mean that the airport development life cycle stages changes that had toard a particular result or even as a series of continuous actions or operations coducting to an end (Merriam-Webster, 2013).

reference

Merriam-webster (2013). On line dictionary. Available at:
https://www.merriam-webster. com/(last accessed July , 8 2013).

Hence, any airport organizations with experience development pricess. When the new airport is built, it must be in the birth life cycle stage. Its passengers number can not increase rapidly. It needs time to grow their number. But, when the new airport operates a period, many different countries begin feel this new airport is existence in the country. They will attempt to catch airplance to visit this country airport to catch airplane to visit tis country airport to travel. If they feel this country airport service performance can satisfy their short time staying feeling or its passengers or airports visitors number may increase rapidly. It meand that this airport is experiencing growth life cycle stage. So, if the airport can attract many visitors in short time. It will reduce time to growth life cycle stage from birth life cycke stage.

So , service performance may be one important factor to inflow the airport grows. When the airport develops to the period, passengers number can not increase rapidly, it may be the airport's mature life cycle stage. Due to it's passengers number can not grow rapidly, its passengers number also may reduce. When its passengers number has significant decrease, if its reduction number is increasing more. It implies that the airport is experiencing decline life cycle stage. All any country's airport may experience whole life cycle stages. If the country's airport can not implement successful strategies, it may experience birht life cycle stage in long time because it can not grow its passengers number significantly. So, any airports need to learn how to help them to change growth life cycle stage, even mature life cycle stage can stay in long time easily. If they hope to attract many different countries passengers to visit their airports or travel themselves countries or enjoy to stay short time in themselves airports in order to grow themselves airline industry development.

- How can processes improvement management strategy influence airport service performance?

Overall processes in an airport may involve passengers, luggage, cargo, aircraft movements, ground handling, and crews . All of these operations can be systematised into processes at airport terminal. Three main types of processes can be established departing , arrival and transfer . Departure consists in catching a flight to a final or intermediate destination, arrival consists in landing and leaving the airport, and transfer consists in landing at the airport only to catch another flight to a final or an intermediate destination. Airports also deal with cargo. It involves in the movement of cargo by air, cargo fies from the shopper to the consignee through one or more airlines. However, when the airport can let them freight forwarder, being familiar with the necessary procedures how permits the airline to concentrate on the provision of air transport and to avoid time consuming details of the facilitation and landside distribution system. It will raise efficiency and improve service performance. The services product by the ground handling are crucial to the success and efficiency of the airport operations.

These services are usually provided by specialised companies. Briefly, it includes the luggage treatment, passengers carrying from plan to terminal when needed and aircraft assistance. Also, focusing on crew, there are two majoe processes, one for departures and the other for arrivals. The crew members also have to pass the security and passport controls. However, they have special channels for this. Once they reach the aircraft, the similarities with the passengers' procedure stop. Hence, they have to perform a set of activities , such as check the aircraft load sheets and help passengers to name a few. Also airport terminal operations processes for passengers and luggage, typically for departures , passengers do the check on the airline area, pass security controls, proceed to the general lounge and lastly to the gate holding area. arriving passengers are able to immediately go from the luggage claim area, but the non-passengers have to pass the passport control at first. After this passengers have to decide if they need to declare goods or not as the paths are different . Hence, if the airport can reduce all of this service processes are less complex as immigration check in-out service, liggage claim can be efficient to carry when passengers need to find themselves luggage. Then, it will reduce waste time and let they satisfy airport service absolutely. So, reducing service process time amy also help the airport to increase customers number significantly. When airport role is the middleman between airlines , cargo transport service providers and passengers, e.g. short time transport cargo service and reducing passengers check in or check out service time. then, it will let them to feel more satisfactory service to the airport.

Hence, airport capacity is as a multifactor function leaves open the exact relationship between the factors but stresses that all factors are relevant to assess airport capacity . So , understanding airport capacity and what drives the capacity usage at airports may provide an insight in the set of instructments available to optimise the use of capacity. All of these factors may influence any capacity of an airport, they may include as below:

For example, technical constraints, e.g. ATM per hour service in a runway in a combined arrival and departure fashion, when many passengers are staying at the airport, they can withdraw money from ATM easily. So, ATM number facilities service supply number and location choice to the airport factors will infuence passengers ' satisfactory level, another factor is environmental constraints, it can directly offer the wellbeing of the communities surrounding the negative emotion to passengers and communities surrounding the airprt. For this factor, the change in technology and/or operational procedures can provide more capacity in the system.

Airline business models factor, it can affect the capacity spoke model when other under a point-point one ,these models directly affect the peak hour operational capacity, particularly in big international hubs. Airlines often compete with high frequencies between destinations, thus increasing the number of movements. In addition, conncectivity also has downsides for this model: the delays in one airport might be exported and sometimes in another, due to the connectivity influencing the real capacity. This factor has been setting economic incentives or pricing models. Furthermore, expanding information systems, from one airport to multiple airports gate-to-gate concept, and the use of larger airport to redcuce frequencies.

Hence, above these factors may influence whether the airport needs how long time to reach maturiry life cycle stage when it is staying the growth life cycle stage. It depends on how its strategies implementation and how environment influence its implementation , if it hopes to achieve to reach the maturity life cycle stage in success in short time.

Finally, I shall explain life cycle cst analysis to any country pavement strategy will bring what significant influential benefits to any airports continue to develop in order to avoid to reach decline life cycle stage time in short time easily , when they are staying in the mature life cycle stage. In the construction or rehabilitation investments of highway's pavements, it is already common to perform a life-cycle analysis or life cycle cost analysis for different alternatives to airport pavements. Becauae when any airport pavements are using for a long time, every day has many airplanes need to fly to land on the pavement. It can bring significant repace influence when the airport has many airplanes are needed to land on the pavements every day in the maturity life cycle stages.

Hence, how to evaluate the repair cost expenditure budget in order to satisfy every day air planes land on the airport pavement need. In the calculations are different cost factors (including direct and indirect cost)to any airport itself pavement. Direct costs are related to the critical construction cost landing on pavement activities and are calculated with information from the airport agency and constructors that work for them. The indirect costs are related with the loss of daily revenue of the airport during work activities, such as landing on the airport pavement.

Runways are the most critical pavements area of airport , so it is critical to ensure the quality of these pavement to let airplanes to land on the airport safety, e.g. they need to be constructed with sufficient strength to carry the moving airport and have a high resistance to skidding and aquaplaining. It is most of the time accomplished with reconstructions or deep rehabilitation. Hence, predicting how much will spend on airport pavement facilities expenditure must need in every day.

However, the life cycle assessment (LCA) is a mult step procedure for calculating the life time environmental impact of a product or service is needed to any airport organizations, when they reachs maturity life cycelt stage . The complex process includes goal and cope definition in inventory analysis impact assessment. The process is vaturally iteractive as quality and completeness of information is constantly being testes. When the definition of the aim and scope of the study is done the next step is the development of an inventory, in which all significant environmental burdens during the lifetime of the product,, such as airport pavements or process , such as airplanes landing on the pavement or airplanes leaving from the pavement in the airport.

(Araujo, Oliveria & Silve) 2014 explained that life cycle snslysis of pavements are focused on the activities of extraction, production, transportation application of materials, concisely the construction of the road. Because its difficult to obtain other relevant data knowing that the use phase of the pavement is predominant with repect to energy consumption and also to gas emissions related to the atmosphere. One of the main factors for the use phase is the rolling resistance, this depends on the surface and structural characteristics of the different pavements.

Hence, , if the airport can have good repairment or renew skills to help its pavement to improve. Then, it may bring long time benefit, such as reducing airplanes energy consumption and also to avoid gas emissions or reduce gas emissions accident occurrene, even air plane landing on pavement accident occurrence chance can reduce to the zero. so, defining the expected pavement performance time improvement strategy can influence whether the airport pavement can satisfy all airplane users how long time landing on or leaving on the airport pavement. Also it is the major factor to influence airport main function success for any airplanes arriving to the country's airport pavement or leaving from the country's airport pavement. Hence, calculating any airport pavement life cycle costs factor. It is necessary to analysis and interpret carefully the results to identfy the most economic pavement strategy in any airport's whole life cycle development stages.

reference

Araujo, J.P.C. Oliveria, J.R.M. & Silva H.M.R.D. (2011) . the importance of the use phase on the LCA of environmentally friendly solutions for asphalt road pavements. transportation research part D: trasport and environment, 32(0), 97-110. Retrieved in March 2015 from://
dx. doi.org/10.1016/j.trd.2014.07.006.

COVID 19 human disease how influences global airline fuel manufacturers to rapid reach decline life cycle stage

Recently, since 2019 end, COVID 19 human disease confirms that any one can be gotten this kind disease by the COVID 19 patient individual mouth or air, hand, even things contact. This kind disease may hurt the heath person individual lung to let him/her to feel difficult to breathe, even death. So, this kind disease had influenced many people feel fear to catch airplanes, because when many passengers are sitting in the airplane, if one or more is/are COV19 human disease patient, then the patient has possible to bring this disease to let the health passengers to get his/her COVID 19 human disease in the none window airplanes environment easily. SO, when this kind of human disease is threatening global travellers to avoid to catch air airplanes to fly to travel frequently. Then, airplanes won't need to fly often. When airplanes do not need often fly in sky. Then gas fuel demand will be influenced to reduce to airlines because airplanes won't need often catch many travellers to go to different countries, due to travellers number reduces as well as many different countries' travellers had begun to reduce travelling times frequently and their airports restrict any high body temperature people to enter their countries, because they will have possible to bring COVID 19 human disease when they arrive any airports. Consequently, airplanes do not need to buy and use any more gas fuel to provide them to fly any more since COVID 19 human disease occurs.

How COVID 19 human disease influences global gas fuel sale number? Because travellers number had been decreasing, airlines do not any airplanes often catch many passengers to fly to any countries again. Surely, gas fuel demand to airplanes may be also influenced to reduce and it can also influence whole tourism leisure industry development will experience to the decline cycle life stage absolutely. Before , due to global has many travellers feel need to travel leisure activity. So, global travellers increasing number impacted to global needs to have many airplanes to be provide to fly every day frequently. Before average per day had above 10,000 times of airplane flying times in our earth every day, so it implied that gas fuel need must be influenced to increase to airlines, because airlines must need to buy a lot gas fuel to provide their airplanes to fly to different countries every day , when any countries have many travellers need to fly to different countries to travel. It is sure that airline gas fuel product must reach the maturity life cycle stage in this airplane gas fuel manufacturing industry, because travelling leisure activities are accepted to be on kind of popular habit leisure to global travellers, when air ticket price had been decreasing, it can also attract many travellers accept to spend money to buy air tickets to go to different countries to travel frequently. So, cheap air ticket price and popular tourism leisure activity factors may influence global travellers number increases. When global travellers number increases, it impacts to global airplanes need to increase flying times to fly frequently and air tickets also increases purchase number. Consequently, airlines also are influenced to need to buy a lot gas fuel to provide to airplanes to fly. SO, due to gas fuel demand increases, but gas fuel supply number is not enough, then gas price can be influenced to raise, when airlines demand gas fuel number is more than gas fuel supply number. It is based on economic theory, when demand to the product increases in the market, but the product has shortage to supply, then price may be influenced to bring sale price increasing chance. So, in this airline gas fuel demand and supply case, due to airplanes need to fly frequently, so global flying numbers had been influenced to rise and global airplanes need to buy many airplanes to catch passengers or travellers to fly to different countries. So, airlines must need to buy a lot gas fuel to provide airplanes to fly to different countries every day in this airline industry mature life stage. Thus, before 1029, it is gas fuel manufacturing industry and airlines travelling transport industry and tourism industry their maturity cycle stage period. Every day, global gas manufacturers need to attempt to find any lands have gas and explore any gas lands, than using technology to manufacture gas fuel in order to supply and satisfy any airlines' gas fuel needs every day. But, since COVID 19 human disease occurred in 2019 end, it influenced many airlines lose confidence the travellers number will increase, due to travellers number had been beginning to reduce every day and airplanes' flying times are also influenced to reduce , these both factors must influence gas fuel need reduces to any airlines their airplanes needs.

Hence, after 2019 end, it may be global tourism leisure industry decline life cycle stage, moreover, it may also be global airline transport flying service industry decline life stage both. So, global gas fuel need on airline sector must be influenced to reduce, when global airplanes did not often fly and global airplanes flying times had been influencing to reduce to per day 500 flying times, even less from the top level per day 10,000 flying times. SO, it can prove that they have relationship between tourism leisure industry and airlines' airplanes transport flying service industry and airline gas fuel product manufacturing industry. It means that when any unpredicted factors influence tourism leisure industry's life cycle stage changes, then the unpredicted factors may influence airline transport flying service industry and airline gas fuel product manufacturing industry life cycle service or gas fuel product stage change suddenly , such as this unpredicted COVID 19 human mouth disease, it can influence global tourism leisure industry and airline airplanes transport flying service industry and airline gas fuel product manufacturing industry had been beginning to experience the decline life cycle stage nowadays.

What COVID-19 human mouth disease can let airlines transport service providers and gas fuel manufacturers and tourism leisure service providers to learn? Airlines clearly have a lot on their airplanes at the moment, but since COVID-19 human mouth disease occurred in 2019 end. Many airlines had brought many airlines to prepare to catch global different countries travellers to go to different countries to travel, but nowadays, they do not need to be driven to fly to countries per day. These airplanes are staying on any countries' airports, but per day airlines need to pay high rent to the countries' airports when they are staying on the countries' airports. SO, their airport airplanes rent expenditure must be high, but their airplanes do not need to fly to different countries every day again , because COVID -19 human mouth disease influenced global travellers number had been reducing continue. With unpredicted consequences, many airlines will choose to sell their airplanes later, it none any one medicine can be invented to kill this kind of human mouth disease later, because if some airlines did not make decision to sell their airplanes, then they may nor regrow to growth life cycle stage from decline life cycle stage easily, due to passengers number reduces and it can influence their income reduces. But airline staffs still need to pay , e.g. pilots, airplane front line staffs and airports front line check in service staffs. Hence, sale of airplanes their assets may be the final strategic decision, when any airplanes can not continue to fly every day after 2020 year. Due to COVID 19 human disease can not be killed by any new medicine. If this kind of disease can not be filled for two or more years, then I believe that there are many airlines will experience to death life cycle stage from decline life cycle stage rapidly, otherwise if they can choose to sell some airplanes , they may keep cash available to prepare to reduce expenditure more easily. Although, some airlines made decisions to dismiss some airline service staffs, even pilots to achieve reducing salary expenditure in this decline life cycle stage. But, it will raise unemployment rate to bring social negative challenge.

If later airlines choose to sell airplanes their assets to raise cash available strategy. However, it implies that gas fuel need must be influenced to reduce, due to COVID-19 human disease will continue to occur. So, it is the right time, gas fuel manufacturers ought not only concern how to manufacture more airplane gas fuel product to satisfy airlines airplanes transport flying need in this COVID-19 human disease occurrence stage. They ought find any new gas fuel users in this gas fuel market, if these airplanes gas fuel manufacturers expect to re-grow their gas fuel manufacturing and sale business to reach the growing life cycle stage from decline life cycle stage again in the future. Otherwise, many of gas fuel manufacturers will experience the death life cycle stage from decline life cycle stage within one to two years soon as possible.

Hence, if the gas fuel manufacturers can attempt to find other new kinds of gas fuel users in this gas energy market , instead of airline airplane gas fuel market and vehicle gas market main both markets. I believe that they can re-grow to growth life cycle stage from decline life cycle stage again in possible. Although, gas price must be influenced to reduce, because excess of gas supply to airline markets before 2019 end, but when airplanes do not need to fly frequently in this COVID -19 human disease occurrence environment. The COVID-19 pandemic human disease had had a significant impact on the aviation industry, due to travel restrictions and a significant full in demand among travellers. Significant reductions in passengers number have results in airplanes do not need to fly , airplanes feel price must drop, due to oil price war occurred. Hence, due to airline fuel price falls down, it causes many gas manufacturers' gas sale number also reduces to airline market. So, it is right time , any gas fuel manufacturers ought attempt to seek other new gas users, instead of airplanes users or cars users basic both gas users market. If they expect that they can change to experience regrowth life cycle stage from decline life cycle stage again and avoid to reach the final death life cycle stage within one to two years, due to COVID-19 pandemic human disease external environment factor influence.

In fact, on early assessment of the impact of COVID-19 on airline industry, it seems to have a more serve and more rapid impact on air traffic of fuel (oil price plummeted during the first quarter of 2020). It implies that global airline fuel price had been falling down due to COVID-19 human disease influences to global airplanes' flying times reduce. Moreover, COVID-19 impact on Asia-Pacific Aviation worsens, we have seen that first airline casually in the region, such as China , Singapore, Japan, Taiwan aviation fuel need has been influenced to reduce much significantly. Consequently, Asia-Pacific Aviation fuel price had been influenced to reduce much significantly. Then, it also influences Western Aviation, e.g. US, UK etc. Their flying times are also influenced to reduce, then fuel price sale to western Pacific Aviation can also influenced to fall down. Hence, it seems that COVID-19 human disease may also influence global aviation fuel price falls down. If the fuel manufacturers still only depend on sale aviation fuel income. I believe that the fuel manufacturers may reach to the death life cycle stage rapidly in short time. So, seeking new fuel users market is real need to any one fuel manufacturers , because global medicine scientists still can not guarantee when the kind of new medicine can be invented to kill COVID-19 human disease successfully. So, In this COVID-19 human disease threat environment, many experiencing mature life cycle stage airlines, such as US airline, Cathy airlines , UK airlines , Australia airline etc. they may be influenced to experience decline life cycle stage , even death life cycle stage within two year rapidly. Also, this kind of disease can also influence many travel agents' travelling leisure business development to experience decline stage cycle stage as well as it can also influence any airplanes fuel manufacturers to experience decline life cycle stage from mature life cycle stage in possible. Hence, it is right time , they need to change any new market users or service strategies in order to keep their businesses can continue regrow to the growth life cycle stage

9 798889 518655

Printed by Libri Plureos GmbH in Hamburg,
Germany